The Paris Years of Thomas Jefferson

William Howard Adams

THE PARIS YEARS
of
THOMAS
JEFFERSON

ORIGINAL PHOTOGRAPHY BY
ADELAIDE DE MENIL

Yale University Press
NEW HAVEN AND LONDON

PUBLISHED WITH ASSISTANCE FROM THE FLORENCE GOULD FOUNDATION.

DESIGNED BY THOMAS WHITRIDGE

SET IN MONOTYPE BELL BY INK, INC., NEW YORK

PRINTED IN THE UNITED STATES OF AMERICA BY THOMSON-SHORE, DEXTER, MICHIGAN.

LIBRARY OF CONGRESS CATALOGING-IN-PUBLICATION DATA

ADAMS, WILLIAM HOWARD.

   THE PARIS YEARS OF THOMAS JEFFERSON / WILLIAM HOWARD ADAMS: ORIGINAL

     PHOTOGRAPHY BY ADELAIDE DE MENIL.

       P. CM.

   INCLUDES BIBLIOGRAPHICAL REFERENCES AND INDEX.

   ISBN 0-300-06903-0 (CLOTH: ALK. PAPER)

   1. JEFFERSON, THOMAS. 1743–1826—HOMES AND HAUNTS—FRANCE—PARIS.

     2. PRESIDENTS—UNITED STATES—BIOGRAPHY. 3. DIPLOMATS—FRANCE—PARIS—

     BIOGRAPHY. 4. PARIS (FRANCE)—INTELLECTUAL LIFE. 5. ENLIGHTENMENT—FRANCE—

     PARIS. [1. PARIS (FRANCE)—HISTORY—1715–1789.] I. TITLE.

   E332.45.A32   1997

   973.4'6'092—DC21

   [B]   97-12330 CIP

A CATALOGUE RECORD FOR THIS BOOK IS AVAILABLE FROM THE BRITISH LIBRARY.

THE PAPER IN THIS BOOK MEETS THE GUIDELINES FOR PERMANENCE AND DURABILITY OF THE COMMITTEE ON PRODUCTION GUIDELINES FOR BOOK LONGEVITY OF THE COUNCIL ON LIBRARY RESOURCES.

10 9 8 7 6 5 4 3 2 1

For
Eileen and John,
Adelaide and Ted

"With all his extraordinary versatility of character and opinions, he seemed during his entire life to breathe with perfect satisfaction nowhere except in the liberal, literary, and scientific air of Paris."

—Henry Adams,
*History of the United States of America
during the Administration of Thomas Jefferson*

Contents

Acknowledgments

T HE GENESIS OF THIS WORK is buried somewhere in the research I carried out while on the staff of the National Gallery of Art as curator of the exhibition *The Eye of Thomas Jefferson*. Jefferson's years in France represented a central portion of the exhibition and catalogue, allowing me to work in key Paris collections, notably the Bibliothèque Nationale and the Archives Nationales.

Friends, colleagues, and institutions have extended help, but so long ago that they may not now recall it, although I remain very much in their debt. I should begin with Dan Jordan, the staff of the Thomas Jefferson Memorial Foundation, and the International Center for Jefferson Studies. Their hospitality and assistance were essential to me as an independent scholar.

Both in substance and in style, Douglas Wilson and Joseph Ellis pulled me back from certain disaster in early drafts. Herbert Sloan's timely reading and suggestions, based on a thorough command of the literature, forced me to reconsider key sections.

My friends Alfred Bush and John Young never failed with generous help whenever other sources turned up dry. Lucia Stanton, John and Eileen Harris, Robert Darnton, Robert McDonald, Frances Smyth, James Holland, Stephen Lloyd, Zanne Macdonald, Mrs. Robert Carter, Nina Herrick, Wendell Garrett, Sybil d'Origny, George Green Shackelford, Michael Plunkett, Annette Gordon-Reed, Brooke Conti, Mary Francis, Jane Sweeney, and Martha Clevenger all have given me much-appreciated assistance along the way.

While I must acknowledge my very real debt to the libraries of Princeton University, the University of Virginia in Charlottesville, the College of

William and Mary in Williamsburg, the University of Houston, and the Library of Congress, two other libraries have meant very much to me, working as I do in a remote corner of the Shenandoah Valley. Joseph Barnes and the staff of the Scarborough Library of Shepherd College near my home have made research possible outside a metropolitan setting. The same is particularly true of the warm assistance of Margaret Didden and Halie Taylor, working at the two-hundred-year-old, one-room town library of Shepherdstown, West Virginia. They regularly and magically produced scarce books from distant shelves through the wonders of the interlibrary loan service.

I must give two special people who have provided "support and encouragement," as the conventional formula goes, my scarcely expressible thanks. Adelaide de Menil and her husband, Edmund Carpenter, have not only made a critical difference in the final appearance of the book, with the photographs which Adelaide took (assisted by Ted), but their steady friendship, hospitality, and concern sustained me to the end.

The following individuals gave permissions, opened doors, and made life easier for Adelaide during her photography expeditions: Messrs. Alain Escalière, François Vuillemin, Jean René Vacher, Gerard de Nussac, Michel Guillon, Benedict Pesle, Michael Bord, Olivier Choppin de Janvry, Pierre-André Lablaude, Frederick Danton, Jean Mouillet, Edmund Baysari, Mmes Marie-Noelle Abat, Nicole Pot, Nadine Pluvieu, Emmanuel, and Constans, Claire Caucheteux.

Aside from Adelaide de Menil's superb photographs, the book's measurable quality of visual appeal is the work of Thomas Whitridge, whose faultless eye lifts book design onto a new plane.

Finally, I want to place on the record my thanks to my editor, Harry Haskell. His skill and patience (marked with forthright Missouri candor, which we both appreciate) helped me to say more clearly and succinctly what I wanted and intended to say but didn't quite know how to.

Chapter 1

Taking Leave

THE AIR IN PARIS had turned suddenly chill as the autumn
equinox arrived. While the days were still washed with the soft
gold light of early fall, fires appeared in drawing rooms, announcing the
season's change.[1] On September 17, 1789 the American minister to the
court of France was expecting four friends for dinner at the Hôtel de
Langeac, his house at the corner of the rue de Berri and the Champs-
Elysées. It would be his last entertainment before he departed on a six-
month leave. Thomas Jefferson had no doubt ordered fires to be laid in
the morning and again in the late afternoon, as he had done throughout
the month, following his old Virginia custom. By establishing the daily
use of each fireplace, he could calculate down to a cord the amount of
wood to be cut annually at Monticello. Counting, calculating, and measuring was a mania he shared with the age. Even the dull, neurotic king
at Versailles suffered from similar if more fatuous compulsions, enumer-
ating every trip he had ever taken, every horse he had ridden, and all the
game he had bagged on each of his mindless rounds of hunting.

Practical and meticulous in the smallest domestic routines, Jefferson
had always relied on the system of things, order bolstered by facts, particularly mathematical, to "combat the chaos of experience."[2] Happiness itself,
both public and private, was something measurable; its attainment even in
the form of personal comfort on a raw day in Paris was a matter of quan-
tifiable regularity. Jefferson's rule was that fires were to be laid twice a day
beginning in September. To his friend Maria Cosway he confided that he
was "an animal of a warm climate, a mere Oran-ootan" who could barely
endure the damp and cold Paris winter.[3] The climate had aggravated his
depression during the first gloomy months he spent in the French capital

1

Thomas Jefferson by John Trumbull, 1788.
Maria Cosway requested this replica when she saw the original version that Trumbull
painted for the *Declaration of Independence*. Taken later to Lodi, Italy, it remained among
Cosway's possessions until 1976, when it was given to the people of the United States as a
gift of the Italian government on the nation's two-hundredth birthday. (Copyrighted by the
White House Historical Association)

in the winter of 1784—a sharp change from the bright Indian summer and winter days on his mountaintop in Virginia, where brilliant blue skies outlined the hills and plains.

Beyond Jefferson's elegant but not ostentatious house, small fires had also begun to appear on Paris street corners. People gathered around them to cook, warm their hands, exchange the latest rumors, and grumble about the alarming shortage of bread—a subject that would come up later at the minister's farewell dinner. Last year's corn was exhausted and the new harvest had not yet been ground. The city was tense. For weeks bakery shops had been guarded by troops rushed to trouble spots. In his last official report to John Jay, the American secretary for foreign affairs, Jefferson wrote that "civil war"—the word "revolution" had not yet entered conversations—was widely talked about and expected.[4] With the onset of winter, he warned, the dwindling supply of bread might spark a full-scale explosion. Jefferson's house had already been robbed three times, claiming the candlesticks that had stood on the dining table. In July the French government had responded to his formal complaint by posting a *corps de garde* at the old Grille de Chaillot, the customs gate at the corner of his house facing the Champs-Elysées. At dusk, the flickering light from their fires could be seen through the windows of his dining room.

The *grille* blocking the avenue marked the western boundary of the city when Jefferson moved into the barely finished house in 1785. At this gate, as at all the customs posts that encircled the city, everything entering was subjected to a duty. This internal tax increased the cost of essential goods for the city's six hundred thousand residents and compounded their grievances against the government. The rest of the country had been relieved of the tariff, but it was such a lucrative source of revenue that the government couldn't afford to abolish it in Paris.

In 1783 Minister of Finance Charles Alexandre de Calonne had approved the construction of a controversial new city wall and tollhouses, or *bureaux*, in an attempt to shore up the decrepit tax-collecting system. Ten feet high and eighteen miles in circumference, the wall was intended to prevent smugglers from avoiding the farmers-general, the government's private tax collectors. Many disgruntled Parisians, however, saw the new customs houses as emblems of a bankrupt government desperate for funds, a need made more urgent by the financial aid France had given to the American cause ten years earlier. Paris wags quickly nicknamed the gateways "Calonnades" to mock the unpopular minister.

The gate beside Jefferson's house had recently been abandoned for one of the new tollhouses located farther up the hill known as the Montagne du Roule (or Etoile). Jefferson caustically referred to them as "the palaces by which we are to be let in and out."[5] To him, the tollhouse symbolized callous oppression on the part of a profligate government, although he confessed that it had given his sparsely settled neighborhood a feeling of security. In fact, he had recently installed security bars and bells in his house.

In letters to friends, particularly in England, where the recent attack on the old Bastille fortress had caused great concern, the Virginian tried to hide his anxiety about the festive lawlessness breaking out in Paris. He lightly assured Maria Cosway in London that while "the cutting off heads is become so much à la mode, that one is apt to feel of a morning whether their own is on their shoulders," the practice would pass like all French fashions and "the spirit of vengeance" would "soon be at rest," except among "a few of the obnoxious characters."[6]

Throughout August and early September 1789, following the fall of the Bastille, the National Assembly (the former Estates-General) continued to debate a new constitution. On the night of August 4, the vicomte de Noailles proposed resolutions essentially exchanging the nobility's old feudal status and privileges for those that would establish the universal title of "citizen." On August 26 the assembly adopted the Declaration of the Rights of Man and Citizen. Jefferson had watched each encouraging step, the "conscientious devotion to these rights...aroused and excited by daily exercise." On September 13 he confidently reported to Thomas Paine in London that "they have decided here some principal outlines of their constitution. 1. That the national assembly shall be in constant existence. 2. That it shall consist of but one house. 3. That the king shall have a negative on their laws, not absolute, but suspensive only till another assembly shall decide ultimately. It is not yet decided whether their elections shall be annual, biennial, or triennial.... Tranquillity is well established in Paris and tolerably so throughout the kingdom." Nothing, he assured Paine, would stop the establishment of a sound constitution suited to the existing French state of affairs, which would be in its principles somewhere between those of England and the United States.[7]

To Maria Cosway, the Virginian wrote how fortunate he had been to "see in the course of fourteen years two such revolutions that were never before seen."[8] It was one of the first times Jefferson had used the word *revolution* to characterize the unrest that betrayed the fault lines running just beneath the surface of French society. He still imagined that a resolute application of rational political strategy would calm the gods of change "without bloodshed." Reason and legitimacy would triumph over terror, although a little punitive violence in the name of liberty, judiciously applied, was justified even for Jefferson.

It was this faith in a constitutional revolution—reinforced, if necessary, by the military—that united the guests Jefferson had invited to his house: the duke de La Rochefoucauld, the marquis de Lafayette, the marquis de Condorcet, and Gouverneur Morris. It was, as his parties usually were, a conspicuously luminous affair. Jefferson had an aversion to goodbyes and the uncomfortable emotions they might stir up. A letter after the fact was his usual way of saying farewell, but the dinner on September 17 was the kind of intimate, polished gathering he favored. It would continue to be his style later as President of the United States. Jefferson's personality always shone under his own roof, where, in the words of Henry Adams, "among friends as genial and cheerful as himself, his ideas could flow freely, and could be discussed with sympathy."[9]

Condorcet was the first to arrive. Mathematician, academician, philosophe, pamphleteer, he had been one of the early defenders of the American rebellion. A tall, awkward, shy man of large frame, he was just Jefferson's age, forty-six. Nervous and ill at ease even with close friends, he had a habit of biting his lips and nails, betraying a bottled-up fury that seemed perpetually on the verge of exploding. In dress he was careless, prompting Julie Lespinasse, the great friend of the Encyclopedists, to complain that he always had powder in his ears and his hair cut unfashionably short. His mentor Jean d'Alembert called him a "snow-capped volcano." John Adams was struck by his strange pallor when they first met in 1778, but decided it was probably caused by too much "hard work." Condorcet's rocklike features, which the sculptor Jean-Antoine Houdon captured so well, might

Marquis de Condorcet by Jean-Antoine Houdon, 1785.
A member of the liberal wing of the philosophes, Condorcet still believed in the utopian reform of society when he finally committed suicide to escape the Jacobin police in 1794.

have appealed to Gutzon Borglum for one of his portraits on the side of Mount Rushmore.

Some of his acquaintances thought Condorcet's astringent personality, his coldness and distance, a facade hiding a deeper rage. His friend Amelia Suard discerned a profound neurosis at the root of his emotionally charged political beliefs. "Between the malice of his mind and the goodness of his heart, there was always a contrast that I found singularly striking," she recalled. "His intolerance on matters of political opinion was incredible."[10] The historian Jules Michelet believed that Condorcet's daughter and only child had been conceived on the night the Bastille fell, and his biographer Keith Baker suggests that Condorcet's political philosophy found its ultimate consummation in his passionate love for his wife, Sophie de Grouchy, who shared his radical political zeal.[11]

Deeply and romantically committed to the American experiment, Condorcet was convinced of its decisive impact on the Old World. Both he and Jefferson saw the American and French revolutions as crucially linked in their success or failure. Jefferson's obsession with the idea of the French Revolution as a validation of American ideals would fester long after he left Paris. Condorcet's pamphlet *De l'Influence de la révolution de l'Amérique sur l'Europe*, published in 1786, was followed by a supplement on the newly minted American constitution, complete with a translation of the text. Condorcet believed that the United States could serve as the model and inspiration for a new French government. "It is not enough that the rights of man be written in the books of philosophers and inscribed in the hearts of virtuous men," he declared; "the weak and ignorant must be able to read them in the example of a great people."[12]

Among the leaders of radical French thought in the eighteenth century whom we call philosophes—Voltaire, Diderot, Raynal, d'Alembert, Helvétius, Holbach, Condorcet—only the last was young enough to become an intimate friend of Jefferson. Condorcet's restless, inquiring mind, disciplined by a love of mathematics and science, immediately appealed to the Virginian. Sharing the rational, critical, universal language of the age, the two men had an uncompromising faith in human progress. Condorcet believed in man's infinite perfectibility with an almost theological intensity. He was also, like Jefferson, a visionary optimist. "Everything tells us that we are bordering the period of one of the greatest revolutions of the human race," he declared. "The present state of enlightenment guarantees that it will be happy."[13] It was probably the last moment in history when a European intellectual could make such an unqualified, foolhardy declaration of faith in the future of civilization.

Gouverneur Morris, the young New York patrician who arrived next at the Hôtel de Langeac, had come to Paris only the previous February to enter the world of international business. A big man with a high-bridged aristocratic nose, he did not share either his host's or Condorcet's optimism about the current political situation, let alone their giddy, radical belief in human progress. At thirty-seven, Morris had already acquired an impressive reputation as a constitution maker and financier. His job in Paris was to represent what James Madison called the "deranged" financial affairs of the Philadelphia businessman Robert Morris (who was no relation). The New Yorker carried gilt-edged letters of introduction from George Washington and Benjamin Franklin.

Morris loved pleasure as much as business. His engaging personality served as a passport to the best Paris drawing rooms and boudoirs, where his wooden leg encouraged receptive sympathy from the women he attracted. His temperament was as full-blooded as any Frenchman's. He shared a mistress, the beautiful countess de Flahaut, with the bishop of Autun—better known as Talleyrand—who also happened to be the father of the countess's young son.[14] Like the bishop, Morris had a "connoisseur's relish for the intricate games people played with each other."[15] Morris's description of the ménage à trois at the countess's apartment captures the casual amorality of Parisian high society: "My friend's Countenance glows with Satisfaction in looking at the Bishop and myself as we sit together agreeing in Sentiment & supporting the Opinions of each other. What Triumph for a Woman! I leave her to go Home with him and thus risque heroically the Chance of Cuckholdom."[16]

Morris made a point of visiting Jefferson's house frequently, even though he had never met the diplomat before coming to France. Morris's usually unannounced calls (most Americans in Paris felt free to drop by the minister's residence without an invitation) seem to have been prompted more by an interest in sniffing out diplomatic developments, especially in the commercial realm, than by real intimacy or friendship. Morris's diary makes it clear that Jefferson kept him at a distance. Elegant, witty, and corrupt by the Virginian's lofty standards, Morris never established close ties with the cool envoy.[17] Invited to sign a letter of tribute to be presented to Jefferson on his last Fourth of July in Paris in 1789, Morris curtly refused, saying only that he was "against the Measure and against the Thing."[18] His pique can be traced in part to the fact that his mission in Paris was to repair the damage the minister had done in breaking Robert Morris's monopoly of American tobacco sales in France. The Philadelphian had cleverly negotiated an exclusive contract with the French government in 1785, without Jefferson's knowledge and in flat opposition to his goal of free trade.

Born in 1752 at Morrisania, the baronial family seat, Gouverneur Morris was educated at King's College (later Columbia University), a hotbed of Toryism among the faculty. He later read law and was admitted to the bar at age nineteen. Even though his mother remained a Loyalist and his half-brother was to marry the dowager duchess of Gordon, Morris wholeheartedly joined the American cause. With John Jay and Robert

Livingston, he helped draft the first constitution of New York State. Leaving New York during the British occupation, he sat in the Continental Congress in 1778 and 1779. Later he served for four years as Robert Morris's assistant superintendent of finance. His association with the financier, who had a reputation for speculation if not sharp practices, made him suspect in Jefferson's eyes. Moreover, the New Yorker seemed to move in the wrong part of high society, whose members all too often represented the views of the reactionary court.

Morris had come to Paris from Philadelphia, where he had been a delegate to the Constitutional Convention. Although he favored senatorial appointments for life and opposed strictly equal representation by the states in the Senate, he nevertheless agreed to the Constitution's final provisions. He also accepted the request of the convention's Committee on Style to put the document in its final form, a task that even Madison conceded was gracefully done. "The *finish* given to the style and arrangement of the Constitution fairly belongs to the pen of Mr. Morris," Madison wrote to Morris's early biographer Jared Sparks.[19]

In his incomparable diary, Morris has left us the only first-hand account of the gathering at what a friend called Jefferson's "charming villetta... within gunshot distance of the city wall." Shortly after Morris arrived at the Hôtel de Langeac, "the Duc de La Rochefoucauld comes in from the States General and at half past four La Fayette, when we sit down to dinner."[20] (On June 17, the Estates-General called by the king had in fact become the National Assembly.) Distinguished, scholarly, and unceremonious, with a touch of the rustic, La Rochefoucauld had struck up a friendship with the American minister. The conspicuously liberal sympathies of Louis-Alexandre, duke de La Rochefoucauld d'Enville, his quiet influence within the upper nobility, and his unwavering support of American independence quickly made him a political confidant as well. "I beg you'd put Mr. Franklin in Mind of Introducing you To the Good duke La Rochefoucauld," the French consul, St. John de Crèvecoeur, wrote Jefferson from New York. "He is the pearl of all the Dukes a Good Man and an most able Chemyst. His House is the Cente[r] of [reunion] where Men of Genius and abilities Often Meet. You have therefore a great Right To Share his Friendship."[21]

Condorcet and Lafayette, along with virtually every American to turn up in Paris, were among the regulars at the Hôtel de La Rochefoucauld. It was after dinner there in "a large Company of Dukes, Abbes and men of Science" that an impressed John Adams noted in his diary the mathematician's chalky face.[22] By coincidence, La Rochefoucauld had first introduced the young Lafayette to the distinguished philosophe, providing the decidedly unphilosophical military leader a link to the rarefied world of ideas where Condorcet reigned as permanent secretary of the Academy of Sciences.

The duke, who represented one of the most illustrious families in France, counted among a long roster of distinguished ancestors François de La Rochefoucauld, the author of *Réflections ou sentences et maximes morales*. His famous collection of axioms was one of the more popular French books that found their way in translation into many libraries in the former colonies. Jefferson had a French edition at Monticello.

The fifty-three-year-old La Rochefoucauld was a reflective, urbane gentleman farmer who shared Jefferson's interest in scientific agricultural experiments. At the Château de La Roche-Guyon, his large estate in Normandy, not far from Paris, the duke operated a model farm where American friends were occasionally invited for country weekends. Jefferson first visited the château in the summer of 1785. The marquis de Chastellux, Condorcet, and other leading philosophes were often included in these relaxed outings as well.

During the American war, with the help of his friend Benjamin Franklin, La Rochefoucauld had translated the various American state constitutions for a clandestine periodical entitled *Les Affaires de l'Angleterre et de l'Amérique*. In 1783 these constitutions were published, with additional key documents, as *Constitutions des treize Etats-Unis de l'Amérique*. The volume contained the Declaration of Independence along with the first draft of the famous Virginia Bill of Rights (comprising all eighteen articles of the original charter, though only sixteen were actually adopted by the Virginia Assembly). The compilation represented the most significant and influential group of documents published in France on the American effort to sever its ties with Great Britain. La Rochefoucauld did not name the author of the Declaration in his book.[23]

The marquis de Lafayette's last-minute arrival on that cool September afternoon had his usual theatrical touch. Jefferson and the other

Louis-Alexandre, duke de La Rochefoucauld. Engraved by Fiesinger after J. Guérin, ca. 1790. (Bibliothèque Nationale de France, Paris)

guests were probably waiting in the oval salon overlooking the garden when he arrived. A pair of tall gilt-framed mirrors, which would later hang in Monticello's parlor, seemed made for the walls flanking the doorway and helped dispel the season's gloom. The pale twilight seeping over the polished floors from the windows in the oval bay silhouetted the men standing there.

Jefferson's private opinion of Lafayette was ambivalent. To Madison's appraisal of the marquis' character—that he was as "amiable a man as his vanity will admit"—Jefferson responded in diplomatic code that it was "precisely agreeable to the idea I have formed," adding that he took "*him* to be of *unmeasured ambition* but that the *means he uses* are virtuous." Later he remarked patronizingly that Lafayette had "a great deal of sound genius."[24] Except that both were tall, sandy-haired, unassuming, and well bred, their manners slightly starched with an initial chilliness, Lafayette and Jefferson had little in common beyond high-minded ideals and mutual respect.[25] Nevertheless, during their long collaboration, first in Virginia and now in Paris, they forged a genuine friendship that shines through the formality of their letters. Jefferson, writing after his return to the United

States to tell Lafayette that he had been named secretary of state, expressed a courteous regret that he would not be "returning to the far more agreeable position which placed me in daily participation of your friendship."[26]

Lafayette had been honored with citizenship by several American states and cities in 1784. (Earlier he had been inducted into the Iroquois tribe.) In October 1784, having heard that Jefferson was at last in Paris, he wrote that he hoped the Virginian would ultimately succeed Franklin as the American minister, "an event which Both as a frenchman, and an American, I most warmly desire." He ended his warm note with an offer of hospitality: "My house, Dear Sir, My family, and anything that is mine are entirely at your disposal, and I Beg you will come and see Mme. de Lafayette as you would act by your Brother's wife. Her knowledge of the Country May be of use to Miss Jefferson whom she will be Happy to attend in every thing that may be agreeable to Her.—indeed, My dear Sir, I would be angry with you, if you or she, did not consider my House as a second Home."[27]

Lafayette had met Jefferson in May 1781, during the last year of the American war. "When I first learned of that quarrel, my heart was enlisted, and I thought only of joining the colors," he wrote in a draft of his early *Memoirs* in 1779.[28] For all his later revolutionary ardor, Lafayette's initial motives were a volatile mixture of vanity, boredom, and vague yearning for military glory. An adolescent urge to fight France's hereditary enemy, England, combined with a huge bank account, had brought the nineteen-year-old aristocrat to America in 1777, a romantic knight-errant bent on going to the rescue of the beleaguered American *résistance*.

At thirty-two the youngest man at Jefferson's farewell dinner, Lafayette had been born into an ancient provincial family in the Auvergne. His ancestors had remained comfortably obscure for generations, rarely stirring beyond their domains except to fight, usually against the British, and often to die for the king. Lafayette's father had been killed by an English cannonball during the Battle of Minden in 1759, when his son was only two years old. His mother's death eleven years later made Lafayette one of the richest orphans in France, and the powerful Noailles family lost no time in selecting the boy-marquis to marry the duke de Noailles' granddaughter Adrienne.

While his mother spent most of her time in her native Paris with her rich family, Lafayette was raised by an adoring grandmother and two aunts at the rustic, isolated Château Chavaniac in the Auvergne. Against this feudal backdrop, the heir and only male hope of his family saw himself at an early age standing in the center and in command of his immediate world. On his first trip to Paris, he was surprised that the peasants he met on the road after leaving his own estates did not automatically lift their caps to him. It was in the Auvergne that he imbibed a near-fatal potion of family myth and romance, of fanciful glory mostly drawn from the battlefield. Lafayette's need to shine, to ride at the head of the parade, was obvious to friends and critics throughout his life. Jefferson famously characterized his obsessive desire for glory and adulation as a "canine appetite," adding in his own coded character sketch to Madison that he would "get above it" in time.

EACH MAN AROUND JEFFERSON'S TABLE in the rue de Berri shared their host's open, candid faith in the natural rights of mankind, his dream of new self-governing republics on both sides of the Atlantic. And each man had staked his fortune and reputation on the success of their respective experiments, which now seemed so closely intertwined.

At that very moment in 1789, a new American government was being organized under the presidency of George Washington. With luck, France too might take the first step toward a stable constitution, avoiding further bloodletting. It in turn would serve as an exemplar for other European nations. But the collapse of the struggle to neutralize, if not remove, the decrepit Bourbon monarchy could have perilous consequences for the fledgling United States. Not only would it be unmistakable proof to the world that republics were a passing aberration, it undoubtedly would undermine America's fragile legitimacy and banking credit. Jefferson's concern with American legitimacy was reflected in everything he did, from his hospitality at the Hôtel de Langeac to his confident appearance at court. As a diplomat representing a parvenu nation, he saw that legitimacy was critical in dealing with a court so ancient and secure that its privileges and authority had never been challenged. But the quick succession of events—the calling of the Estates-General in May, the creation of the National Assembly in June, the fall of the Bastille in July, and, by August, the prospect of a written constitution prefaced, as in Virginia, with a Declaration of the Rights of Man—had suddenly called the legality of the king's government into question. No one could predict the outcome.

Jefferson, with his unvarnished optimism, had written a German diplomat in early August, only three weeks after the surrender of the Bastille, that never had "so great a fermentation...produced so little injury," claiming that he had "quietly slept...thro' the whole as I ever did in the most peaceable moments." Neither the Virginian nor his friends saw the civil convulsions in particularly apocalyptic terms. The National Assembly's methodical work on a proposed constitution must have appeared to Jefferson "a little like revising the Virginia Code," the only difference being that nearly every member seemed to have a declaration of rights or a constitution in his pocket, ready to be introduced at a moment's notice. With good timing and perseverance, Jefferson confidently ended his letter, the French experience might well be "but the first chapter of the history of European liberty."[29]

The guests at the Hôtel de Langeac quickly got down to the dangerous events that had turned Paris into a powder keg in recent days. There were unsettling rumors that Louis XVI was secretly planning to flee to the garrison town of Metz near the German border, where sympathetic foreign troops could come to his rescue. On September 19 Jefferson reported to Jay that he believed such a plot was quite possible and could well spark a St. Bartholomew Massacre; he had probably first caught wind of the king's plans at his dinner two days before.[30]

Lafayette had a more disturbing story to relate. A few nights earlier, at a dinner with his battalion commanders of the Paris National Guard, a small group had taken their commandant general aside and told him that a number of guardsmen were planning to rejoin the king's bodyguard at Versailles, their old unit. There was clearly a lack of discipline among the troops. Some professed that they merely wanted to keep a closer watch on the king in case he should attempt to escape to Metz. But their motives were obviously confused, even sinister. Lafayette's account presaged major trouble at a critical moment when the National Assembly and the king could not agree on a safe transition to a constitutional monarchy.

Later the night of September 17, Morris in his diary expressed doubts that Lafayette could control his troops in defending Paris, although the general had assured Jefferson and the other guests that his men "would readily follow him into action"—if, he added, it didn't rain.[31] It may have been this odd qualification that prompted Morris to write with evident foreboding: "This man is very much below the Business he has undertaken and if the Sea runs high he will be unable to hold the helm.... I have known my Friend Lafayette now for many Years and can therefore estimate at the just Value both his Words and Actions. If the Clouds which now lower should be dissipated without a Storm he will be infinitely indebted to Fortune, but if it happen otherwise the World must pardon much on the score of Intention."[32]

The ominous bread shortage was on the mind of everyone that afternoon. Morris, always the alert businessman on the lookout for a potential market for American grain, hastened to make an appointment with Lafayette "to confer on the subject of Subsistence." When Lafayette offhandedly suggested that they discuss it later over a meal at his house, Morris—displaying an early symptom of the ingrained American suspicion that the French are never quite serious even in a crisis—privately dismissed the invitation as "idle" because the general usually had "a Crowd and is but a few Minutes at Home."[33]

On August 25, ignoring any embarrassment it might cause a scrupulous diplomat representing a foreign country, Lafayette had sent Jefferson an urgent note: "I Beg for liberty's sake You will breack Every Engagment to Give us a dinner to morrow Wednesday. We shall Be some Members of the National Assembly—eight of us whom I want to Coalize [bring to a compromise] as Being the only Means to prevent a total dissolution and civil war." The crisis in the assembly had been triggered by the thorny issue of whether the proposed constitution should provide for a royal veto. In spite of his professed reluctance to involve himself too closely in French domestic controversies, Jefferson had agreed not only to allow his house to be used for the critical negotiations but to collaborate silently by his presence.

The next morning, with diplomatic prudence, Jefferson lost no time in getting to the office of the count de Montmorin, the French minister of state, to explain "with truth and candor, how it had happened that my house had been made the scene of conferences of such a character." The canny minister, claiming that he already knew about the meeting, replied that, far from being upset, he wished Jefferson would hold more conferences, as he was "sure I should be useful in moderating the warmer spirits, and promoting a wholesome and practical reformation only."[34]

AS JEFFERSON AND HIS GUESTS moved to the small dining room, reminiscent of the public rooms of a comfortable Virginia plantation house, the atmosphere was quickened by the personal ties among the group. Few figures in American public life understood the fine art of entertaining better than Jefferson.[35] In Paris he carried on the tradition summed up in the commonplace expression "Virginia hospitality," which he defined so well in a letter to a neighbor in Albemarle County: "You know our practice of placing our guests at their ease and showing them we are so ourselves, and that we follow our necessary vocations instead of fatiguing them by holding unremittingly on their shoulders."[36] Gouverneur Morris noted the respect that Jefferson commanded among *le monde* of Paris and Versailles. "The french, who pique themselves on possessing the Graces, very readily excuse in others the Want of them; and to be an *Étranger* (like Charity) covers a Multitude of Sins. On the whole therefore I incline to think that an American Minister at this Court gains more than he loses by preserving his Originality."[37]

That Jefferson was original not only in his thinking but also in his manners and slightly *outré* appearance may have been part of his appeal to jaded Parisians. The most picturesque portrait of the Virginian in middle age was recorded less than a year after he left Paris. William Maclay, a senator from Pennsylvania, described Jefferson, now secretary of state, making his first and only appearance before a Senate committee:

> Jefferson is a slender man, has rather the air of stiffness in his manner. His clothes seem too small for him. He sits in a lounging manner, on one hip

Table and mirror, French, ca. 1780. Jefferson purchased these handsome pieces for his Paris residences and later shipped them to Monticello. As an ensemble now installed in an eighteenth-century Virginia manor house, they evoke their original settings in Paris. (Courtesy of Mrs. Robert H. Carter. Photo provided by Monticello/Thomas Jefferson Memorial Foundation, Inc.)

commonly, and with one of his shoulders elevated much above the other. His face has a scranny aspect. His whole figure has a loose, shackling air. He has a rambling vacant look, and nothing of that firm collected deportment which I expected would dignify the presence of a Secretary or Minister. I looked for gravity, but a laxity of manner shed about him. He spoke almost without ceasing. But even his discourse partook of personal demeanor. It was loose and rambling, and yet he scattered information wherever he went, and some even brilliant sentiments sparkled from him.[38]

Maclay's unflattering sketch needs to be balanced by the portrait John Trumbull painted during his stay with Jefferson in Paris in the winter of 1787–88. The author of the Declaration of Independence appears relaxed and collected in Trumbull's recreation of the famous scene in Philadelphia. There is even a hint of smug satisfaction in his face. His clothes are fastidious, the conspicuous red vest adding a bit of sartorial dash. The earliest portrait of Jefferson, painted by Mather Brown in 1786, similarly suggests a self-conscious dandy, with his overly ruffled jabot and tightly curled wig. A comparison between the soft face in the Brown portrait and the taut, heroic bust of Jefferson by Houdon reveals two utterly different personalities. There is no "loose, shackling air" in the chiseled, urbane features of Houdon's likeness; Jefferson's steady gaze and the backward tilt of his head convey instead an air of toughness and intellectual arrogance. The substantial London tailor's bills recorded in Jefferson's *Memorandum Books* likewise contradict Maclay's charge of ill-fitting clothes.

The "rambling vacant look" and absence of "firm collected deportment" that the congressman detected are more difficult to explain. Maclay may have sensed a reaction to the confusing, alien world that Jefferson found on his return to the United States in 1790. It was a different country from the one he had conjured in his idealized recollections, and certainly foreign to the liberal society he had known in Paris for the past five years. Jefferson later wrote of dinner parties in New York: "I cannot describe, the wonder and mortification with which the table conversations filled me....A preference of kingly over republican government was evidently the favorite sentiment."

As Henry Randall observed in his nineteenth-century biography,

Jefferson's "manners had the grace, finish, suavity and unpresumingness... of a well-bred Frenchman." Even the envoy's appetites were
French. "He ate delicately and sparingly of light materials, and chose the
lightest wines of French vintage. His physical, and in some particulars his
mental constitution seems to us to have more resembled the man of
Southern than the man of Northern Europe."[39] Jefferson made a point of
laying a lavish table and serving excellent wines from the moment he
arrived in Paris. Young Nabby Adams was amazed by how thoroughly the
American diplomatic community had taken on French fashions. "There is
no such thing here as preserving our taste in anything," she wrote after a
dinner given by the American account commissioner in August 1784. "We
must all sacrifice to custom and fashion. I will not believe it possible to do
otherwise for my papa, with his firmness and resolution, is a perfect con-
vert to the mode in everything, at least of dress and appearance."[40]

One of the new Parisian fashions that Jefferson immediately adopted—
and later introduced at Monticello and in Washington—was the use of
small, individual serving tables placed between guests in dining rooms,
eliminating the need for servants in the room during the meal. Years later
in Washington, Margaret Bayard Smith recalled Jefferson's remark "that
much of the domestic and even public discord was produced by the mutilated and misconstructed repetition of free conversations at dinner tables,
by these mute but not inattentive listeners."[41] In the waning years of the
old regime, both the promise of liberty and inklings of its suppression
were subjects best discussed out of earshot of servants. The often conspir-
atorial quality of these dinner-table conversations, especially among *les
grands* and regardless of their politics, made the removal of inquisitive
attendants all the more urgent.

William S. Smith, later John Adams's son-in-law, was impressed by
this social innovation when he dined with Lafayette shortly after arriving
in Paris. "There were only us two," he wrote; "the table was laid with
great neatness. By the side of each was fixed, (I'll call it) a dumb waiter.
On which was placed half a dozen clean plates, knives and forks, and a
small bell on the one near the Marquis, and the servants retired. The
first course being over, he rung the bell and it was removed for the second. Thus we spent an hour and a half with great ease and friendship; not

incommoding the servants, nor being subject to their inspection. Indeed the arrangement was charming."[42]

The domestic staff of the Hôtel de Langeac was headed by Adrien Petit, the *maître d'hôtel* who ran the house under Jefferson's meticulous supervision. He oversaw the kitchens, the wine cellar, and the stables, handling all the household accounts and directing the other servants: Legrand, the *valet de chambre*, Saget, the *frotteur* who polished the parquet and tile floors, and Vendôme, the coachman. James Hemings, a talented young slave from Monticello, served as Jefferson's private servant. Hemings was later given training in French cooking, although Jefferson often used Parisian caterers for his private dinner parties. After an apprenticeship in the impressive kitchens of the prince de Condé, Hemings assumed the duties of *chef de cuisine* in the rue de Berri. When Jefferson retired from public life in 1793, he drew up an agreement giving Hemings his freedom. In the contract, Jefferson referred to the "great expense" of teaching Hemings "the art of cookery" and stipulated that Hemings train a successor as the price of his freedom.[43]

Jefferson also had a full-time gardener to tend the extensive grounds that had first attracted him to the Hôtel de Langeac. The gardens beyond the house and stables, where he grew sweet corn from the Cherokee country and other American vegetables, took up a major part of the complex and gave the house the feeling of a small villa. There was enough space for Jefferson to experiment with cultivating grapes, as he had done at Monticello, using cuttings sent by his friend Baron Geismar after the two men visited vineyards in the Rhine Valley in 1788. Jefferson responded to the irregular configuration of space by designing a well-defined garden of urban dimensions—a challenge he had not faced at his sprawling estate in Virginia. Having studied the fashionable new *jardins anglais* scattered throughout Paris, he was anxious to try out his own original interpretation of the style.

Another resident of the rue de Berri was Jefferson's private secretary, William Short, who had followed his mentor to Paris from his native Virginia in 1784. Although small in stature, Short possessed a grace and an innate savoir-faire that quickly gained him entrée to the fashionable world he found so alluring. He was soon taken up by La Rochefoucauld's mother, the formidable old duchess d'Enville, and by the duke's vivacious young second wife, Rosalie. Nabby Adams, who met Short just before she moved to London with her parents, noted in her diary his "good figure...looks and manners." Her mother, Abigail, approvingly called his manners "modest and soft." The dashing young Virginian spoke well—he had spent his first six months in Paris polishing his French—and, with his talent for dancing and laughter, he quickly became a fixture in the La Rochefoucauld household.

By the fall of 1789, Jefferson's protégé, now the official secretary of the American legation, was caught up in a furtive love affair with Rosalie de La Rochefoucauld. Short may well have been preoccupied with his *éducation sentimentale* on September 17, or he may have declined Jefferson's dinner invitation on the excuse that he had the usual "squall of work." It is also possible that Jefferson had not invited him out of deference to the duke's feelings.[44] To Jefferson such extramarital affairs were a sign of moral decay, a blot on the otherwise near-perfect *vertu* of French society. Like a frontier preacher from the Piedmont, he was constantly taking the higher ground in letters to American friends. "Intrigues of love occupy the younger, and those of ambition, the elder part of the great," he wrote disapprovingly to Carlo Bellini, professor of modern languages at William and Mary College. "Conjugal love having no existence among them, domestic happiness of which that is the basis, is utterly unknown."[45] He often urged Short to return to Virginia as soon as possible to find a suitable wife.

The Hôtel de Langeac had been comfortably furnished during Jefferson's five years of constant collecting, but by September 1789 it had taken on a stripped-down, Spartan look. Paintings, busts, clocks, and a harpsichord, along with much of Jefferson's impressive library, had been packed since April. The baggage also contained foodstuffs unavailable in Virginia, such as macaroni, Parmesan cheese, dates, vinegar, olive oil, and tea, as well as a selection of wine destined for Monticello's cellars. Other hampers held an exotic assortment of plants, part of an ongoing horticultural exchange that Jefferson had operated with French friends during his stay and would continue long after his return to America. Among the plants bound for Virginia were two cork oak trees, a white fig, four specimens of *Mimosa farnesiana*, and cuttings of the newly fashionable Lombardy poplars that Jefferson would later plant along the avenue between the president's house and the unfinished Capitol building in Washington.[46]

The main purpose of the trip back to Virginia, as Jefferson recalled in his autobiography, was to settle his two daughters "in the society & care of their friends." Martha ("Patsy"), named for her deceased mother, and Mary ("Polly") had been enrolled in the convent school of the Abbaye Royale de Panthémont but visited the rue de Berri regularly, often with school friends. Expecting to depart for the United States at any moment, Jefferson had withdrawn the girls from the school in April 1789, but their music and dancing lessons had continued at home. He intended to return to Paris after spending six months in Virginia to check on affairs at Monticello and to negotiate with creditors over his pressing personal debts.[47]

ON SEPTEMBER 24 Gouverneur Morris dined at the rue de Berri, apparently unaware that his host planned to depart two days later. After the meal, the two men visited Houdon's nearby studio to take a final look at his unfinished marble sculpture of George Washington. It had been commissioned by the Virginia Assembly in 1784 and was destined for the new capitol building in Richmond. Jefferson had played the key role in securing the commission for Houdon, and Morris's commanding frame had provided a suitable model for the general's body.

Already crated for shipment to Virginia were Houdon's plaster busts of Washington, Franklin, Lafayette, and John Paul Jones. They would later decorate the new "tearoom" at Monticello, which Jefferson called his "most honorable suite." Also in his personal luggage was a set of gold and silver commemorative medals that Congress had ordered to honor Washington and other Revolutionary War heroes. Jefferson had carefully overseen their design by French medalists. He would present them to President Washington in their specially made velvet-lined boxes on April 21, 1790, the day he was appointed secretary of state.

Between September 24 and his departure, Jefferson tied up loose ends, entering in his account book that he had paid 192 livres to his daughters' dancing master. He also gave the eminent harpsichordist Claude Balbastre 144 livres, representing a month's wages, for the girls'

Lafayette by Jean-Antoine Houdon, 1787. The Virginia Assembly commissioned a portrait of the "Hero of Two Continents" when Lafayette was twenty-nine years old. The first version was presented to the City of Paris in 1786. Another was completed for Richmond a short time later. (The Library of Virginia, Richmond, Virginia)

last music lessons at Panthémont. On September 25 he "pd. servants wages, 343 livres," and early the following morning, on what Morris reckoned in his diary as "a prodigiously fine day," Jefferson, Martha, and Polly set off for Le Havre in his new London-made carriage. James Hemings and his sister, Sally, who had accompanied Polly to Paris as her maid, traveled in Jefferson's old phaeton. Petit accompanied the party as far as the port before returning to Paris, having received from Jefferson 402 livres "for traveling expenses."[48]

At Le Havre, high gales "with a fury almost unexampled" delayed the Channel crossing for ten days, giving Jefferson an opportunity to inspect the impressive work being carried out on the busy harbor. Le Havre, he predicted to Nathaniel Cutting, an American businessman who was traveling to London, would "one day be the first seat of commerce of France."[49] While "roving thro the neighborhood of this place," Jefferson decided to take a pair of sheep dogs back to Virginia. After walking ten miles in a blinding rain storm, he found a German shepherd bitch "big with pups" and bought her just before leaving.[50] Two puppies were born a few days later at Cowes, on the Isle of Wight, and were taken on to Monticello.

On October 5 Jefferson paid the final shipping charge at Le Havre for thirty-eight pieces of luggage and crates, the carriage, and phaeton. Most of the baggage had been dispatched from Paris early in September by river on a *diligence d'eau.*[51] Shortly after midnight on October 8, the sea now calm, the entourage finally left France, stopping briefly at Cowes to change ships for the long Atlantic voyage.

Four days earlier the French Revolution had suddenly lurched forward into its next epic stage. Jefferson had not yet received Short's letter of October 8 describing the royal family's forced removal from Versailles, and he dismissed the first alarming accounts in English newspapers, assuring his friend Madame de Corny that he "read all their details as I would those of a romance." On October 14, a week before he expected to "be underway, with a hopeful breeze," he wrote to Thomas Paine from Cowes. Irritated by the "romantic" English reports of the latest events in France, he confessed to experiencing a rush of elation as the second wave of rebellion swept over Paris, much as he had felt when the Bastille fell: "I have no news but what is given under that name in the English papers. You know how much of these I believe. So far I collect from them that the king, queen, and national assembly are removed to Paris. The mobs and murders under which they dress this fact are all rags in which religion robes the true god."[52]

Without realizing it, the forty-six-year-old envoy had finished his European education. Having eluded the snares designed to trap an innocent American bred in a simpler culture, he would be ready to return a few months later and pledge allegiance to the new order about to be born. His family had "left a turbulent scene," he wrote optimistically to Maria Cosway on October 14. "But a return of quiet and order...the ensuing spring might give us a meeting at Paris with the first swallow. So be it, my dear friend, and Adieu under the hope which springs natural out of what we wish. Once again then farewell, remember me and love me."[53]

Chapter 2

A Provincial Prelude

JEFFERSON DID NOT FOLLOW a straight Cartesian road from
Virginia to Paris. But the collaboration of the French army in the
American Revolution had helped pave the way and build a bridge of
understanding between New World and Old. When Filippo Mazzei, Jefferson's Albemarle neighbor, reported from Paris in 1780 that the
French were afraid the Americans might settle for a separate peace with
Britain, Jefferson, then governor of Virginia, was shocked. "Beleive me
no opinion can have less foundation," he replied immediately. "The disinterested exertions of France for us have not only made real impression
on the leaders of the people, but are deeply felt by the people themselves.
...Whenever the French and American troops have acted together the
harmony has been real, and not given out merely to influence the opinion
of the world."[1]

Lafayette exemplified this spirit of harmony conspicuously, and he had
played a critical role in repelling the British invasion of Virginia. Gen.
Charles Cornwallis had found his French adversary, whom he derisively
called the "boy," dangerously elusive in the crucial spring of 1781, when the
outcome of the conflict hung in the balance. Later in Paris, Jefferson found
Lafayette's friendship steadfast and would be "powerfully aided by all the
influence and the energies of the Marquis de La Fayette, who proved himself equally zealous for the friendship and welfare of both nations."[2]

Few Virginians during Jefferson's formative years of the 1760s and
1770s saw France as the cultural touchstone of European civilization. For
Americans, the unquestioned standard remained England. The French
language was not an evident element or even an occasional veneer in the
conversation and reading of the Virginia gentry, the provincial society that

Jefferson grew up in. His famous "Bill for the More General Diffusion of Knowledge," drafted in 1778, specified neither French literature, even in translation, nor French history among the books to be uniformly used throughout the state. "At every of these schools, the books which shall be used...for instructing the children to read shall be such as will at the same time make them acquainted with Graecian, Roman, English, and American history," the bill declared.[3]

Training for a career in international diplomacy was no apparent part of Jefferson's education. Nor was he prepared for life in an international capital like Paris after the American triumph at Yorktown, when the nation was about to risk its future on an unprecedented experiment. As a revolutionary society, America had not had time to clarify its own ideals, nor had it developed a working notion of European politics and society, beyond fairly narrow prejudices and confused assumptions. This fact alone makes Jefferson's open, confident entry into an unknown society, a world utterly removed from anything he had experienced before, all the more remarkable and should be kept in mind as his engrossing European education progresses.

Jefferson would have agreed with the American poet Delmore Schwartz's observation that Europe was "the greatest thing in North America," representing the long succession of historical forces that had created it.[4] He also would have acknowledged the other important half of the truth: that Europe from the beginning was (as it still is) the most rejected thing in America. In his efforts to come to terms with Europe during his five years in Paris and his subsequent public career in Philadelphia and Washington, Jefferson combined something of each of these pieties, looking both backward to the past (Europe) and forward to the future (America).

Jefferson actually had twice turned down opportunities to go abroad before agreeing to join Franklin and John Adams in Paris as minister plenipotentiary in 1784. His wife's recurring illness had kept him home in 1776. Five years later, in August 1781, he elected to stay and defend his reputation when his performance as wartime governor of Virginia was brought into question and made the subject of an official inquiry by the Virginia Assembly. During the spring session of 1781, the assembly, or what was left of it, along with the governor, had been on the run from town to town, with British forces in hot pursuit. On Junè 4, in a famous and humiliating episode, an English advance guard under the command of Col. Banestre Tarleton missed their prey by minutes at Charlottesville after the harried Virginia officials "adjourned" out of harm's way over the mountain to Staunton. The vague charges of incompetence against the governor were later dropped by the assembly.

Jefferson was not cut out to requisition horses, boats, and wagons in time of war. He was mercifully relieved when his term as governor expired in June 1781, allowing him to retire to Monticello. A desperate legislature selected Gen. Thomas Nelson, Jr., commander of the state troops, to finish out the war as governor. Jefferson, not for the last time, was ready to renounce public life forever. As he wrote to Lafayette, then serving with the American forces in Virginia, in August: "The independence of private life under the protection of republican laws will I hope, yeild me that happiness from whi[ch] no slave is so remote as the minister of a Commonwealth."[5] By turning down the French post, he believed he was losing his only opportunity to combine public service with private gratification.

One accomplishment in which Jefferson had taken pride during his administration was the reorganization in 1779 of the run-down William and Mary College and the introduction of French into the curriculum. In effecting these changes at his alma mater, he had abolished the old grammar school and, more significant, the professorship of divinity in order to create a professorship of modern languages. Both the prospects of international commerce and the war itself had convinced a number of Virginia leaders that a knowledge of French and Italian was essential. Moreover, the participation of French troops in the Revolution fostered a wave of francophilia, at least among the better-informed and -educated classes, and tentative friendship seemed to be moving toward a more permanent relationship.

Virginia society, made up mainly of uneducated yeomen-farmers and slaves, hardly provided a suitable cultural background for a diplomatic post in the most important capital in Europe. Nor did it offer any of the amenities that Jefferson considered essential to the good life—books, music, works of art, fine wine, food, and above all good conversation. America's rustic settlements seemed a planet away from the urbane civility of Paris, and Jefferson's Hôtel de Langeac would have stunned most of his neighbors in Virginia. Even the food he learned to serve in Paris would have been suspect to provincials like Patrick Henry, who rebuked his fellow Virginian for "abjur[ing] his native victuals." (In fact, Jefferson regularly stocked his Paris larders with a supply of Virginia hams and bacon that he ordered from home.)

Scarcely a single house in the entire former colonies could match the Hôtel de Langeac's sophistication and style, its furnishings or cuisine. In a well-known passage in his *Notes on the State of Virginia*, written before he had seen France, Jefferson complained bitterly of the architectural "maledictions" that had been "shed" upon his own state. Houses in Virginia, he wrote, were "rarely constructed of stone or brick; much the greatest proportion being of scantling and boards, plastered with lime. It is impossible to devise things more ugly, uncomfortable, and happily more perishable."[6] The cultural impoverishment the sensitive Virginian had endured is touchingly conveyed in a letter written to Giovanni Fabbroni in Paris in June 1778. Although music "is the favorite passion of my soul," Jefferson laments, "fortune has cast my lot in a country where it is in a state of deplorable barbarism." He asks Fabbroni to help find some skilled workmen who are needed at Monticello and who can also "perform on the French horn, clarinet or hautboy and bassoon." Should they be willing to come to America, they could double as a private orchestra at Monticello while working at their crafts, since "the Bounds of an American fortune will not admit the indulgence of a domestic band of musicians."[7]

Enlightened French patricians, for their part, had a rapturous and largely mythical vision of life in the former British colonies. In their minds, the New World was an Arcadia settled by simple but learned farmers at peace with the world, except for the common enemy, England. Much of this nostalgic propaganda had been spread by Franklin, who convinced his French friends that all working men in Pennsylvania read a newspaper every day at noon and a bit of philosophy by candlelight at night. Another story, promulgated by Jefferson himself, had New Jersey farmers forming sturdy wagon wheels by bending wet willow branches according to Homer's directions in the *Iliad*.

In much of Jefferson's boyhood Virginia, a different kind of mirage had formed. The colonial perception of France was seriously clouded by suspicion and ignorance, an attitude formed at least as early as the French and Indian Wars. The French government was viewed as a model of despotism and tyranny, its Catholic religion a relic of the Dark Ages and its moral standards a threat to every honest, hard-working American. Try as he might to overcome it, this recurring image haunted Jefferson as he plunged into the cultivated pleasures of Paris, "indulgences" that were alien to the simple life in Albemarle County. Perhaps because of its admitted attractions, Jefferson repeatedly singled out French high society—particularly kings, bishops, and women—in his indictments of the Old World.

Unlike Franklin, who transformed his fellow countrymen into simple Quakers to the delight of his enthralled Parisian audience, no clever French propagandists roamed the Virginia woods painting Paris or Versailles as Montparnasse. In 1760, when Jefferson entered college, anti-French sentiments were widespread among ordinary Americans. All Frenchmen were either victims of a benighted Jesuit education and schooled in treachery or immoral followers of Voltaire, free-thinkers, frivolous and undependable. As late as the closing days of the Revolution, an American officer wrote his superior in Virginia, "The people do not like Frenchmen; every person they cant understand they take for a Frenchman." This, of course, was a "wool hat," backwoods reaction, a far cry from the grand receptions given to the French troops in the port cites of Newport, Philadelphia, Baltimore, and Charleston.

Jefferson's father, who built a sizable estate in the Virginia Piedmont, had seen to it that his son got the best education available in the colony. Jefferson considered it his father's greatest legacy. At an early age he was exposed to the wider world reached through the classics, just as they had served the equally provincial Lafayette growing up at the Château Chavaniac in the Auvergne. The latter's tutor, the abbé Fayon, had given his young charge a love of Latin commensurate to Jefferson's, even though Lafayette's formal schooling beyond his "merely military" education was somewhat inferior to the Virginian's.

Both boys had been marked for special roles in the "exalted spheres of life." At his first rather primitive school when he was six or seven, Jefferson was introduced to French by the Reverend William Douglas of Glencairn, whose limited knowledge of the language was further disguised by a heavy Scottish accent. A later teacher, Dr. James Maury—Jefferson called him "a correct, classical scholar"—whetted the young man's intellectual appetite for the full range of Enlightenment literature. His was by no means an isolated case; there were many pockets of learning throughout the colonies. Teachers and tutors had agreed upon a broad, eclectic, and dynamic, if sometimes ephemeral, body of literature. The new country itself was on its way to becoming one of the most characteristic products of the Enlightenment.

In America as in Europe, book collecting by individuals of means was symptomatic of the Enlightenment. In Paris Jefferson established direct contact with European booksellers and, though he could ill afford it, continued to buy books for the rest of his life, mainly in Paris, London, and Amsterdam. Many of the other Founding Fathers shared his addiction. Among the crates that returned to America with Jefferson in October 1789 were hefty boxes of books for the libraries of Franklin, Madison, and George Wythe.

Jefferson's first library was destroyed when his family house, Shadwell, burned in 1769—an incalculable loss in terms of measuring his early intellectual development. But two years later he drew up for a kinsman, Robert Skipwith, a list of 148 books suitable for the general reader. Skipwith had asked him to recommend titles that would be "improving and amusing" for someone who had little understanding of the classics and no "leisure for any intricate or tedious study." The "Skipwith List" allows us at least partially to reconstruct the library at Shadwell. Although Douglas Wilson has cautioned that not all of the volumes were in Jefferson's own collection,[8] it is fair to assume that many were, along with a small selection of translations of French authors, mostly in sets—Molière, Fénelon, Montesquieu, Marmontel, Rousseau, Bossuet's *History of France*, Buffon, and Voltaire. John James's *Theory and Practice of Gardening* was also on the list, a translation of Dezallier d'Argenville's treatise on laying out a classic French garden following the principles of André Le Nôtre; it may well have been Jefferson's first book on gardening. The young Virginian discovered the French playwright Jean Racine at an early age and sometime in the 1760s copied four extracts from Racine's tragedies into his *Literary Commonplace Book*, the only entries in the French language.[9]

Until Jefferson began his legal studies under George Wythe in 1762, his most talented teacher and friend in college was another Scot, William Small. Small was twenty-six when he arrived at William and Mary in 1758 to teach mathematics. He had studied medicine in Aberdeen, where he had absorbed the basic tenets of eighteenth-century scientific and philosophical inquiry. To Jefferson, who matriculated just as he was turning seventeen, Small must have been a breath of fresh air in the demoralized atmosphere of the college. He taught Jefferson virtually every subject and would carry him further into the mainstream of the Enlightenment.

It was Small who introduced the precocious student to the worldly circle of Gov. Francis Fauquier and Wythe, the lawyer/classicist. In old age Jefferson remembered dinners with the three older men at the governor's palace, where he heard "more good sense, more rational conversations" than he would ever hear again. Fauquier's father was a Huguenot physician who had worked for Sir Isaac Newton at the Royal Mint in London after escaping from France. Having inherited a fortune from an uncle, Fauquier was free to follow his personal interests in science and philosophy and became a fellow of the Royal Society. Thus did the European and American Enlightenments come together around the governor's table in Williamsburg. Embracing shared ideals and a universal faith in mankind, expressed in a common language, the cultivated Old World and the primitive outpost of the New seemed at least philosophically united.

Jefferson's sources and inspirations remained unconditionally international, in the spirit of the Enlightenment. In his *Summary View of the Rights of British America* of 1774, the young Virginian's first bold expression of his political philosophy, as in the Declaration of Independence, he invoked the political and philosophical heritage of England, France, Rome, and Greece and manipulated it for his own objectives. In the last year of his life, Jefferson wrote to Henry Lee describing the intellectual atmosphere in which the Declaration had been drafted: "Neither aiming at originality of principles or sentiment, nor yet copied from any particular and previous writing, it was intended to be an expression of the American mind, and to give to that expression the proper tone and spirit called for by the occasion. All its authority rests then on the harmonizing sentiments of the day, whether expressed in conversation, in letters, printed essays, or in the elementary books of public right, as Aristotle, Cicero, Locke, Sidney, &c."[10] Some of the most protean concepts expressed in the Declaration were drawn from French writers and philosophes—Montesquieu, Voltaire, Helvétius, Diderot—whose world Jefferson would finally enter in 1784.

IN THE SPRING OF 1782, following the American victory at Yorktown, the marquis de Chastellux, the soldier-philosopher who had been a general in Rochambeau's army, arrived at Monticello. The vision of Jefferson among his family and books on his secluded summit was one that could be fully appreciated only by a product of the Old World order fired with dreams of a new one. A member of the French Academy and author of *De la Félicité publique,* Chastellux was particularly impressed by Monticello's growing library, which, as Jefferson told Robert Skipwith, had been "formed on a more extensive plan" than its predecessor at Shadwell.[11]

The Frenchman admired the unfinished house "in the Italian style" resonating with classical references drawn from the books of Palladio, Gibbs, Morris, Kent, and Chambers. Jefferson had also acquired and used a number of French sources in his architectural experiments.[12] The magnificent folio edition of Perrault's *Architecture de Vitruve* was among his early books on architecture, and all of the interior frieze designs for the entrance hall, parlor, and his own bedroom at Monticello would be taken from the plates in Antoine Desgodetz's *Edifices antiques de Rome.* Chastellux found the original Monticello "quite tasteful…a large pavilion, into which one enters through two porticoes ornamented with columns. The ground floor consists chiefly of a large and lofty *salon,* or a drawing room, which is to be decorated entirely in the antique style; above the *salon* is a library of the same form; two small wings, with only a ground floor and attic are joined to this pavilion." Then, in a much-quoted line, he declared: "Mr. Jefferson is the first American who has consulted the fine arts to know how he should shelter himself from the weather."

Chastellux was even more impressed that his host preferred cultivating the arts and sciences on the edge of the wilderness to accepting his country's "honorable commission of Minister Plenipotentiary in Europe." At first the Frenchman found Jefferson's manner "grave and cold," but as

Marquis de Chastellux, by John Trumbull (detail from *The Surrender of Lord Cornwallis at Yorktown, 19 October 1781*). Trumbull painted the portrait from life in Paris in the winter of 1787–88. (Yale University Art Gallery, Trumbull Collection)

the two men began to talk, Chastellux quickly discovered a "conformity of feelings and opinions...so perfect that not only our tastes were similar, but our predilections." Since his youth Jefferson had, it seemed, "placed his mind, like his house, on a lofty height, whence he might contemplate the whole universe." Here was an American who, without leaving his own country, had made himself "a Musician, a Draftsman, Surveyor, Astronomer, Natural Philosopher, Jurist, and Statesman; a Senator of America, who had sat for two years in that famous Congress which had brought about the Revolution."[13]

ON MAY 8, 1782, a few weeks after Chastellux's visit, Martha Wayles Jefferson gave birth to her last child, a girl named Lucy Elizabeth. She had already given Jefferson two daughters—Patsy, then aged nine, and Polly, who was three—and ten years of "unchequered happiness."[14] Martha's advanced pregnancy and apparent depression prevented her from making much of an impression on the Frenchman; he refers to her simply as "a gentle and amiable wife." Little else about her is known, except that she shared her husband's love of music and was accomplished on the keyboard. Jefferson ordered the latest pianoforte for her from London shortly after they were married on New Year's Day 1772. A few other scattered references attest to Martha's talent on the harpsichord, which she studied with the Italian Francesco Alberti.

Martha's precarious health troubled her husband deeply. Throughout the summer of 1782, he seems to have been so depressed that he could not write a single letter. His destruction of Martha's letters shortly after her death in September has left biographers with little more to go on than subjective speculation. Not even a portrait of her survives. The passing mention of the idyllic domestic scene at Monticello in Chastellux's journal is the only intimate vignette of the young Jeffersons together.

Late in the morning of September 6, a few moments before Martha died, Jefferson's sister, Martha Carr, led her brother "in a state of insensibility" from the bedroom to his library at Monticello, where he fainted. For the next three weeks, he stayed in his room, among his books, where he slept fitfully on the floor. When he finally emerged, he took to riding aimlessly about the countryside on his horse, trying to bring his violent grief under control. Patsy did not leave his side until his despair was finally exhausted.

Edmund Randolph thought his friend's inconsolable grief, in contrast to the stoic silence with which the Virginia gentry normally dealt with loss and death, somehow abnormal. A shocked Madison dismissed the stories of Jefferson's behavior as "altogether incredible."[15] Martha Wayles Jefferson's death was a turning point, completely changing the inner rhythm and direction of her husband's life. Her loss, he told an acquaintance, "was the only circumstance which could have brought me to Europe."[16]

TEN WEEKS AFTER MARTHA'S DEATH, Jefferson wrote to Chastellux that he was "emerging from that stupor of mind which has rendered me as dead to the world as she." The catastrophe, he told the marquis, had altered his "scheme of life" at Monticello. He had "folded" himself "in the arms of retirement, and rested all prospects of future happiness on domestic & literary objects. A single event wiped away all my plans and left me a blank which I had not the spirit to fill up." The Frenchman's letter had reminded him that there "were persons still living of much value" to him and that he was struggling to reenter the world of the living.[17]

On November 13, 1782 Jefferson received word from Robert Livingston that Congress had appointed him minister plenipotentiary to join

Benjamin Franklin, John Jay, and John Adams in Paris to conclude the peace negotiations with England. In his "Notes of the Debates," Madison mentions that the action was taken because it was thought that Martha Jefferson's death might have altered the Virginian's recent decision to leave public life.[18] Jefferson told Chastellux that the appointment had tempted him out of his enforced retirement; he hoped to be able to join the Frenchman on his voyage from Philadelphia to Paris in late December. He sent his two younger daughters to live with their maternal aunt, Elizabeth Wayles Eppes, at Eppington, in Chesterfield County. After a number of delays, he and Patsy finally reached Baltimore, only to learn that a provisional peace treaty had been signed within days of his appointment. He had no choice but to return to a bleak, memory-ridden Monticello.

The following June, however, while Jefferson was working on revisions of the Virginia constitution, the Virginia Assembly elected him to Congress as head of the delegation. To keep himself busy while he waited at Monticello for Congress to open, the only thing that would save him from deeper depression,[19] he decided to draw up a catalog of his library, which now numbered an astonishing 2,640 volumes. The list would be useful in Paris, where he would spend so much time and money enlarging the collection. He also made an inventory of his extensive slave holdings, which he found to have grown to 204.

During the nearly two years between his wife's death and his departure for France, Jefferson established enduring friendships with three younger Virginians: James Madison, thirty-one, James Monroe, twenty-four, and William Short, twenty-three. All three would become lifelong disciples of Jefferson, and each would benefit from his experiences as envoy in Paris. Madison and Monroe would serve as his main anchors to Virginia and American politics during his long absence. He urged the three men to buy land near Monticello and join a small, select society he hoped to create out of whole cloth in Albemarle County. "Monroe is buying land almost adjoining me. Short will do the same," he wrote to Madison in February 1784. "What would I not give you could fall into the circle. With such a society I could once more venture home and lay myself up for the residue of my life, quitting all its contentions which grow daily more and more insupportable. Think of it. To render it practical only requires you to think it so. Life is of no value but as it brings us gratifications. Among the most valuable of these is rational society. It informs the mind, sweetens the temper, chears our spirits, and promotes health."[20]

But it was Paris and the society of cosmopolitan men and women, not the company of bookish neighbors and provincial lawyers, that would finally lift the forty-one-year-old Virginian out of his melancholy. On May 7, 1784 Congress appointed him to replace Jay as minister plenipotentiary, along with Adams and Franklin, in negotiating treaties of amity and commerce with France. That same day, Congress adopted new instructions to the ministers that he himself had drafted.

The moment Jefferson had both dreamed of and repeatedly resisted finally arrived. At 4 A.M. on July 5, 1784, an aloof, slender, middle-aged widower, accompanied by eleven-year-old Patsy (she would celebrate her twelfth birthday in Paris on September 27) and James Hemings, his valet and slave, sailed quietly out of Boston harbor on the *Ceres* bound for Europe, a scene he could avoid no longer.

Chapter 3

The City

> I cannot leave this great and good country without expressing my
> sense of its preeminence of character among the nations of the earth.
> A more benevolent people I have never known nor greater warmth
> and devotedness in their select friendships. Their kindness and
> accommodation to strangers is unparalleled and the hospitality of
> Paris beyond anything I had conceived to be practical in a large city.
>
> —Jefferson, *Autobiography*

JEFFERSON FELL UNDER THE SPELL OF PARIS the
moment he set foot on its "vaunted scene" on August 6, 1784. The public openness of the carefully orchestrated mise-en-scène, framed by the
broad, tree-lined avenue Champs-Elysées leading into the metropolis from
the Etoile, seemed to contradict the idea of a city laid out and ruled by an
authoritarian government. But the rational planning of cities has always
required ruthless political power, something the French have never hesi-
tated to wield when it came to making a great urban setting. The Paris
that Jefferson entered was in the throes of dynamic modernization, both
physical and ideological. Although the disintegration of the old regime
was well advanced, the countervailing energy to renew and change was
just as apparent in the streets of the capital.

Even as undercurrents of unrest began to surface, building fever lifted
the city's energy level, providing unmistakable evidence of public optimism. The atmosphere was not that of a society in thrall to memories and
myths of former glory. The city's obvious vitality contradicted the later
movie-set image built out of nostalgia's plaster and lath as the only true

Bird's-Eye View of Place Louis XV. Engraved by Née after L.-N. Lespinasse.
The square created a new entrance for the city. Jefferson suggested to Major L'Enfant that
Gabriel's facades (left) might serve as a model for the president's house in Washington.
(Bibliothèque Nationale de France, Paris)

douceur de vivre. Much of the visible energy was driven by a flurry of business deals often tied to private real estate speculation. The popular jour-
nalist Louis-Sébastien Mercier estimated that fully a third of the city had
been rebuilt in the two decades before Jefferson arrived: "Huge blocks of
dwellings rise from the ground as if by magic and new districts of the
most magnificent houses take shape. The building mania gives an air of
grandeur and majesty to the city.... The speculators cry out for the contractors who, with plan in one hand and a contract in the other, bring balm
to the hearts of the capitalists."[1]

In the wake of France's humiliating defeat by the British in the Seven
Years' War, the capital's stagnant economy suddenly revived in the 1760s.
Building cranes bristled in all directions, competing with old landmarks,
and ancient limestone quarries were threatened with exhaustion. By the
mid-eighteenth century, French writers and critics were expressing a new
attitude toward urban space and forms. The revolutionary self-awareness
calling for rational solutions in all aspects of life had been announced in
1759 by Jean Le Rond d'Alembert in his introduction to an essay for the

Encyclopédie: "A most remarkable change in our ideas is taking place, one of such rapidity that it seems to promise a greater change still to come. It will be for the future to decide the aim, the nature and the limits of this revolution, the drawbacks and disadvantages of which posterity will be able to judge better than we can."[2]

D'Alembert, who had collaborated with Diderot on the *Encyclopédie*, was speaking of philosophy and science, reflecting the rational views of the philosophes, who sought to alter the world by rebuilding it rather than merely attacking superstition and worn-out dogma. But it was clear that the arts would be subjected to the same sweeping changes. This critical questioning of the very fabric of society inevitably extended to the physical structure of the city, its buildings and streets. How urban spaces should relate to and serve the city's inhabitants, who were simultaneously grappling with their new roles as incipient "citizens" rather than subjects, was a matter of spirited debate.

As early as 1753, the shrewd essayist Marc-Antoine Laugier had criticized the old royal squares of Paris for failing to serve the needs of a modern city. He saw that a growing, more independent populace energetically pursuing their individual interests needed strategically placed public spaces for civic activities. In his essay, Laugier was as much concerned with political issues as with architectural aesthetics. "For a square to be beautiful," he wrote, "it should be a communal center from which people can make their way into different quarters and where, coming from different quarters, they can get together; for that reason several streets must lead to it like the roads of a forest to a *carrefour*. Porticoes are the right decoration for squares and if joined to these there are buildings of different height and shape, the decoration will be perfect. Symmetry is necessary but also a certain disorder that varies and heightens the spectacle."[3]

By emphasizing easy, open circulation, combined with the careful siting of articulated buildings, Laugier was proposing an unprecedented urban system that soon would be expressed in the new royal square dedicated to Louis XV.[4] Only hindsight would illuminate the irony in his call for a "certain disorder" to vary and heighten the "spectacle," after the Place Louis XV had been thoroughly washed in blood in the last decade of the century and its name changed to the Place de la Révolution.

The grand new entry gate to the city formed by the Place Louis XV lay ahead of Jefferson as he turned east on the Champs-Elysées from his house in the rue de Berri. (With a pedometer, he calculated the distance from his house to be 820 double-steps.) Plans for the square had been approved in 1755 and became a catalyst for the new neoclassical hôtels that would spring up to the north and west.[5] Framing the north side of the inviting public space were (and are) the splendid classical facades of Jacques-Ange Gabriel's buildings flanking the rue Royale. Straight ahead, the gardens of the Tuileries palace spread out before the old, dilapidated château, partially hidden by the mature trees that now, in the late eighteenth century, broke up Le Nôtre's taut allées and parterres. To the right was the Seine. The first bridge from the square to the Palais Bourbon on the opposite bank, already named the Pont Louis XVI, had not yet been built, although the plans by the engineer Jean-Rudolphe Perronet had been published and were ready to be executed.

Standing in the center of the Place Louis XV was Edme Bouchardon's equestrian statue of the king, *le bien aimé*, whose miraculous recovery from illness in 1748 had inspired the city of Paris to build this gleaming new entrance on the west on vacant land made available by the king. Jefferson, intent on rescuing his countrymen from their "deplorable barbarism" by emulating the best of European architecture, carefully noted Gabriel's handsome facades. But he had serious reservations about the scale of the statue in the large open space. Asked to explore with Houdon the making of an equestrian statue of George Washington, he confidently told Congress that although Bouchardon's was the smallest such sculpture in the city, "it is impossible to find a point of view from which it does not appear a monster, unless you go so far as to lose sight of the features and finer lineaments of the face and body....To perceive those circumstances which constitute its beauty you must be near it, and in that case, it should be so much above the size of life, as to appear actually that size from your point of view. I should not therefore fear to propose that the one intended by Congress should be considerably smaller than any of those to be seen here."[6]

Pierre Patte's folio *Monuments égrigés en France à la gloire de Louis XV*, containing engraved views of the square and statue, was among the avalanche of books that Jefferson shipped home to Monticello and eventually sold to the Library of Congress. Despite his deep-seated aversion to large cities, he instinctively grasped the political implications of the exuberant development of Paris, in particular the Palais Royal, the Place Louis XV, and the new public theaters. Later, when the American government was faced with transforming the countryside along the banks of the Potomac into the Federal City, he recommended Gabriel's fronts and other Paris examples to the architects as a fitting inspiration.

The *Plan de la ville de Paris*, published in 1787 to celebrate the aggressive new era in the city's history, proudly outlined the successive rings of urban growth. The map defines the city that Jefferson knew and explored for five years within the new wall of the farmers-general. By 1784 the city of Louis XVI had become a construction site. Quays along the river were filled with building material brought in by boats. Piles of stone and timber strewn around half-completed buildings, some of it spilling into the congested streets, were becoming serious traffic hazards. As an architect, Jefferson was entranced by the robust panorama of the capital "every day enlarging and beautifying."[7]

The concentric circles on the *Plan*, indicating historic patterns of development, called attention to the contrast between the insignificant Roman village of Lutetia, huddled with the later Visigothic strongholds in the middle of the map, and the modern metropolis around the edges. This optimistic comparison of old and new was intended as civic propaganda and appealed to advocates of civic and political change, irrespective of party or ideology. After all, some of the most outspoken champions of progress and liberty had made fortunes as the crown's private tax collectors. These nouveau riche money merchants were also the clients of the architects responsible for the spectacular new city palaces. Their stylish salons were fitted out with rich carpets, gilded furniture, and the latest fashions in painting. Their overflowing libraries contained the books and pamphlets that were fueling the revolutionary changes in society.

It was this mixture of motives and policy that made the wall of the farmers-general so controversial. On the west, the fields of Les Invalides and the Champs de Mars at the bend of the river were grandly appropriated into the scheme. On the east, classical columns mounted on top of the

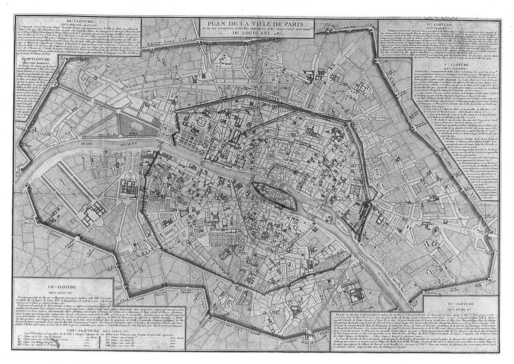

Plan de la ville de Paris (Map of the City of Paris), 1787. Engraved by P.-F. Tardieu.
(Bibliothèque Nationale de France)

Barrière du Trône, one of the new toll stations, could be seen as far as the
Château of Vincennes on the city's edge. The templelike tollhouses were
much too grand for mere tax collectors; critics derided the ornate follies
as entrances to a graveyard. No wonder Claude-Nicholas Ledoux, the
visionary architect who designed the wall and its forty-seven tollgates,
had been blind to the reality that he was simply creating a more efficient
means of oppression.

The wall had been proposed by the marquis Antoine Lavoisier, France's
most celebrated chemist, and carried forward by Calonne as minister of
finance. Lavoisier's fame as a scientist grew out of his work on oxygen and
his discovery of the composition of water. He was also a senior partner in
the lucrative and loathed tax-collecting apparatus of the old regime.
Lavoisier seemed trapped by the notorious institution he served. The Farm
was a distilled solution of the vices and virtues of the age, a virulent
hypocrisy that characterized the deeply fractured France of Louis XVI.

In Jacques-Louis David's brilliant double-portrait, the urbane scientist and his beautiful wife appear to be the ideal couple of a new order. Madame Lavoisier was also the daughter of a farmer-general and no doubt had been a coveted trophy. Lavoisier divided his days between the offices of the Farm in the Hôtel des Fermes on the rue Grenelle-Saint-Honoré and his magnificent four-story house near the Bastille, where he carried on scientific experiments in his private laboratory with his wife's assistance. The English agronomist Arthur Young was impressed by Lavoisier's splendid equipment when he inspected the laboratory in 1787. "A State can never be in better hands than of men who apply the superfluity of their wealth," he naively declared.[8] Several times a week Lavoisier would meet with friends and colleagues to listen to scientific papers and discuss current political issues. Aside from the unscrupulous business of the Farm, somewhat masked by his genuine liberal sympathies, it was a well-ordered, productive routine that Jefferson appreciated.

Jefferson knew Lavoisier not only as a member of the Academy of Sciences but as a close friend and colleague of Benjamin Franklin. Franklin's network of well-placed friends was one of his most useful diplomatic and propaganda tools, and it became an important legacy for his successor. Along with La Rochefoucauld, Condorcet, Buffon, and other French luminaries, Lavoisier had been elected to the American Philosophical Society on the recommendation of Franklin, who generously used the society to cement American-French relations among scientists and intellectuals during the war. At the beginning of 1787, Lavoisier was included in Franklin's "honor list" of twenty-five Frenchmen named to the Philadelphia institution. Jefferson forwarded to him his certificate of membership.[9]

The paradoxical combination of intellectual speculation and highly profitable, if often suspect, financial ventures was by no means unusual among the *grands* of the decade before the Revolution. Like others of his class, Lavoisier was, in Simon Schama's apt portrait, "at once pioneering and arcane, intellectually free and institutionally captive, public-spirited but employed by the most notoriously self-interested private corporation." The philosophe Claude-Adrien Helvétius left a huge fortune made in financial speculation to his widow, the countess de Ligneville d'Helvétius, who used it to conduct one of the most illustrious and subtly subversive salons in

The Barrière de la Villette.
The best preserved of the original forty-seven tax-collecting posts placed around the city.
Each temple was distinctively different. La Villette is based on Palladio's Villa Rotonda.
(Photo by Adelaide de Menil)

the city. The powerful and liberal Laborde family got their start as West Indian merchants trading in slave-produced sugar. Like Jefferson, Jean-Benjamin Laborde supported his diverse intellectual and creative interests—he was a composer, scientist, and writer on medicine, geology, and archaeology—with funds originally generated by slavery. It was Laborde, a third-generation farmer-general, who probably introduced Ledoux to Lavoisier, leading to the commission for the tax wall.[10]

The ideal of the good life is seen to perfection in the portraits of these self-satisfied tax collectors and their wives painted by David, Duplessis, and Vigée-Lebrun. But the smooth, porcelain complexions that matched their Sèvres teacups, the women's liberated hair and lithe, elegant bodies of unmistakable *ton*, belie the brutal, deeply corrupt underside of the enormously profitable operations of the farmers-general. As the count de Ségur said forty years later, for the select few in the 1780s, and especially those who lived off of tax collecting, it was as if they were standing on a flowered carpet, but one stretched over a bottomless abyss.

Ledoux had started to design the wall and its forty-seven tollhouses in 1783, but by 1787 the enormity of the project, tainted with a strong whiff of financial scandal, had stirred up strong public reaction and forced the architect's removal. From the beginning, Ledoux had ignored the real purposes of the wall and had seen it as a classical propylaeum, a garland ("les Propylées") around the most modern city in the world. Calonne, he wrote, desired "that the gateways to the capital of the world announce to the foreigner the grandeur of an opulent city."[11] In July 1789, however, the tollgates became the first targets of the mob in the Paris uprisings. The wall was breached in several places and forty of the new customs posts were pillaged. Later many of the farmers-general, including Lavoisier, went to the guillotine.

In collecting taxes for the crown, it is estimated that the Farm assigned more than twenty thousand armed personnel to police each jurisdiction and the commodities produced there, notably salt from the marshes of Brittany. This paramilitary cadre, reaching into every village throughout the country, had the right to enter, search, and confiscate any property or household considered suspicious. Mercier called the Farm an "infernal machine which seizes each citizen by the throat and pumps out his blood." Thousands were probably involved in the dangerous, but highly lucrative, business of smuggling to avoid the tax-collecting apparatus. To discourage the black market in salt, the Farm applied its most efficient brutality. Smugglers could be whipped, branded, sent to the galleys, and even put to death by breaking on the wheel, all without trial. The French courts were powerless to stop these assaults on individual liberties.[12]

When innocent Americans were swept up in the net, the American minister was called upon to help extricate them. In his battle to free the American tobacco trade from the monopoly of the farmers-general shortly after he arrived in Paris, Jefferson was quickly taught the power of the "Company." "I have struck at its roots here, and spared no pains to have the farm demolished," he ruefully told Patrick Henry. "But it has been in vain. The persons interested in it are too powerful to be opposed, even by a whole country."[13] John Jay confirmed his own earlier frustrations with the system in a letter to Jefferson in June 1786. "When I was in France I heard that System censured by almost every Gentleman whom I heard speak of it, and yet it seems so firmly fixed, perhaps by golden Rivets, even on Sovereignty itself as that the speedy Destruction of it seems rather to be wished for than expected."[14]

The Paris real estate boom of the 1780s was almost entirely in the hands of private investors and entrepreneurs. Contrary to conventional belief that the nobility stayed clear of business and commercialism, many of the titled grandees were deep into enterprise generated by the wealth of the private tax collectors, particularly real estate speculation, during the closing years of the old regime. Newly minted titles—Lavoisier's father, for example, purchased his in 1772—were conspicuous in these financial dealings. Memoirs and diaries of the decade record the social confusion at every level, signaled by small but profound alterations in rules of everyday life. "Ladies no longer escorted each other or rose for greeting," the marquise de Crequy wrote in her souvenirs. "People said *women* instead of *ladies* and *men* of the court instead of Nobles. The greatest ladies were invited to supper and mixed with the wives of financiers."[15] For many, this breaking of class barriers and taboos was one more sign that the ancient social and political structure was collapsing as fast as the old buildings being razed all over the city in the name of progress and gain.

The real estate market was regulated by royal and municipal authority. Encouraged by the government guarantees for real estate loans that Louis XV had established, the duke de Richelieu, the marquis d'Orrouer, the count de Gouffier, and other nobles joined forces with architects and contractors to carve up ancient estates and moribund religious communities. Even the king's brother, the count d'Artois, was involved in breaking up the former royal nursery into building sites between the Champs-Elysées and the rue Saint Honoré. It was in this subdivision that Jefferson's Hôtel de Langeac stood.

The Virginian and his daughter Patsy spent their first days in France at an inn in the rue de Richelieu, near the Palais Royal, before moving to more comfortable but still temporary quarters at the Hôtel d'Orléans in the rue des Petits-Augustins on the Left Bank. Jefferson lost no time in establishing a rudimentary domestic base, hiring both a *valet de chambre* and an *homme d'affaires*, and buying eighteen dozen bottles of Bordeaux wine, along with a few bottles of Frontignac and "Muscat," even before he had a cellar to store them in.[16] He did not hire a cook until the end of his first year in Paris, relying instead on caterers to supply meals for his household, the resident diplomatic staff, and a steady but unpredictable stream of guests.

The minister's residence served as a boardinghouse for visiting Americans. Also living there full-time were the secretary of the American commission, Col. David Humphreys, "a dark complexioned, stout, well-made, warlike looking gentleman," and William Short, Jefferson's personal secretary. Another boarder was the mysterious Charles Williamos, who had insinuated himself into the household not long after Jefferson arrived. Abigail Adams thought the Swiss-born adventurer "clever, sensible, obliging," noting that he was very much a part of the family and "always dines with Mr. Jefferson." A perennial office seeker, Williamos had gained the Virginian's confidence by running errands and otherwise making himself useful. He was abruptly sent packing in July 1785, after apparently charging some personal tailoring in Jefferson's name. It seems likely that Jefferson suspected Williamos of being an English spy, a tip that the French Foreign Office had passed along to the embarrassed minister.[17]

On October 16, 1784, Jefferson signed a nine-year lease on the Hôtel Landron, or Taitbout, as he called it. A new residential district developed by the Laborde family in what is now the Ninth Arrondissement, the cul-de-sac Taitbout ran north from the tree-lined boulevard des Italiens, where the outer walls of the city had once stood. The old city gates had been moved north to the base of Montmartre, and by the 1780s they had been pushed half-way up the slope to make way for more new houses.

By November the house was comfortably furnished and four more servants had been added to the staff. But Jefferson, sensitive to the French emphasis on appearances, had already begun to feel the financial pinch resulting from the unfamiliar expenses of city living. This insecurity would gnaw at him for the rest of his stay in Paris. When he discovered that his initial "outfit" had cost a thousand guineas, the specter of personal insolvency became deeply worrisome. In November 1784 he confided to James Monroe, "whose secrecy and delicacy" he could trust, a glimpse of his private circumstances: "I live here about as well as we did at Annapolis. I keep a hired carriage and two horses. A riding horse I cannot afford to keep. This stile is far below the level, yet it absorbs the whole allowance."[18] The following June he again unburdened himself to Monroe:

> For the articles of household furniture, clothes and a carriage, I have already paid twenty eight thousand livres and have more to pay. For the greatest part of this I have been obliged to anticipate my salary from which however I shall never be able to repay it. I find that by a rigid economy, bordering on meanness, I can save perhaps five hundred livres a month in the summer at least. The residue goes for expenses so much of course and of necessity that I cannot avoid them without abandoning all respect to my public character. Yet I will pray you to touch this string, which I know to be a tender one with Congress, with the utmost delicacy. I'd rather be ruined in my fortune, than in their esteem.[19]

A tally of the outlays recorded in the *Memorandum Books* shows that Jefferson had spent fully one-quarter of his first year's salary on household linen, window hangings, and upholstery alone. If he was not reimbursed, he told John Jay, he would not have "a copper to live on" in the first year. Jefferson was not overstating his financial predicament. Although his landholdings and some two hundred slaves made him, on paper, one of the richest men in Virginia, the annual income from these operations did not cover the debts of the estate. In Paris, consequently, he was entirely dependent on his minister's salary and living allowance.[20]

AS THE BUILDING FEVER SPREAD from the boulevards toward Montmartre, a number of large, fine residences sprang up in the area around the Hôtel Taitbout, several of which Jefferson came to know. Up the rue des Martyrs to the north was the estate of Chrétien-Guillaume de Lamoignon de Malesherbes, the "good and enlightened minister unquestionable" whom Jefferson considered "the first character in the kingdom for integrity, patriotism, knowledge, and experience in business."[21] A protector of the philosophes, he was minister of household affairs to Louis XVI, in which capacity he defended religious toleration and was instrumental in modifying the notorious revocation of the Edict of Nantes. Jefferson gave his neighbor a copy of his newly published *Notes on the State of Virginia*, spelling out his own defense of religious freedom, along with a number of American plants for Malesherbes' arboretum, including the pecan nut and cranberry. He also divided with the statesman "a prodigious quantity" of shrubs and trees, including seeds of *juniperus Virginiana*, one of the favorite species that Jefferson introduced to his Paris friends, its tall, dark silhouette recalling the classical Italian cypress.[22]

Jefferson's first residence was modest compared to such spectacular neighbors as the Hôtel Thélusson, designed by Ledoux, which attracted so many visitors that tickets were needed to get in. In spite of the government's financial crisis, the expansive private economy had produced a new breed of patrons and clients eager to explore the latest fashions in architecture and furnishings. The more avant-garde tastes in the new quarter went in for the neoclassical style of architects such as Alexandre-Théodore Brongniart and Ledoux. At the entrance to the chaussée d'Antin from the boulevard des Italiens was Ledoux's impressive Hôtel de Montmorency. Lining the cornice of the mansion, proudly displayed like trophies, stood statues of all the *connétables* of Montmorency since the Middle Ages. The house not only had a small pavilion *à la Chinoise* in its garden but was also fitted out with the latest bathroom plumbing, an innovation that Jefferson would later enjoy at the Hôtel de Langeac.

A more exotic house nearby in the chaussée, also by Ledoux, was the pavilion built for the dancer and opera singer Mademoiselle Guimard, mistress of the prince de Soubise and other notable lovers. Baron Friedrich Melchoir von Grimm, who sent a newsletter retailing Paris gossip to several German courts, reported that "Amour has met the costs, Volupté designed the plans; and in Greece itself, that latter divinity has never had a temple more worthy her cult."[23] The apsidal porch of this striking building, inspired by Roman models, was covered with a semidomed roof and closed by four chaste columns. The pavilion represented a brief departure from Ledoux's resistance to elevations *à l'antique*. It has been suggested that Jefferson's memory of this facade may have informed his elevation for Pavilion IX, the faculty house, at the University of Virginia. (The Temple of Venus at Stowe, in England, is another plausible model.)

The Hôtel Thélusson, drawn by Gabriel St. Aubin.

The hôtel, seen here under construction, was designed by Claude-Nicolas Ledoux. It was in the new section of the city not far from the chaussée d'Antin, where Jefferson's first house in Paris was located. (Statens Konstmuseer/The National Swedish Art Museums)

The Hôtel Guimard, designed by Claude-Nicolas Ledoux.
Built between 1770 and 1774 for a dancer at the Opéra, it was not far from Jefferson's first
residence in the chaussée d'Antin. (Bibliothèque Nationale de France, Paris)

Although actresses and dancers were not received by ladies of society,
they were beginning to be welcomed in the more liberal literary world of
the capital. If, like Guimard, they had acquired a fortune, building a house
and conducting a smart salon was an acceptable way to spend it. Guimard's
house also had a little private theater, where ladies of the court could watch
unseen behind cleverly placed grilles. Writers and artists were among her
casual lovers. Sébastien-Roch Nicolas Chamfort, the playwright, aphorist,
revolutionary, and near contemporary of Jefferson and Franklin, enjoyed
both her bed and her stage: two of his plays were performed there. Their
brief liaison may have recalled the courtesan's earlier affair with the
painter Jean-Honoré Fragonard. To Fragonard's declaration of love "if
only for a week," Guimard replied: "A week! none of my lovers could ever
boast of anything of the kind. A week! It would be as bad as a marriage."[24]
    The house that Jefferson knew best in the neighborhood of the Hôtel
Taitbout was the stylish but staid establishment of the Cornys. Ethis de
Corny had served for more than a year as commissary for the French

army in America and was now comfortably ensconced in the office of *pro-cureur du roi et de la ville*. His second wife, Marguerite-Victoire, who had a serious interest in politics, became one of Jefferson's most intimate friends in Paris, a member of the "little coterie" that included John Trumbull, Maria Cosway, and Angelica Schuyler Church.

IN THE AUTUMN OF 1785, Jefferson moved to the Faubourg du Roule, the new quarter west of the Place Louis XV developed by the count d'Artois. The Hôtel de Langeac had been built for the marquise de Langeac, mistress of the count de Saint-Floretin. After the marquise was forced into exile in 1774, work on the structure was abandoned, then resumed four years later. Smaller than the older baroque and rococo models, the two-story Hôtel de Langeac was freestanding and had a dignified neoclassical facade. Its asymmetrical interior plan would have been inconceivable to Jefferson's revered Andrea Palladio. The unusual layout reflected both the irregular shape of the lot, typical of many parcels in the suburb, and a new concern for interior freedom. The traditional Paris hôtel comprised two regular parallel sets of rooms, one oriented toward the courtyard and one toward the garden. But in the Hôtel de Langeac, the architect Jean Françoise-Thérèse Chalgrin had cleverly adapted the composition of the new *folies* and small pavilions like Mademoiselle Guimard's. The curved and angled spaces that Chalgrin created for the marquise de Langeac provided easier communication between rooms that were scaled to fit their particular functions.

The impression of a pavilion—or, as Filippo Mazzei called Jefferson's house, "villetta"—was further emphasized by the compact profile of the *petite maison*, with its low, mezzaninelike second story. The space on this floor was much smaller than on the main level because of the round skylight that lit the reception room below; there were only two bedrooms in addition to Jefferson's large, oval study/bedroom overlooking the garden. The circular entry hall penetrating the second floor was surrounded by a maze of narrow corridors. The only surviving plan of the second floor is by Jefferson, who probably drew it when one of the bedrooms was divided into two smaller ones for Patsy and Polly. The partition was formed by a bed, anticipating the use of a built-in bed in Jefferson's own

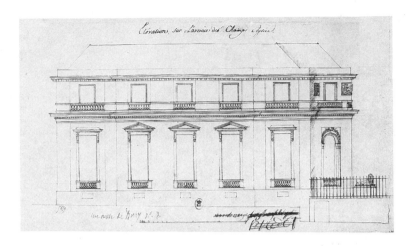

The Hôtel de Langeac.
These elevations reveal the house as it appeared during Jefferson's residence. A projected additional floor in the surviving drawing has been removed, restoring the house's original scale as a villa or pavilion. Although the hôtel lacked porticoes, its low mezzanine floor nevertheless gave it something of the quality of Monticello. (Bibliothèque Nationale de France, Paris)

Church of Saint Philippe du Roule, 1772–84, by Jean Françoise-Thérèse Chalgrin, the architect of Jefferson's second house, the Hôtel de Langeac. (Photo by Adelaide de Menil)

room at Monticello and at Poplar Forest, his retreat in Bedford County, Virginia.[25]

As the visitor entered the courtyard off the rue de Berri, the front door was to the right rather than in a conventional central facade. The large garden, partially visible through a grille fence at the back of the entrance court, had a fashionably picturesque form. Jefferson enthusiastically tackled the design problems presented by the irregular configuration of his new urban garden, which included a generous rectangular vegetable plot, or *potager*. Experiments in garden design had become the rage in Paris. In this, as in architecture and constitution making, English influence was strong. Both Thomas Whately's *Observations on Modern Gardening* (1770) and William Chambers's *Dissertation on Oriental Gardening* (1757) were closely

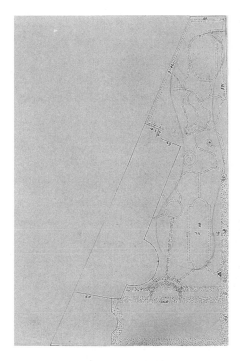 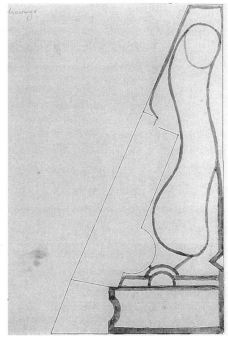

Plans of the garden of the Hôtel de Langeac by Thomas Jefferson, ca. 1787.
(Left) Of the three versions drawn by Jefferson, it is fair to assume that this could have been the plan of the garden at the time that the envoy moved to the small estate. The outline of the house is at the lower left corner. Stables and courtyard are outlined by the blank space on the left side of the property, facing the rue de Berri. In its flowing lines and irregularity, the design represents a stylized interpretation of an English garden popular in Paris in the 1780s. (Right) This bolder plan may well have been an attempt by the American envoy to simplify the original, overcomplicated garden design by eliminating many of the paths, giving the garden greater unity. (The Huntington Library)

studied in Paris. The *cahiers* of George-Louis Lerouge reproduced plans of the best-known *jardins anglaises*, a number of which Jefferson explored. One of the most notable was the "Folie Boutin," the residence of the financier Simon-Charles Boutin not far from the Corny house (and Jefferson's first residence). Set on the western flank of Montmartre, Boutin's semirural estate consisted of a mock-Italian garden overlooked by an English garden of "strolling groves" and "an antique tomb shaded with cypresses, a sheepfold and many rare shrubs mingled with exotic plants and flowers." The

Pompeiian atrium in Boutin's house further expressed the cutting edge of fashion. His cabinet of natural history held "a collection of minerals, tastefully assembled and arranged to make a study room rather than a display of luxury." It was the kind of idiosyncratic collection that appealed to Jefferson's intellectual taste, prefiguring the museum of natural history that he later installed in the front hall of Monticello.[26]

THE CITY'S NEW THEATERS AND OPERA HOUSES, its broad boulevards and public spaces, encouraged a popular cultural mix with distinct political overtones. The radical social, cultural, and political shifts under way in French society were especially evident in the erotic microcosm of the notorious Palais Royal. Every class was represented in its arcades, bars, and gardens, particularly the demimonde. As Mercier observed: "There you can see everything, learn everything....There is no spot in the world comparable to it. Visit London, Amsterdam, Madrid, Vienna, you will see nothing like it: a prisoner could live here free from care for years with no thought of escape."[27]

The heart of Cardinal Richelieu's old palace complex had housed various members of the royal Orléans family since the late seventeenth century. In 1776 the duke d'Orléans gave it to his son, the duke de Chartre, who later took his father's title. A failed naval officer with no obvious professional ability, the young duke turned to real estate speculation to shore up his sagging fortune. Combining a flamboyant style and an instinct for enterprise, "Philippe-Egalité," as he was popularly known, dreamed up an unprecedented extravaganza of development designed to serve "a quotidian carnival of appetites."[28] Neighboring properties were acquired so that the inner courtyard of the old palace could be enlarged, and the covered promenade around the perimeter was invaded at the duke's invitation by shops, gambling dens, brothels, cafés, and private clubs.

The new Palais Royal opened for business and pleasure in 1784. Mercier called it an "enchanted place...a small luxurious city enclosed in a large one," exclaiming, "There seems to be some charm that attracts money from all pockets, especially foreigners who are mad over this convenient assemblage of delights." The novelist Restif de La Bretonne, in Les Nuits de Paris, dubbed it the "center of a big city's chaos." Writers,

The Palais Royal.
Reconstructed by the duke d'Orléans in the 1780s for commercial purposes, the old Orléans palace became the popular heart of Paris and the center of the revolutionary carnival in 1789. (Photo by Adelaide de Menil)

journalists, and flaneurs were drawn to the Palais Royal to revel in the unprecedented democratic experience. As one writer asserted, "All the orders of citizens are joined together, from the lady of rank to the dissolute, from the soldier of distinction to the humblest official in the Farms."[29] The count de Ségur was shocked by the extraordinary license he encountered: "A crowd attracted by curiosity were closely ranged round a man who was mounted upon a table; this declaiming demagogue was railing, with vehemence, at the perfidy of the court, the pride of the nobles, the cupidity of the rich, the sloth of the legislators; he excited passions by the most incendiary gesticulations, to which some replied by applauding and others by insulting him."[30]

Gossip spread in the duke d'Orléans' new shopping mall—known successively as the Palais Royal, the Palais Marchand, the Palais Egalité, the

Jardin de la Révolution, and then again the Palais Royal—enriched the pages of the popular news sheets. Daily newspapers as we know them did not exist in Jefferson's Paris. Before the Revolution, the most important journals containing political news and commentary were imported from abroad. For much of his intelligence, Jefferson had to rely on rumor and exchanges of information that were often inaccurate, though his sources were better than most. By the 1780s the Palais Royal had become the center for underground news sheets and other clandestine publications that had not passed under the eye of the court censor. Since the palais was the private preserve of the duke, police patrols were virtually banned, making it a haven for what Robert Darnton describes as "Grub Street hacks, pirate publishers, and under-the-cloak peddlers of forbidden books."[31]

It is evident from Darnton's research that a significant, if indiscriminate, reading public was emerging in France at the same time that enlightened political reform was becoming a gripping topic in more liberated intellectual and aristocratic circles. But the precise connection between the "High Enlightenment" and its scruffier counterpart is hard to establish. In *The Old Regime*, de Tocqueville points out that "France had been for a long time the most literary-minded of all of Europe; but so far our writers had not displayed that intellectual brilliance which won them world-wide fame toward the middle of the eighteenth century."[32] The newly literate constituency was much larger than Jefferson seems to have suspected, judging from the few references he makes to it. Indeed, the political influence of the underground press may well have been greater than that of all the liberal political philosophers and theorists combined.

Living in gutters and garrets, working in an isolation and poverty that would turn any man into a revolutionary, the underground writers inhabited a world utterly alien to the privileged drawing rooms that Jefferson knew. To him they were merely part of the abstract "mob," wretched victims of urban life bred in conditions that must not be allowed to spread to the United States. The writers' target was the entire *grand monde*, encompassing the monarchy, the court, the church, the aristocracy, the academies, and the salons. Their graphic "chronicle of cuckoldry, buggery, incest and impotence in high places" anticipated the scurrilous attacks to which Jefferson would later be subjected by the Federalist press and his enemy James Callender as a result of the Sally Hemings scandal. It was inevitable that the Revolution's first liturgical act of waving heads on pikes to cheering crowds took place at the Palais Royal in the summer of 1789.

Jefferson apparently understood at least the broader popular attractions of the palais and its spontaneous street theater, even if he remained aloof from the ubiquitous underground literature and its authors. He joined the fashionable chess club, the Salon des Echecs, above the Café de Foi, and he liked the new freedom of dress he saw in the crowded galleries. He detected political significance in the changing fashions: "In society the habit habillé is almost banished, and they begin to go even to great suppers in frock: the court and the diplomatic corps however must always be excepted. They are too high to be reached by improvement. They are the last refuge from which etiquette, formality and folly will be driven."[33]

Jefferson quickly discerned the financial possibilities in the novel urban mall. To a friend in Richmond, Virginia, he wrote: "A particular building lately erected here...has greatly enriched the owner of the ground, has added one of the principal ornaments to the city and increased the convenience of the inhabitants."[34] Among the "conveniences" Jefferson described were cafes of all kinds, billiard halls, magic lantern shows, bookstalls (which Jefferson of course patronized), peddlers selling bawdy political satires, and a defrocked abbé singing gamy songs as he strolled with his guitar. Courtesans and street walkers moved easily through the crowds disguised as countesses. Jefferson was impressed by the large underground hall or circus for public entertainments that had been excavated in the center of the garden. He and William Short briefly considered promoting such a shopping complex in the new Virginia capital—modified, of course, to conform to the strict family values of the new republic.

THROUGHOUT JEFFERSON'S STAY IN PARIS, the practical, utilitarian side of his mind was always grappling with his vision for the United States. The new government either had to set up shop in an existing city like New York or Philadelphia, or start from scratch. Jefferson was drawn to the latter option: a national capital free of old, corrupt institutions that would choke its growth. The founders of the new republic were agreed that they did not want to build a metropolis like London or Paris, where

The Grand Colonnade of the Louvre by Claude Perrault and others, built during the reign
of Louis XIV.
Jefferson placed it among "the celebrated fronts of modern buildings" and bought
engravings of it for the planners of Washington. (Photo by Adelaide de Menil)

immorality and squalor, not to mention a gutter press, seemed to dominate urban life. Yet for all their acumen, they simply could not conceive of
a metropolitan center that would serve both as a seat of government and
as a powerful "mirror of a national civilization."[35]

While trying to come to terms with the confusing but vital civilization
he encountered in Europe, Jefferson was also gathering—in a rather dis-
jointed, uncritical way—examples and fragments that might prove benefi-
cial when he returned to the United States. But he was not at all sure how
the pieces could be reassembled and fitted into the hybrid urban setting of
a republican society based on agrarian values. Jefferson's anti-urban sentiments were, of course, widely shared by his American contemporaries even
before he spelled them out in *Notes on the State of Virginia*. "The mobs of
great cities add just so much to the support of pure government," he thun-
dered, "as sores do to strength of the human body."[36] Revolutionary soldiers had been paid off in tracts of land, where Jefferson and others hoped
they would carve out an agrarian utopia untainted by cities and their mobs,
"sores" on the body politic.

The proposal to move the capital of Virginia from Williamsburg to the
straggling village of Richmond had finally been passed by the reluctant legislature in 1779, after Jefferson had been elected governor. He had pushed
the idea for several years on the grounds that Richmond was both more
secure and more centrally located to serve settlers on the moving frontier
along the state's western boundaries. The redundant symbolism of the old
colonial buildings in Williamsburg—Jefferson called them "rude, misshapen piles...brick-kilms"—rendered them completely unacceptable to
house a republican government.[37] But he appears to have had no notion of
how the miserable collection of shanties huddled at the falls of the James
River might be transformed into a center of state government. As we will
see, Richmond's six large public squares would be filled with buildings
inspired by models Jefferson saw in Europe, but there was no coherent vision
of their relationship to the city that would suddenly grow up around them.

Shortly after returning from Europe, Jefferson would play a critical
role in the political horse-trading that resulted in the creation of another
city, the future federal capital along the Potomac. In 1783 he had proposed
to the Virginia Assembly that Virginia join Maryland in clearing some land

on the Potomac, throw up a few buildings, and offer the wilderness capital to Congress as a fait accompli. This appalling, parochial impulse reveals Jefferson's utopian notion that a capital is merely a seat of government, not a metropolitan center that both stimulates and reflects a nation's cultural life. Even Williamsburg, which he disdained, had put in place at the beginning of the century the basic principles of baroque design in its use of key buildings as focal points and its ample allocation of public space for the day-to-day life of the community.

The idea that a capital city—or any city, for that matter—could simply be created by legislative fiat on virgin ground was virtually without precedent. Benjamin Latrobe, who called Washington during Jefferson's administration "an anomalous kind of settlement that was neither fish nor foul," understood the problem very well. He wrote to Filippo Mazzei, who had recruited two Italian sculptors to work on the Capitol building: "The present president, whose talents, virtues, and great patriotism you know too well, to render it necessary for me to say anything to you on his character, has been the only real patron of the city. He has caused excellent roads to be made between the public buildings, and has lent his influence and example to every measure that could promote its growth and prosperity. But it is, I fear, beyond the power and influence of his or any administration to *force* a city on the spot."[38]

At least Jefferson was thinking about the larger functions of a capital as he tried to absorb the lessons of Paris in the 1780s. To follow him through the streets on one of his long daily hikes is to realize how many city landmarks were making their debuts. The dome of the Halle aux Bleds, a startling inverted glass bowl, its sections held together with wood-ribbed framing, had been completed in 1783 to cover the municipal grain market. Designed by Nicolas Le Camus de Mézières, the halle originally had an open courtyard where wagons could bring in the grain. Later, when it was decided to roof it over, the architects Jacques-Guillaume Legrand and Jacques Molinos revived a construction technique invented in the sixteenth century by Philibert Delorme. Its contemporary translation struck Jefferson as "the most superb thing on earth." To his eye, the light-filled room seemed to manifest the idealism of the age. It was a recurring image that he could not shake. The marriage of practical engineering and aesthetic

The new Halle aux Bleds, drawn by J.-B. Maréchal, 1786.
Arthur Young described the grain market as "a vast rotunda, the roof entirely of wood,
upon a new principle of carpentry...so well planned and so admirably executed that I know
no public building that exceeds it in either France or England." Jefferson agreed and more
than once tried to get it adapted for public buildings in the new Federal City of Washington.
(Bibliothèque Nationale de France, Paris)

beauty was a relationship that would often inspire his architectural fantasies. The halle's sparkling glass and thin wooden ribs somehow captured
for Jefferson the spirit of an "enlightened space" that was both symbolic
and utilitarian.

In 1802, the year the first roof of the Halle aux Bleds burned, President Jefferson insisted in his proposal for a new naval dry dock that it
have a "roof of the construction of that of the meal market in Paris."
Three years later, he urged Latrobe to model the ceiling of the House of
Representatives on that of the halle. Latrobe, however, argued that "a single leaky joint, dropping upon the head or desk of a member would dis-
turb the whole house." He complained more forthrightly to his clerk of
works, John Lentall: "I am sorry that I am cramped in this design by
[Jefferson's] prejudices in favor of the architecture of old french books,
out of which he fishes everything." Jefferson sacrificed his vision reluctantly, writing to Latrobe: "I cannot express to you the regret I feel on

the subject of renouncing the Halle aux bled lights of the Capitol dome. That single circumstance...would...have made it the handsomest room in the world, without a single exception. Take that away, it becomes a common thing exceeded by many."[39]

For all the filth and congestion in the narrow Parisian streets, civic enterprise and French military engineering had produced some impressive new boulevards. Circulation was improved by pulling down churches that stood in the path of urban planning, installing new street lighting, and clearing old bridges encrusted with ancient, ramshackle houses. The instant ruins produced by urban renewal in a society that had suddenly become fascinated with ruins, particularly of the antique variety, offered a new genre for painters like Hubert Robert and Pierre-Antoine de Machy; the latter's painting of the demolition of the Church of the Saints-Innocents turned up in the Salon of 1787. Indeed, it could be argued that the Revolution interrupted this surge of civic progress.

A number of buildings under construction caught Jefferson's eye as he crossed over the newly cleared Pont au Change leading to the Ile de la Cité, then over the Pont Notre Dame to the Right Bank. Jacques-Germain Soufflot's Church of Sainte Geneviève (now the Panthéon) had risen impressively up to the base of the dome. When John Trumbull first arrived in Paris, he lost no time in climbing up to "the highest scaffolding" of the church, whence he could enjoy "the extent of the city, the vast and opulent country terminating partly in rough and broken hills, partly in a fine campaign."[40] Trumbull's mentor added an engraving of the completed Sainte Geneviève to his growing collection of views of outstanding modern buildings.

Another building destined to become a Paris landmark was the Hôtel de Salm, now the headquarters of the Legion of Honor. "Violently smitten" by its design, as he wrote to Madame de Tessé, Jefferson spent hours watching its construction from the terrace of the Tuileries gardens across the river. Begun in 1782 to plans drawn by the architect Pierre Rousseau for the profligate prince de Salm, a sometime champion of the queen, the house combines the suave elegance of the French hôtel with the monumental grandeur of the antique world. The gate on the side away from the river (on the rue de Lille), inspired by a Roman triumphal arch, frames an

The Hôtel de Salm by Jallot.
Begun in 1782, following the neoclassical plans of Rousseau, it was built over a period of five
years corresponding almost exactly to Jefferson's stay in Paris. (Musée Carnavalet)

inner courtyard in the form of a colonnaded peristyle.[41] Both fronts would
be singled out by Jefferson as models for the new public buildings of the
Federal City. The combination of domestic comfort and fashionable classical references appealed deeply to the Virginian. He later translated it into
his own idiom in the second version of Monticello.

Politically advanced but architecturally more conservative, Jefferson
did not notice the startling group of houses called the Maisons Saiseval,
which Ledoux had built next door to the Hôtel de Salm on the Left Bank.
The architect incorporated references to Roman, Greek, Renaissance,
and classic French architecture—an amalgam that was at once elemental,
primitive, and natural. Although it represented a major stylistic break-
through, the ensemble failed to touch Jefferson the architect, schooled in
Palladian authenticity filtered through English architectural theory and
examples.

In 1790 Jefferson, as secretary of state, took charge of planning the
Federal City. In Europe he had developed firm ideas of what he wanted to
incorporate into the new public buildings of the Republic. He had also

The entrance to the Hôtel de Salm on the rue de Bourbon (now the rue de Lille).
The hôtel was one of Jefferson's favorite houses in Paris. (Photo by Adelaide de Menil)

absorbed, particularly in Paris, some aesthetic notions about the scale of streets and building regulations. His first sketch of an "agenda for the seat of government" proposed that streets not be less than one hundred feet wide. He disapproved of the requirement that houses be built a certain distance from the street, which produced a "disgusting monotony." The height of buildings, however, should be carefully regulated. "In Paris it is forbidden to build a house beyond a given height and it is admitted to be a good restriction. It keeps down the price of ground, keeps the houses low and convenient, and the streets light and airy. Fires are much more manageable where houses are low."[42]

When the time came to lay out the city of Washington in 1791, Jefferson thrust into the hands of Maj. Pierre L'Enfant, the French engineer in charge of the initial planning, some two dozen building elevations that he had diligently gathered abroad, as well as a number of exemplary city plans. In a letter to L'Enfant, he outlined the design sources he had observed in

Paris. "Whenever it is proposed to prepare plans for the Capitol, I should prefer the adoption of some one of the models of antiquity which have had the approbation of thousands of years; and for the President's house I should prefer the celebrated fronts of Modern buildings which have already received the approbation of all good judges. Such are the Galerie du Louvre, the Gardes meubles, and two fronts of the Hotel de Salm."[43]

Jefferson did not reveal the identities of the "good judges" who had approved the "Gardes meubles" by Jacques-Ange Gabriel, on the north side of the Place Louis XV, the colonnade of the Louvre, and the Hôtel de Salm as paradigms of public architecture. In his view, virtually no other modern public buildings in Paris were appropriate as either aesthetic or ideological models. Most candidates carried the symbolic taint of an authoritarian government. It is still startling to realize that the Virginia capitol, Jefferson's plan for which was based on the Roman temple at Nîmes, was the first structure of its type on either continent designed specifically to house the offices of a modern government. Only the architecture of classical antiquity had the beauty Jefferson demanded and symbolized contemporary republican principles. Just as the founding fathers had called on the ancient world for revolutionary legitimacy in government, so they returned to it for architectural validation.

CHURCHES EXCEPTED, architecture to serve public purposes of any kind was rare in France before the 1750s and 1760s. The king's palace complex at Versailles and other royal palaces, though open on a limited basis, were not designed primarily for the public at large. This explains the excitement generated in the 1770s by Gabriel's facades decorating the new public space between the Tuileries gardens and the Champs-Elysées. Not until the closing decades of the old regime did elite and popular tastes converge on the theater as the prototype of a public building designed to serve these two worlds.

The Théâtre des Italiens, located on the boulevard des Italiens just opposite the cul de sac Taitbout, was barely completed when Jefferson moved into his first house a short distance away. One of three theaters subsidized by the king, the Italiens, designed by Jean-François Heurtier and Charles de Wailly, specialized in light opera. It was there, and at the nearby Royal

Opera, or Academy of Music, where Lully, Rameau, and Gluck were performed, that Jefferson began to indulge his passion for music.

Before the middle of the eighteenth century, court spectacles had been staged in special rooms or improvised spaces in palace complexes such as the Tuileries and the Palais Royal. In the old regime, attending the opera was a social event with strictly prescribed etiquette, and the theater was almost exclusively the domain of the aristocracy. But as the century advanced, the "spatialization of power" underwent a major overhaul, reflecting the changes within society. By the 1780s, both audience and seating hierarchy had become relatively egalitarian compared to the middle of the century, when the nobility had passed along their theater boxes as symbols of their position in society. Another sign of subtle social revolution was the spread of private theaters, whose owners set their own rules for guests. Although in no way designed to serve the public, these small theaters represented a further departure from the privileged milieu of the court.[44]

The second half of the eighteenth century saw an explosion of great public temples of theater based on antique forms: the Bordeaux Theater by Victor Louis, designed in 1772–73; Ledoux's theater at Besançon, completed in 1784; and the Théâtre Français, or Odéon, by M.-J. Peyre and Charles de Wailly, opened in Paris in 1782. Whether Jefferson saw the new theater in Bordeaux when he stopped there in 1787 is not known, but there was little in Louis' plan that he had not already experienced at the Théâtre Français. The latter building, with its imposing neoclassical colonnade of eight columns, dominated its new square, a public urban space that had been set aside for it.

Jefferson frequented several of the leading Paris theaters, where he saw plays by Racine, Molière, Lasage, and Dancourt. But the most notable production he attended was Beaumarchais' *Mariage de Figaro, ou La Folle Journée*, in which the nobility and the established order were skewered while the insolent servant Figaro was portrayed as virtue personified. Repeatedly suppressed by court officials, the play grew in fame as an underground manifesto with each rumor of a clandestine reading or production. After being accepted by the Comédie Française for a public performance in 1781, *Figaro* was summarily turned down by the censors and was not presented to the general public until three years later.

The Odéon Theater.
Originally called the Théâtre Français and designed by the architects Charles de Wailly and
M.-J. Peyre, the theater opened its doors in 1782. (Photo by Adelaide de Menil)

Throughout the controversy, Beaumarchais cleverly cast himself as
the injured *honnête homme*. As a man of the theater, he knew how to manip-
ulate the fans of his "people's" drama. Ironically, some of his most vocal
defenders were powerful members of the nobility who had not quite
grasped the play's subversive message. Amused boredom, fashionable
excitement, and an obsession with scandal all played a part in its attraction, notwithstanding critics who saw *Figaro* as a "scandalous farce where,
behind an appearance of defending morality, morality itself is held up to
ridicule."[45] The queen requested a special performance in the Théâtre des
Menues on June 13, 1783, but an order by the king stopped it at the last
minute. The première finally took place on September 22, 1783 in the private theater of the count de Vaudreuil, a powerful member of the queen's

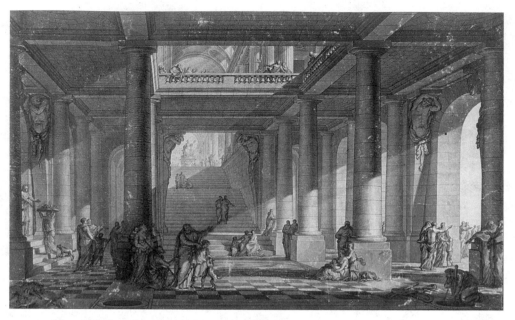

The vestibule and staircase of the Théâtre Français (Odéon).
Jefferson attended Beaumarchais' *Mariage de Figaro* here on August 4, 1786. (Musée du Louvre)

entourage. He and his court friends had little notion of the social conditions that demanded political redress, and few realized that the play's attack was directed not so much at the monarchy as at themselves.

Figaro opened at the Théâtre Français on April 27, 1784. The nobility turned out in force and a crowd fought for the few remaining seats, breaking through the barred entrances to the theater. De Wailly's huge circular auditorium, a "quarry of white sugar," was alive with anticipation. From the very first scene, the performance was interrupted by applause, extending the playing time for over five hours. The Alsatian baroness d'Oberkirch was carried away by the play's seeming "naturalness" at the opening-night performance. No liberal, she was astonished to see the *grands seigneurs* in the stalls obsequiously applauding Figaro's stinging speech in the fifth act, which violated contemporary codes governing relations between master and servant. Some of the grandees in the audience "struck themselves across their own cheeks; they laughed at their own expense and what is even worse they made others laugh too...strange blindness."[46] When the king had heard these lines earlier at a private reading, he had stormed out, declaring that the Bastille would have to be pulled down before the public would be allowed to see Beaumarchais' play.

Paradoxically, by the time the play had cleared the hurdles of censorship, Beaumarchais was no longer the exemplary Everyman implied in his populist attack on the establishment. Restlessly ambitious, he had become a conspicuous member of *le monde*, complete with a recently purchased title, considerable wealth, and widespread influence. From the large townhouse he built on the edge of the working-class district of Saint Antoine, the arriviste would have a ringside seat for the street theater at the Bastille, only a few hundred yards away, in July 1789.

Like many characters Jefferson met in Paris, Beaumarchais led a life marked with ambiguities and enigmas unique to late eighteenth-century French society. He began writing *Figaro* in 1777 while deftly managing clandestine shipments to the American insurgents (or "Bostonians," as they were sometimes called) as a secret agent of the French government. His liberal sentiments, tacitly encouraged by the French foreign minister, Count Charles Gravier de Vergennes, allied him with the colonists in their dispute with Britain. At one point, Beaumarchais hired a fleet of forty ships at his own expense to carry supplies to the beleaguered revolutionaries. In December 1778 he sent an agent, Monsieur de Francy, to the United States to negotiate for compensation in Virginia tobacco. There had been a dispute with the state assembly regarding the terms of payment and the quality of the tobacco offered. Jefferson, as governor of Virginia and a friend of France, was asked to intercede. But the claim was not settled for many years. In 1787 Jefferson reported to John Jay that he had met the playwright for the first time to discuss the long-overdue American debt. As late as 1801, Beaumarchais' daughter was still pressing for payment for arms furnished the United States during the Revolution.

Jefferson saw the sixteenth performance of *Le Mariage de Figaro* at the Théâtre Français on August 4, 1786. At some point he added a copy of the play to his library, along with Beaumarchais' *Oeuvres complètes*. He also acquired a clandestine edition of Voltaire's writings, with notes by Condorcet, which Beaumarchais had had privately printed at Kiel, out of reach of the French censors. Jefferson appreciated the allusions in *Figaro* to freedom of expression, equality of birth, and the evils of summary imprisonment. But the play also dramatized for him the fundamental social and political divisions between the Old and New Worlds. Freedom, liberty, and equality had different meanings and implications in each society. The principles that Jefferson had proclaimed in the Declaration of Independence may not have applied in his mind to the whole of mankind, but expressions of democratic ideals were becoming more evident every day in the French capital.

In 1786 European papers noted the Virginia Assembly's passage of a revised legal code for the state, which incorporated Jefferson's statute ensuring freedom of religion. The reports apparently failed to mention the American minister, although his work on the revision of the code was later cited in an article on the United States in the *Encyclopédie méthodique*. Reflecting on the conditions that had produced the American Revolution, Jefferson contemplated the gap between the two societies: "If all the sovereigns of Europe were to set themselves to work to emancipate the minds of their subjects from their ignorance and prejudices, and as zealously as they now endeavor the contrary, a thousand years would not place them on that high ground on which our common people are now setting out. Ours could not have been so fairly put into the hands of their common sense, had they not been separated from their parent stock and been kept from contamination either from them or the other people of the old world, by the intervention of so wide an ocean." Europe was "yet loaded with misery by kings, nobles and priests," and the same conditions conducive to despotism—"monarchy" was Jefferson's code word—could appear in the New World if it failed to guard itself against the age-old fascination with "nobility, wealth and pomp." In fact, the Virginian would be stunned by the loose approval of monarchy that he heard in New York shortly after he returned in 1789.[47]

A SEQUEL TO BEAUMARCHAIS' PLAY might have had Figaro sailing off with Susanna to freedom in the bucolic town of Boston or the forests of upper New York State. And it would have been a resounding hit, as all things American were by the time Jefferson arrived in Paris. The period roughly bracketed by the signing of the Treaty of Paris in 1783 and the adoption of the Declaration of the Rights of Man by the National Assembly in August 1789 was a shining episode in Franco-American relations. Lafayette's triumphant return from the American war in 1782 aroused passion, especially among privileged discontents, for what most Frenchmen had seen as vague patriotic sentiments coupled with even fuzzier notions of liberty: "We applauded the republican scenes represented upon our theaters, the philosophical speeches of our academies, the bold productions of our literary men," the count de Ségur recalled in old age. "We were pleased with the courage of liberty, whatever language it assumed, and with the convenience of equality. There is a satisfaction in descending from a high rank, as long as the resumption of it is thought to be free and unobstructed; and regardless therefore of consequences we enjoyed our patrician advantages together with the sweet plebeian philosophy."[48]

American liberty was equated with patriotism, and Lafayette's defiance of the king in joining the insurgents, together with the royal pardon on his return, magnified his reputation as a patriotic French hero devoted to the cause of liberty. Jefferson recognized his continuing importance to American interests in France early in the game. In March 1785 he sent a coded message to James Madison: *"He is returned fraught with affection to America and disposed to render every possible service."*[49]

The United States and France had signed a Treaty of Amity and Commerce in 1778, followed by a Treaty of Alliance. French intervention in the American Revolution, at first secret, became irreversible once the alliance was official. Commercial treaties with Prussia and Sweden quickly ensued after the end of the war. It is important to appreciate the momentum of these events as a backdrop to Jefferson's Paris years. The city seemed not only physically less decrepit than he had expected but more exuberant and vital in its outlook, and more sympathetic to Americans than he could have imagined.

Benjamin Franklin embodied the romantic idealism that America and its war against England inspired in the French public during the Revolution. If the antiquated European social and political order was to be overhauled, Franklin represented the virtues men should emulate. The count de Ségur was struck by his "rustic apparel, the plain but firm demeanor, the free and direct language." Franklin's "antique simplicity of

Benjamin Franklin by Jean Valade,
ca. 1786.
Jefferson purchased the portrait, copied
after the better-known work by
Duplessis, in September 1786.
(Monticello/Thomas Jefferson
Memorial Foundation, Inc. Photo by
Edward Owen)

dress and appearance seemed to have introduced into our walls, in the midst of the effeminate and servile refinement of the 18th century," a figure "contemporary with Plato, or...of the age of Cato and of Fabius."[50] Franklin's provincial presence caught the popular imagination at every level of French society. As John Adams wrote: "His reputation was more universal than that of Liebniz or Newton, Frederick [the Great] or Voltaire, and his character more beloved than any or all of them. His name was familiar to government, and people, to kings, courtiers, nobility, clergy, and philosophers, as well as plebeians, to such a degree that there was scarcely a peasant or a citizen, a *valet de chambre*, coachman or footman, a lady's chamber maid or scullion in a kitchen, who was not familiar with [him], and who did not consider him as a friend to human kind. When they spoke of him, they seemed to think he was to restore the golden age."[51]

Dressed in his long brown coat and beaver hat, Franklin was his own master stage director. Yet long before he came on the Parisian scene, Voltaire had created the myth of the "Good Quaker" in his *Lettres philosophiques*, published in 1734. The first four letters eulogized the gentle, tolerant, and simple, if at times eccentric, Pennsylvania sect. In 1764 the first American

"Quaker" appeared on the French stage in *La Jeune Indienne*, by Franklin's friend Chamfort. If Franklin was the architect of his international celebrity, he had a substantial foundation to build on in France.

Such a role did not have the slightest appeal for Jefferson, whose style, temperament, and intellectual makeup stood at the opposite pole from Franklin's. As he told Abigail Adams, he much preferred to be "an on-looker." Franklin generously introduced Jefferson into several of his many social and scientific circles—Adams called them "atheists, deists and libertines"—where the Virginian made a number of lasting friends. But his self-effacement and psychological need for privacy separated him from Franklin's world. His interest in the arts, particularly architecture, which he seems to have shared with only a few friends, further set him apart from the Franco-American milieu that Franklin had dominated for more than eight years. The Paris seen through the eyes of the sly, worldly Franklin and the Paris that Jefferson experienced do not appear to be the same place.

The two men probably differed most in their relationships with women. Whereas the shy Jefferson complained about their excessive influence in French public affairs, Franklin was famously and rarely out of women's company. Jefferson inherited two of Franklin's devoted friends, Madame d'Houdetot and Madame Helvétius, who gave him an entrée to the Paris salon. Both women were survivors from another era, and their wit and easy manners conveyed to Jefferson the flavor of a time when the salons had been dominated by the first brilliant wave of *lumières*. Madame d'Houdetot appears as "Sophie" in Rousseau's *Confessions*. In spite of her plain looks, she was the mistress of the poet and philosopher Jean-François Saint-Lambert and became one of the most romantic figures of the century. She collected Americans and attempted to include Jefferson in her soirées more often than he was willing at first. But after visiting Sannois, the country house where she lived with her husband and lover, he saw the social advantages of Madame d'Houdetot's friendship, writing to Abigail Adams that he hoped she had "opened a door of admission for me to the circle of literati with which she is environed."[52]

Madame Helvétius had long been famous for her irreverence and for the lively salon she conducted at her house in the suburb of Auteuil, not

far from the disapproving Adamses. The flamboyant widow of the distinguished philosophe was Franklin's most enduring friend, although she
refused his proposal of marriage; he called her "Notre-Dame d'Auteuil."
The abbé André Morellet complained that her beauty, wit, and stimulating temperament "disturbed serious, philosophical discussions."[53] By the
time Abigail Adams met her neighbor in 1784, Madame Helvétius was a
well-worn sixty, and although she belonged to an ancient noble family of
Lorraine (and was a relative of Marie Antoinette), Abigail immediately
wrote her off in a letter to her sister:

> When we went into the room to dine, she was placed between the Doctor
> [Franklin] and Mr. Adams. She carried on the chief of the conversation at
> dinner, frequently locking her hand into the Doctor's, and sometimes
> spreading her arms upon the backs of both the gentlemen's chairs, then
> throwing her arms carelessly upon the Doctor's neck—I should have been
> greatly astonished at this conduct, if the good Doctor had not told me that in
> this lady I should see a genuine Frenchwoman wholly free from affectation or
> stiffness of behavior, and one of the best women in the world; but I should
> have set her down as a very bad one, although sixty years of age, and a
> widow. I owe I was highly disgusted and never wish for an acquaintance with
> any ladies of the cast.[54]

According to John Adams, Madame Helvétius's *ménage* included
"three or four handsome Abby's who daily visited the house and one at
least resides there." This inspired one of the better Puritan quips in
Adams's diary: "These Ecclesiasticks ... I suppose have as much power to
Pardon a Sin as they have to commit one, or to assist in committing one.
Oh Mores! said I myself. What Absurdities, Inconsistencies, Distractions, and Horrors would these Manners introduce into our Republican
Governments in America: No Kind of Republican Government can exist
with such national manners as these. Cavete Americani."[55]

If Henry Adams was right in judging Jefferson's Paris years his happiest, it had little connection with the cynical, often risqué era of
Franklin's triumphs. The fact that the Virginian is rarely mentioned in
contemporary French letters and memoirs, while Franklin turns up regularly, attests to his private, diffident manner. By temperament and by

choice, Jefferson distanced himself from the shallow, sarcastic wit that defined *mondain* society. Rather, he took pleasure in exchanging ideas with the extraordinary array of talented individuals in that talented age—writers, scientists, artists, philosophers—who thrived in the urban setting.

It was in Madame Helvétius's salon, for example, that Jefferson met Count Constantin de Volney, A.-L.-C. Destutt de Tracy, and Pierre-Georges Cabanis. Later he worked on a translation of Volney's *Ruines, ou Méditation sur les révolutions des empires*, which anticipated the replacement of monarchy and church with a new age of liberty and justice. He helped revise the translation of Destutt de Tracy's *Commentaire sur l'esprit des lois de Montesquieu* and found an American publisher for them. He greatly admired Cabanis' *Rapports du physique et du moral de l'homme*, which was sent to him when he was president. Cabanis outlined an advanced theory of physiological psychology, striking a hard blow against the "spiritualists" who were then attracting attention. Jefferson recommended the treatise to his friends.

For the first time in his life, Jefferson was living in a rarefied cosmopolitan environment where every day he could meet and talk on equal terms with men and women who shared his own wide-ranging interests. He had found his true calling in this vital, unpredictable city in transition, aroused by its aesthetic and intellectual life, its climate of experiment and change, and its magnetic, heightened possibilities.

Chapter 4

The Patriot Aesthete

Were I to proceed to tell you how much I enjoy their architecture,
sculpture, painting, music, I should want words. It is in these arts
they shine.

—Jefferson to Carlo Bellini, September 30, 1785

HIS KINSMAN PEYTON RANDOLPH said that Jefferson
"panted" after the fine arts and "ran before the times in which he
was born." If there is a hint of heavy breathing in his letter to Carlo
Bellini, then teaching modern languages in Williamsburg, it is because of
his sudden discovery of the high-charged Parisian art world. Among the
founding fathers, for all their learning and abilities, Jefferson's passion for
the arts was unique. John Adams was unapologetically indifferent. "I
would not give six pence for a picture of Raphael," he wrote the sculptor
Binon in his old age, "or a statue of Phidias."[1]

The gap between the Virginian and his contemporaries appears even
greater because it is virtually impossible to detect any aesthetic aware-
ness or sensitivity among his American friends and colleagues in Europe.
One day, when driving to Neuilly with Gouverneur Morris, Jefferson
pointed out the splendid Pont de Neuilly, designed by Jean-Rodolphe
Perronet and completed in 1774. Morris was amazed. "I had crossed four
Times without remarking it and which he says is the handsomest in the
World," he recalled. Morris agreed that the bridge had "Solidity and
Lightness" but confessed that he was no judge and left "all final Decision
to old Father Time."[2]

Almost without exception, Jefferson expressed his love of painting,
sculpture, architecture, and music only to foreigners such as Bellini, Filippo

Mazzei, Giovanni Fabbroni, the marquis de Chastellux, Maria Cosway, and Madames de Tessé, de Corny, and de Tott. His most perceptive exchanges were with the women in this roster. John Trumbull, the well-traveled artist from New Haven whom he first met in London, is the only American who fit genially into this circle.[3] Jefferson's friend Baron Grimm, who advised Catherine the Great on the latest artistic fashions, should also be mentioned, although Jefferson merely tells us that they talked often about the contemporary art scene in Paris.

Jefferson's dependence on the sympathetic though infrequent company of cosmopolitan Europeans is evident in the years before he went to Paris for the simple reason that none of his Virginia friends, especially his Albemarle County neighbors, shared his intense aesthetic interests.[4] From an early age he remained aloof from his mother's Randolph family, who were for the most part well off and conventionally philistine in their tastes. Garry Wills remarks that Jefferson seemed to move "in and out of his own life, keeping an oblique but observant distance between himself and his surroundings, and his artistic interests were a private matter he shared with very few, adding to a certain remoteness in his personality."[5] But in the inventions secretly recorded in his early gardening and building notes, his imagination not only outran the times but, in their physical scale, soared beyond the physical limits of Monticello. Take, for example, the fantastic crenellated tower some 120 feet high he envisioned on the summit of Carter's Mountain, which dominates the view from the west portico of the house. An alternative scheme was to make the tower a gigantic version of Trajan's Column in Rome.[6] In either form the tower would have been the envy of that other romantic of the age, William Beckford, who was actually building his fantasies at Fonthill Abbey in England.

In 1774 Jefferson purchased the Natural Bridge hidden in the Valley of Virginia, some seventy-five miles from Monticello. In his mind, it was a kind of extravagant garden ornament in a visionary landscape to which he might occasionally escape and become a hermit living in a nearby hut. "I sometimes think," he wrote from Paris to a friend in 1786, "of building a little hermitage at the Natural Bridge...and of passing there a [part] of the year at least."[7]

The Opening of the Pont de Neuilly by Hubert Robert.
The bridge was completed in 1774. Jefferson told Gouverneur Morris that he thought it
"the handsomest in the World." (Musée Carnavalet. Copyright Photothèque des Musées de
la Ville de Paris)

Given the isolation of Monticello, Jefferson was always on the alert
for visitors who might stir up the artistic and intellectual atmosphere.[8] In
1774 he encouraged the Tuscan immigrant Filippo Mazzei to settle on a
farm adjoining Monticello in what turned out to be a disastrous experiment to introduce Italian vineyards and fruit trees to Virginia. Clearly,
Mazzei was also to serve as a link to European culture. He imported Italian vignerons and laborers to work the vineyards. Later he was joined by
his countryman Bellini, the two men serving as informal artistic advisers
to their neighbor. In an early notebook dealing with a possible collection
of reproductions of "Statues, Paintings, etc." for Monticello, Jefferson
notes that "Bellini tells me that historical paintings on canvas 6 ft. by 12
ft. will cost £15 sterl. if copied by a good hand."[9]

When the Venetian violinist and harpsichordist Francesco Alberti
turned up in Albemarle County in the 1770s, Jefferson immediately
engaged him for music lessons, later claiming that he practiced at least
three hours a day. After the Battle of Saratoga in 1777, paroled British and
German officers living near Monticello were invited to join evenings of
chamber music and were impressed by their host's skill.[10] The British general Friederich Adolph von Riedasel, who was stranded in the Monticello

neighborhood in 1780, was pressed into service painting a design on a ceiling on which Jefferson had installed a compass. Some of Riedasel's fellow officers joined the Virginian and his talented wife in musical evenings.

Any attempt to trace Jefferson's early aesthetic development before his encounter with Europe must begin with two things: the rigorous classical education his father insisted upon, and the practical, "eye"-dominated skills dictated by the rustic plantation life. His father's example was undoubtedly important. As a surveyor and map maker working on the frontier of the Virginia Piedmont in the 1740s and 1750s, Peter Jefferson had perfected an expertise in reconnaissance and topographical analysis. Young Thomas grew up on the edge of the wilderness, and its romantic beauty stirred his imagination. Adopting the latent literary jargon of romantic enthusiasm, he found the Natural Bridge "so beautiful, an arch, so elevated, so light, and springing as it were, up to Heaven!"[11] In a similar passage worthy of Wordsworth, he described the magical view from Monticello: "How sublime to look down into the workhouse of nature, to see her clouds, hail, snow, rain, thunder, all fabricated at our feet!" he wrote in the famous "Head and Heart" letter to Maria Cosway in 1786. "And the glorious Sun, when rising as if out of a distant water, just gilding the tops of the mountains, and giving life to all nature."

The Garden and Farm Books are full of Jefferson's reveries on his physical surroundings. Just how strongly he responded to his environment can be seen in the passage in *Notes on the State of Virginia* that documents the optical phenomenon called "looming": "There is a solitary mountain [Willis Mountain] about 40 miles off, in the South [of Monticello], whose natural shape, as presented to view there, is a regular cone; but, by the effect of looming, it sometimes subsides almost totally into the horizon; sometimes it rises more acute, and more elevated; sometimes it is hemispherical; and sometimes its sides are perpendicular, its top flat, and as broad as its base. In short it assumes at times the most whimsical shapes, and all these perhaps successively in the same morning."[12]

By the time work on Monticello began in 1769, Jefferson's intense curiosity and powers of observation had been honed by his day-to-day experience on a self-contained plantation. Everything possible was made on the place, often with ingenious skills. Monticello would become famous for its owner's many gadgets and "inventions." The moldboard plough "of the Least Resistance" that he designed and presented to the Musée d'Histoire Naturelle in Paris has all the elegant qualities refined by his firsthand experience and close observation. There is evidence that he could use his hands deftly in demonstrating how he wanted something made. Chastellux remarked after his visit to Monticello in 1782 that his host was not only the architect but "often the builder."[13] While inspecting the construction of the University of Virginia, he is said to have taken a workman's hammer and chisel to show how a volute on a capital should be turned. Woodworking was a private and apparently life-long hobby. Before going to London in 1786, he sent the French Foreign Office a list of items he intended to bring back, so that they could be cleared for customs. It included a "box containing small tools for wooden and iron work, for my amusement."[14]

Jefferson's building notes for the first version of Monticello attest to the finely tuned coordination between his eye and his mind as he strove to combine aesthetic and utilitarian values. He translated plates found in books by Gibbs, Palladio, Inigo Jones, and Perrault into precisely measured designs that he incorporated into his drawings. In 1769 he made a closely observed time-and-motion study of the workmen's rhythms as they excavated the well: "in digging my dry well, at the depth of 14f. I observed one digger, one filler, one drawer at the windlace with a basket at each end of his rope very accurately gave one another full emploiment, but note it was yellow rotten stone with a great many hard stones as large as a man's head and some larger, or else the digger would have had time to spare. they dug and drew out 8. cubical yds. in a day."[15] The vagrant appetite of his eye was constantly tempted by appealing objects that caught his attention wherever he went. He had barely settled into his quarters on the boat returning to America in October 1789 when he sat down and made careful notes and specifications of the table in his cabin and asked the captain to have it copied and shipped later to Monticello.

Before going to Paris, Jefferson had hardly seen a single piece of sculpture or a painting by a European master.[16] Yet, like many provincials arriving in Europe for the first time, he had long been compiling an encyclopedia of information gathered from assorted books containing canonical lists of artists. A few clues can be pieced together from his library. Twenty-eight when the family house burned in 1769, he immediately began rebuilding what was to become one of the best collections of books in the colonies. The list of basic titles for a gentleman's library that Jefferson drew up for Robert Skipwith in 1771 reveals a solid grounding in the classics. But he cautioned that "the learned lumber of Greek and Roman reading" was too limited with regard to works of the imagination; he reminded Skipwith that "every thing is useful which contributes to fix us in the principles and practices of virtue."[17] He believed that man's aesthetic feeling or "taste" was, like moral sense, innate, yet both were directed to the common goal of happiness and virtue. "We have indeed the sense of what we call beautiful,...that is exercised chiefly on subjects directed to the fancy," he wrote in his retirement, "whether through the eye in visible forms ...or in the imagination directly."[18]

Under the heading "Criticism on the Fine Arts," the Skipwith List includes works by Lord Kames, Edmund Burke, Daniel Webb, and William Hogarth—but no French titles. (Molière, Rousseau, Montesquieu, Button, Voltaire, Fénelon, and Marmontel were present in translation.) Jefferson did, however, own one folio volume by a Frenchman, François Perrier's book on the *mirabilia* of ancient Italy, illustrated with one hundred engravings of classical sculpture. These rather crude images supplied much of the inspiration for the collection of classical casts that he thought of assembling at Monticello in the early 1770s.[19]

Jefferson's wide-ranging artistic enthusiasms are reflected in the steady—some feel indulgent—accumulation of furnishings and artworks for his houses in Paris. Some critics have claimed that his collecting somehow lacked "moral purpose," but given the size and function of his Paris establishments, and the extraordinary range of his high-minded ambitions, curiosity, and taste, any moral judgment seems misplaced. For him, collecting was a moral imperative. An acute sensitivity to keeping up appearances and preserving his gravitas—a serious matter of diplomatic legitimacy—also governed his personal behavior within the conventions of French society.[20]

Routine purchases of sofas, chairs, tables, stoves, coal grates, carpets, mattresses, silver plate, dinnerware, candlesticks, tablecloths, and china for

Coffee urn, 1789. Made in Paris by the silversmith J.-L.-A. Leguay. Possibly based on Jefferson's own design inspired by classical vases and urns, it is one of four urns that Jefferson bought in Paris.

the Hôtel Taitbout were carefully itemized in Jefferson's *Memorandum Books*. Judging from the pieces that have survived, the furnishings were for the most part well made but unexceptional, lacking any feeling of *luxe*, as that word was understood in Paris. Three days after signing the lease on October 16, 1784, Jefferson bought "2 small laughing busts," followed by a statue of "Hercules in Plaster." On October 29 he purchased his first paintings and entered them in his Account Book as "heads." A nearby auction of the collection of the late Monsieur Billy, *premier valet de garderobe du roi*, supplied a "Virgin Mary weeping on the death of Jesus." Flush with the pleasure of buying artworks for the first time in his life, Jefferson attended another auction at the beginning of 1785, acquiring five more canvases on religious themes. All were no doubt passable copies of the period, although only the large *Heriodiae* after Guido Reni is still at Monticello.[21]

Jefferson's initiation into the realm of aesthetic judgments came too late for him to develop any real originality in his artistic taste. For the most part, he accepted the canonical views of writers like Jonathan Richardson, who declared that "a copy of a very good picture is preferable to an indifferent original."[22] Copying was a major cottage industry in

France and Italy during the era of the Grand Tour. This, of course, had been the young Virginian's guiding principle when he planned to populate Monticello and the surrounding hills with casts of antique gods and goddesses. No doubt Jefferson had also read the influential essays on the utility of art in Diderot's *Encyclopédie*. Etienne-Maurice Falconet's argument in his article on sculpture that it had essentially moral value, serving as a durable reminder of men's achievement, summed up the Virginian's conclusions.

On November 29, 1784 Jefferson received a letter from Gov. Benjamin Harrison of Virginia notifying him of the legislature's resolution to commission a statue of George Washington. Harrison and the Assembly were confident that his reputation as a home-grown connoisseur qualified him, in collaboration with Franklin, to select "the most masterly hand" to carry out the assignment.[23] Jefferson, for whom the commission exemplified the highest form of art patronage in a republic, had no doubt who the artist should be. In fact, by the time he replied to Harrison a few weeks later, the eager patriot-aesthete had negotiated all the necessary arrangements with Jean-Antoine Houdon. There could be no question as to "the Sculptor who should be employed, the reputation of Monsr. Houdon of this city being unrivaled in Europe. He is resorted to for the statues of most of the sovereigns of Europe." Jefferson and Franklin had held lengthy meetings with the affable, enthusiastic Houdon, who was so "anxious to be the person who should hand down the figure of the general to future ages" that he was prepared "to leave the statues of kings unfinished."[24] The three men discussed the size of the sculpture and the need to work directly from life, which would require a trip to Mount Vernon.

Jefferson had met Houdon shortly after arriving in Paris and considered him an artist "without rivalship," a warm, generous, candid man "panting after glory." Houdon had already exhibited busts of Franklin in the Salon of 1779 and of the naval hero John Paul Jones in the Salon of 1781, the same year he received a commission from the state of Virginia for a bust of Lafayette. With the image of Franklin, the full-scale statue of Washington, and his later bust of Jefferson, the French artist was to create the most powerful and enduring iconography of three of America's

George Washington by Jean-Antoine
Houdon, signed and dated 1788.
(Photo by Robert C. Lautman)

founding fathers. Houdon's busts of Franklin, Jones, Lafayette, Turgot,
Voltaire, and Jefferson eventually came to Monticello. Also in Jefferson's
collection was a small plaster version of a nude Diana that he admired on
his frequent visits to Houdon's studio while the sculptor was at work on
the Washington and Lafayette commissions.[25]

The Virginia Assembly originally intended to present Lafayette's
bust to the young general in gratitude for his military service. But by the
time the work was finally undertaken in 1784, the legislature had
changed its mind and decided that Houdon's sculpture "be presented in
the name of the Commonwealth, to the City of Paris, with a request that
the same be accepted and preserved in some public place of the said city."
In January 1786 the marble bust of Lafayette was nearly finished and Jefferson wrote to Gov. Patrick Henry that he intended to present it without delay. But in a country where protocol was sacred, the minister found
himself on uncharted ground. "No instance of similar proposition from a
foreign power had occurred in their history," he reported to Henry.

Jefferson asked the foreign minister's deputy, Joseph-Mathias Rayneval,
if it was necessary to request permission of the king and ministers before
approaching the mayor of the city. This, of course, turned out to be the

case, necessitating delicate negotiations that delayed the presentation until September 27, 1786. An elaborate ceremony, with eulogies, music, beribboned guests, and tears, was staged in the great hall of the Hôtel de Ville, but Jefferson was unable to attend. A few days earlier he had fallen over a low fence and fractured his wrist while walking along the Seine with Maria Cosway. That injury, combined with a severe attack of migraine, made it necessary for William Short to read an elegant letter from Jefferson praising Lafayette. Ethis de Corny, who had served as the general's aide-de-camp in the American army and was a fellow member of the newly founded Society of the Cincinnati, delivered the principal address. "Such fame is the right of a free Nation...that has been fathered by Washington, Franklin, Adams and Jefferson. Rome herself would have been honored," he declaimed.[26]

In 1774 Corny had administered the oath to Lafayette as a captain in the French army, requiring that he never serve a foreign power. So "was disobedience to kings made into a virtue by the servant of a king—with Jefferson in the background." Houdon's bust of the first (and only) international hero in America, commissioned by a state government and presented to Lafayette's own country, was the perfect *beau geste* to cement the friendship between the two allies following the victory at Yorktown. The commission and its presentation were reported throughout Europe and created a sensation in Paris. Anticipating the possibility of distorted accounts, Jefferson took steps to control the report and circulated his own official narrative of the event to the press.[27]

JEFFERSON HAD NO PROBLEM in using painting and sculpture as a political tool to celebrate the public virtue of a Washington or Lafayette. Yet, although he never denied the personal satisfaction he found in the arts, there was still in his mind an ambivalence and uncertainty about their place and role in a new republic that lacked firmly rooted native traditions. Like most of the revolutionary generation, he vaguely hoped that in due time the blessings of liberty somehow would release the nation's creative energies, producing a golden age not only of industry but of art as well. John Adams's old-fashioned republicanism made him skeptical that freedom could survive if undisciplined market forces, essential to producing the wealth that European "high culture" seemed to require, were turned loose in American society. Would such wealth not also breed luxury, extravagance, and folly? he asked Jefferson in his troubled old age. "Luxury will follow riches and the fine arts will come with luxury in spite of all wisdom can do."[28]

Although Jefferson did not share Adams's parochial attitude, he understood that the last thing his utopian society of yeomen farmers needed or wanted was fancy paintings and sculpture, and he was reluctant to encourage young Americans to spend much time in European museums and art collections. When Edward Rutledge and Thomas Shippen, Jr., were planning a tour of Europe, Jefferson advised them that paintings and sculpture "are worth seeing but not studying," contradicting his own practice of seeing and studying everything in his path.[29]

If Jefferson was too pragmatic to announce the imminent appearance of an American Athens, he nevertheless believed that the astonishing growth of the population would ultimately transform the cultural wasteland. For the foreseeable future, the demand for new buildings would give architecture priority among the arts. History proclaimed that architecture was the measure of a great civilization. Painting and sculpture, on the other hand, were too expensive for a republic to foster, at least at the beginning. The amassing of wealth would generate great cities, which in turn might undermine the very foundation of American liberty. This was the central dilemma of Jeffersonian democracy. When an artistic outpouring finally did occur, the "lesser arts," Jefferson reasoned, would serve a moral purpose by recording man's great achievements, as well as providing "a pleasing and innocent direction to accumulations of wealth which would otherwise be employed in the nourishment of coarse and vicious habits."

Jefferson's views reflected the tentative conclusions that the marquis de Chastellux expressed in an essay on the future of the arts and sciences in America, written on the eve of his return to France in 1783. Jefferson had seen the manuscript and urged Chastellux to append it to his *Travels in North America*. "Far from rendering nations vain and frivolous," the marquis argued, the fine arts would actually "preserve them from the excesses of luxury and caprices of fashion...such as valuable furniture, gold and silver jewelry, sumptuous services of plate etc."[30]

Model of the Virginia state capitol. Jefferson had this plaster model of the design for the capitol made in Paris and shipped to Richmond. (The Library of Virginia)

In a much-quoted letter to James Madison, written in 1785, Jefferson unabashedly confessed his enthusiasm "on the subject of the arts." The letter has often been read as referring to the entire spectrum of the arts, but in fact Jefferson was speaking specifically of architecture. Two days before writing to Madison, the "much mortified" diplomat had learned from Gov. Henry that the contractors in Richmond were proceeding to lay the foundation of the new capitol building without waiting for the plans they had requested him to send from Paris. Here was the first building in the new nation designed exclusively to serve a republican form of government, and an irretrievable opportunity was about to be lost.

With a moral urgency, Jefferson asked Madison to use his influence to stop the work until he and his new architectural partner, Charles-Louis Clérisseau, completed their revolutionary adaptation of the Maison Carrée at Nîmes to house the government of the Commonwealth of Virginia. Jefferson, who saw architecture as an outward sign of a society's values, argued that it was imperative to establish "useful, noble" models at the outset. "But how is a taste for this beautiful art to be formed in our countrymen, unless we avail ourselves of every occasion when public buildings are to be erected, of presenting to them models for their study and imitation," he complained to Madison. The Assembly, by "erecting a monument to our barbarism" instead of one that would reflect "national good taste," could long delay "a reformation in this elegant and useful art."[31]

It was an issue that had troubled Jefferson for several years and had provoked some of his most caustic observations in the *Notes on the State of Virginia*. In the revised manuscript, completed in the winter of 1783–84, while he was still a delegate to the Continental Congress, the Virginian had indicted his native state for the architectural "maledictions spread over the land." Not until January 1786 was he finally able to send the legislature "the ground plan, the elevation of the front, and the elevation of the side" for the new capitol, "knowing that this was all which would be necessary in the beginning." A plaster model followed in March.

IN THE SUMMER OF 1786, Jefferson's explorations of the Parisian artistic scene took a critical turn with the arrival of the young American painter John Trumbull at the Hôtel de Langeac. They had first met in London earlier that year, when Jefferson had joined John Adams in commercial treaty negotiations with envoys from Tripoli and Portugal. Trumbull immediately assumed the role of guide and adviser, taking Jefferson to the studios of Benjamin West (his teacher), John Singleton Copley, and Mather Brown. It was during this stay in London that the Virginian engaged Brown to paint his first portrait. In all probability, West showed his American visitor his unfinished painting commemorating the signing of the peace treaty between the United States and Great Britain, which had taken place in Paris on November 30, 1782. It was one of a series on the American Revolution that West, who had been born in the colony of Pennsylvania, intended to paint.[32]

While making these rounds, Jefferson canvased the distinguished artists regarding the costume that Houdon's Washington should wear. The American Republic's identification with its ancient Roman counterpart was reflected not only in architecture, painting, and sculpture but in the popular decorative arts and fashions. Men of affairs in the former colonies often posed—and some, especially in Virginia, believed they actually lived—as Roman citizens, minus togas. How Washington, the noblest Roman of them all, was to be dressed for posterity was not an insignificant

Self-Portrait by John Trumbull at age
twenty-one, 1777.
Trumbull struggled for years against
his father's disapproval before going
to Europe. Jefferson's encouragement
was a turning point in the artist's
career. (Courtesy Museum of Fine
Arts, Boston. Bequest of George
Nixon Black)

issue. Jefferson had raised the question with Washington himself at
Mount Vernon, but the president had dodged it, deferring "to the taste of
connoisseurs" while indicating a preference for "modern costume." Back
in Paris, Jefferson reported in a letter to Washington that West, Copley,
Trumbull, and Brown all favored modern dress.

While in London, Jefferson had invited Trumbull to come live at the
Hôtel de Langeac. There was ample room in the new house for the artist
to work, and Jefferson was clearly impressed by Trumbull's patriotic plan
"to take up the History of Our Country, and paint the principle Events
particularly of the late War." By giving the artist room and board so that
he could pursue his work, the minister was undertaking an act of patronage on behalf of his government, a casual yet significant gesture that was
without precedent. Trumbull recalled their first meeting in his autobiography: "He had a taste for the fine arts, and highly approved my intention
of preparing myself for the accomplishment of the national work. He
encouraged me to persevere in this pursuit, and kindly invited me to come
to Paris, to see and study the fine works there, and to make his house my
home, during my stay."

Trumbull arrived in Paris in July 1786, carrying with him the canvases of *The Death of General Warren at the Battle of Bunker's Hill* and *The
Death of General Montgomery in the Attack on Quebec*. His immediate plan
was to have the paintings engraved, while seeing as much contemporary
artwork as possible "in this capital of dissipation and nonsense." Jefferson
also asked him to finish a portrait of Washington that he had acquired
from the artist Joseph Wright in Philadelphia. Only the head had been
completed, and Jefferson was in such a rush that Wright did not have
time to adequately dry the unvarnished painting in the sun before the
minister left for Boston and Paris.

Trumbull's most celebrated work, *The Declaration of Independence*,
was not identified by the artist as one of the principal events of the Revolution to be included in his American history series. In all likelihood it
was Jefferson who suggested the subject, and the artist immediately
began a rough composition, drawing on the enthusiastic minister's
"information and advice." Jefferson even made a sketch (since shown to be
inaccurate) of the floor plan of the chamber in the Pennsylvania State
House as it had appeared in 1776, "to convey an Idea of the Room in
which congress sat." Because the signing of the Declaration took place
over several weeks, Trumbull actually portrayed the meeting of June 28,
when the committee named to draw up the document presented Jefferson's unedited draft to John Hancock, president of the Continental Congress. After lengthy debate, the Congress, now constituted as the
Committee of the Whole, carried out considerable surgery on Jefferson's
text. Late on July 4, the revised—Jefferson called it "mutilated"—draft
was finally approved.

In late 1786 Trumbull went back to London to continue work on the
Declaration, which would occupy him for another ten years. By the time he
returned to Paris the following fall, the small original version of the composition was ready to receive Jefferson's portrait. The companion piece was
also ready for the principal French officers who had witnessed the British
surrender at Yorktown. All fifteen officers were in town and came to the
artist's makeshift studio in the Hôtel de Langeac. Jefferson personally
helped arrange the appointments. Both Trumbull and Jefferson later
accepted the scene as representing July 4 rather than June 28. On the

The Declaration of Independence by John Trumbull (detail).
Jefferson probably suggested the subject when the young artist arrived in Paris in 1786 with
his plans to record the great events of the American Revolution. (Yale University Art
Gallery, Trumbull Collection)

advice of Adams and Jefferson, all the signers were portrayed in the room, whether or not they were actually present.[33]

Jefferson's memory of the circumstances surrounding the signing of the Declaration had recently been refreshed by a garbled account of the events in Philadelphia that appeared in the *Journal de Paris* on August 29, 1787. An unsigned book review quoted with approval the erroneous claim that John Dickinson had been solely responsible for the passage of the Declaration by breaking a tie vote. In fact, Dickinson had opposed it. In a long and uncharacteristically emotional letter to the editor, signed simply "An American," Jefferson exploded at what he considered a reckless, ignorant rewriting of history. His notes on the summer of 1776, which he had brought with him to Paris, helped him set the record straight according to his own recollections. "If contemporary histories are thus false," he wrote, "what will future compilations be."[34]

Jefferson soon cooled down, however, and never posted the heated letter. Since his authorship of the Declaration still was not widely known in Paris, he may have felt that the matter was not worth a public confrontation with the *Journal*'s editor. In fact, Dickinson was as famous in France as the American minister and had long been identified as one of the strongest advocates of the American cause. But Jefferson believed the Pennsylvanian had shown more cleverness than sound judgment in the arguments for conciliation with Great Britain that he set out in the *Letters from an American Farmer in Pennsylvania*, published in 1769. This, along with other disagreements, was probably the subtext of the Virginian's indignation. The article in the *Journal* also may have stirred up memories of his first clash with Dickinson in June 1775, when the Continental Congress named both men to the committee charged with drafting a manifesto declaring the need to take up arms. When Jefferson was asked to draft a response for Congress, Dickinson thought it was too harsh, and the older, more cautious farmer from Pennsylvania managed to water it down.[35]

Jefferson had had another opportunity to claim authorship of the Declaration around the time of Trumbull's first visit to Paris, when the French historian François Soulés asked him to comment on his *Histoire des troubles de l'Amérique anglaise*. Jefferson responded by providing detailed information about the events in Philadelphia, concluding tersely: "The declaration of Independence was debated during the 2nd. 3rd. and 4th. days of July and on the last of these was passed and signed."[36] Soulés followed Jefferson's corrections closely, to the extent of not mentioning either him or the other members of the committee that drafted the Declaration. The full text of the document was printed in an appendix of Soulés' book, but again without the author's name.

ALTHOUGH THE AMERICAN DECLARATION and the later *Déclaration des droits de l'homme et du citoyen* shared "essential principles," each being, in Julian Boyd's words, "a part of the air breathed" by patriots on both sides of the Atlantic, it should also be remembered that the American document was unique in presenting an orderly, legal justification for dissolving "political bands" with Great Britain. The urgent motive behind its passage in June 1776, as Garry Wills has written, was in fact to secure desperately needed military aid from France. Jefferson's own notes support Wills's point. "That a declaration of Independence alone could render it consistent with European delicacy for European powers to treat with us, or even to receive an Ambassador from us."[37]

Just as it was initially marginal in the United States, the Declaration of Independence had little real influence in France; its significance there as a revolutionary document was largely rhetorical. Lafayette translated the symbolic language of Jefferson's Preamble into his own Déclaration (only to see it rejected by the National Assembly). Tocqueville considered the most original idea in the Declaration to be the concept of "equality," although he charged that the Revolution had done little or nothing to secure equality in American society. When the Declaration was referred to at all in France, it was because it had proclaimed for the first time the right of a political society to break its old ties and to create a new government through revolution, and because it had enumerated those natural rights on which that government would be founded.

Nevertheless, the Declaration remained a great revolutionary totem and manifesto for French liberals like Lafayette. He had a copy engraved in gold in 1783 and conspicuously displayed it in the entry hall of his house in the rue de Bourbon, which he had transformed into an American shrine, complete with two Indian pages he had brought back from the wilds of New York state. The empty frame hanging beside Jefferson's words, the French patriot explained to visitors, was only "waiting for the declaration of the Rights of France."[38]

Jefferson, for his part, never suggested that the incendiary language of the Declaration might serve as an inspiration for France. He understood the gulf that separated the history, culture, and political aspirations of the two countries. If others were impatient for a revolutionary solution to France's ills, he seemed comfortable for the time being with more modest reforms—correcting the "vices in the form of governments"—that would have left the old social order in place for the time being.[39] Even the monarchy itself might be preserved, provided it was redefined by constitutions, parliaments, and laws. The slow, unpredictable political progress of the masses argued against short-cuts inflamed by too much radical, utopian rhetoric applied in the wrong places. Not long after returning from Paris, and before the upheavals of the French Revolution had carried the country into more dangerous waters, Jefferson reminded a fellow Virginian "that the ground of liberty is to be gained by inches, that we must be contented to rescue what we can get from time to time, and eternally press forward for what is yet to get. It takes time to persuade men to do even what is for their own good."[40]

JEFFERSON'S AUTHORSHIP OF THE DECLARATION was not widely known in America or France in the decades following the Revolution. His name was not linked in print with the document until 1783, when Ezra Stiles published a sermon praising Jefferson for having "poured the soul of the continent into the monumental act of Independence."[41] The only recorded mention while he was in Paris seems to be in an address of eulogy privately presented by a small group of American friends who had been invited to celebrate the anniversary of the signing at the Hôtel de Langeac on the Fourth of July, 1789. The tribute, probably drafted by the poet and diplomat Joel Barlow with the assistance of Filippo Mazzei and John Paradise, was addressed "to the man who sustained so conspicuous a part in the immortal transactions of that day—whose dignity, energy and elegance of thought and expression added a peculiar lustre to that declaratory act which announced to the world the existence of an empire."[42]

Paradise was just sober enough to read the tribute to the minister after the Lafayettes and Gouverneur Morris had left the party. The next day, Jefferson wrote a note of thanks to Paradise, typically protesting that his "little transactions" had not been "made for public detail. They are best in the shade. The light of the picture is justly left to others." Then, in a characteristic disclaimer bordering on the specious, he added: "To glide unnoticed through a silent execution of duty, is the only avocation which becomes me, and it is the sincere desire of my heart."[43]

Morris did not sign the accolade. His evident reservation anticipated the Federalists' later charge that Jefferson was not the author of the Declaration and had been guilty of plagiarism. John Adams in his old age claimed that Jefferson had merely "clothed" the committee's articles in "proper dress." His jealousy and egotism unassuaged, Adams said that he had always considered the Declaration "a theatrical show" in which "Jefferson ran away with all the stage effect...and all the glory of it."[44]

Jefferson's over-the-shoulder participation in the composition of Trumbull's great icon was indeed a coup de théâtre, and it undoubtedly gave him the private satisfaction of helping to shape the public's only visual image of the mythical tableau. Standing tall in his red vest and unpowdered red hair, he is the central figure in the composition. The short, stout Adams and Franklin appear as supporting characters. Contrary to Adams's recollection, this symbolically conforms to Jefferson's recollection that the three men had not met as a subcommittee to work on the document. "The Committee...unanimously pressed on myself alone to undertake the draught. I consented. I drew it," he wrote to Madison.[45] Years later, when Trumbull was working on the monumental version of the *Declaration* for the rotunda in the Capitol, he informed Jefferson that his figure dominating the composition was now larger than life.[46]

Trumbull's painting, with all its stage effects, conflates the presentation of Jefferson's draft on June 28, 1776 with the actual signing of the amended version later in August—two dates that Jefferson later muddled in his own memory. He would always hold that his original text was superior, including it in his autobiography to answer his accusers. Not until he wrote the epitaph for his tombstone, in fact, did he finally lay unqualified claim to authorship. He had often claimed that the Declaration was not so much his creation as the "common sense of the subject." Similarly, by translating into visual form the ideals expressed in the document, Trumbull's *Declaration* was American to its core, the emblem of the great, if vague, national myth. Regardless of the struggle ahead, the infant nation is seen to be in the hands of men "driven at least in theory by the dictates of reason," making the Declaration also, in Irma Jaffe's words, "the ultimate statement of the European Enlightenment."[47]

Trumbull's plan to have his series of patriotic paintings engraved and widely distributed appealed to Jefferson's democratic instincts. As secretary of state, he would later promote this popular deployment of art to educate the public. Upon learning that the nation's capital would be built along the Potomac near Georgetown, he urged the government to purchase inexpensive engravings of Roman architecture by Piranesi and distribute them free to local citizens, in order to elevate their taste before the new city was built.

DURING HIS FIRST VISIT TO PARIS IN 1786, Trumbull took advantage of his host's connections, and together they visited artists' studios and art collections all over the city. On August 9 Trumbull noted in his diary that he and a group of friends had gone to Jacques-Louis David's apartments, introducing themselves to the "pleasant, plain, sensible" painter whose star was very much on the rise. The king had offered David lodgings in the old Louvre on the artist's return from Rome in 1783. Two years later his *Oath of the Horatii* created a sensation when it was first exhibited to the public; a few critics even hailed it as a veiled prediction of social upheaval. David and Trumbull immediately struck up a friendship, and the older artist generously offered the American the opportunity "of seeing all that related to the arts, in Paris and its vicinity."[48]

Trumbull introduced Jefferson to the work of David, who was instantly converted. If, as Anita Brookner has observed, David had "the ability to produce a style to meet the needs of an historical moment," the Virginian was quite prepared to accept the artist's revolutionary break with aesthetic orthodoxy.[49] One detects a growing critical assurance that has developed under the guidance of his young adviser when he later writes to his friend Madame de Bréhan, now in New York: "I do not feel an

The Salon of 1787 by P.A. Martini, 1787.
The Royal Academy of Painting and Sculpture held an exhibition every other year, opening
on Saint Louis' Day, August 25. During Jefferson's stay in Paris, salons were held at the
Louvre in 1785, 1787 and 1789. (Bibliothèque Nationale de France, Paris)

interest in any pencil but that of David."[50] In 1786 Jefferson did not
anticipate a revolution in the French political system, but David's austere
images of ancient virtue profoundly impressed him, particularly by contrast with the conspicuous lack of virtue in contemporary Paris.

Writing to Trumbull in London in 1787, Jefferson urged him not to
miss that year's Salon, singling out David's *Death of Socrates*, a painting
that represents the neoclassical *beau idéal*: "The best thing is the Death of
Socrates by David, and a superb one it is."[51] David's new masterpiece
exceeded, in its power, even that of the *Horatii*. Its flawless composition
and formal unity, its theatrical exploitation of the vague but quintessential
emotion called sublime, all contributed to its triumph. As David's biographer observes, *The Death of Socrates* "reverberate[s] with a tension that
threatens to disrupt the tight schema of the composition."[52] This tension,
which the artist has managed to control and to transcend in his painted

Marius Imprisoned at Minturnae by Jean-Germain Drouais, 1786.
The young artist's masterpiece captured Jefferson's imagination when he first saw it in the
winter of 1787. (Musée du Louvre)

manifesto, can also be seen as analogous to the growing strains within
the French body politic—a double frisson to which the observant American envoy responded.

David's brilliant young pupil Jean-Germain Drouais also attracted
the budding connoisseur with a precocious masterpiece when it was privately exhibited in Paris in 1787. Some even considered *Marius Imprisoned at Minturnae* a challenge to David's *Horatii*. Painted in Rome in
1786, Drouais' dramatic work elicited an enthusiastic reaction from Jefferson: "Have you been Madame, to see the superb picture now exhibit-
ing in the rue Ste. Nicaise, No. 9. chez Mde. Drouay?" he wrote Madame
de Tott. "All Paris is running to see it; and really it appears to me to have
merit. It fixed me for a quarter of an hour, or a half an hour, I do not
know which, for I lost all ideas of time, even the consciousness of my

existence." When his friend wrote back with some cool reservations, he told her that she "had confirmed a part of my own ideas, given some which escaped me, and corrected others wherein I have been wrong."[53]

Trumbull's diary entries during the late summer of 1786 document the Parisian public's growing access to art. Royal collections were opened and private ones could be seen without difficulty. Artists held open houses in their makeshift studios in the old Louvre, while canvases, drawings, and engravings were hawked in a nearby archway. The battered palace had become a veritable artists' republic. Not only painters and sculptors but cabinet makers, tapestry weavers, goldsmiths, and even writers had gradually taken over deserted sections of the building. Unaware that they were witnessing the final moments of European optimism, Trumbull and Jefferson could hardly contain their delight in this intoxicating atmosphere, heightened by the enthusiasm of their sophisticated companions.[54]

Prominent among them were Richard and Maria Cosway, with whom Trumbull first saw the enormous canvas of the *Horatii* in David's studio shortly after the English couple arrived from London. Richard Cosway was a miniaturist, connoisseur, and eccentric with something of an international reputation. Maria, seventeen years younger than her husband, was an accomplished painter and musician. Slight, impatient, and vain, he was upstaged by the insouciant glamour of his somewhat taller wife. Some thought he had the air of a monkey. "Fancy bore sway in him," William Hazlitt wrote, adding that he was "gifted with a *second sight*" and ready to believe "whatever was incredible." In a revealing self-portrait with more than a touch of eighteenth-century camp, Richard Cosway gives free rein to his fantasies and vanity, dressing himself in a Van Dyck suit and a plumed hat that might have come out of Rubens's studio as he pays homage to busts of the Dutch master and Michelangelo standing on an altar.

Cosway had worked his way into the confidence of the dissolute young prince of Wales, largely, it was said, through the pornographic snuff boxes Cosway painted for him. In her old age, Maria Cosway still possessed a box depicting an erotic Leda and the Swan.[55] Cosway's career had accelerated in 1780 when he was commissioned to paint his first portrait of the prince. The painter's tastes ran to decadent royalty: he had been invited to Paris in

Richard Cosway, self-portrait with busts of
Michelangelo and Rubens, ca. 1789.
Cosway dramatized his vanity as he
associated himself with the old masters
placed on the altar of fame.
(Fondazione Cosway, Lodi)

1786 by the unsavory duke d'Orléans, a friend of the prince of Wales, to
paint the duchess and her children at the Palais Royal.

Richard Cosway was himself an astute collector of old master paintings, prints, objets d'art, and furniture of every description, which overflowed his fashionable London house in Pall Mall. Its cupboards were
jammed with the extravagant costumes he and his wife loved to wear. His
responsibilities as artistic factotum for the prince of Wales included assembling the prince's art collection and decorating his palace, Carleton House,
as well as painting the portraits of the prince's succession of mistresses.
At the time of his visit to Paris in 1786, Cosway was also negotiating to
make a well-publicized gift to the French royal family of four large six-
teenth-century tapestry cartoons from his private collection.

When Jefferson, Trumbull, and the Cosways visited the Palais Royal
on August 6, they found workmen dismantling the old galleries in order

to rebuild the palace in a modern style. Cosway had arranged to see the duke's extraordinary collection, much of which would end up in major European museums after the Revolution. Paintings were placed on easels around the middle of the rooms or stacked on the floor against the walls. Some of the enormous canvases by Poussin, Correggio, Rubens, and the Carracci were difficult to take in at such close range. The next day the high-spirited band visited the count d'Orsay's house, "overloaded with elegance," including some superb small Dutch paintings, bronzes, and fine porcelain.[56]

Later their feverish schedule included trips to churches and public buildings, fitted in around long midafternoon dinners. The painter Elisabeth Vigée-Lebrun invited them to dine with her friend David.[57] Afterwards, the party proceeded to Jefferson's house to admire Trumbull's American battle pictures. Jefferson later recalled that Baron Grimm, the "oracle" of taste in Paris, often came to the Hôtel de Langeac while Trumbull was working there.[58] The painter Hubert Robert, the antiquarian Pierre-François Hugues d'Hancarville (he styled himself "baron"), and the count de Moustier, soon to become minister to the United States, also stopped by the American artist's temporary atelier.

Another dinner was given by the abbés Chalut and Arnoux, close friends of Franklin who provided letters of introduction for Jefferson when he traveled to the south of France. Still later, Robert and Vigée-Lebrun were guests at the dinner for the group given by the count de Vaudreuil, amateur painter, collector, and enthusiast of the latest garden fashions. The composition of the coterie changed from day to day, with the count de Vaudreuil, the count de Moustier, Madame de Bréhan, and other grands joining in along the way. Trumbull recalled years later that Jefferson joined the group "almost daily" in their rounds of entertainment.

Even after two years in Paris, Jefferson had never found himself in such a sympathetic set whose sensibilities seemed to match his own. It was an emotionally charged experience, generating inner tensions that would finally well up in the famous "dialogue...between my Head and my Heart," which Jefferson sent to Maria Cosway after her return to London. But the Virginian's uncritical innocence seemed to insulate him from the often racy wit, titles, and polished manners of his careless, attractive companions. There can also be little doubt, as John Randolph maliciously remarked, that

Jefferson was well endowed with "easy credulity." He was unaware of Richard Cosway's notorious reputation, and of his profitable career in the fast circle of the prince of Wales, who reputedly used the painter's house for assignations. Nor had he heard the London gossip that Maria Cosway had once been the prince's mistress. Maria's friend Madame de Bréhan immediately captivated the susceptible minister, but he would have been shocked to know that she was the mistress of her brother-in-law, the count de Moustier. Vigée-Lebrun, liberated in spirit if not in fact from her tyrannical husband, who managed her business affairs, was a close, perhaps intimate friend of the count de Vaudreuil.[59]

NOTWITHSTANDING the conservative guardians of taste still lodged in the court and the French Academy, the Paris of Louis XVI surged with a defiantly creative, libertarian energy in every field of the arts. "People crowded to the galleries of Houdon, of Moitte, of Vien, David, and Julien," recalled the count de Ségur. "France became enriched with monuments of art. Foreigners admired the dome of Sainte-Geneviève, the theater of Bordeaux, the school of anatomy, and the bridge of Neuilly. Our theaters resounded with the strain of new music."[60]

The arts, along with government, law, and education, appeared to be moving steadily toward the rational systems envisioned by ideal philosophy and supported by an ideal public. Noble simplicity in painting, furniture, silver design, and architecture became an overt criticism of the now discredited Rococo, just as the clear, chaste language favored by Jefferson was used to condemn corrupt governments. Superfluous ornament in rhetoric was as bad as overwrought opera scores. Gluck's revolutionary music, both applauded and jeered by Paris audiences in the 1780s, rejected the operatic past as radically as Jefferson's rhetoric in the Declaration of Independence dismissed the British government. "When I undertook to write the music for *Alceste*," Gluck declared, "I resolved to divest it entirely of all abuses, introduced either by the mistaken vanity of singers or by the too great complaisance of composers, which have so long disfigured Italian opera...tarnished with florid descriptions, unnatural paragons and sententious, cold morality."

On both sides of the Atlantic, abuse of every kind, from violated human rights to misshapen architecture, was condemned with appeals to the remote purity of classical Greece and Rome. The only way to become great, according to the archaeologist Johann Winckelmann, was to imitate antiquity. Jefferson, like Diderot and Sir Joshua Reynolds, embraced this key axiom that defined the neoclassical attitude to the ancient world. Throughout Western society, from Stockholm to Philadelphia, antiquity had become, as Hugh Honour put it, "part of the furniture of the educated mind."[61]

Within his limited philosophical grasp, even Louis XVI accepted many of the high-flown tenets of the Enlightenment. That he was seen by many, including the pragmatic Jefferson, as a potential constitutional monarch shorn of any power did not contradict hopes for political reform. It was the king, after all, who had appointed the count d'Angiviller to succeed the conservative marquis de Marigny as the new director of arts (called the superintendent of buildings). D'Angiviller encouraged young artists to introduce themes of public virtue drawn from antique examples into their history paintings. It was during David's five years in Rome, beginning in the late 1770s, that the French Academy began to assign subjects representing patriotism, frugality, integrity, and courage associated with Roman virtue. *The Oath of the Horatii*, portraying a historical event that embodied all of the Roman virtues, broke new ground for rigorous purity of style.

Architecture of all periods figures in Jefferson's letters to Maria Cosway recalling the brief time of six weeks they spent together in Paris. In fact, Trumbull had first introduced him to the Cosways beneath the Renaissance column that still stands next to the "noble dome" of the Halle aux Bleds. Typically, he later told Maria that he had visited the new grain market not for his own pleasure but for the sake of "public utility," since he was interested in it as a possible model for a new market to be built in Richmond. The landmarks that Jefferson and Maria Cosway visited over the next few weeks included the Church of Sainte Geneviève (now the Panthéon), Val de Grâce, Les Invalides, Notre Dame, the aqueduct at Marly, and the palaces of the Tuileries, Meudon, Saint Cloud, and the Louvre.

Early in the reign of Louis XVI, a period that many thought promised a new Golden Age after the debauched rule of Louis XV, the rather ramshackle old Louvre had become a kind of center for advanced studies of

Baron d'Hancarville by Isabella Teotochi Albrizzi. The connoisseur/antiquarian turned up with the Cosways in Paris, where he met the American envoy and joined the coterie making the rounds of galleries and artists' studios. (Bodleian Library, University of Oxford)

the arts and sciences. Jefferson selected its great seventeenth-century colonnade by Le Vau, Perrault, and Lebrun as a fitting model for future reference. Not only were star artists and scientific prodigies given apartments there, the Louvre also housed the French Academy, the academies of architecture, painting, and sculpture, and the office of inscriptions and medals. The biennial Salon exhibition was staged in the Salon Carré. The scientific academies, which had been expanded in 1785 to include mineralogy, natural history, and agriculture, were also honored with royal accommodations in the old palace.

The addition of the baron d'Hancarville to the party of sightseers undoubtedly pleased Jefferson. An old friend of the Cosways, he was recognized as an eminent antiquarian and classical scholar. His catalogue of Sir William Hamilton's collection of ancient art, begun in Naples in 1766, had taken ten years to complete. D'Hancarville seems to have mesmerized his listeners not only with tall tales of antiquity but with well-edited accounts

Catherine de Médici Column.
The Halle aux Bleds was built on the site of Catherine de Médici's Hôtel de Soisson. The column rescued from the earlier building marks the spot where Jefferson first met Maria Cosway. (Photo by Adelaide de Menil)

of his own far-fetched life. As his friend Isabella Teotochi Albrizzi wrote: "His penetrating, voracious eyes, his flaring nostrils, his lips which barely touch each other are the outward signs of his longing to see everything; and then, having seen everything, having known everything, he wins you over with his learning and his prolific and imaginative way of speaking."[62]

The cunning old operator did not reveal everything about his past to Jefferson—for example, the time he had spent in prison for having stolen silver from his patron, the duke of Wurtemberg, the abandonment of his pregnant mistress, or his investigation of the ancient cults of phallic worship and fertility on the theory that they were the origin of all religions. And it was just as well that some of his less scholarly works, which had struck a blow for freedom of expression in their explicit and graphically illustrated accounts of the sex lives of the twelve Caesars, never tested Jefferson's loftier notions of civil liberties. They were placed on the government's list of forbidden books and remained there through most of the twentieth century.[63]

JEFFERSON DISCOVERED the "remains of Roman grandeur" at first hand the following winter, on his second and most extensive trip in Europe. The wrist he had fractured the previous fall had not healed properly, so on February 28, 1787, following his doctor's advice, he left Paris for the south of France. One object of the trip, he explained to James Monroe, was "to try the mineral waters there for the restoration of my hand"; another was "to visit all the seaports where we trade, and to hunt up all the inconveniences under which it labours, in order to get them rectified. I shall visit, and carefully examine too the canal of Languedoc."[64]

No doubt d'Hancarville had briefed Jefferson on the Roman ruins he would find in the region. The minister followed the advice he later gave to two compatriots planning a trip to Europe: "When you are doubting whether a thing is worth the trouble of going to see, recollect that you will never again be so near it, that you may repent the not having seen it, but can never repent having seen it." Architecture, both classical and modern, deserved the young men's "great attention," since it was "among the most important arts; and it is desirable to introduce taste into an art that shows so much." Jefferson clearly expressed his personal priorities when he reported to William Short from the south of France that "architecture, painting, sculpture, antiquities, agriculture, the condition of the laboring poor fill all my moments."[65]

Jefferson preferred traveling alone and anonymously, in each principal town hiring valets "who know nothing of me." The need to distance himself from friends and quotidian affairs was a recurring theme in Jefferson's life. "Between the society of real friends and the tranquillity of solitude the mind finds no middle ground," he lamented to Madame de Tott.[66] During his Paris years, particularly in the autumns of 1787 and 1788, the diplomat occasionally withdrew to the seventeenth-century Hermitage of Mont Valérien, overlooking Longchamp and the Bois de Boulogne and now run as a retreat by clubbable monks. Patsy Jefferson recalled that "whenever he had a press of business," her father would move into one of the monastery's forty-odd guest apartments for a week or more to finish his work. Jefferson hoped to find a "middle state" at Monticello, where he could enjoy friends and the necessary amenities while maintaining his intellectual privacy. Eventually, however, the growing number of visitors prompted him to build a more isolated retreat at Poplar Forest, in Bedford County, after he retired from public life.[67]

Heading south through Burgundy to Aix-en-Provence, Jefferson made meticulous notes on the wine industry. A typical entry reads: "The wines which have given such celebrity to Burgundy grow only on the Cote, an extent of about 5 leagues long, and half a league wide. They begin at Chambertin, and go through Vougeau, Romanie, Veaune, Nuys, Beaune, Pommard, Voulenay, Meursault, and end at Montrachet. Those of the last two are white, the other red. Chambertin, Voujeau and Veaune are the strongest, and will bear transportation and keeping."[68]

At the Château de Laye Epinay in the Beaujolais country, he confessed to Madame de Tessé in Paris, he fell in love with "a Diana…a delicious morsel of sculpture, by Michael Angelo Slotz."[69] Two years older than Jefferson, Madame de Tessé shared his interests in art, antiquities, gardening, and philosophy. She was, her biographer says, "captivated by philosophical ideas of the century, and intoxicated by seductive innovations which were to bring about, in her eyes, the regeneration and happiness of our country." Having made the Grand Tour to Italy some ten years earlier, Madame de

Tessé no doubt offered Jefferson expert advice during his many visits to her hôtel in Paris or to Chaville, her legendary château.[70]

In the former Roman city of Nîmes, Jefferson wrote his friend a bantering letter that began: "Here I am, Madame, gazing whole hours at the Maison quarrée like a lover at his mistress. The stocking weavers and silk spinners around it consider me as an hypochondriac Englishman, about to write with a pistol the last chapter of his history." Only now was he seeing what he believed to be the "the most perfect and precious remain of antiquity." The Maison Carrée had fired his imagination seven years before, when, as governor of Virginia, he had signed the legislation moving the capital from Williamsburg to Richmond. The little temple in Nîmes, dating from the Augustan period, had only recently been discovered by the public after the medieval buildings crowding around it had been pulled down. Knowing how much Madame de Tessé adored "whatever is Roman and noble," he wrote that "from Lyon to Nismes" he had been "immersed in antiquities from morning to night." Given her love of "architecture, gardening, a warm sun, and a clear sky," he couldn't understand why she didn't move Chaville to Nîmes.

Another Paris friend who was well equipped to advise the novice classical antiquarian on his explorations was Charles-Louis Clérisseau. He had spent nearly twenty years studying ancient monuments and working with the Adam brothers in Italy before returning in 1767 to study Roman remains in southern France. Jefferson bought his copy of *Monuments de Nîmes* from the architect cum archaeologist and, the year before his own trip to the south, he had asked Clérisseau to supervise the construction of the plaster model of the Maison Carrée that he had shipped to Richmond.

While inspecting the temple, Jefferson spotted an elegant Roman bronze vessel for wine or oil. A copy of the *askos* would, he thought, be a perfect gift for Clérisseau, and on the spot he commissioned a wooden model for a silversmith to copy. The model never materialized, but on his return to Paris Jefferson instead designed a coffee urn for the architect based on Roman vases and urns recently discovered at Pompeii and Herculaneum. It was made by Jean-Baptiste-Claude Odiot, Jefferson's favorite silversmith in Paris, who also executed a pair of silver goblets of classical design. Long after he had returned to America, Jefferson as president

The Maison Carrée at Nîmes.
"Erected at the time of the Caesars and which is allowed without contradiction to be the most perfect and precious remain of antiquity," Jefferson wrote of the little temple, "I determined, therefore, to adopt this model and to have all its proportions justly drewed." He stared so long at it that workmen thought him "an hypochondriac Englishman, about to write with a pistol the last chapter of his history." (Photo by Adelaide de Menil)

ordered a second wooden model of the askos and had it executed by a Philadelphia silversmith.[71]

Besides the Maison Carrée, Jefferson visited the ruins of the Temple of Diana and the Arena at Nîmes. Nearby he admired the "sublime" Pont du Gard, as well as the antiquities at Vienne and the amphitheater at Orange. At Vienne and later at Arles he made detailed measurements of several Roman structures and methodically recorded them in his travel notes, "useful facts to carry home to his countrymen." He was particularly impressed by the quality of Roman bricks, observing that "the grain is as fine as that of our best earthen ware." In 1792, as secretary of state, he dredged up from memory the details of the Roman bricks and their measurements and recommended that the commissioners of the Federal City consider using brick for the public buildings. "The remains of antiquity in Europe prove brick more durable than stone. The Roman brick appears in these remains to have been 22. inches long, 11 I. wide and 2 I. or 2 1/2 I. Thick."[72]

As a number of scholars have pointed out, Jefferson's systematic survey of Roman models on his trip encouraged his eclectic use of classical sources in a single building or group of buildings, as in his later plans for the University of Virginia. In measuring the Pretorian Palace at Vienne, he was acting more as a scientist than as an antiquarian or aesthete. Nor was this simply another example of his utilitarian preoccupations. To Jefferson, the structure was merely one more mathematical expression of architectural proportions, the type of source his idol Palladio had studied in determining the rules of lasting beauty. If the ratios of the decadent sepulchral pyramid outside Vienne (dating from 400 A.D. and finished by Charlemagne) proved faulty, he could establish the fact by comparative analysis.[73]

By the time the rejuvenated diplomat reached Marseilles, six weeks after leaving Paris, he had decided to extend his travels briefly into Italy. This "Peep into Elysium"[74] was not, as Congress had specifically authorized, related to his health and ailing wrist. For some months before leaving Paris, he had been supplementing his diplomatic interests in the American tobacco and whale oil trade with research into the cultivation of rice. As the French imported both Carolina and Piedmont varieties, he wanted to visit northern Italy, where the government protected both its seed rice and special husking equipment from potential foreign competitors. In a letter dated April 7, 1787, he informed Short that he planned to "meet with rice fields and the machines for cleaning it just beyond the Alps."[75]

Three days later Jefferson crossed the Var River into the Kingdom of Sardinia. He traveled by mule to Turin through Scarena, Sospello, Breglio, Saorgo, Fontan, Ciandola, Tende, Limone, Cuneo, Centallo, Savigliano, Racconigi, and Poirino. The winding road over the Tende Pass at 4,230 feet was considered an engineering triumph. "You may go in your chariot in full trot from Nice to Turin, as if there were no mountains," he reported to Maria Cosway. At the picturesque Gorge of Saorgo, his

Triumphal Arch and Tomb of the Julii at St. Rémy by Charles-Louis Clérisseau.
Jefferson visited St. Rémy on March 24, 1787, following his own advice to take a "tour into
Southern Parts of France" to see the "fine ruins." (Courtesy of the Board of Trustees of the
Victoria and Albert Museum)

descriptions echoed some of the word-pictures of Virginia that he had
written earlier to Maria; he insisted that she must come and paint the
romantic Italian scene.[76]

After visiting Turin, Milan, and Genoa, Jefferson confessed to his old
preceptor George Wythe that he had "scarcely got into classical ground"
but had taken with him "some of the writings in which endeavors have been
made to investigate the passage of Annibal over the Alps." He casually
reported that he had "found much amusement" in Italian architecture,
painting, and sculpture, but gave frustratingly few other details. In Milan,
he caustically pronounced the Cathedral "a worthy object of contemplation,
to be placed among the rarest instances of the misuse of money. On viewing
the churches of Italy it is evident without calculation that the same expense

would have sufficed to throw the Apennines into the Adriatic and thereby render it terra firma from Leghorn to Constantinople." Jefferson's preference for the Rome of Cicero over that of the Church Fathers—solid Enlightenment theology—could not be made more explicit.[77]

On May 6 Jefferson was back in Marseilles, having barely stepped into the classical world. Palladian scholars have deplored his neglect of the architect's city of Vicenza, but his dependence on books for the study of Palladio's work made the actual examples somehow less significant in his mind. His refusal to make a brief excursion to Rome, if only to see some of the old masters of which he had copied, is indeed inexplicable. But he had already stretched his travels beyond the limits set by Congress and he was intent on taking a trip on the Languedoc Canal, one of the original objects of his tour, before returning to Paris.

The pleasures of traveling on the noble canal of Louis XIV taught Jefferson quite a different moral lesson than the Milan Cathedral. In a lyrical passage to Short, he described an experience that went far beyond canal engineering:

> I have had some superb days of superb weather, enjoying two parts of the Indian's wish, cloudless skies and limpid waters: I have had the luxury which he could not wish since we have driven him from the country of mockingbirds, a double row of nightingales along the canal in full song. This delicious bird gave me a rich treat at Vaucluse. arriving there a little fatigued, I sat down to repose myself at the fountain which in a retired hollow of the mountain, gushes out in a stream sufficient to turn three hundred mills. The ruins of Petrarch's chateau perched on a rock two hundred feet perpendicular over the fountain, and every bush filled with nightingales in full chorus. I find Mazzei's observation just, that their song is more varied, their tone fuller and stronger than on the banks of the Seine. It explains to me another circumstance, why there never was a poet north of the Alps and why there never will be one. What a bird the nightingale would be in the climates of America! We must colonize him thither.[78]

"I HAVE COURTED THE SOCIETY OF GARDENERS, VIGNERONS, coopers, farmers &c, examining the culture and the cultivator," Jefferson wrote to the marquis de Chastellux from Marseilles. He repeated the

The Pont du Gard, one of the best-preserved antique monuments in the Languedoc.
Jefferson visited it in the spring of 1787. (Photo by Adelaide de Menil)

same sentiments a few days later in a letter to Lafayette. Gardens and gardeners ranked next to architecture and architects at the top of his scale of
the fine arts. This is where he placed them in the earliest catalogue divisions of his library, and it is where they remained throughout his life.[79]

His most important garden tour in Europe took place in 1786, when he
joined John and Abigail Adams in London. He took nearly two weeks away
from diplomatic negotiations with Portuguese envoys to see some of the
major English landscape creations of the eighteenth century. The art of
the garden was virtually the only English aesthetic achievement the confirmed anglophobe was willing to recognize. Dismissing English architecture as wretched, he had to admit that "gardening in that country is the
article in which it excels all the earth. I mean their pleasure gardening.
This, indeed, went far beyond my ideas."[80]

Carrying a copy of Thomas Whately's *Observations on Modern Gardening*—Jefferson said he "always walked over the gardens with" the book in hand—he set out to explore the subject at close range, often in the company of the Adamses. "Mr. Jefferson and myself," John Adams wrote, "went in a postchaise to Woburn farm, Caversham, Wotton, Stow, Edgehill, Stratford upon Avon, Birmingham, the Leasowes, Hagely, Stourbridge, Worcester, Woodstock, Blenheim, Oxford, [and] High Wycombe" before returning to Grosvenor Square. Jefferson on his own added to the list visits to Lord Burlington's Chiswick ("the garden shews still too much art: an oblisk to ill effect"), Alexander Pope's garden at Twickenham, Hampton Court, Esher Place ("Clumps of trees. The clumps on each hand balance finely."), Cobham, Painshill, and Weybridge.

Both men kept brief notes on each place. Jefferson's included his usual utilitarian details, while Adams injected an occasional moral observation, as at Painshill: "The owners of these enchanting seats are very indifferent to their beauties." Or at Edgehill: "Why do Englishmen so soon forget the Ground where liberty was fought for?" And at Stowe: "The Temples to Bacchus and Venus, are quite unnecessary as Mankind have no need of artificial Incitements to such Amusements."[81]

In his "Objects of Attention for an American," written two years after his English garden tour, Jefferson naively attempted to distill the significance and utility of garden art for America. Given the horticultural riches of the country, an entire continent of limitless waste could be reconciled with civilization and its landscape turned into an Eden merely for the asking: "Gardens. Peculiarly worth the attention of an American, because it is the country of all others where noblest gardens may be made without expense. We have only to cut out the superabundant plants."[82]

Jefferson's excursion through English gardens coincided with a revolutionary attempt to transform the English countryside into a Virgilian ideal, a vogue that saw the literary and painterly image of the pastoral illusion realized in landscaped parks and gardens. The cult of "Anglomanie," as Walpole called it, had quickly swept through Europe, reaching not only

The Pagode de Chanteloupe, near Amboise.
Jefferson saw the pagoda on his return from southern France in 1787. The tower dominated the vast gardens of the château of the duke de Choiseul. (Photo by Adelaide de Menil)

The Palladian Bridge, Stowe.
The great landscape park of Stowe was on everyone's list to visit. Jefferson stopped there
with his friends John and Abigail Adams during their garden tour in the spring of 1786.
The Palladian Bridge is attributed to James Gibbs. (Photo by Adelaide de Menil)

Marie Antoinette at her Hameau and Voltaire at Ferney but Catherine the
Great in Russia, who eagerly laid out fashionably wiggling garden paths
largely to bolster her international reputation as an enlightened ruler.

Back in Paris in the late summer of 1786, Jefferson found time to see a
number of French gardens around the city in the congenial company of
John Trumbull and the Cosways. As minister, he went regularly to Versailles on diplomatic errands and occasionally wandered into the gardens.
But he left no recorded comments on the baroque geometry of the layout, a
symbol of royal autocracy that L'Enfant would later interpret in his plans
for Washington, D.C. In his enthusiasm for the radically new English

The Orangery at Kew Gardens, London, by William Chambers.
The handsome classical building was one of a number of buildings at Kew designed by
Chambers for Princess Augusta between 1757 and 1762. (Photo by Adelaide de Menil)

Grotto, Folie de Sainte-James, by François-Joseph Bélanger.
The most successful element in the extravagant garden on the edge of the Bois de Boulogne
was the great stone grotto, complete with a gallery and bathroom. When its builder, baron
de Sainte-Gemmes, went bankrupt, Jefferson suggested that his friend Madame de Corny
buy the estate so that she could be closer to the Hôtel de Langeac. (Photo by Adelaide de
Menil)

picturesque garden, the Virginian could hardly have seen any redeeming
elements in the now exhausted formula of André Le Nôtre.

Le Nôtre's allées, more than a hundred years old, had been replaced in
1772 but had not regained their former splendor. The royal garden
designer Hubert Robert documented the forlorn park both before and after
the trees had been cut down. But the sightseers noticed no signs of devastation when they toured the royal art collection and grounds of Versailles
in August 1786. The gardens must be seen, "they cannot be described,"

Trumbull wrote in his diary. "I had expected to see immense monuments of labor and bad taste, where nature was overwhelmed in Art"; instead, he was ironically "disappointed" to find the gardens "so vast, so magnificent as to bear down all criticism."[83] The newly installed Bain d'Apollon, François Girardon's baroque group of marble statues hidden in a bower created by Robert, also made a strong impression on the visitors.

The royal botanical garden in Paris, known as the Jardin du Roi, or King's Garden, was headed by Jefferson's friend, the internationally celebrated George-Louis Buffon. The two men had dined together in the superintendent's house, and Jefferson had pored over Buffon's *Histoire naturelle* while working on his *Notes on the State of Virginia*. Jefferson also knew the count d'Artois' Bagatelle and its jardin anglais, not far from the ruins of the old Château de Madrid in the Bois de Boulogne, the former royal hunting park near the Hôtel de Langeac. Both John Adams, who lived in the village of Passy on its western edge, and Jefferson walked there regularly. The Virginian told Madame de Corny that he went to the Bois nearly every day "to survey its beautiful verdure, to retire to its umbrage, from the heat of the season."[84]

England and France dominated the new garden fashions of the late eighteenth century. So, between his impressive survey of the latest English gardens in 1786 and his persistent search for the most advanced designs in and around Paris, Jefferson gained a knowledge of gardens that was unequaled in America.

The new jardins anglais were essentially an urban phenomenon; their wealthy owners could afford to escape to their ideal worlds while keeping the amenities and excitement of city life close at hand. The La Rochefoucauld estate of La Roche-Guyon, with its model farm and landscape garden laid out by the duke's mother, the duchess d'Enville, according to the latest formula found in J.-M. Morel's *Théorie des jardins*, was a typical example. In attaching a shining classical portal to the ruins of the ninth-century Norman tower in the grounds of the château, the duchess announced the triumph of the new aesthetics over the medieval past.

Jefferson had long recognized that the organization of the limitless countryside in his ideal American republic would have to accommodate both primitive nature and human intervention. No doubt this explains why he placed the new landscape revolution and its seeming promise of environmental civility so high on his list of concerns about America's political destiny. In Paris, he fleshed out that early Virgilian vision with extraordinary energy and an insatiable appetite to see and experience everything. In later years he would sort through his eclectic baggage, looking for just the right fragment of inspiration to decorate his house, as well as the republic he had helped to invent. He was, as the authors of *The Age of Federalism* observe, concerned above all with creating "a total effect for his America," just as he was at Monticello. There seemed to be no element of European civilization that he would not try to fit into his conception of a republican society based on liberty, virtue, and the good life.[85]

Chapter 5

The Liberal, Literary, Scientific Air of Paris

ON AN APRIL MORNING IN 1782, the marquis de Chastellux finally reached his destination—a striking new house, a small temple perched on a low mountaintop in the Virginia foothills. Following the wagon ruts through the forest thick with spring growth, he was eager to meet the American who had been, in the Frenchman's words, the "author of the revolution." After playing "a distinguished role on the theatre of the New World," this remarkable man had withdrawn to his rural estate, where, as "a Philosopher retired from the world and its business," he could devote himself to his private intellectual pursuits. Chastellux's vivacious sketch of his host was one of the first to reach the French public when his journal was published four years later.[1] Jefferson considered the portrait greatly exaggerated, telling Chastellux that it presented "a lively picture of what I wish to be, but am not."[2] Nevertheless, it would serve as a kind of passport photograph, an introduction to the liberal circles that the Virginian would find so congenial when he arrived in Paris in little more than two years.

Chastellux knew of the Virginian's scholarly reputation, but he was not prepared to find a man of such cultivated, catholic interests. Almost from the moment the French soldier-philosopher arrived at Monticello, fresh from the battlefield of Yorktown, the two men's passion for politics, art, science, and literature fanned their conversation. For the astonished Parisian to find "the *dernier cri* of cosmopolitan sensibility" in the wilderness, as John Dos Passos put it, "must have been like stumbling onto a rubber plantation owner reading *Ulysses* in the African jungle."[3] Here was a self-made American who could more than hold his own in the highest intellectual circles of Paris, but whom circumstances had so far prevented from visiting the unquestioned capital of that golden age of ideas. For European liberals like Chastellux, eager to prove that the New World was capable of producing men of breadth and discrimination, Jefferson was reassuring evidence that their patient, costly support of the American experiment had not been in vain.

In 1784, when Jefferson agreed to join Franklin and Adams as a commissioner in Paris, Chastellux knew that his friend would fit smoothly into the capital's heady intellectual circles. Jefferson's interests and sensibilities had seemed exotic in rural Virginia, where, as Henry Adams observed, absence of city life was the one characteristic Virginians had in common. At Monticello, as Chastellux shrewdly guessed, Jefferson had isolated himself from "his fellow citizens," who were "not yet in a condition either to bear light, or to suffer contradiction."[4] His self-imposed exile would come to an end in France.

THOUGHTS OF PARIS were remote in the fall of 1780, when the thirty-seven-year-old governor of war-torn Virginia received an unexpected request for "statistical accounts" of his native "country" from François Barbé de Marbois, the secretary of the French legation in Philadelphia. Although Jefferson did not realize it at the time, the questionnaire was important preparation for his later work in Europe. When it was completed, Jefferson's *Notes on the State of Virginia* would provide an intellectual report on how the ideals of the European philosophes were being translated into the realities of America's still uncertain destiny. The government of Louis XVI had begun systematically to collect information about conditions and potential commercial prospects in the former British colonies. In all likelihood, the celebrated naturalist Georges-Louis Buffon and his staff of scientists at the King's Garden in Paris had drafted the twenty-two questions, which were also being circulated to other states.

Joseph Jones, Virginia's delegate to the Continental Congress, had recommended Jefferson to Marbois as the man best equipped to respond to the questionnaire. It began with a request for an "exact description" of Virginia's physical boundaries, but Jefferson soon found himself pondering some of the thorniest issues raised by the founding of the new republic. The very leanness of the queries seemed to encourage him to put the country's present chaotic state into perspective. Asked to describe "the particular customs and manners that may happen to be received in the state," he issued one of his most succinct indictments of slavery and its effect on society. More important, Jefferson was inspired to record for the first time his intellectual, social, political, and moral convictions, a world view on a "macroscopic plane" modestly couched as a foreigner's guide to his native state.

As the manuscript of what eventually became the *Notes on the State of Virginia* grew, the novice author probed his own ideas about representative government, the relationship between the form of government and economic production, religious freedom, the "political and moral" evils of slavery, public education, the separation of church and state, constitutional government, even architectural reform—all issues that at that very moment were being vigorously debated in Paris salons. The questionnaire also allowed him to explore and clarify his ambitions for the great abstraction he called "the empire of liberty" more fully than he would ever be able to do again. And he would soon be ready to test his conclusions in the sympathetic but critical setting of Paris before exposing them widely to his own countrymen.[5]

Having what he called a "canine appetite" for learning, Jefferson had always observed nature closely for evidence of rational laws and constitutions that might govern mankind. That these seemingly random notes might be organized into coherent answers for the French mission proved the usefulness of his obsessive pastime. Proceeding methodically through the list of questions (he would later rearrange them for publication) temporarily distracted Jefferson from the siege of the British forces. "I am at present busily employed for Monsr. Marbois without him knowing it," he wrote to the chevalier d'Anmour, stationed with the French troops in Baltimore, on November 30, 1780, "and have to acknowledge to him the mysterious obligation for making me more acquainted with my own country than I ever was before. His queries as to this country put into my hands by Mr. Jones I take every occasion which presents itself of procuring answers to."[6]

In the same letter, Jefferson first mentioned his interest in obtaining a copy of Diderot's "grande Encyclopédie," no doubt to help him answer Marbois' questionnaire. The expensive, cumbersome tomes were difficult to import in wartime, and Jefferson had evidently asked d'Anmour to find "some vessel of war" to bring a set directly from Paris. By chance, a few weeks later a bookseller in Alexandria advertised for sale in the *Virginia Gazette* a set of "the supreme work of the Enlightenment." Although in the original French, this particular edition had actually been published in Lucca, Italy, by a group of provincial aristocrats whose interests were not unlike those of their Virginia counterparts. The Luccanese publishers had appropriately dedicated it to the senate of their tiny republic.

The twenty-eight-volume *Encyclopédie* was an extraordinary thing to be peddling at that moment in Virginia, whose militia had just been defeated at the disastrous battle of Camden. But Governor Jefferson, in an unconscious gesture of unfailing optimism (and no doubt contemplating retirement to his "literary objects"), immediately negotiated for its purchase on behalf of the state; the considerable price was fifteen hogsheads (15,068 pounds) of tobacco. The heavy, unbound folios were delivered early in the spring of 1781, as the governor and his council were preparing to flee the approaching enemy. Later that May, Jefferson, fearing that the treasure might fall into the hands of marauding British troops, ordered it taken to the western military outpost of Winchester, Virginia, for safekeeping. After leaving office in June 1781, Jefferson retrieved the volumes and kept them in his possession while he was revising his answers for Marbois. On July 5 the Virginia Council directed the state's agent "to take measures for getting from Mr. Jefferson the *Encyclopédie* belonging to the public." As Douglas Wilson has pointed out, his reluctance to give it up was certainly linked to his work on the *Notes*.[7]

By the time Chastellux visited Monticello, Jefferson had completed the first draft of his answers and sent them to Marbois. Chastellux also received a manuscript copy, but Jefferson warned him to "distrust the information" because he had already begun to revise it. "I found some things should be omitted, many corrected, and more supplied and enlarged. They are swelled nearly to treble bulk." The manuscript was now too large to circulate, but in the spring Jefferson hoped to have "a dozen or twenty" copies printed for friends. He made further emendations before sailing for France in 1784, incorporating information supplied by friends, including Chastellux. Although he considered publishing the book in Philadelphia, he ultimately decided to have "a few copies struck off" in Paris, where printing was cheaper.[8]

Shortly after arriving in France in August, Jefferson was introduced (probably by Franklin) to the printer Phillippe-Denis Pierres, who agreed to publish the work of the novice author. A mere two hundred copies were printed privately, typically without the author's name on the title page. Despite his endless hours of research, writing, and revision, Jefferson affected modesty about his literary efforts, just as he had deprecated his work on the Declaration of Independence. In June 1785, a month after the *Notes* appeared, he wrote to Charles Thomson, a fellow member of the American Philosophical Society: "In literature nothing new: for I do not consider as having added any thing to that feild my own Notes of which I have had a few copies printed." Thomson, who had read the first draft of the manuscript carefully, appending his own amplifications, did not over-state when he told the author that he thought it "a most excellent Natural history not merely of Virginia but of No. America and possibly equal if not superior to that of any Country yet published."[9]

It is important to remember that the *Notes* was written for a foreign audience and at a stage in the Virginian's life when he felt ready to reflect on events—his most congenial role—rather than helping to shape them. The book expresses not only his hopes but his gloomier concerns for America's future. Now that the war was over, Jefferson had a foreboding that the country was already slipping downhill; the ancient virtues of freedom, friendship, and public happiness—those natural elements of a republic—seemed vaguely threatened, their importance diminished. Fearing that "fashion and folly," fed by easy credit, would lead to public and private debt, he foresaw the very foundation of American liberty being undermined, morally and politically. Many of his liberal European friends, however, took a less pessimistic view. Theorists were working on blueprints for a society in which men could pursue narrow self-interests without worrying about moral considerations. If those goals resulted in "luxury," it might or might not "presage national declinsion and ruin," as the Scottish philosopher Adam Ferguson wrote in 1767, for the simple reason that no one could agree "on the application of the term."[10]

The moral problem of excessive wealth leading to decadence had been addressed in the article on "luxe" in the *Encyclopédie*. In his *Notes* and letters, Jefferson envisioned society's ultimate happiness as residing in the elevated moral principles of a well-ordered state, transcending the debilitating conditions of the market-oriented society he encountered in Europe. He aimed his most scathing indictments in the *Notes* at the concentration of people in cities and the "workshops" of the new industrial capitalism. Jefferson had, of course, framed his ideological rejection of cities long before he actually laid eyes on any of the city-bred vices of France. His condemnations echoed those of another Scottish philosopher, Lord Kames, who observed that "great opulence opens a wide door to indolence, sensuality, corruption, prostitution," and, in that final state of lost souls, a Presbyterian "perdition."[11]

In Query XIX of the *Notes*, entitled "Manufacturing," Jefferson outlined the critical economic differences between Europe and America, particularly Virginia. This section of the book, with its physiocratic tone, was especially significant for Europeans; it anticipated the arguments that Jefferson would encounter in Paris. How to insure for the majority a quality of life reflected in "manners and spirit," not measurable by economic criteria associated with urban society, was a problem that would continue to perplex him. He spelled out his own priorities in a letter to William Short in early 1787, while he was traveling in France. He had "not visited all the manufactures of" Lyon, he told his secretary, "because knowledge of them would be useless and would extrude from the memory other things more worth retaining. Architecture, painting, sculpture, antiquities, agriculture, the condition of the labouring poor fill all my moments."[12]

The *Notes* played well in Paris, and Jefferson immediately sent copies to his new friends. Among the first to receive it was Chastellux, who in his acknowledgment warmly recalled his visit with the author at Monticello. Jefferson asked James Madison to read the book carefully, concerned about its public circulation in the United States because of the sentiments he expressed about slavery and his harsh criticism of the Virginia constitution.[13] Franklin, now in Philadelphia, and John Adams in London received early copies. Adams wrote an enthusiastic letter on behalf of his entire family; Abigail thought that Benjamin West and John Singleton Copley should have been included in the passage on American talent in response to the abbé Raynal's condescending claim that America had yet to produce a single "genius."[14] Other "friends and estimable characters beyond that line" to whom Jefferson sent the book included Lafayette, Condorcet, Buffon, Mazzei, Malesherbes, the count de Rochambeau, the abbé André Morellet, the naturalist Louis-Jean-Marie Daubenton, and the historian François Soulés.[15] Outside of Paris, copies were eventually given to Maria Cosway and Richard Price, the liberal clergyman in London, and to G. K. van Hogendorp, a Dutch friend living in the Hague. Madame de Tessé, Baron Grimm, and the duke de La Rochefoucauld were surely on the author's preferred list of recipients of the limited private edition, but the record has disappeared. He also saw to it that the libraries of both the French Institute and the Museum of Natural History received the original letterpress edition.[16]

In vivid passages inserted among the arid statistics and lists of flora and fauna, Jefferson gave Europeans their first glimpse of America's natural beauty. Buffon's dismal description of the New World—which was all most Frenchmen knew of the country's varied landscape—reads like a passage from a steaming gothic novel: "The air, the earth, overloaded with humid and noxious vapours, are unable either to purify themselves, or to profit by the influence of the Sun, who darts in vain his most enlivening rays upon this frigid mass, which is not in a condition to make suitable returns to his ardour. Its powers are limited to the production of moist plants, reptiles and insects, and can afford nourishment only to cold and feeble animals."[17]

Buffon and other writers drew their pseudoscientific conclusions from a grab bag of fact and fancy. The age was obsessed with the possible influence of soil quality, climate, and temperature in various parts of the world on the evolution of animal life, including man. Cornelius DePauw, Montesquieu, and Voltaire, as well as Buffon and the abbé Raynal questioned the New World's ability to achieve a civilization that was mature by Old World measures. They held that America's natural environment was fatally flawed and not a hospitable habitat for man or beast. Over time, both would degenerate physically, contradicting the Enlightenment's promise of progress. Not only were the native animals of the New World smaller than European species, Buffon argued that the American Indians were physically undeveloped and lazy; the men's "organs of generation" were "small and feeble," and they had "no ardour for the female."[18] Descendants of European settlers likewise supposedly showed a marked physical, intellectual, and moral decline in the New World; only a few spots offered conditions that were "proper either for culture or habitation."[19]

Jefferson, of course, was infuriated by such theories. Not only did they run counter to his fundamental belief in man's inevitable physical and intellectual progress, they negated the central tenet of liberal faith: that by exercising reason freely, people could not fail to reach ever higher levels of prosperity, justice, and happiness. Buffon, Raynal, and others later recanted their more controversial conjectures, thanks in large part to Benjamin Franklin's persuasive intervention, but the theory of "degeneration" persisted in vulgarized forms. It also had a continuing attraction for leading intellectuals: when Raynal offered a prize for an essay on the question "Has the discovery of America been useful or harmful to the human race?" the entries were evenly divided in their conclusions.[20]

Desperate for international recognition, assistance, and credit, successive American envoys worked hard to convince the French government that the United States was a good financial risk, holding long-range promise of growth and development. Franklin, Adams, and Jefferson were, of course, in the forefront of the crucial effort to establish America's political legitimacy and international standing. Jefferson saw his *Notes* as an important means of countering what he considered pernicious scientific heresy, though his refutation of Buffon was cushioned by a diplomatic regard for the respected French scientist, "the best informed of any Naturalist who has ever written."[21] Nevertheless, he continued, "I am induced to suspect, there has been more eloquence than sound reasoning displayed in support of this theory; that it is one of those cases where the judgment has been seduced by a glowing pen: and whilst I render every tribute of honor and esteem to the celebrated Zoologist, who has added, and is still adding, so many precious things to the treasures of science, I must doubt whether in this instance he has not cherished error also, by lending her for a moment his vivid imagination and bewitching language."[22]

Jefferson dismissed Raynal's work as the "effusions of an imagination in deliris."[23] To Raynal's contention "that America had not yet produced one good poet, one able mathematician, one man of genius in a single art or single scientist," the Virginian replied with towering indignation, channeled into one of his most eloquent passages:

> In war we have produced a Washington, whose memory will be adored while liberty shall have votaries, whose name will triumph over time, and will in future ages assume its just station among the most celebrated worthies of the world, when that wretched philosophy shall be forgotten which would have arranged him among degeneracies of nature. In physics we have produced a Franklin, than whom no one of the present age has made more important discoveries, nor has enriched philosophy with more ingenious solutions of the phenomenon of nature. We have supposed Mr. [David] Rittenhouse second to no astronomer living: that in genius he must be the first because he is self-taught. As an artist he has exhibited as great a proof of mechanical genius as the world has ever produced. He has not indeed made a world; but he has by imitation approached nearer its Maker than any man who has lived from the creation to this day."[24]

Jefferson considered certain portions of the abbé Raynal's account of the United States, "worthless." The book's widespread influence can be measured by the fact that it went through fifty-five editions in at least six languages. The American section had been picked up separately by other writers and eventually appeared in the article on the United States in the *Encyclopédie méthodique.*[25]

Since Jefferson had not yet met Buffon in 1785, he asked Chastellux to present a copy of the *Notes* on his behalf, together with an impressive panther skin for which he had paid sixteen dollars in Philadelphia just before sailing for Europe. His idea was to confront the scientist with incontrovertible evidence of the wildlife of the New World. Buffon, no doubt appreciating the American boldness of the gesture, immediately invited the envoy to dine with him at his residence at the King's Garden.[26] Yet in spite of the gifts and long discussions with Jefferson, the naturalist remained skeptical. Undaunted, the Virginian began to assemble a veritable museum of American natural history, asking friends to send him grouse and pheasant from Pennsylvania and buck horns of a Virginia deer. But his biggest piece of evidence came from New Hampshire: at his request, Gen. John Sullivan organized an expedition to hunt down large specimens of moose, caribou, deer, and elk. It took the general and twenty men to catch the moose, boil the bones, and stuff the skin before shipping it to Paris along with horns of the caribou, elk, deer, and spiked horned buck. Jefferson transmitted the "spoils" to the doubting Buffon, ironically expressing his hope that they "may have the merit of adding any thing new to the treasures of nature which [have] so fortunately come under your observation, and to which she seems [to] have given you the keys."[27]

IN HIS *MEMOIRS*, Filippo Mazzei's imaginative recollection fixes the origin of the *Notes on the State of Virginia* to 1788, three years after its actual publication. His fanciful genesis places Jefferson, Mazzei, Condorcet, and William Short at La Roche-Guyon as weekend guests of the duke de La Rochefoucauld. According to Mazzei, the future of the American republic was discussed, and Jefferson agreed to answer questions if the duke would write them down. There is a certain allegorical charm to this tale of the two Enlightenments coming together, for the five men had often discussed many of the issues Jefferson addressed in the *Notes*. That the most important scientific and political book written by an American in the eighteenth century was hatched by men of such caliber in the idyllic French countryside is an inspired invention. Once again, Europe was projecting its own ideal vision onto the American screen; the tableau of leading Old World intellectuals eager to learn from an acclaimed spokesman for the New confirmed the mythic ties between the two cultures.

George-Louis Buffon's house in the King's Garden. (Photo by Adelaide de Menil)

The *donjon* (dungeon) of the Château de La Roche-Guyon. The medieval tower hangs on the cliff above the La Rochefoucauld château and the Seine. The neoclassical door that the duke's mother, the duchess d'Enville, attached to the old ruins in 1780 as background for her modern *jardin anglais* symbolizes the spirit of this liberal family who befriended Jefferson. He shipped a number of trees and shrubs from Virginia for the duchess's garden. (Photo by Adelaide de Menil)

La Rochefoucauld, Condorcet, and Chastellux had played major roles in consolidating French support for the American cause, and each had published important books that promoted Franco-American understanding. (They also happen to be the same group that John Adams later condemned as the "chimera of Liberty, Equality and fraternity" who had led France over the "inevitable abyss.") According to Condorcet, America alone was on the verge of realizing the ideals of the age. "The spectacle of the equality that reigns in the United States and which assures its peace and prosperity can be useful in Europe," the philosophe declared. Condorcet yearned for confirmation that mankind's great work-in-progress was moving ahead on course and on schedule. The dreams of European intellectuals were being put to the test and depended on a favorable outcome. "What had been for them only words and paper had, in America, become flesh and blood."[28]

Born in the same year, Jefferson and Condorcet shared a lifelong interest in the classics. Both had absorbed the Enlightenment's catechism and struggled to take rational control of their respective worlds. No doubt their mixture of reserve and frankness further cemented their friendship. In their early forties when they first met, both men had already enjoyed extraordinary careers. While Jefferson was taking part in the drama leading to the break with England, Condorcet was working on the revised edition of the *Encyclopédie* and writing advanced political tracts. Voltaire's anointed heir, Condorcet was bold enough to proclaim himself a "republican" before the Revolution, and lived long enough to sit in the Convention of 1792.[29] The Virginian would found a political party that would elevate him twice to the head of government, Condorcet would die by his own hand when his country's revolution took an unexpectedly violent turn and he was run to ground by his enemies. Jefferson would have appreciated the worn copy of Homer found in the philosopher's pocket when he was cornered in 1794.

Condorcet subscribed to the analytical method of enquiry exhibited in the *Notes*. But Jefferson's instinctive American approach—pragmatic, discursive, self-confident, concrete—differed sharply from the Frenchman's abstract, sanguine idealism. Consumed by a desire to discover the laws of human progress, Condorcet had studied American political writings, including the Declaration of Independence, "a simple and sublime exposition of these [human] rights." He had also read Jefferson's anonymous preamble to the Virginia charter, which had been incorporated into the state constitution. He was particularly struck by the chaste, neoclassical literary style of the documents: "the Americans have based their peace and happiness on a small number of maxims which seem to be the simple expression of what good sense could have dictated to all men." As for George Mason's Virginia Bill of Rights, its author was "entitled to the eternal gratitude of mankind."[30]

Even among Jefferson's most liberal colleagues, Condorcet stood out in his unequivocal determination to eliminate every form of discrimination in society and to count on reason and justice to carry the day. Abolishing slavery and achieving equal rights for women were at the top of his list. He must have been pleased to read the Virginian's draft for a state constitution, appended to the *Notes*, proscribing the slave trade and including a provision giving women equal rights of inheritance.[31] Yet whereas Jefferson's proposals were tentative and equivocal, Condorcet played with revolutionary fire in blunt, incendiary words: "He who votes against the rights of another, whatever be his religion, color, or sex, has at that moment abjured his own rights."[32]

As John Chester Miller has pointed out, Jefferson assuredly "did not write the Declaration with slavery in mind," even though his "self-evident truths" unquestionably precluded tolerating the evil in the United States. If human liberty and dignity were to be sustained, how could they be denied to members of the human race who were held as bondsmen? By 1776 Jefferson had come to believe that slavery was too deeply established among his own class of southern planters to be dismantled with a few idealistic laws. His modest proposal in the draft Virginia constitution to abolish the slave trade (though not the institution) gradually had been rejected that year. As he argued consistently for the rest of his life, he had concluded from experience that the abolition of slavery would be a long, painful process, requiring the utmost patience and determination. "The revolution of public opinion which this cause requires," he wrote two weeks before he died, "is not to be expected in a day, or perhaps in an age; but time which outlives all things will outlive this evil."[33]

Jefferson realized that his criticism in the *Notes* of the Virginia Constitution, and of slavery in particular, would not go down well among his fellow Virginians, even though it did not go far enough in the eyes of his Parisian friends. Slavery was the touchiest personal dilemma Jefferson had to deal with. It represented the greatest threat to the pastoral republic he had conjured in the *Notes*, undermining his utopian society of hardworking, virtuous, forward-thinking farmer-citizens. But he was unable to devise a workable plan to eradicate the evil, short of invoking a just

God's wrath. In a memorandum of June 1786 addressed to Jean-Nicholas Démeunier, the talented young editor of the *Encyclopédie méthodique*, he made his forced retreat to divine intervention explicit: "But we must await with patience the workings of an overruling providence, and hope that that is preparing deliverance of these our suffering brethren. When the measure of their tears shall be full, when their groans shall have involved heaven itself in darkness, doubtless a god of justice will awaken to their distress, and by diffusing light and liberality among their oppressors, or at length by his exterminating thunder, manifest his attention to the things of this world, and that they are not left to the guidance of blind fatality."[34]

Démeunier had asked why Virginia's new slave law, which Jefferson had helped to draft, lacked a provision for emancipation. The Virginian explained that his proposed amendment would have required gradual emancipation and deportation, but the "slaveholding spokesman of freedom," as Edmund Morgan called him, was not prepared to risk open political conflict by pressing the issue. Jefferson's personal stake in the institution of slavery separated him from his liberal French friends. When he left for Europe, he owned some two hundred slaves, two of whom, James and Sally Hemings, became members of his Paris household. Once they set foot in France, the Hemingses could have had their freedom for the asking under French law—as Jefferson well knew, even if they did not. In 1786 Paul Bentalou of Baltimore wrote the minister to inquire about the status of a "Little Negro Boy" his wife had brought with her to France. After checking with the French authorities, Jefferson advised Bentalou to keep quiet, since the boy was so young that it was "not probable" that he would "think of claiming freedom."[35]

The major statement of Condorcet's opposition to slavery is *Réflexions sur l'esclavage des nègres*, published in 1781, about the time Jefferson began working on the Virginia constitution.[36] "To reduce a man to slavery, to buy him, to sell him, to keep him in servitude, all these are real crimes that are worse than stealing," Condorcet declared in Jefferson's translation. Even if "the human race unanimously voted approval, the crime would remain a crime." Jefferson avoided such inflammatory language in the *Notes*, focusing instead, in the section appropriately titled "Manners," on

the "blot" slavery had left on the white population. In exercising absolute power over other human beings, he argued, even virtuous men had been corrupted and morally degraded.

Jefferson tried to persuade Condorcet that dismantling the institution of slavery was a far more complex problem than he thought. The philosophe had no direct knowledge of slavery and its entrenchment in the American South. In his writings, he repeatedly referred to what he imagined to be happening in America, and he convinced himself, no doubt with Jefferson's help, that progress was actually being made toward abolition. In *De l'Influence de la révolution de l'Amérique sur l'Europe*, he wrote: "It is true that Negro slavery still exists in some of the United States; but all enlightened men feel its shame, and its danger, and this blemish will not long continue to sully the purity of American laws."[37]

In a postscript to the 1788 edition of his *Réflexions*, Condorcet again reviewed the state of affairs in the United States and proposed a number of laws that he believed would lead to abolition there and in the French West Indies. The first step was to legally prohibit further trade in slaves, while freeing those under the age of five and granting them a government stipend. Older slaves would be assisted in gradual emancipation, and their former masters compensated. Condorcet also proposed that a public ombudsman be appointed to monitor the rights of blacks during the transition period. Jefferson, impressed by Condorcet's rational argument, purchased two copies of the new edition and later embarked on a translation—a gesture of approval that he bestowed on few other French books.

A letter Jefferson wrote to Edward Bancroft in 1788 suggests that his conversations with Condorcet had helped to convince him to free his slaves when he returned to America. Around the same time he seriously contemplated allowing his slaves to become tenant farmers instead of leasing them with the land. Jefferson's dilemma was not only moral: in Virginia he was saddled with large, scattered agricultural operations that held him hostage

Entryway of the Hôtel de la Monnaie.
As Inspecteur général des monnaies, the marquis de Condorcet and his wife, Sophie de Grouchy, were given an apartment in the new headquarters of the Royal Mint. The American envoy went there regularly. (Photo by Adelaide de Menil)

to the system of slavery and with heavy debts that he could not manage. The far-fetched scheme that he outlined to Bancroft involved importing German peasant laborers to eventually replace the slave force at Monticello and at Poplar Forest, the plantation he had inherited from his wife. In July 1787, he had raised the possibility of leasing portions of his land to tenants as soon as his slaves had discharged "my debts with their labour...the moment they have paid the debts due from the estate." In the spring of 1793 he would explore with his son-in-law Thomas Mann Randolph a lease arrangement that included slaves as part of the deal.[38]

The year 1788 had seen other stirrings on the slave question in Paris. Several members of Jefferson's circle were actively participating in the growing debate. The ambitious lawyer Brissot de Warville, who had written a popular travel book about the United States, founded a philanthropic club called the Society of Friends of the Blacks (Société des Amis des Noirs). Dedicated to the abolition of slavery through political action, particularly in the French colonies, it included Lafayette, Condorcet, and the duke de La Rochefoucauld-Liancourt among its charter members. Jefferson was also invited to join but diplomatically declined. "Those that I serve having never yet been able to give their voices against this practice," he said, it was not proper for him to take a public stand. Without being of much help in France, "it might render me less able to serve it beyond the water."[39] As we will see, Jefferson did not have the same qualms about becoming involved in the strategic politics of the French Revolution. On the moral issue of abolition, he was not prepared to collaborate with his far more liberal friends.

Shortly after Jefferson returned to America, a scurrilous pamphlet circulated in the Palais Royal claiming that Brissot's society was an English conspiracy to foment trouble in the French islands. A list of its members was also made public, so the envoy's caution had been well founded.[40] Brissot was in fact in touch with English abolitionists and his society was a branch of the English antislavery organization, giving color to the charge of subversion.[41]

QUERY XVII OF THE *NOTES*, entitled "Religion," unexpectedly raised
another bristling issue that was beginning to be widely discussed in
Europe but had already reached the first stages of public policy in America.
On the face of it, Marbois' request for information about "the different religions received into" Virginia called for nothing more than a straightfor-
ward inventory of the state's religious institutions. But Jefferson seized the
opportunity to write a brilliant essay on intellectual and religious liberty
that was even more inflammatory than his stand on slavery. The prologue
of the Virginia statute establishing religious freedom alone, paraphrasing
Voltaire, Diderot, and other philosophes, was enough to send chills down
the spine of any official of the old regime. It began: "Almighty God hath
created the mind free, that all attempts to influence it by temporal punish-
ments or burthens, or by civil incapacitations, tends only to beget habits
of hypocrisy and meanness."[42]

After summarizing the "religious slavery" embedded in English law,
Jefferson recounted the events of the convention at Williamsburg in 1776,
in which he had participated. Although George Mason's Declaration of
Rights, set out in the Virginia Constitution, boldly stated that "all men are
equally entitled," conservative members of the convention refused to enact
laws enforcing it. In his autobiography Jefferson recalled that his efforts to
implement the constitution and its bill of rights had been "the severest
contests in which I have ever been engaged." He did not mention in the
Notes that as governor he had actually introduced in 1779 the statute on
religious toleration which he had apparently drafted several years earlier.[43]

Jefferson's daring call for religious freedom resonated throughout
Europe. Taking the argument to its logical conclusion, he defended freedom of human conscience as an essential cornerstone of civil liberty. The
celebrated passage confessing his indifference to his neighbor's religious
beliefs later came to dog him during his rising political career in the
United States. In fact, this portion setting out the crux of his argument
would cause him more political trouble than anything else he said or did
during his lifetime:[44]

> The error seems not sufficiently eradicated, that the operations of the mind,
> as well as the body, are subject to the coercion of the laws. But our rulers can

have authority over such natural rights only as we have submitted to them. The rights of conscience we never submitted, we could not submit. We are answerable for them to our God. The legitimate powers of government extend to such acts only as are injurious to others. But it does me no injury for my neighbor to say there are twenty gods, or no gods. It neither picks my pocket nor breaks my leg. If it be said, his testimony in a court of justice cannot be relied on, reject it then, and be the stigma on him. Constraint may make him worse by making him a hypocrite, but will never make him a truer man. It may fix him obstinately in his errors, but will not cure them. Reason and free enquiry are the only effectual agents against error. Give a loose to them, they will support the true religion, by bringing every false one to their tribunal, to the test of their investigation. They are the natural enemies of error, and of error only.[45]

On June 23, 1786 Jefferson received word from Madison that in the final hours of the Virginia Assembly, the statute he had first introduced seven years earlier had finally been "pursued into a Bill." When a copy of the Act for Establishing Religious Freedom arrived in Paris, Jefferson lost no time in having it translated and printed in both French and Italian. He was eager to have "propagated with enthusiasm" throughout Europe that his native state had, as he wrote to Madison, "produced the first legislature who had the courage to declare, that the reason of man may be trusted with the formation of his own opinions." He also saw the act as a powerful answer to French critics of America, "the best evidence of the falsehood of those reports which stated us to be in anarchy."[46]

European papers gave wide coverage to the Virginia Assembly's action. Even skeptics, Jefferson told George Wythe, were convinced that

such a work is that of a people only who are in perfect tranquility.... The ambassadors and ministers of several nations of Europe resident at this court have asked of me copies of it to send to their sovereigns, and it is inserted at full length in several books now in press; among others, in the new Encyclopedie. I think it will produce considerable good even in these countries where ignorance, superstition, poverty and oppression of body and mind in every form, are so firmly settled on the mass of people, that their redemption from them can never be hoped. If the almighty had begotten a thousand sons, instead of one, they would not have sufficed for this task. If all the sovereigns of Europe were to set themselves to work to emancipate the minds of their subjects from their present ignorance and prejudices, and that as zealously as they now endeavor to the contrary, a thousand years would not place them on that high ground on which our common people are now setting out. Ours could not have been so fairly put into the hands of their common sense, had they not been separated from their parent stock and kept from the contamination, either from them, or the other people of the old world, by the intervention of so wide an ocean.[47]

A week or so after writing to his old mentor in Williamsburg, Jefferson sent a copy of the act along with a translation to the count de Mirabeau. In his accompanying letter, he quoted the count's recent remarks that there was no place on earth where it was sufficient for a man to practice the social virtues in order to participate in all the advantages of society. Mirabeau, he wrote, was probably not familiar with the enclosed act recently passed by "one of the American republics"; and the politician might "on some occasion to avail mankind of this example of emancipating human reason."[48]

As the somewhat underground reputation of the *Notes* spread, Jefferson became increasingly concerned that a bad translation would appear, causing further misunderstanding over some the more controversial sections. In the fall of 1785, he learned that the French bookseller Barrois was in fact planning to publish an unauthorized translation. He was relieved, and probably flattered, when the abbé Morellet, a recently elected member of the French Academy who had received one of the first copies, made a "friendly proposition" that they collaborate on the French edition. Morellet, a friend of Franklin, was one of several liberal ecclesiastics who frequented the smart Parisian drawing rooms. Captivated by Franklin's advanced political prescriptions dished up in simple homilies, Morellet had also written articles on religion for Diderot's *Encyclopédie*. Mazzei, in his memorandum for Jefferson on personalities in Paris, called the abbé "one of the most sensible men in France."[49]

Morellet, the son of a small-time paper merchant who styled himself "count," was some ten years older than Jefferson. A protégé of Madame Geoffrin, he had charmed his way into high society and the heady circle of

Turgot, Diderot, and d'Alembert. When Jefferson first met him at La Roche-Guyon in the summer of 1786, Morellet was living with his sister, the wife of the successful playwright Jean-François Marmontel. She maintained a chic apartment overlooking the Tuileries gardens, where he held a weekly salon. Morellet was devoted to his comforts far more than to the church, which claimed, as one wag put it, "only half his faith, half his wardrobe, and only one priory." A fashionable crowd representing the arts, letters, and bon ton gathered in Morellet's salon and library, one of the finest in Paris. "There, in the midst of perfect quiet and with peace in one's heart and soul," the duchess d'Abrantés recalled, "one listened to the most ravishing music, or discussions of the latest poetry and prose."[50]

At the outset of their collaboration, Jefferson seems to have been satisfied with the amiable, worldly cleric. He was keen to have a map of Virginia for the new translation, based on the one by his father and Joshua Fry. The production of the map proved to be a headache, but the abbé's awkward translation posed even bigger problems. In August 1786 Jefferson complained to Wythe that "a bad French translation" was about to appear in Paris. The finished edition, printed on poor paper, filled with errors, misprints, and faulty translations, and with the material rearranged, confirmed his worst fears.[51] It came out just a few weeks before the first authorized English edition was published by John Stockwell, the London printer. Carrying Jefferson's full name on the title page, the London edition, published in the summer of 1787, contained the draft of his constitution for Virginia and the Act for Establishing Religious Freedom.

Morellet's *Observations sur la Virginie* was no best-seller, but it received at least one generous notice. The reviewer for the *Mercure de France* thought Jefferson's demolition of Buffon's theory of degeneration "a model of good logic and excellent discussion." The writer was also impressed by his defense of religious freedom, placing Jefferson alongside Adams, Washington, Franklin, and Rittenhouse in the group of the American lumières who had created "the empire of reason and the inestimable blessing of liberty."[52]

The publication of the *Notes* coincided with growing efforts to modify the revocation of the Edict of Nantes, which had driven the Protestants of France into exile in 1685. In June 1787 Jefferson's friend Malesherbes, who had received one of the first copies of the book, had returned to the King's Council, and by November he had drafted an Act of Toleration for the king's signature, giving Protestants the barest of legal standing. Although Malesherbes was a sensible skeptic and stood solidly for religious toleration, there was clearly no connection between the royal act and the recently adopted Virginia statute or the Resolution to Disestablish the Church of England, which Jefferson had prepared in 1776.[53] In Jefferson's opinion, Malesherbes' timid overture to the Protestants, a "small effort of common sense," was an insult to the very idea of intellectual freedom.

The Virginian probably did not know that Malesherbes, as director of the French book trade, had rescued the *Encyclopédie:* after officially banning the first two volumes that contained opinions which undermined royal authority, he had offered secretly to store the manuscripts of future articles for Diderot. Privately, the old statesman no doubt sympathized with Jefferson's more radical position. He had once been in charge of official censorship for the government but had found the job impossible: "A man who had read only books that originally appeared with the formal approval of the government," he declared, "would be behind his contemporaries by nearly a century." Publishers in Holland, Germany, Switzerland, and England, who enjoyed greater freedom, flooded France with books proscribed by its own government; many of them entered the Virginian's library.[54]

Writing to John Rutledge, Jr., in February 1788, Jefferson complained that the newly drafted American Constitution itself lacked the safeguards of a Bill of Rights. His letter closed with a stinging commentary on the king's feeble effort to alleviate religious persecution:

> The long expected edict for the protestants at length appears here. It's analysis is this. It is an acknowledgement (hitherto withheld by laws) that protestants can beget children and that they can die and be offensive unless buried. It does not give them permission to think, to speak, nor to worship. It enumerates the humiliations to which they shall remain subject, and the burthens to which they shall continue unjustly exposed. What are we to think of the condition of the human mind in a country such a wretched thing as this has thrown the state into convulsions, and

how must we bless our situation in a country the most illiterate peasant of which is a Solon compared with authors of this law. There is a modesty often which does itself injury. Our countrymen possess this. They do not know their own superiority. You see it; you are young, you have time and talents to correct them. Study the subject while in Europe, in all the instances, which will present themselves to you, and profit your countrymen of them by making them to know and value themselves.[55]

ON FEBRUARY 23, 1788 the *Mercure de France* published an enthusiastic review of Filippo Mazzei's history of the United States. Some time in the winter of 1785–86, Jefferson's former neighbor in Albemarle County had turned up in Paris, as usual pressed for funds. With Jefferson's encouragement, Mazzei decided to recoup his fortune by writing an ambitious study of his adopted country. *Recherches historiques et politiques sur les Etats-Unis*, first published in Italian, had been translated by Condorcet and his wife.[56] Baron Grimm, who was in a position to know, maintained that Condorcet also wrote the unsigned review.

The *Mercure* focused on Mazzei's treatment of freedom of religion and of the press, calling attention to "the illustrious citizen" who had initiated the liberal dialogue. Mazzei had reprinted the Virginia Bill of Rights and borrowed generously from Jefferson's *Notes*. Jefferson, he claimed, had approved of his reply to the abbé de Mably's reactionary comments on freedom of the press. The *Mercure* quoted Jefferson to the effect that government should be denied any power over individual opinion. The reviewer also lifted from the *Notes*, as quoted by Mazzei, Jefferson's unabashed and, to many, blasphemous words on religion. The *Mercure*'s rival, the conservative *Année littéraire*, immediately published a letter expressing horror that anything "so harsh, so revolting, so absurd" had appeared in a Paris newspaper. According to Grimm, the proprietor of the *Mercure* was threatened with the loss of his royal license. The whole episode was deeply painful to Jefferson, whose frustration was compounded by the public reticence demanded of an accredited diplomat.[57]

For Jefferson, as for his predecessors, tracking, policing, and correcting misinformation about the United States was a major preoccupation.[58] Unlike Franklin, who used self-dramatization for propaganda purposes, and Adams, who grumbled freely about slights to national pride, Jefferson characteristically preferred to work behind the scenes, quietly countering misleading accounts whenever he saw an opportunity. In his own mind and in the *Notes*, the Virginian had created a coherent image of his country's identity, enabling him to devise effective and consistent strategies to promote international understanding of America.

Even before going to Paris, Jefferson had recommended to his Virginia friends Démeunier's acclaimed *Encyclopédie méthodique*, the first four volumes of which had appeared in 1784. But he was unhappy that the editor had relied on the abbé Raynal for the chapter on the United States. In 1786 Démeunier asked Jefferson for advice about Virginia's slave laws and subsequently decided to put the "article under Mr. Jefferson's inspection." Jefferson "struck out and altered the most flagrant errors. It remains at present as different from what he had written, as to matters of fact, as virtue to vice," William Short reported to a friend in Virginia.[59] Jefferson told Adams that it was crucial to set "to rights a book so universally diffused and which will go down to late ages."[60] The voluminous corrections and amplifications that he sent to Démeunier over the next six months swelled the American article to eighty-nine printed pages. Not surprisingly, the space devoted to Virginia exceeded that devoted to all the other states combined. By comparison, the article on England ran to fifty pages, while that on France took up only forty.

Démeunier's *Encyclopédie méthodique* was intended as disinterested scholarship, not propaganda, but Jefferson saw his duty as minister to uphold the best interpretation of American political ideals and policies, nebulous and confused though they still were. He proposed, for example, to "new-model" the section on the controversial Society of the Cincinnati. As Jefferson explained in his essay for the encyclopedia, the society was conceived as a purely social organization of former Revolutionary officers, both French and American. Politicians, however, including Jefferson, saw an aristocracy incubating in the fine print of the society's by-laws providing for hereditary membership; were "a race of nobles" to spring up in the United States, republican values could be destroyed. The déclassé count de Mirabeau, future leader of the French Revolution, had recently aggravated the debate in Paris by translating and amplifying a pamphlet from South Carolina opposing the society.[61]

Jefferson himself was strongly opposed to the society, but in his cool, measured account for the encyclopedia, he made every effort to clarify the peculiarly American issues involved in the debate. For centuries, the feudal structure of French society—state, church, families, institutions—had been organized on the ability of entrenched privilege to perpetuate itself through inheritance. Europe's class-ridden society had no real counterpart in the American colonies, and the Society of the Cincinnati could not possibly threaten republican ideals. To French liberals such as Lafayette, who was one of it ardent supporters, the controversy seemed to have been sparked by a handful of ribbons and medals. Yet it presented Jefferson with another opportunity to reinforce America's moral and political distinctiveness.

If the patient Démeunier had allowed him yet one more revision, Jefferson might well have expanded on his general views of feudal privileges. As a soft-spoken but determined member of the Virginia Assembly, the thirty-three-year-old lawyer had declared full-scale war on what he saw as feudal holdovers in American society. The ancient laws governing the ownership of land, on which Virginia's provincial aristocracy was based, had become one of his first legislative targets. On November 1, 1776 Jefferson's bill to abolish entail—the right to control descent through successive generations—was enacted, bringing down one of the already crumbling pillars of the landed gentry. In 1785 James Madison would push through Jefferson's bill wiping out feudal land tenure by right of primogeniture. Jefferson believed that this body of law, along with "the restoration of the rights of conscience," represented "a system by which every fibre would be irradiated of antient or future aristocracy; and a foundation laid for a government truly republican."[62]

In the fall of 1785, a few weeks before Démeunier invited him to contribute to the *Encyclopédie méthodique*, Jefferson wrote to James Madison, outlining his views on the need for wide ownership of land.[63] Outside the town of Fontainebleau, where the court was temporarily in residence, he had fallen in "with a poor woman walking at the same rate" and began one of his sociological enquiries "to know the condition of the working poor." The Virginian had been moved to reflect "on that unequal division of property which occasions the numberless instances of wretchedness which I had observed in this country and is to be observed all over Europe." The conversation also brought into focus the intolerable conditions of a country plagued by poverty, homelessness, and unemployment while vast tracts of land reserved by the nobility for hunting lay idle.

In the *Notes,* Jefferson had commented on the relationship between individual rights and the means of production in the new republic. There, however, he had concluded that the seemingly limitless supply of western American land would stave off, for a few generations at least, the rise of a landless proletariat such as he had seen in Europe. In his letter to Madison, the Virginian called for the creation of more "work-shops" and manufactures in Europe to preserve an essentially agrarian society of small landowners. He reminded Madison that, as a universal proposition, the earth was the common property of mankind. It followed that legislatures had an obligation to lessen the inequality of property ownership, if necessary through progressive taxation. "The consequences of this enormous inequality producing so much misery to the bulk of mankind, legislators cannot invent too many devises for subdividing property, only taking care to let their subdivisions go hand in hand with the natural affections of the human mind." Left out of these musings were the American slaves, who in Jefferson's mind remained property to be subdivided.

Jefferson's vision might make sense in America, where something close to the Virgilian model of independent yeomen farmers already existed. But the shocking concentration of wealth in Europe would require stronger remedies than a dose of the *Georgics.* Here was an entrenched feudal system that denied personal autonomy—the very basis of democratic government—to "the bulk" of the population. It denied individuals the means to live, or even to find meaning and purpose in the griefs and burdens that the peasant woman in Fontainebleau had described to him. A ruthless market economy designed to serve the few, unregulated by humanitarian restraints, would be little better. Nor would turning Europe's vast hunting estates into profitable agricultural land, as the physiocrats had advocated, solve the problem unless the people's economic and political rights were completely restructured.

> Whenever there is in any country, uncultivated lands and unemployed poor, it is clear that the laws of property have been so far extended as to violate natural right. The earth is given as a common stock for man to labor and live on. If, for the encouragement of industry we allow it to be appropriated, we must take care that other employment be furnished to those excluded from the appropriation. If we do not the fundamental right to labour the earth returns to the unemployed. It is too soon in our country to say that every man who cannot find employment but who can find uncultivated land, shall be at liberty to cultivate it, paying a modest rent. But it is not too soon to provide by every possible means that as few as possible shall be without a small piece of land. The small landholders are the most precious part of a state.

Conspicuous evidence of inequality existed in Virginia, as Jefferson had observed when he led the Assembly to take up the issue of land ownership in the 1770s. It is instructive to set his criticism of rural French poverty against Chastellux's comments on similar conditions in Jefferson's own backyard in 1782; it is a picture of a society into which Monticello and Jefferson himself easily fitted.

> Humanity has still more to suffer from the state of poverty in which a great number of white people live in Virginia. It is in this state, for the first time since I crossed the sea, that I have seen poor people. For among these rich plantations where the Negro alone is wretched, one often finds miserable huts inhabited by whites, whose wane looks and ragged garments bespeak poverty. At first I found it hard to understand how, in a country where there is still so much land to clear, men who do not refuse to work could remain in misery; but I have since learned that all these useless lands and those immense estates, with which Virginia is still covered, have their proprietors. Nothing is more common than to see them possessing five or six thousand acres of land, but exploiting only as much of it as their Negroes can cultivate. Yet they will not give away or even sell the smallest portion of it, because they are attached to their possessions and always hope to eventually increase the numbers of their Negroes.[64]

Writing to his neighbor James Madison at Montpelier in 1789, Jefferson returned to the question of entrenched privilege and the ownership of production, again using France as his example:

> This principle that the earth belongs to the living, and not to the dead, is of very extensive application and consequences, in every country, and most especially in France. It enters into the resolution of the questions Whether the nation may change the descent of lands holden in tail? Whether they may change the appropriation of lands given antiently to the church, to hospitals, colleges, orders of chivalry, and otherwise in perpetuity? Whether they may abolish the charges and privileges attached to lands, including the whole catalogue ecclesiastical and feudal? It goes to hereditary offices, authorities and jurisdictions; to hereditary orders, distinctions and appelations; to perpetual monopolies in commerce, the arts and sciences; with a long train of et ceteras.[65]

Jefferson's feelings about aristocracy and the conflict between feudal and natural rights lay just beneath the surface of his essay on the Society of the Cincinnati, which Démeunier incorporated without change into the article on the United States in the *Encyclopédie méthodique*. Americans who had not traveled in Europe had no idea of the insidious dangers posed by the specter of "monarchy" in the the former colonies; "to detail the real evils of aristocracy they must be seen in Europe...and as they would have followed in America if this institution [the society] remained."[66] Démeunier accepted virtually all of the diplomat's additions, as well as including his draft of the Virginia Constitution. Jefferson, however, complained to Adams that he had "still left in a great deal of the Abbé Raynal, that is to say a great deal of falsehood, and he has stated other things on bad information. I am sorry I had not another correction of it. He has paid me for my trouble, in the true coin of his country, most unmerciful compliment. This, with his other errors, I should surely have struck out had he sent me the work, as I expected, before it went to the press. I find in fact he is happiest of whom the world sais least, good or bad."[67]

Jefferson's next opportunity to set the American record straight came in the summer of 1786. He had asked his London publisher, John Stockwell, to send him a new history of the American Revolution by the respected French historian François Soulés. Upon learning that the author was planning a revised edition, Jefferson apparently volunteered some observations, to which Soulés responded by submitting a number of questions to Jefferson.[68] The envoy began a page-by-page commentary but stopped abruptly in early September—the period corresponding to the crucial gap in John Trumbull's diary, when Jefferson joined Maria and Richard Cosway and their bohemian party nearly every day on their rounds seeing the sights of Paris.

Later, "over family soupe" at the Hôtel de Langeac, Jefferson continued to feed Soulés with material from the notes he had supplied to Démeunier, including the text of the Act for Establishing Religious Freedom. Soulés, however, was far more selective than Démeunier in adopting the American's arguments. He concluded his revision with a biting criticism of the failures of postrevolutionary American society. After quoting the American patriot's own words from the Declaration of Independence—"Nous tenons comme une vérité certaine et évidente, que tous les hommes dont créés égaux"—the historian claimed that instead of cultivating the soil and being content with their homespun lot, like good republicans, Americans were hankering after luxury and high living. They were sending ministers to Europe addicted to "pomp and style" and contracting foreign debts, and were not even able to pay their own troops. Soulés had put his finger on one of Jefferson's own growing preoccupations; in the *Notes* he had written that since the war Americans, struggling to right their capsized economic boat, had become oblivious to everything except making money.[69]

THREE OTHER GIFTED MEN—Count de Volney, A.-L.-C. Destutt de Tracy, and Pierre-Samuel du Pont de Nemours—made lasting impressions on Jefferson during the Paris years, although the record of their friendships is thin. Of the three, du Pont unquestionably shared the most lasting intellectual intimacy with the American. It was to him that the weary President Jefferson wrote one of his most moving letters a few days before leaving office in 1808: "Within a few days I retire to my family, my books and farms, and having gained the harbor myself I shall look on my friends still buffeting the storm, with anxiety indeed, but not with envy. Never did a prisoner released from his chains, feel such relief as I shall of shaking off the shackles of power. Nature intended me for the tranquil pursuits of science, by rendering them my supreme delight, but the enormities of the times in which I have lived have forced me to take a part in resisting them, and to commit myself on the boisterous ocean of political passions."[70]

Only two minor letters between Jefferson and du Pont survive from the Paris period. Following du Pont's emigration to the United States, however, the economist and founder of the physiocratic school would become one of Jefferson's most stimulating correspondents on every aspect of government. Du Pont believed that the soil was the source of all virtue and that it was the essential function of government to assure all citizens the enjoyment of their natural rights. The strongly agrarian spirit of his physiocratic principles was Jeffersonian up to a point, but the two men differed on one critical issue. Du Pont insisted that the population of a republic should be divided into two classes or orders: real citizens, natural aristocrats who could vote and govern, and "inhabitants," who owned no real property and were governed, albeit with reasoned enlightenment. Such a division, of course, contradicted the sacred Jeffersonian principle that the will of the people must be supreme—a principle that Europeans had difficulty comprehending or accepting.[71]

While he was composing the Declaration of Independence in June and July 1776, Jefferson had relaxed by drafting model constitutions for Virginia, his "country." In all of these drafts, the people were the source of authority. As he was to write years later to Samuel Kercheval, "a government is republican in proportion as every member composing it has an equal voice in directing its concerns."[72] This fundamental principle of republican government could not be qualified, and any attempt to restrict the vote, such as du Pont proposed, could never be reconciled with Jeffersonian democracy.

The two men were, however, in complete accord on the necessity for a comprehensive system of public education in a republic. If, as du Pont, Helvétius, Condorcet, and Destutt de Tracy held, all social life and morality were based on self-interest, then it was imperative to educate the minds of citizens in order for them to become virtuous, enlightened members of society. Jefferson had come to the same conclusions and in 1779 and had translated them into his groundbreaking Bill for the More General Diffusion of Knowledge for the state of Virginia. In its recognition of the three stages of the educational process—primary, secondary, and higher—Jefferson's practical plan would become the foundation of modern education.

The Virginian had developed his educational philosophy at length in his *Notes* and had discussed it with French friends in Paris. Among other things, he had declared that the objective of knowledge was to make the young "useful instruments for the public." In plain language, this meant that one of the uses of knowledge, as Joseph Kett has written, was "to instill republican attitudes such as political responsibility, love of liberty, and hatred of tyranny."[73] These cardinal tenets of liberal public education, which Jefferson introduced to France in the 1780s, would be incorporated into the various educational proposals submitted to French legislatures in the 1790s.[74] In his last decade, when he was planning the new University of Virginia, Jefferson reviewed du Pont's scheme for higher education, which itself borrowed liberally from the Virginian's bill, although conceived upon a far greater scale. Thus did Jefferson's educational ideas come full-circle back to Charlottesville.

Shortly after arriving in Paris, the novice envoy had gravitated to two young intellectuals, Constantin-François Chasseboeuf, the "count" de Volney, and Destutt de Tracy. Like him, they were just beginning to circulate in the salon of Madame Helvétius. Destutt de Tracy was a distant relative of Lafayette, while Volney had recently invented his nobility out of his nom de plume. Volney, an ambitious savant and disciple of the philosophe d'Holbach, was "shy, affected, a little starched." Like Jefferson, he was made more for writing than for talking.[75] His first publishing success was *Voyage en Syrie et en Egypte*, published in 1787 and based on visits to the ruins of Baalbek and Palmyra. Engravings of these antiquities graced the volume and no doubt caught Jefferson's eye: he immediately bought two copies.[76] In 1791, when Jefferson, now secretary of state, saw Volney's *Ruines, ou Méditations sur les révolutions des empires*, he started work on a translation but finally turned it over to Joel Barlow. Volney spent several days with Jefferson at Monticello while collecting material for his study of the American climate. No doubt he described the Egyptian pyramids to his host, for as a belated house present he sent Jefferson a model of one in 1801.

Destutt de Tracy completed the first two volumes of his philosophical work *Eléments d'idéologie* in 1803 and sent copies to Jefferson. Jefferson wrote Adams that in his judgment Destutt de Tracy was "the most profound of our Ideological writers," but he confessed he found the theoretical, abstract treatise heavy going since it did not apply "immediately to some useful science."[77] Similar reaction to abstruse French philosophical discourse is echoed in the Virginian's opinions of some of du Pont's more theoretical arguments. He never overcame his impatience with intellectual, as distinguished from political, abstractions.

In 1809 Destutt de Tracy sent Jefferson the manuscript of his commentary on Montesquieu's *Esprit des lois*, asking the retired president to help have it translated and published in the United States. (It could not be published in Napoleonic France because of its libertarian, republican slant.) William Deane, the Philadelphia publisher, agreed to undertake the work, with Jefferson's assistance in the translation. The book was published anonymously in July 1811; Jefferson wrote the "author's preface." Du Pont, however, became convinced that Jefferson had written the entire book. Before he realized his mistake, he began to translate it back into French and sent Jefferson a letter noting errors in need of correction. Destutt de Tracy took particular aim at the philosopher's argument that representative democracies could survive only in small societies of limited geography. He also took exception to Montesquieu's English bias and further confirmed Jefferson's brand of American republicanism.

Jefferson had read Montesquieu all his life and had lifted more abstractions from the Frenchman's writing for his legal commonplace book than from any other source. He regularly recommended the philosopher's work to prospective law students. But his enthusiasm seems to have waned, and by the time he left Paris he had denounced Montesquieu's "heresies."[78] David Mayer believes that the Virginian's disenchantment began in the late 1780s, when French constitutional reformers broke into two camps. One followed Montesquieu closely, advocating an English system of government—a position similar to the one John Adams took in his *Defense of the Constitutions of Government of the United States of America.* The other side seemed to take its lead from Turgot, adopting the slogan "One king, one nation, one house." This group looked to the American model, naturally with Jefferson's tacit approval.

PARIS IN THE 1780s had provided Jefferson an ideal setting to test his profound belief in republican government in the company of intellectual equals. He was at liberty to express himself on how those principles could be put into practice in France, while at the same time remaining detached as the French governmental crisis deepened. He could, and of course did, support those who favored the American Constitution and quietly disagreed when friends like Destutt de Tracy refused fully to embrace his liberal republicanism. What held his attention was the way his friends and colleagues seemed to be remaking their society along the broad lines of Enlightenment ideology.

Just as he pursued the pleasures of good books, music, wine, silver, and architecture offered by the quintessential metropolis of the late eighteenth century, Jefferson found in Paris the stimulating intellectual company that could not exist in provincial Albemarle County. "To read, write, speculate in new lines of thought, to keep abreast of the intellect of Europe, and to feed upon Homer and Horace, were," in the words of Henry Adams, "pleasures more to his mind than any to be found in public assembly."[79] Adams may have been thinking of the Virginian's confession to Margaret Bayard Smith in his retirement: "The whole of my life has been a war with my natural taste, feelings and wishes. Domestic life and literary pursuits were my first and my latest inclinations."[80]

Jefferson was never able to reconcile his delight in the cultural and intellectual life of Paris with his doctrinaire loathing for "the great mobs of the city." In 1800 he wrote a chilling letter to Benjamin Rush saying that yellow fever was a blessing in disguise because it would "discourage the growth of great cities in our nation & I view as pestilence to the morals, the health and the liberties of man."[81] Yet at the Hôtel de Langeac, in the

The Pont Neuf and Hôtel de la Monnaie Seen from the Quai du Louvre by A.-J. Noël, ca. 1780.
The hôtel housing the Royal Mint, designed by Jacques-Denis Antoine, faces the river at the
right end of the bridge. Its rich, subdued elegance did not reflect either the precarious state
of French finances or the radical politics of the Inspecteur général, Condorcet. (Musée
Carnavalet. Copyright Photothèque des Musées de la Ville de Paris)

not-quite-urban "middle landscape" between the energetic expanse of
Paris and the forest of the Bois de Boulogne, Jefferson's ideals seemed to
blossom. In this cultivated environment, so unlike any other he had
known or would ever experience again, he could share with intellectual
equals his expansive plans to improve the lot of humanity.

Paradoxically, Jefferson's determination to inoculate America against
city life would undercut the values unique to the vital urban culture he had
discovered in Paris. Yet between "independence" in the "wilds" of the country and the pleasures of the city, his preference was clear, at least on the
anniversary of his first year abroad. It is summed up in his often quoted
expression of agrarian rectitude: "I am a savage enough to prefer the
woods, the wilds, and the independence of Monticello, to all the brilliant

pleasures of this gay capital. I shall therefore rejoin myself to my native country with new attachments, with exaggerated esteem for its advantages, for tho' there is less wealth there, there is more freedom, more ease and less misery."[82]

Jefferson's vision of a humane society that would somehow reconcile the needs of an active, industrious, virtuous people with a simple yet satisfying agricultural order was a fleeting, abstract goal. He had not been able to achieve it in his own life before he went to Europe, and he remained uneasy as he thought about now it at a distance. By its very structure, the republic of isolated yeomen farmers that he was promoting on the frontiers of America made it impossible to form the critical intellectual and creative mass that a prosperous, progressive society ultimately required.

In the end, Jefferson's divided feelings about Paris reflected what Richard Hofstadter called the "deep ambiguities in his thinking, which made any effort of consistency impossible. Ever since Jefferson's death, scholars have been trying to discern order in—or impose it upon—his elusive, unsystematic thought, but without much success, It simply does not lend itself to ordinary standards of consistency."[83] But far from being symptomatic of a neurotic personality, Jefferson's inconsistencies confirm the many and often conflicting levels on which his mind was able to operate creatively. To paraphrase F. Scott Fitzgerald, he frequently held two opposing ideas at the same time without suffering intellectual paralysis. However dogmatic and mistaken he could be in his judgments, this intellectual tension is part of Jefferson's attraction and distinguishes him from any other American leader.

Chapter 6

The Diplomat

WHEN IT CAME to his revolutionary colleagues, John Adams was not given to gratuitous compliments. But his characterization of Jefferson in Philadelphia during the tense days of 1775 as "prompt, frank, explicit, and decisive" sums up the Virginian's operating style in Paris.[1] Methodical habits, self-control, and an obsessive determination to keep busy were his nature to a fault. This intuitive aggressiveness in the management of affairs was the very signature of Jefferson the diplomat. He took literally Virgil's advice in the *Georgics* that "hard work overcomes everything." His powerful ambition to secure the ultimate eighteenth-century prize of "fame" may well have been an unacknowledged defense against depression, signaled by periodic attacks of migraine and a desire to withdraw from society.

Jefferson's voracious appetite for facts and details made him an exemplary foreign representative, as he demonstrated in his accumulated "notes" on Virginia and his diplomatic position papers. His critical reports to John Jay and his long letters to Madison, Monroe, and Adams reveal a remarkable grasp of issues, based largely on his own research and expressed with sharpness and pith. Unlike Gouverneur Morris, whose diary and letters are sprinkled with vivid private observations, Jefferson was indifferent to Paris drawing-room intrigue. His seemingly high-minded detachment "led him," in Morris's prejudiced conclusion, "to assign too many to the humble Rank of fools."[2] Although his comments could be double-edged, his prose elegant, Jefferson rarely indulged in the irony that was so much a part of the Old World social temperament. Humor was not in his makeup.

Jefferson's letters reveal few glimpses of his private life or emotions. Even during the dramatic prelude to the French Revolution, he maintained a cool, stylized reserve in his diplomatic dispatches. In the midst of writing his autobiography, he considered abandoning it altogether because he was "already tired of talking about" himself.[3] G. K. van Hogendorp, who met Jefferson in Annapolis in the spring of 1784, sensed that the Virginian "was revolted by idle chatter" and took his taciturn manners to mean that he was a "man of business." The young Dutch nobleman did, however, manage to lift a corner of the diffident Virginian's mask, writing to him in a remarkably familiar tone: "At the same time I became acquainted with Your state and with yourself, I grew fond of your benevolent character.... I pitied your situation, for I thought you unhappy. Why, I did not know; and though you appeared insensible to social enjoyments, yet I was perfectly convinced you could not have been ever so. One evening I talked of love, and then I perceived that you still could feel, and express your feelings."[4]

The change of scene in Paris gradually brought the dispirited widower back into the social swim, reviving the hidden qualities detected by van Hogendorp. If hard work was a cure for depression, the problems confronting the American commercial commissioners were made to order. In April 1784 a congressional committee had studied the country's alarming economic problems, noting that "the delicate situation of commerce to the United States at this time, claims the attention of several states, and will be admitted that few objects of greater importance can present themselves to their notice. The fortune of every citizen is interested in the fate of commerce: for it is the constant source of industry and wealth; and the value of our produce and our land must ever rise or fall in proportion to the prosperous or adverse state of trade."[5]

The report's guarded language only hinted at the dilapidated state of the American economy following the Revolution. The break with Britain had left the country saddled with a crushing debt for staples purchased before the war from merchants in London and Glasgow. With its traditional markets for tobacco, wheat, whale oil, and rice cut off, the country desperately needed alternative outlets. Virginia was particularly hard hit: many slaves had escaped or been carried off by the British, inflation was rampant,

Thomas Jefferson
by Jean-Antoine Houdon.
Jefferson met the sculptor soon after he
arrived in Paris. Strangely, the details
and date of the execution of his own
portrait are unknown. A bust of "M.
Sefferson [sic], Envoyé des Etats de
Virginie" was shown in the Salon of
1789. (Courtesy Museum of Fine Arts,
Boston. George Nixon Black Fund)

and the countryside, particularly in the Tidewater, had been badly damaged
by marauding armies. The problems had been compounded by the terms of
the peace treaty, which required all Americans, including the new envoy, to
pay their prewar British debts with interest for the eight years of war.[6]

When Jefferson learned on May 7, 1784 that he was to be "adjoined
…to Mr. Adams and Dr. Franklin on the foreign commercial negotiations," he understood the crisis on both a public and a private level. As
his mission was to coax trade treaties out of resisting or indifferent
European governments, his first step was to collect information about
the economic health of each state he passed through on his way to Boston
to catch the boat to France; he even made an unplanned detour to New
Hampshire and Vermont. Although his investigations merely confirmed
the general mood of despair and unrest, Jefferson claimed also to have
documented "the blessings of liberty." As always coloring the bleakest
landscape with vivid optimism, whatever problems he may have uncovered, he believed that Americans' virtue and self-sacrifice, coupled with a
willing reception by Europe, would eventually turn things around.

Jefferson was naturally equipped for the hot new field of political economy, assimilating its novel language, method, and point of view. It is not surprising to find in his library a copy of the Scottish theorist Sir James Steuart Denham's *Political Oeconomy*. Published in the 1760s, it is considered the first English work on the subject. Its cumbersome subtitle— "Being an essay on the science of domestic policy in free nations. In which are particularly considered population, agriculture, trade, industry, money, coin, interests, circulation, banks, exchange, public credit, and taxes."—is as good an index as any to the new diplomat's eclectic interests.[7]

Even when the causes of the shaping of national character were debatable—Jefferson once claimed (only half-jestingly) that the English ate too much red meat and that the only way to reform them was through their cuisine—his assessments could be shrewd and provocative. Despite his own frequent indulgence in patriotic hyperbole, he chided Chastellux for judging Americans too generously. Jefferson based his analysis of the "characters of the several states" on the popular theory of the influence of climate and temperature, caricaturing the European conjectures about the New World that so infuriated him. The North was cool, sober, hardworking, and persevering, but also "chicaning, superstitious and hypocritical in its religious beliefs." As for his own region, the South, it was "fiery, Voluptuary, indolent, unsteady, independent, zealous…without attachment or pretensions to any religion but that of the heart," generous to a fault. The one common denominator that seems to have transcended the climatic differences between North and South was their resolute commitment to personal independence.[8]

When he reached New York in late May 1784, Jefferson again met up with van Hogendorp, whose keen if uncomfortable perceptions had impressed the Virginian in Annapolis. In his easy familiarity, the Dutchman did not fit into Jefferson's stereotype of the European. The two men discussed the kinds of information the envoy would find useful in the forthcoming negotiations. Then van Hogendorp drew up a memorandum to help the novice commissioner in compiling his notes on the "commerce of the northern states." Among other things, he suggested that Jefferson ascertain whether the government of the state was respected by its citizens and obtain a detailed schedule of wages, running from "Labourers in the Earth" (as farmers were poetically labeled) to weavers and ship carpenters.[9]

Jefferson understood that the American Revolution had turned old European customs and methods of foreign relations upside-down. The diplomacy that regularly drew his condemnation was summed up in the nineteenth century by the historian Albert Sorel: "Reason of State directed all policy, and state interest was the only guarantee of any engagements. In other words, no guarantee existed at all.... War was the great instrument of rule, the supreme argument of reason of state. It was considered right as it was judged necessary. It was waged to conquer or to preserve, in self defense against an attack or to forestall one." In the beginning, at least, this monarchical policy was wholly incompatible with the ideals of the American republic.[10]

Isolated from the rituals and intrigues of corrupt European power politics, the United States had an opportunity to change the rules of the game. But the new country faced daunting problems as it struggled to secure its borders and shake off the remnants of British economic control. (In 1784 the British still held military posts in the Northwest Territory and upstate New York.) The American and European economies were inseparable, and the success of the American experiment could well depend on its foreign policy. As Jefferson wrote to Chastellux, "You were a witness to the total destruction of our commerce, devastation of our country, and absence of precious metals. It cannot be expected but that these should flow in but through the channels of commerce, or that these can be opened in the first instance of peace."[11]

Jefferson's appreciation of political economy was far more complex than the "agrarian" philosophy or the shibboleth of "small government" with which he is regularly identified. As he was to write in 1816: "In so complicated a science as political economy, no one axiom can be laid down as wise and expedient, for all times and circumstances, and for their contraries."[12] Yet his dedication to the expansion of American foreign trade grew directly out of his commitment to wide ownership of land, distributed more or less equally among independent individuals. In his view, an uncorrupted republic was tied to the preservation of an agrarian economy free of debt, which in turn was linked to a supply of land to serve a growing population. America's virtue would remain healthy, as he wrote Madison, "so long as there shall be vacant lands in any part of America" and its citizens were not "piled up on one another in large cities as in Europe."[13]

As early as 1785, Jefferson's sensitivity to the possibilities of an "empire of liberty" reaching to the American West Coast surfaced in his recognition of the long-range implications of the vacant western lands. In June of that year, Louis XVI launched a scientific expedition led by the count de La Pérouse, who was to explore the Pacific coasts of Alaska and California in search of the Northwest Passage. Jefferson, believing that the French might intend to establish settlements in the region (to which the United States, of course, had at the time no claim), immediately alerted John Paul Jones to investigate "all the circumstances relative" to the expedition. In August 1785 he wrote Jay of his concern: "They give out that the object is merely for improvement of our knowledge of the geography of that part of the globe. Their loading [of men and supplies] ... and some other circumstances appear to me some other design; perhaps that of colonizing of the West coast of America." It was, as so often with Jefferson, a prescient curiosity, with more than a glint of imperial ambitions.[14]

Jefferson's goal as commissioner in Paris was to advance the realization of an essentially agrarian democracy by opening up world markets for American agricultural commodities. In Query XIX of his *Notes*, on "Manufactures," he describes his ideal citizen:

> Those who labour in the earth are the chosen people of God, if ever he had
> a chosen people whose breasts he has made his peculiar deposit for
> substantial and genuine virtue. It is the focus in which he keeps alive the
> sacred fire, which otherwise might escape from the face of the earth.
> Corruption of morals in the mass of cultivators is a phenomenon of which
> no age nor nation has furnished an example. It is the mark set on those,
> who not looking up to heaven, to their own soil and industry, as does the
> husbandman, for their subsistence, depend for it on the casualties and
> caprice of customers. Dependence begets subservience and venality,
> suffocates the germ of virtue, and prepares fit tools for the design of
> ambition. This, the natural progress and consequence of the arts, has
> sometimes perhaps been retarded by accidental circumstances: but,
> generally speaking, the portion which the aggregate of the other classes of
> citizens bears in any state to that of the husbandman, is the proportion of

Auction Room of the Hôtel Bullion by Pierre-Antoine de Machy.
Jefferson frequented auction rooms like the Hôtel Bullion, where he bought a number of
works that would later hang at Monticello. (Musée Carnavalet. Copyright Photothèque des
Musées de la Ville de Paris)

its unsound to its healthy parts, and it is a good enough barometer
whereby to measure its degree of corruption. While we have land to
labour then, let us never wish to see our citizens occupied at a work-bench,
or twirling a distaff. Carpenters, masons, smiths, are wanting in
husbandry: but, for the general operations of manufacture, let our work-
shops remain in Europe. It is better to carry provisions and materials, and
with them their manners and principles. The loss by the transportation of
commodities across the Atlantic will be made up in happiness and
permanence of government.[15]

An acceptable foreign policy had to incorporate these values. Jefferson
paraphrased its fundamental assumptions again in a letter to John Jay a
year after he arrived in Europe; put simply, an agricultural society committed to freedom but lacking an industrial base had to secure its well-

being and preserve its integrity by developing a strong transatlantic trade, protected by a naval force, that being pragmatically, the "only weapo[n] with which we can reach an enemy."[16] Or, in the plain words of Gouverneur Morris: "If Europe wishes us to be her customers, she must enable us to pay for the articles we buy of her. If France wishes us to drink her wine, she must let her Islanders eat our bread."[17] Free trade, in Merrill Peterson's words, was the only potent weapon of diplomacy, short of force "to be employed in pursuit of the national interest."[18]

Jefferson's frequent use of *virtue* and *virtuous*, watchwords of republican ideology, had far greater resonance than we now give them.[19] Honest work and virtue are frequently linked to his vision of the ideal society. Moral and physical discipline would make Americans superior both to the benighted savage and to the indolent few in civilization's most advanced stages. The Preamble to Virginia's original Bill of Rights spelled out this basic political principle in no uncertain terms: "No free government, or blessings of liberty, can be preserved to any people, but by a firm adherence to justice, moderation, temperance, frugality and virtue." The old regime of France was the best example of national decadence. "It is the manner and spirit of a people," Jefferson concludes his ringing response to Query XIX of the *Notes*, "which preserve a republic in vigour. A degeneracy in these is a canker which soon eats to the heart of its laws and constitutions." Herbert Sloan has pointed out that Jefferson could at least take satisfaction in the war's disruption of the Virginia gentry's habit of overspending, particularly on imported luxuries—an affliction that undermined republican morals.[20]

Jefferson's radical view, in Leo Marx's classic analysis, embraced a pastoral society in a metaphorical "middle landscape" that was distinctly egalitarian, democratic, and noncapitalistic, avoiding both the savagery of the wilderness and the inevitable taint of the city.[21] In both Jefferson's diplomatic negotiations and his personal philosophy, this evolving ideal had to be refined and confirmed. "The trick was," as Drew McCoy has ably summarized, "to advance far enough in the cycle to enjoy the many advantages of commerce without moving so far as to begin an ominous descent into decay and corruption, powerful images of which were evoked by historical memories of ancient Rome."[22]

Given the potential riches of the untapped American continent, there seemed little doubt that the greatest threat to the republic lay in the loss of virtue through opulent living. Europe, following France's example, had brought this extravagance—which in Jefferson's mind was subsumed under the heading of "monarchy"—to perfection. "I was much an enemy to monarchy before I came to Europe," he declared to Washington. "I am ten thousand times more so since I have seen what they are." The Virginian's "pastoral ideal," as Marx has argued, anticipated the literary theme implicit in the work of Henry Thoreau, Mark Twain, Ernest Hemingway, and Robert Frost.[23] It is also the subtext of his censorious letter to John Bannister, Jr., warning against a European education for American youth:

> He acquires a fondness for European luxury and dissipation and a contempt
> for the simplicity of his own country; he is fascinated with the privileges of
> the European aristocrats, and sees with abhorrence the lovely equality
> which the poor enjoy with the rich in his own country: he contracts
> partiality for aristocracy or monarch; he forms foreign friendships which
> will never be useful to him, and loses the season of life for forming in his
> own country those friendships which of all others are the most faithful and
> permanent: he is led by the strongest of all the human passions into a spirit
> for female intrigue destructive of his health, and in both cases learns to
> consider fidelity to the marriage bed as an ungentlemanly practice and
> inconsistent with happiness: he recollects the voluptuary dress and despises
> the chaste affections and simplicity of those of his own country.[24]

Believing that the peculiar simplicity of American manners was also reflected in the American language, Jefferson concluded that "there never was an instance of man's writing or speaking his native tongue with elegance who passed from 15. to 20. years of age out of the country where it was spoken."

WHEN HE LEFT FOR PARIS, the fledgling diplomat had in his baggage the hastily gathered information on commerce in several key states and the uncompleted manuscript of his *Notes on the State of Virginia*. The latter would provide a kind of philosophical blueprint to guide him in devising a coherent foreign policy. Jefferson also took with him notes from the research he had carried out in 1783, as he prepared to join Adams and Franklin in the peace negotiations that in the end were concluded before his departure. In Philadelphia he had studied in some detail official government correspondence and documents relating to the country's relations with European governments. At the same time, he and Madison had drawn up a list of more than three hundred essential books for the congressional library, a list that is instructive in connection with his contemplated diplomatic mission.[25]

"At length our foreign affairs are put upon as excellent an establishment as we could desire," James Monroe wrote to Gov. Benjamin Harrison of Virginia. "As respectable talents as these states possess, with characters eminent for integrity and attachment to the public interest, collected also in such manner from the different parts of the union as to possess a knowledge of local interests of the whole, are center'd in the three gentlemen Mr. Adams, Mr. Franklin, and Mr. Jefferson."[26] As a member of Congress the May before his appointment, Jefferson had actually drafted the remarkable "Instructions to the Ministers Plenipotentiary appointed to negotiate Treaties of Commerce with European Nations." Article 3 of the instructions addressed the central objective of bolstering the American union in matters of foreign policy. In all treaties of amity and commerce, the United States were to be "by their constitution consolidated into one federal republic." Throughout his term in Paris, Jefferson never wavered in his primary goal of "strengthening the band of Union" by addressing international issues collectively.[27]

Jefferson invited his twenty-five-year-old protégé William Short to join him as private secretary. A distant kinsman who had attended William and Mary College, the bright, enthusiastic Short was prepared to sell a recent inheritance in order to pay his way. Since the newly formed commission already had a secretary, Jefferson reminded Short that he might have to begin as "the index of a book," meaning a private clerk. But Jefferson offered him bed and board, an assurance that he would give him "little trouble," and a salary of a thousand dollars a year.[28] Short realized that unless he had an official title other than private secretary, Parisian society might peg him as a "domestic" in the minister's household—a position to be avoided at all costs by a Virginia gentleman. He therefore kept his seat

William Short by Rembrandt Peale.
(Muscarelle Museum of Art, The College
of William and Mary in Virginia)

in the Virginia Executive Council of State as a "mark of honor" in the rank-conscious, "foolish world" of Paris.[29]

When Jefferson arrived in 1784, the shaky Confederation's foreign delegation in Paris consisted of stout old Ben Franklin, minister to France, and prickly John Adams, who had served as a member of the commission to negotiate peace. Congress had decided that Jay's former responsibilities as minister to Spain could be handled by a chargé d'affaires. Each minister, including Jay, whom Jefferson replaced, had his own private secretary and shared a fourth one.

Franklin, eager to preserve his mystique of home-grown simplicity, had made do with a single secretary as minister to France, despite his overwhelming correspondence and heavy social schedule. He had shrewdly persuaded Vergennes, the French foreign minister, to conduct all American business personally with him, ostensibly to avoid the delays caused by the bureaucracy of the Foreign Ministry at Versailles. But their intimacy undoubtedly lubricated the negotiations, fostering the illusion of diplomatic equality between the two countries.

Just how Franklin juggled his professional and social responsibilities by artful confusion and creative neglect cannot be discerned from the jaundiced account in Adams's diary. The two men's working relationship

in Paris was constantly strained. Adams's version of the day-to-day friction provides a background to Jefferson's own introduction to the tense
American diplomatic arrangements in Paris:

> I found that the Business of our Commission would never be done unless I
> did it.... The Life of Dr. Franklin was a Scene of continual dissipation. I
> could never obtain the favour of his Company in the Morning before
> Breakfast which would have been the most convenient time to read over
> the Letters and papers, deliberate on their contents, and decide upon the
> Substance of the Answers. It was late when he breakfasted, and as soon as
> Breakfast was over, a crowd of Carriges came to his levee or if you like the
> term better to his lodgings, with all sorts of people; some Phylosophers,
> Academicians and Economists; some his small tribe of humble friends in
> the literary Way whom he employed to translate some of his ancient
> Compositions.

After detailing the evenings Franklin spent with his high-born lady
friends gossiping, listening to music, and playing chess, Adams wrote that
he would have been happy to perform all the diplomatic "drudgery" in
exchange for a few moments of consultation a day. But, he lamented, "this
condescension was not attainable. All that could be had was his signature,
after it was done, and this it is true he rarely refused though he sometimes
delayed."[30]

Forever mixing business with pleasure, Franklin nevertheless had
achieved astonishing results with his alchemy. In eight and a half years,
he had negotiated the Treaty of Amity and Commerce and the Treaty of
Alliance with France. During the American Revolution he had arranged
exchanges of prisoners with Great Britain and helped negotiate the
Treaty of Peace, followed by treaties of amity and commerce with Sweden and Prussia. But the exhausted, seventy-nine-year-old Franklin was
suffering from stone and gout when Jefferson arrived, and there were
rumors that he would soon retire. He had little energy to shepherd the
junior commissioner into an unfamiliar world.

Adams's assistance on the social level was equally limited. He had
been serving intermittently in Europe since 1777, returning to Paris for the
third time in 1782 to join Franklin and Jay in negotiating Great Britain's

View of Paris Skyline from Franklin's House in Passy by John Trumbull, 1786.
This sketch was made the same day that the artist dined with Franklin and Jefferson in
Passy. Scaffolding can be seen on the dome of the Church of Sainte-Geneviève (now the
Panthéon). (Yale University Art Gallery. Bequest of Susan Silliman Pearson)

formal recognition of American independence. But he had avoided the
extracurricular social scene in which Franklin thrived. Upon hearing of
Jefferson's appointment, Adams warmly praised his abilities. As he wrote
James Warren, he had labored "at many a knotty Problem" with the Virginian, "in whose Abilities and Steadfastness I have always found great
Cause to confide."[31] Later, having received a letter from Arthur Lee, a
colleague of Jefferson in Congress, bitterly criticizing Jefferson, who Lee
believed had blocked his political ambitions, Adams immediately rose to
the defense of "his old friend and coadjutor whose character I studied
nine or ten years ago and which I do not perceive to be altered. The same
industry, integrity, and talents remain without diminution."[32] Jefferson,
however, had observed Adams's temperamental outbursts and was more
reserved in his own judgment. In 1783 he had passed on to Madison a
double-edged compliment of Adams: "His dislike of all parties, and all

men, by balancing his prejudices, may give the same fair play to his reason as would a general benevolence of temper."

Abigail Adams's gift for entertaining improved her husband's social
style. The Adamses had been separated for more than four years when she
and her daughter Abigail, nicknamed "Nabby," sailed for Europe a few
days before Jefferson. After being reunited in London, where John Adams
was pursuing Dutch loans, the family arrived in Paris the day after Jefferson and Patsy. They immediately leased a house at Auteuil, then a quiet,
leafy suburb west of the city. Nabby described their new home as "very
large and very inconvenient," but it had a nice drawing room on the
ground floor, opening onto a generous garden unusual for Paris houses. It
was also close to the Bois de Boulogne, where her father liked to walk.
Her mother thought that with twenty thousand livres to repair and furnish it, the run-down house might be made acceptable for a minister. Like
Franklin and Jefferson, however, the Adamses found it difficult to make
ends meet on the small salary approved by Congress, even with their
"very plain stile of life," as Jefferson observed.[33]

With Patsy enrolled at the Abbaye Royale de Panthémont, the most
fashionable convent school in Paris, through the efforts of the marquis de
Chastellux, Jefferson could relax in the family atmosphere of the Adams
house, where he dined often before the Adamses moved to London in
May 1785. Abigail Adams had met Jefferson in Boston in the summer of
1784, and they seem to have been drawn into an instant friendship that
grew over the years. Jefferson had proposed that they travel together to
Europe, but, as Abigail explained to her husband, she had already paid
for her passage on an earlier boat. Her warm, sympathetic personality
and keen interest in her surroundings no doubt helped pull Jefferson
through his first lonely days in Paris, particularly when he fell ill that
first fall and winter.[34]

The Abbaye Royale de Panthémont.
The fashionable convent and school in the Faubourg Saint-Germain, which the Jefferson
girls attended, faced an inner garden behind the church fronting on the rue de Grenelle.
The structure was part of an ambitious building program undertaken at the old abbey in the
1740s. (Photo by Adelaide de Menil)

AS A MEMBER OF CONGRESS AFTER THE REVOLUTION, Jefferson had worked out a policy of commercial liberty linked to world trade, drafting the report and instructions for the newly created commission. But once he entered the field of international negotiations, he cautiously deferred to his more seasoned colleagues. On August 30, 1784 he joined Adams and David Humphreys, the new commission's secretary, at Franklin's house in Passy to review their instructions. They "agreed to meet every day at this place until the objects of the Commission shall be properly arranged, and put as far as may be into the best train of execution." The next day they decided to notify the French court of the objectives of the American mission and to inform the British minister, David Hartley, that they were ready to negotiate a treaty of commerce with Great Britain. Similar messages were delivered to representatives of other European countries.

Two weeks later the commissioners "exhibited officially to Comte de Vergennes" their mandate "to conclude a supplementary Treaty between the United States and His Most Christian Majesty." Congress had authorized commercial treaties with sixteen European nations as well as the Barbary powers. The ultimate goal of these agreements was, in effect, to ratify the commercial principles underlying the American Revolution, which had severed the old imperial system of trade between unequals. Any nation refusing to enter into a treaty relation, it was understood, would be subject to discriminatory commercial policies in the American market.

The new envoy's quiet, steady presence seemed to reduce the friction between Adams and Franklin. "Since our Meeting upon our new Commissions, our affairs have gone on with the utmost Harmony," Adams wrote to Elbridge Gerry, "and nothing has disturbed our Peace. I wish this Calm may continue and believe it will." But it was a fragile détente. In the same letter Adams accused Franklin of continuing to impugn him with "the most malicious misrepresentations which were ever put on paper."[35] Jefferson often found Adams "a bad calculator of the force and probable effect of the motives which govern men." Nevertheless, he wrote to Madison in 1787, "he is as disinterested as the being which made him: he is profound in his views: and accurate in his judgment except where knowledge of the world is necessary to form a judgment."[36]

Always the scholar, the new diplomat turned instinctively to the language and substance of the proposed treaties. His initial contributions were mainly analytical and literary—his natural way of fitting unobtrusively into the work of the delegation. This same conscientious, academic approach had given him a certain distance from the political "scurrings and schemings" in Philadelphia, in Garry Wills's apt description, and had ultimately won him the honor of drafting the Declaration of Independence.[37] Just as he had spoken then of Americans as "one people," contrary to all appearances in 1776, so in 1784 he was determined to make the commercial treaties of the far-from-unified Confederation pragmatic instruments of de facto union in its dealings with other nations.

In their commercial arrangements with foreign powers, the states had remained independent and insular, refusing to give Congress the power to regulate foreign trade collectively. It was this critical issue that Jefferson had attempted to deal with in a congressional address in April 1784, when he proposed to "vest Congress with so much power over their commerce as will enable them to retaliate on any nation who may wish to grasp it on unequal terms."[38] John Jay argued that the Confederation should establish its own system for regulating trade with other nations *before* concluding treaties, rather than allowing the treaties to dictate the collective policies of the states. But by May 7, 1785, when Jefferson's first treaty with Prussia was finally approved by Congress, the Virginian had come to a different conclusion. As he wrote to Monroe:

> Congress, by the Confederation have no original and inherent power over
> the commerce of the states. But by the 9th article they are authorized to
> enter into treaties of commerce. The moment these treaties are concluded
> the jurisdiction of Congress over the commerce of the states springs into
> existence, and that of the particular states is superseded so far as the articles
> of the treaty may have taken up the subject.... [With two exceptions],
> Congress may by treaty establish any system of commerce they please.
> But...it is by treaty alone they can do it. Tho' they may exercise their own
> powers by resolution or ordinance, those over commerce can only be
> exercised by forming a treaty and this probably by accidental wording of our
> confederation. If therefore it is better for the states that Congress should
> regulate their commerce, it is proper that they should form treaties with all

nations with whom we may possibly trade. You see that it is my primary object in the formation of treaties to take the commerce out of the hands of the states, and place it under the superintendence of Congress, so far as the imperfect provisions of our constitution will admit, and until the states shall by new compact make them more perfect. I would say then to every nation on earth, *by treaty,* your people shall trade freely with us, and ours with you, paying no more than the most favored nation, in order to put an end to the right of individual states, acting by fits and starts to interrupt our commerce or to embroil us with any nation.[39]

By the broadest interpretation of the Articles of Confederation, Jefferson was prepared to use the tool of commercial treaties to shore up both the concept and the reality of the "united states." Putting aside the Virginian's claim that this was the "primary" objective of treaty making, it did conform to the commissioners' instructions that the United States was to be "one Nation" in its dealings with other countries. But, as Merrill Peterson has pointed out, the European principle that no nation should be treated less favorably than any other under the rubric of "most favored nation" fell far short of Congress's directive that trade be conducted on the basis of "the most perfect equality and reciprocity." The green but determined diplomat would continue to look for ways around the frayed, compromised "favored nation" argument.

THE FIRST RESPONSE to the American ministers' broadside invitations had been encouraging. "Old Frederic of Prussia met us cordially," Jefferson recalled in his autobiography, "and without hesitation, and appointing Baron de Thulemeyer, his minister at the Hague, to negotiate with us, we communicated to him our Project, which with little alteration by the King, was soon concluded."[40] The treaty with Prussia was the first to be drafted with the new envoy's participation, and its language reflected his distinctive brand of idealism, now addressed to the community of nations. Jefferson proposed to incorporate into the agreement articles laying

Foreign Ministry wing, Palace of Versailles.
The minister and his staff had offices in this wing running along the right side of the château's central courtyard. (Photo by Adelaide de Menil)

down rational, universal rules of conduct in war. These humanitarian propositions, unprecedented in international treaties of commerce, flew in the face of entrenched European cynicism. In a paper entitled "Reasons in Support of the New Proposed Articles in the Treaties of Commerce," Jefferson attempted to break out of the established routine:

> By the original Laws of Nations war and extirpation were the punishment of injury. Humanizing by degrees, it admitted slavery instead of death. A further step was the exchange of prisoners instead of slavery. Another, to respect more the property of private persons under conquest, and be content with acquired dominion. Why should not this law of nations go on improving? Ages have intervened between its several steps; but as knowledge of late increases rapidly, why should not those steps be quickened. Why should it not be agreed to as the future law of nations, that in any war, hereafter the following descriptions of men be undisturbed, have the protection of both sides, and be permitted to follow their employment in surety.

He goes on to list the categories of men to be exempted from war's ravages:

> 1st. Cultivators of the earth, because they labour for subsistence of mankind.
>
> 2nd. Fishermen, for the same reason.
>
> 3rd. Merchants and Traders in unarmed ships, who accommodate different Nations by communicating and exchanging the necessities and conveniences of life.
>
> 4th. Artists and Mechanics inhabiting and working in open towns. It is hardly to add that the Hospitals of the Enemies should be unmolested, they ought to be assisted.
>
> It is for the interest of humanity in general, that the occasions of war, and the inducements to it, should be diminished.
>
> If rapine is abolished, one of the encouragements of war is taken away, and peace therefore more likely to continue and be lasting.[41]

The Prussian minister hailed the new provisions, which had been "dictated by the purest zeal in favor of humanity. Nothing can be more just than your reflections on the noble disinterestedness of the United

States of America. It is to be desired that these sublime sentiments may be adopted by all the maritime powers without any exception. The calamities of war will be much softened and hostilities, often provoked by the cupidity and inordinate love of gain, of more rare occurrence."[42] Adams viewed the issue from a more practical Yankee perspective. After Frederick the Great had accepted the treaty, he wrote to the minister that "the Platonic Philosophy of some of our articles which are a good lesson to Mankind…will derive more Influence from a treaty ratified by the King of Prussia, than from the writings of Plato or Sir Thomas Moore."[43]

Even before the treaty with Prussia had been concluded, Jefferson boldly broached another revolutionary measure in international relations. In an astonishing document secretly sent to Adams in late July 1785, he envisioned nothing less than a fundamental redefinition of citizenship. His proposal that countries temporarily extend full rights of citizenship on a reciprocal basis to foreigners traveling within their territory was a variation on the vague concept of world citizenship floated by Thomas Paine and others. Jefferson's idea seems to have originated in discussions with Adams and Franklin as an alternative to the "most favored nation" language in their model treaty of commerce. There the concept of reciprocity had been limited to commercial transactions, but in presenting his volatile proposal to Adams, Jefferson expanded it to create, in effect, a new class of citizenship transcending national laws and boundaries. "Believing that a free and friendly intercourse between them…cannot be established on a better footing than that of mutual adoption by each of the citizens or subjects of the other, insomuch that while those of the one are traveling or sojourning with the other, they shall be considered in every intent and purpose as members of the nation, where they are, entitled to all the protections, rights and advantages of its native members."[44]

Such a mind-boggling notion, with its far-reaching and uncharted implications, not only exceeded the powers of the American commissioners, however broadly defined, it flatly contradicted the Confederation's constitutional powers as well. All of this was freshly on Jefferson's mind. Writing to Monroe only a month earlier, he had conceded that the reserved powers of the states placed severe limits on the treaty-making authority of Congress.[45] And he admitted to Adams that the proposal went "beyond our powers and that of Congress too." But he considered it "so evidently for the good of all the states" that he was "not afraid to risk [himself] on it" if Adams went along.[46]

It is unclear just what Adams thought of the idea; possibly he suggested that Jefferson test the waters with France. Jefferson did indeed open the subject in a letter to Vergennes that November. "Both nations," he wrote, "perhaps may come into the opinion that their friendship and their interest may be better cemented by approaching the condition of their citizens reciprocally to that of *natives*, as a better ground of intercourse than that of *the most favoured nation.*" If, as Condorcet believed, the United States was to serve as a revolutionary model for France, the temporary exchange of citizenship would be a useful bridge for French idealists who had no first-hand idea of the new "Americanism" and the "precious blessings" of liberty, "which no other people on earth enjoy." It might also open the eyes of Americans, who Jefferson thought had already begun to take their "precious blessings" too much for granted. As he glumly wrote to his brother-in-law, Henry Skipwith, in 1787, "The accounts from our country [Virginia] give me to believe that we are not to hope for imitation in any thing good. All letters are filled with details of our extravagance. From these accounts, I look back to the time of war as a time of happiness and enjoiment when amidst the privation of many things not essential to happiness, we could not run into debt because no body would trust us."[47]

Despite their promising start, the treaty negotiations ultimately produced disappointing results. Old European habits and an entrenched mercantile philosophy of trade remained intact, especially when it came to trade with European colonies such as the French West Indies. No other European country followed Prussia's example. As Jefferson recalled in his autobiography, "Other powers appearing indifferent we did not think it proper to press them. They seemed in fact to know little about us, but as rebels who had been successful in throwing off the yoke of the mother country. They were ignorant of our commerce, which had been always monopolized by England, and by the exchange of articles it might offer advantageously to both parties. They were inclined therefore to stand aloof until they could see better what relations might be usefully instituted with us."[48]

WITH THE AILING FRANKLIN'S DEPARTURE from Paris—eased by a special mule-drawn litter supplied by Marie Antoinette to carry the lame hero to the port—Jefferson was named minister plenipotentiary in May 1785. Two months earlier Adams had been appointed to the same post in London, moving there with his family after less than a year in Auteuil. Jefferson's new diplomatic responsibilities undoubtedly helped cushion the devastating blow he had received in January in a letter from his friend Dr. James Currie in Richmond: Lucy Jefferson, only two years old at the time she had been left behind with her aunt Elizabeth Wayles Eppes when her father and sister sailed for Paris, had fallen "Martyr to the Complicated evils of teething, Worms and Hooping Cough."[49] On January 27, Nabby Adams wrote in her journal: "Mr. J. is a man of great sensibility, and parental affection. His wife died when this child was born, and he was in a confirmed state of melancholy; confined himself from the world, and even from his friends, for a long time; and this news has greatly affected him and his daughter."[50]

Lafayette had delivered Currie's letter on his return from Virginia. He had also brought an earlier letter from Jefferson's brother-in-law, Francis Eppes, reporting only that Lucy, her sister Polly, and their cousin Lucy Eppes were sick. On February 5, when Jefferson finally acknowledged to Eppes that he had learned of Lucy's death, he slammed the lid on his ravished emotions just as he had done when Martha died. It was, he wrote, "in vain to endeavor to describe the situation of my mind; it would be to pour balm, neither into your wounds nor mine. I will therefore pass on from the subject."[51]

In mid-March, after enduring a "seasoning as they call it...the lot of most strangers," Jefferson wrote to Monroe that the gray, damp Paris winter had evaporated. For three weeks the city had enjoyed a "warm visit from the sun (my almighty physician)," and he found himself "almost reestablished." Buying books, as he claimed he did every afternoon he was in Paris, often lifted his spirits. On March 3 he placed an order for some forty titles from Samuel Henley, a former professor at William and Mary who was now living in London. Bound in a single volume were several items, all on subjects that stirred him: an essay on poetry and music by Webb, Moor's essay on Tragedy, another on garden design, and one on medals by Jennings. Jefferson also mentioned to Monroe that he was think-ing of taking a restorative three- or four-week trip to the south of France.[52]

"On the 14th. of May I communicated to the Count de Vergennes my appointment as minister plenipotentiary to this court," Jefferson reported to Jay, adding in his usual laconic style, "and on the 17th. delivered my let-ter of credence to the king at a private audience and went through the other ceremonies usual on such occasions."[53] David Humphreys, who was also presented at Versailles that day, added a few details in a letter to Washington: "I have passed through the ceremony of going to court and being presented to the king and Royal family. The King, who is rather fat and of a placid, good tempered appearance, is thought to possess an excel-lent heart and to aspire only to the distinction of being considered as the father of his people."

According to the count de Cheverny, who stage-managed these diplo-matic presentations, the ceremonies usually took place in the morning beginning at ten o'clock:

> Preceded by the pages of the ambassador, followed by the gentlemen of the
> embassy, we climbed the great stairway, the secretary of the legation
> following. The ambassador found the great staircase lined with a hundred
> Swiss guards in full dress, the officers, at their head, within the hall the
> bodyguard, with its officers, the sentinels saluting. The two Swiss guards
> before the King's apartment stood at their posts in the *Oeuil-de-boeuf*
> [antechamber]. The captain of the bodyguard stood at the left with the
> *introducteur*, as he could never leave the left of the ambassador having to
> instruct him what to do.
>
> On arrival in the King's bedroom, we found him seated surrounded
> by his leading officers, the grand chamberlain, all the dukes and people of
> title—in short the courtiers. When the King observed the ambassador,
> he removed his hat and rose. The ambassador escorted by a prince and
> the *introducteur*, advanced, followed by his secretary of legation and staff.
> He made three deep bows at equal distances. Then the King seated
> himself and replaced his hat. The ambassador did likewise. The princes,
> and the dukes and the others also put on their hats. The ambassador then
> began his discourse. Each time he mentioned the name of their Majesties,

he uncovered his hat. The King did the same, and the courtiers followed faithfully. At the conclusion of the ambassador's remarks, the King responded. The Ambassador then presented the secretary of the legation and all the personnel, whereupon they retired as they had come in, again making three bows. Then we went to the Queen's apartment, and to those of all the royal family, going through much the same ceremony each time.

At two o'clock a table for fifty guests was set up in the Council Chamber. With one of the king's maîtres d'hôtel present to orchestrate the banquet, "Swiss in uniform passed the platters about."[54]

Members of the diplomatic corps were Vergennes' guests when Jefferson and Humphreys were presented, followed by the usual dinner. "It is curious to see forty or fifty ambassadors, ministers or other strangers of the first fashion from all nations of Europe," the secretary reported, "assembling in the most amicable manner and conversing in the same language. What heightens the pleasure is their being universally men of unaffected manners and good dispositions."[55] Jefferson, however, thoroughly detested the rituals of the court and diplomatic corps. They were the last vestiges of the old regime to be touched by the new, relaxed atmosphere he was beginning to detect in Paris society. Even so, his self-confidence and cultivated republican asceticism allowed him to fit smoothly into these stiff affairs of state.

Years later, near the close of his first term, President Jefferson would draft a set of social rules to be followed by official Washington. These republican "Canons of Etiquette" contrasted starkly with the forms that had so irritated him at Versailles.[56] The attempt to introduce old-fashioned, countrified Virginia customs into Washington society emphasized the widening gap between European and American manners. Jefferson's code annoyed foreign diplomats and especially their wives, who suddenly found themselves cut adrift and scrambling for their places at receptions and dinner parties. "To maintain the principle of equality, or pele mele," as Jefferson called it, "and prevent the growth of precedence out of courtesy, the members of the Executive will practice in their own houses, and recommend an adherence to the ancient usage of the country, of gentlemen in mass giving precedence to the ladies in mass, in passing from one apartment to another."[57]

At a disastrous dinner given by the president in honor of the new British minister, Anthony Merry, and his wife, Jefferson's "canons" provoked further Tory resentment. Merry reported to London that "Mrs. Merry was placed by Mr. Madison below the Spanish minister, who sat next to Mrs. Madison. With respect to me, I was proceeding to place myself, though without invitation, next to the wife of the Spanish minister, when a member of the House of Representatives passed quickly by me and took the seat, without Mr. Jefferson's using any means to prevent it, or taking any care that I might be otherwise placed."[58]

From the beginning, Jefferson was liked at all levels of French society. "His manners had the grace, finish, suavity and unpresumingness, if they had not the freedom in some un-English particulars, of a well-bred Frenchman," Henry S. Randall wrote. "He had none of those abrupt angularities and inequalities of temper and demeanor, which embroiled Mr. Adams with the people and the government, almost as soon as he set foot in France, and made his entire stay there a series of torments and misunderstandings." Jefferson's way of expressing himself in "resounding abstractions" and bold, sweeping generalizations was very much in the contemporary French rhetorical style.[59] In comparing the French and British characters for Abigail Adams in London, Jefferson only slightly caricatured his own sentiments: he "would not give the polite, self-denying, feeling, hospitable, goodhumoured people of this country [France] and their amiability for every point of view...for ten such races of rich, proud, hectoring, swearing, squibbling, carnivorous animals as those among whom you are."[60]

Before Jefferson arrived in Paris in 1784, the French minister to the United States gave Vergennes a candid, perceptive profile of the new envoy. The chevalier de la Luzerne emphasized his learning, love of the arts and sciences, and reputation for integrity: "He is full of honor and sincerity and loves his country greatly, but too philosophic and tranquil to hate or love any other nation unless it is for the interest of the United States to do so. He has a principle that it is for the happiness and welfare of the United States to hold itself aloof from England as a peaceful state of affairs permits, that as a consequence of this system it becomes them to attach themselves particularly to France, even that Congress ought as quickly as possible to direct this affection of the people toward us in order to balance the penchant and numerous causes continually attracting them to England."[61]

The count de Vergennes, who controlled French foreign policy, was a jaded, seventy-one-year-old professional, a master in the byzantine ways of European diplomacy. Jefferson, however, was not intimidated, even though he was at the bottom of the hierarchy of foreign representatives at the French court, not even an ambassador. When it came to his country's interests, he could match any wary courtier of the old school in worldly toughness and Machiavellian analysis and strategy. After two years of observation, Jefferson gave Madison his shrewd appraisal of the count, who seemed impressed by the American's frankness and integrity: "He is a great Minister in European affairs but has very imperfect ideas of ours [and] no confidence in them. His devotion to pure despotism render him unaffectionate to our government but his fear of England makes him value us as a make weight. He is cool, reserved in political conversation, free and familiar on other subjects, and a very attentive, agreeable person to do business with. It is impossible to have a clearer, better organized head but age has chilled his heart."[62]

The Virginian's precise role in the American Revolution may have been vague to most Frenchmen, but there was an aura of self-confidence about him, a historical fascination, that gave him the stamp of legend. His very existence, as Bernard Bailyn remarked, was a symbol of enlightened liberalism. The angular planes of his face and his way of moving and standing against the ultra-European backdrop of Versailles somehow emphasized his made-in-America label, with its indelible stamp of Tidewater and Piedmont breeding. Young Thomas Shippen of Philadelphia, visiting Paris in the winter of 1788 and easily impressed by "titled men and Ladies of birth," was taken to Versailles by Jefferson to be introduced at court. Shippen was particularly struck by how the American envoy stood out in such a glittering setting: "I observed that although Mr. Jefferson was the plainest man in the room, and the most destitute of ribbons, crosses and other insignia of rank that he was the most courted and most attended to (even by the Courtiers themselves) of the whole Diplomatic corps."[63] The Philadelphian's portrait accords with the firm features set above the deep jacket collar and linen cravat of Houdon's bust, probably modeled that same year.

WHEN THE AMBITIOUS SCHEME to bring all of Europe into a network of commercial treaties collapsed in 1786, Jefferson concentrated his attention on France, where he believed he would find the key to America's vexing commercial problems by overthrowing the British monopoly of trade. If trade could be diverted to France and her West Indian colonies by the abolition of restrictive regulations, in exchange for an open American market for French manufactures and tropical produce, the British hold would be broken. This bold strategy would dominate Jefferson's dealings with the French Foreign Ministry. He pressed his suit at every chance, not hesitating to insist on private meetings with Vergennes.

At first, Jefferson had difficulty getting a private appointment with the foreign minister. Tuesday was "ambassadors' day" at Versailles, and the Virginian was punctilious in attending. But he complained to Jay that there were always a "number of audiences of ambassadors and other ministers, which take place before mine," rarely leaving time for the junior diplomat at the end of the day. Whenever he had the count's ear, Jefferson made the most of the opportunity. In an eight-page letter to Jay in January 1786, he described the problem centering on American tobacco, the country's chief export. Jefferson called the trade "the point of union" or crux of expanded American commerce with Europe.[64] As a Virginia planter, Jefferson fully understood the ramifications of breaking England's domination of the former colonies' tobacco market. France was a large user of the weed, and the tax revenues to its hard-pressed treasury were very profitable. But in its desperation for ready cash, the government had farmed out the collection of custom duties and taxes on tobacco to the avaricious farmers-general, who held a monopoly on the commodity. Complicating the matter even further, the farmers-general had given the American financier Robert Morris an exclusive three-year contract to supply the French market.

Jefferson's laissez-faire inclinations were strengthened by the spectacle of European monopolies and their cost to American trade. "It is contrary to the spirit of trade," he boldly reminded Vergennes, "and to the disposition of merchants, to carry a commodity to any market where but one person is to allowed to buy it, and where that person [the farmers-general] fixes the price."[65] The argument appealed to Vergennes, who disliked the monopoly and was already prepared to reduce the farmers-general's cut of the revenue. Assisted by Lafayette, Jefferson finally persuaded the minister to appoint an "American Committee" to study the matter and make recommendations to improve French-American trade. In a clever maneuver, the twenty-eight-year-old Lafayette was named to the committee, which he had also helped to recruit. The assignment was tailor-made for the ebullient Franco-American hero, with his insatiable "joy in wire pulling," always eager to please his American friends."[66]

Tobacco was the first item on the committee's agenda. Eventually Morris's monopoly was weakened, turning him into Jefferson's unforgiving enemy. The revolution in French domestic policy that Jefferson proposed, however, came to nothing. To break the ancient monopoly of the farmers-general was, as Vergennes pointed out, too radical a step for the beleaguered government seriously to consider.

In his January 1786 report to Jay, Jefferson mentioned that Vergennes was disturbed by commercial regulations that seemed to differ from state to state and complained that American justice was both inconsistent and slow when French merchants pressed for settlement of overdue bills. The minister had touched on one of the fundamental weaknesses of the loose Confederation, a weakness that affected American trade ambitions abroad. Jefferson responded with his usual thoroughness, writing a comprehensive treatise on the trade laws and regulations of American states to refute Vergennes' charges.

Jefferson was careful to balance his efforts on behalf of the tobacco trade with similar labors to enlarge the markets for American whale oil and rice. The Revolution had wrecked the New England whaling industry, and the opening of the European market now dominated by the British, and to a lesser degree by the Dutch and French, was viewed as key to its recovery. If the French market could be cracked, it not only would benefit the New England economy but in time American competition would damage France's old enemy by shutting off a major market to the British whale oil industry.

France's increasing consumption of whale oil made it the largest potential market for American whalers, as Jefferson pointed out in his memorandum "Observations on the Whale-Fishery."[67] Paris had made impressive progress in street lighting; whale-oil lamps even illuminated the heavily traveled road between the capital and Versailles. In an outline for a contemplated essay on France, Jefferson put lighting at the top of Paris's outstanding new public features.[68] The illumination of Marseilles alone consumed some seventy tons of oil a year. New England spermaceti whale oil was particularly well suited for street lamps, burning twice as long as the widely used vegetable oils. Jefferson shrewdly linked this capability with the French public's growing concern for crime during the dark hours. Using information gathered by Lafayette, he also emphasized how much the loss of the French market would cost the British. Ultimately, it was this argument that persuaded the French to restrict their market to American and French oil. Jefferson the aggressive pragmatist, as Merrill Peterson has observed, simply ignored his frequent sermons on "free trade" as a cornerstone of American commercial policy.

Nowhere is Jefferson's doctrine of free trade spelled out more succinctly than in the letter he drafted on behalf of the commissioners to the Prussian minister, De Thulemier, in the spring of 1785. In a characteristic strategy, he first established his argument on the progressive footing of reform: a liberated trade policy flowed inevitably from an enlightened, broadminded resourcefulness. Restrictive trade practices had their origins in "remote and unenlightened periods, when religion, physics and every branch of science was sophisticated and abused." But "the progress of information and of liberal sentiment has led to reformations in those, and in this also seems to have matured principles which should produce a reformation equally." The evidence for the American position was obvious: "Casting an eye over the states of Europe, we find them wealthy and populous nearly in proportion to the freedom of their commerce; and we conclude from thence that were it perfectly free, they would probably attain the highest points of wealth and population of which their other circumstances would admit." Ignoring the whale-oil cartel that Jefferson had engineered with France, the letter piously declared that it was in all parties' interests to root out monopoly as "the most powerful engine ever employed for the suffocation of commerce."[69]

Around the time he was warming to these "liberal sentiments" on free trade, Jefferson received a private lesson in the extent of French duties and imposts. When a shipment of Bordeaux wine from his wine merchants Bondfield and Girandeau arrived in Paris, he calculated on the back of the bill of lading that the excise taxes were as much as the cost of transportation. Nothing like this had yet occurred in trading between the American states, and the incident reinforced Jefferson's belief that interstate commerce should be regulated by Congress. Later, when he moved to the Hôtel de Langeac, he found a convenient way around the duties collected on wine at the nearby tollhouse by telling the wine merchant that he would receive the shipment just outside the city wall, before a tax could be imposed.[70]

High on the American trade agenda, Jefferson recalled in his autobiography, was "the admission of our rice on equal terms with that of Piedmont, Egypt and the Levant." Although there was no duty on rice, the Mediterranean variety was more to French taste than American rice. Wisely restraining his reforming tendencies when it came to the French table, Jefferson concentrated instead on improving the rice grown in the Carolinas and the American South for the French market. On his trip to the south of France in 1787, ostensibly to heal his injured wrist, he extended his travels into Italy for three weeks to research rice production there. Unable to "satisfy [himself] at Marseilles of the causes of the difference of quality between the rice of Carolina and that of Piedmont," he wrote to Adams, he proceeded directly to the Italian rice country in the Po Valley. There he "found the difference to be not in management as had been supposed but in the species of rice."[71] Jefferson smuggled a sample of Italian rice out of the country and sent it to friends in the United States. "I am satisfied that the rice of Lombardy is of a different species than yours," he reported to Ralph Izard, a South Carolina planter. "The exportation of it, in the husk being prohibited, I could not bring with me but as much as my pockets would hold which I sent to your society of agriculture."

On the eve of his first term as president, Jefferson asked himself if the United States was any better off for his having lived there. In a private tally sheet headed "A Memorandum (Services to My Country)," he listed, together with the Declaration of Independence and the act prohibiting the importation of slaves, the introduction of olive trees and an improved strain of rice. "The greatest service which can be rendered any country is, to add an useful plant to its culture," he summed up in an unforgettable line.[72]

From the moment the gardener/diplomat arrived in Paris, he was involved in the international exchange of plants, a passion he shared with many of his French acquaintances. When he wasn't sending plants back to Monticello or to American friends, he was ordering familiar Virginia vegetables for his garden at the Hôtel de Langeac. "I cultivate in my own garden here Indian corn for the use of my own table, to eat green in manner," he told his Albemarle neighbor Col. Nicholas Lewis. "But the species I am able to get here for seed is hard, with a thick skin and dry." He asked Lewis to send an ear of the "small rare ripe corn we call Homony-corn," which was grown at Monticello, along with the seeds of the common sweet potato, watermelon, cantaloupe, acorns of various sorts, "and a dozen or two bacon hams."[73]

Jefferson's continuing fascination with the growing of grapes recalled his collaboration with Filippo Mazzei at Monticello before the Revolution, when the Italian had arrived with ten vignerons and a collection of root stock to begin his Virginia wine experiment. During his excursion down the Rhine Valley in 1788, Jefferson visited some of the well-known German vineyards with his friend Baron Geismar. "The vines which I took from Hocheim and Rudesheim," he later wrote the baron from Paris, "are now growing luxuriously in my garden here, and will cross the Atlantic next winter, and that probably if you ever revisit Monticello, I shall be able to give you a glass of Hock or Rudesheim of my own making."[74]

On August 20, 1784, two weeks after arriving in Paris, Jefferson noted in his account book that he had received his first supply of 276 bottles of French wine from Thomas Barclay, the American consul in Bordeaux. Although he had imported French wines regularly to Monticello, only now was he able to study many of the vineyards first-hand. The envoy recognized the diplomatic importance of a good table and was determined to uphold his country's honor. Gouverneur Morris, who was privy to some of the best tables in Paris, rated the American minister's as outstanding, particularly in the wine department. Jefferson especially admired the wines of Bordeaux. If he encountered an outstanding vintage at someone's house, he would often note it and immediately place an order. Following a dinner at Franklin's, for example, he placed an order with the Bordeaux merchant Bondfield and Girandeau for a gross of bottles of the same wine Franklin had purchased.

As he grew in experience and knowledge, and always ignoring the cost, Jefferson bought the very best wine available. From the Château d'Yquem he ordered 250 bottles of 1784-vintage sauterne, writing to Monsieur d'Yquem that he "would prefer to receive it directly from your hands." When he visited the renowned Château Margaux, he wrote to his Virginia friend Alexander Donald that he had bought a good supply, also from 1784, "on the spot, and a part of the very purchase from which I send you. It is of the best vintage that has happened in nine years.... I may safely assure you therefore that, according to the taste of this country and of England there cannot be a better bottle of Bordeaux produced in France."[75]

In preparation for his trip to the south of France in 1787, Jefferson studied and tasted the wines of Burgundy. Marking out his route through the vineyards, he engaged a local agent in Beaune to be his guide. Price, he assured the agent, was not a consideration, even though he was complaining regularly to friends in Virginia that his expenses as minister were leading him to bankruptcy. His research paid off. The Burgundy labels he bought in quantity were the finest—Chambertin, Romanie, Pommard, Meursault, Montrachet. In Burgundy he also selected a number of vine plants to continue his experiments at Monticello.

ONE OF JEFFERSON'S TRUSTED ADVISERS ON WINE was another diplomat, Count Elie de Moustier, a well-placed member of the French court. Upon returning from the south of France in the spring of 1787, he sent Moustier a bottle of Frontignac, the most famous muscat produced by the Lambert vineyard. With the gift of wine, Jefferson enclosed a note telling the count that Thomas Paine was in Paris and wanted to meet him. By then, Paine had achieved international renown and Moustier wrote back immediately to invite both men to dinner, no doubt anticipating his impending mission to the United States. That August, in a letter describing the

continuing decline of the French court's popularity, Jefferson reported to
Adams that Moustier was to be the next minister to the United States:

> The carriage of Madame de (I forget her name) in the queen's livery was
> stopped by the populace under a belief that it was Madame de Polignac whom
> they would have insulted, the Queen, going to the theatre at Versailles with
> Madame de Polignac was received with a general hiss. The King, long in the
> habit of drowning his cares in wine, plunges deeper and deeper, The Queen
> cries but sins on.... The Marechal de Castries retired yesterday.... The
> Marechal de Segur retired at the same time prompted to it by the court.
> Their successors are not yet known. M. de St. Prist goes Ambassador to
> Holland in the room of Verac transferred to Switzerland, and the Count de
> Moustier goes to America in the room of Chevalier de la Luzerne.[76]

When Jefferson heard that his friend Madame de Bréhan, the count's
sister-in-law, planned to accompany the engaging Frenchman, he wrote
enthusiastically to John Jay introducing the pair. "You will find him open,
communicative, candid, simple in his manners, and a declared enemy to
ostentation and luxury."[77] Neither a taste for fine wine nor a close but
innocent friendship with a beautiful married woman, of course, fell into
the category of ostentation on the Virginian's scale of values. There is
little doubt that Jefferson played a role in the count's selection for the
post in America.[78]

Madame de Bréhan, he assured Jay, would "deserve the friendship of
Mrs. Jay," who should in turn "treat her without the shadow of etiquette."
To Abigail Adams in London he confided that he "rejoiced" in Madame
de Bréhan's character, which would help discourage the alarming taste
for fashion and luxury in the States. "Simple beyond example in her
dress, tho neat, hating parade and etiquette, affable, engaging, placid, and
withal beautiful, I cannot help hoping a good effect from her example."[79]
Still full of New World innocence after nearly three years in Paris, Jefferson told Madison that Madame de Bréhan was accompanying the new
minister "in hopes that a change of climate may assist her feeble health,
and also that she may procure a more valuable education for her son, and
safer from seduction in America than in France." Her husband, he
explained, was an officer "obliged by the times to remain with the army."

Jefferson reminded Moustier on his departure that they were "the two end links of that chain which holds the two nations together" and urged him to preserve his appealing French ways.[80]

Jefferson's esteem for the count was short-lived, however. In early 1789, he received an encoded letter from Madison revealing that Moustier's appointment had been disastrous. Not only was the count "unsocial, proud and niggardly," betraying, in Madison's opinion, a marked "fastidiousness toward this country," his private life was scandalous. "He suffers also from his illicit connection with Madame de Bréhan which is universally known and offensive to American manners." The "ladies of New York" had seen through the whole charade, no doubt led by the formidable Mrs. Jay, and had "for some time withdrawn their attentions from her," making her life so miserable that she and her brother-in-law had left town to travel around the country, including a stop at Mount Vernon. "On their journeys," Madison continued, "it is said they often neglect the most obvious precautions for veiling their intimacy." They had even succeeded in alienating their fellow countrymen, who now felt that the minister should be recalled.[81]

From Madame de Bréhan's perspective, she had no doubt been misled by her American friend's simple republican manners and her naive literary notions of American society. Despite Jefferson's warning that America was not Arcadia and that she would not be pleased with the imitation European etiquette she was likely to find there, she was unprepared for the pretentious courtiers that George Washington was beginning to gather around him. Not for the last time, the French mirage of American society had turned out to be a sour delusion. Mutual ignorance ensured predictable disenchantment for all parties. Jefferson saw the trouble coming when he wrote Maria Cosway that their friend's "love of simplicity and her wish to find it" led her to think she was going to a Rousseauesque paradise.[82]

Jefferson's personal disappointment aside, the embarrassing turn of events was badly timed for diplomatic reasons. During the meeting of the Assembly of Notables in 1787, called to raise taxes, charges had been publically made that the United States was acting in bad faith by not paying interest on its loans from the French government. To the sensitive American's further discomfort, French officers who had served in the Revolution had not been paid since 1785. A number of the veterans were his friends and many were well connected with the court, where they could easily damage American relations. When these increasingly disgruntled officers threatened to protest, the harassed envoy was able to sidetrack them briefly, but his appeals to Jay and even Washington were ignored.

Although Moustier may have misread American moral standards, the real reason he was recalled was that he had been audacious enough to make representations about the American debt and to press for payment. The festering tension between the two countries over the debt grew as France itself teetered toward bankruptcy. Jefferson outlined the problem in his letter to Adams in 1787: "I have had it much at heart to remove from between us every subject of misunderstanding and irritation. Our debts to the King, to the Officers, to the Farmers, are of this description. They having complied with no part of our engagements in these, draws on us a great deal of censure, and occasioned a language in the Assemblée des Notables very likely to produce dissatisfaction between us."[83] Montmorin, the French minister of state, was surprisingly accommodating when Lafayette, on behalf of his mortified friend, asked that Moustier be granted a leave of absence. Using a well-known diplomatic ploy, Jefferson had engineered the envoy's removal by suggesting to his go-between that a close reading of one of Moustier's letters could be interpreted as a request for a change of post.

The controversy over the American debt in Europe plunged Jefferson into the arcane world of international finance and bond speculators. The weakness of the Confederation and what Adams called its "downright Ignorance of the Nature of Coin, Credit and Circulation," coupled with the meddling of well-placed American speculators, hampered Jefferson's efforts to unravel the debt problem to the end of his term as minister. But he had gained an education in European high finance from his meetings with shrewd Amsterdam bankers to consolidate the American loans and from the tough, seasoned Adams, who for ten years had been "vexed with such terrible complaints and frightened with such long Faces."[84] When Adams returned to the United States in 1788, Jefferson was left to handle the debt problem on his own. It was around this time of intense preoccupation with his debilitating personal debts and his country's insoluble public obligations that a deeply troubled Jefferson began to consider ways to limit indebtedness to one generation—ideas that he would later set out in his famous letter of September 6, 1789 to James Madison.[85]

ANOTHER TOUCHY ISSUE CONFRONTING JEFFERSON was the long-standing friction between England and France, which threatened to explode without warning. In 1785 a radical manifesto had been published in Leiden echoing Jefferson's Declaration. "Liberty is an inalienable right of all citizens. No power on earth much less any power derived truly from the people...can challenge or obstruct the enjoyment of this liberty when it is so desired." These sentiments resonated throughout Dutch society, encouraged by an uncensored press. The long-simmering Dutch civil conflict suddenly flared up in the fall of 1787, when the niece of the king of Prussia and wife of the stadtholder was unexpectedly arrested and insulted by Dutch "patriots" outside The Hague, precipitating an invasion by Prussian troops. The intrepid princess had been aided in her misdirected plan to raise the Orange flag by none other than van Hogendorp, the Orange nobleman whom Jefferson had met in Annapolis. The Dutch patriots, of course, were not simply peasants, small farmers, and fishermen—Dutch versions of the Concord minutemen—but also burghers, members of an oligarchy whose awesome commercial power clashed with the pretensions of the stadtholder, the weak William V of Orange-Nassau. The only function of the stadtholder—who had been brought up in England, the son of Princess Anne—was to head the armed forces, heavily subsidized by the British government. Dutch financial support of the American rebels further tied the two countries together.

On the surface, the Dutch conflict scarcely posed a major threat to the peace. But the Dutch "republicans" who resisted the stadtholder's attempt to intervene in government affairs counted on French support since the English, who had egged on the Prussian king, would no doubt side with Berlin. America could hardly remain neutral if the French and English squared off again. Should the turmoil escalate, a French diplomat reported to Versailles, "it is to be feared that it may cause an explosion which will have incalculable consequences."[86] As the situation continued to deteriorate over the next several months, another general conflict into which America would be drawn seemed a real possibility. It was eventually averted when the French ignominiously abandoned their Dutch allies. Lafayette had already charged off to the Dutch border on a nonstop, 150-mile ride, hoping to be named to command the patriot troops, only to find that the prince de Salm—Jefferson called him "a prince without talents, without courage and without principle"—had gotten the job.[87]

Jefferson's republican indignation, always near the surface, was triggered by these European intrigues and overflowed in a letter to David Humphreys. Complaining of the trappings of kings and queens disguised as "reasons of state," he wrote: "From these events our young republics may learn many useful lessons, never to call on foreign powers to settle their differences, to guard against hereditary magistrates, to prevent their citizens from becoming so established in wealth and power as to be thought worthy of alliance by marriage with the nieces, sister &c of kings, and in short to besiege the throne of heaven with eternal prayers to exterpate from creation this class of human lions, tygers and mammouths called kings from whom, let him perish, who does not say 'good lord deliver us.'"[88]

The Dutch crisis and its potential to upset the country's loan arrangements with the hard-pressed American government had prompted Jefferson's flying trip to The Hague in March 1788 to head off, as he reported to Washington, inevitable bankruptcy. But to even his surprise, he and Adams were able successfully to renegotiate the loans. Adams modestly admitted to Abigail that his own experience with Dutch bankers was critical. "Mr. Jefferson is so anxious to obtain Money here to enable him to discharge some of the most urgent demands upon the United States and preserve their Credit from Bankruptcy for two years longer after which he thinks the new Gov't will have Money in their Treasury from Taxes; that he has prevailed upon me to open a new Loan, by virtue of my old Power—I was very much averse to this but he would take no denial."[89]

Jefferson's analysis of the precarious financial condition of the United States during the transition to a stronger, reorganized government under the new constitution recognized the significant impact it had on the country's foreign relations. "I am anxious about every thing which may affect our credit," he told Washington. "My wish would be to possess it in the highest degree, but to use it little. Were we without credit we might be crushed by a nation of much inferior resources but possessing higher credit." In the same letter, Jefferson criticized the American Constitution for lacking a Bill of Rights and giving the president an unlimited term of office, which would lead inevitably to the monarchy he detested. "There is scarcely an evil known in these countries which may not be traced to the king as it's source, nor a good which is not derived from the small fibres of republicanism existing among them…there is not a crowned head in Europe whose talents or merit would entitle him to be elected a vestry man by the people of any parish in America."[90]

In all his European observations, Jefferson found evidence that only the structural reform of government would rescue man from "infinite wretchedness." His radical diagnosis laid the cause of mankind's ills on repressive institutions such as monarchy (he might well have included the church), reversing the conventional arguments of the day that traced man's inherent fallibility to the fall of Adam—the classic explanation for the failure of republican governments. As Joyce Appleby has pointed out "In his conception of human nature, his expectation of progress, his enthusiasm for economic growth, and his irreverence toward the past, Jefferson explicitly distanced himself from civic humanism" leading to government by a political elite and endorsed by John Adams in his *Defense of the Constitutions of Government of the United States of America.*[91]

Jefferson feared that the very importance and power of the office of the presidency would lead to a hereditary institution inviting "interference with money and arms by foreign countries to whom the choice of an American president would be interesting. Examples of this abound in history; in the case of the Roman emperors, for instance, of Popes, while of any significance, of German emperors, the Kings of poland, & the Deys of Barbary. I had observed too in feudal History, and in the recent instance particularly of the Stadtholder of Holland, how easily offices or tenures for life slide into inheritances."[92]

Jefferson's reference to "the Deys of Barbary" was not offhand: the Barbary pirates who were enslaving free Americans obsessed him during his stay in Paris. Only the lack of an effective naval force kept him from instigating an all-out war to protect American commercial interests in the Mediterranean. The pirates had long plagued European powers, but Jefferson first took note of their depredations in a report to Congress on behalf of the American commissioners a little more than two months after he arrived in Paris, in November 1784. He had heard about "the piratical states" earlier in Annapolis and been briefed by Adams and Franklin, who described the tribute in the form of annual gifts that Morocco, Algiers, Tunis, and Tripoli would demand for putting an end to the piracy. As the novice envoy wrote to Congress, "Presents or war is their usual alternative."[93]

Matters came to a head a month later, when the Virginian read in the papers that a ship registered in his own state had been captured by a frigate of the emperor of Morocco. By February 1785, he was convinced that there was only one solution to the problem: the American government had to quickly develop a naval force if it intended to pursue international trade. "Paul Jones with half a dozen frigates...by constant cruising" could cut "them to pieces piecemeal." Feeling "suspended between indignation and impotence," Jefferson repeated his earlier argument to Monroe that the time was ripe "to plead for war," in view of the enemy's weak, divided condition. "Can we find a better occasion of beginning one? Or find a foe more certainly within our dimensions? The motives pleading for war rather than tribute are numerous and honourable, those opposing them are mean and shortsighted."[94]

An expanding international free trade of agricultural surplus was basic to Jefferson's vision of a nation of small farmers, as he explained in the *Notes on the State of Virginia*. It is in this agrarian context that his advocacy of a strong naval force to use against anyone interfering with American maritime interests must be considered. But Congress balked at the cost of a navy, electing instead to pay tribute by appropriating eighty thousand dollars for presents during the negotiations with the Mediterranean despots. Americans were being held prisoners and a ransom would have to be paid to free them, regardless of any naval success.

When Adams got to London in May 1785, the ambassador of Tripoli hinted to him that treaty negotiations were possible. "By a little Italian and French, and some lingua Franca, they got into conversation and understood each other wondrously," Abigail Adams reported. It was this prospect that caused Adams to dispatch William Stephens Smith to Paris with an urgent request that Jefferson come to London in the spring of

1786. Timing was crucial, Adams believed, since there was a serious possibility that England would encourage attacks on American vessels trading in the Mediterranean.

Arriving in London on May 11, Jefferson met with his old colleague the following day, and together they worked out an agenda for the meetings. The Tripolitan ambassador proved a much tougher bargainer than the Americans had expected. When the commissioners inquired on what grounds Tripoli was making war against nations without provocation, the ambassador replied that, according to the Laws of the Prophet as written in the Koran, it was his countrymen's religious duty to kill or enslave their enemies, who were all sinners. Jefferson later reported to William Carmichael in Madrid that the price of a peaceful settlement far exceeded the "drop in the bucket" of funds that Congress had authorized. Nothing came of the negotiations. Moreover, what appeared to be a successful commercial treaty with Portugal, worked out during Jefferson's trip to London, foundered when it was sent back to Lisbon for approval.[95]

Adams had also been optimistic that Jefferson's presence would offer an "occasion to renew our overtures" for a commercial treaty with Great Britain. Several weeks earlier Abigail Adams had hinted to her friend in Paris that certain "symptoms" indicated that discussions "in respect to a treaty with America" might be possible. Adams wrote to the marquis of Carmarthen, the British minister of foreign affairs, that "Mr. Jefferson, Minister Plenipotentiary at the Court of Versailles, is now here, and as they have something to communicate to his Lordship, relative to the affairs of the United States, they request a time when they may have the honour to pay their respects to his Lordship, before the levee on Wednesday."[96]

The meeting was a diplomatic debacle: the commissioners' overtures elicited no response. "I suppose this the last offer of friendship which will ever be made on our part," Jefferson, clearly rankled, concluded in his letter to Carmichael. "I think the king, ministers, and nation are more bitterly hostile to us at present than at any period of the late war....Our enemies (for such they are, in fact,) have, for 12 years past, followed but one uniform rule, that of doing exactly the contrary of what reason points out. Having early, during our contest, observed this in British conduct, I governed myself by it in all prognostications of their measures. And I can say with truth, it never failed me but in the circumstances of their making peace with us."[97]

On April 25 Jefferson and Adams reported that further negotiations were futile. "His Lordship after harping a little on the old String, the insufficiency of the powers of Congress to treat and to compel Compliance with the Treaties, said he would lay the matter before the Ministry and King." After further meetings and proposals, it became clear to the exasperated commissioners that only a complete capitulation on their part would produce an agreement. One of the sticking points was the issue of requiring American debtors to pay back the interest that had accrued on British loans during the war. The two diplomats met several times with merchants in an effort to find an acceptable formula, but the back interest remained a bitter pill that the Americans refused to swallow. To do so, Adams and Jefferson maintained, would be to admit that the war had been their fault in the first place. "There is no part nor Individual here in favor of a Treaty, but upon the Principle that the United States will retaliate if there is not one. All agree that if America will suffer England to pocket (that is their Expression) all her navigation, England would be unwise not to avail herself of the advantage."[98]

Jefferson's bitter memory of the meeting lasted to the end of his life. "On the first conference with the Marquis of Carmarthen...the distance and disinclination which he betrayed in his conversation, the vagueness and evasions of his answers to us, confirmed me in the belief of their aversion to have anything to do with us. We delivered him however our *projét*, Mr. Adams not despairing as much as I did of its effect. We afterwards by one or more notes, requested his appointment of an interview and conference, which without directly declining, he evaded by pretenses of other pressing occupations for the moment."[99]

ON MARCH 17, 1786 JEFFERSON RECORDED in his Memorandum Book that he had "paid porters at St. James on my being presented 42/," but it would take him fifty years to sum up his feelings about the "time lost...in ceremony" that day. The *Gazetteer* announced that the notorious Thomas Jefferson of Virginia "was introduced to the King at St. James by his Excellency, John Adams," observing that the levée was "very thin of nobility," in contrast to the previous day's brilliant social display. Jefferson recalled the occasion with distaste: "On my presentation as usual to the King and Queen at their levées, it was impossible for anything to be more ungracious than their notice of Mr. Adams & myself. I saw at once that the ulcerations in the narrow mind of that mulish being left nothing to be expected on the subject of my attendance."[100]

Jefferson's garden tour with the Adamses, a trip to Windsor Castle, and shopping expeditions for books and other supplies no doubt helped ease his official frustrations in England. A few days before his presentation at court, he attended a performance at Drury Lane by the celebrated Mrs. Siddens in a new tragedy, *The Captives*. On April 20 he saw her as Portia in *The Merchant of Venice*, and two nights later as Lady Macbeth. He saw King George III again on March 18, at a command performance of the new comic opera *La Scuola dei gelosi* by Salieri at the King's Theatre in Haymarket. The prince of Wales, extravagantly dressed in maroon velvet and sparkling buttons, was also on hand. The Virginian later added a portrait of the prince to the rogues' gallery of royalty that he penned for John Jay in a not-so-subtle attack on heredity as a principle of government: "He has not a single element of Mathematics, of natural or moral philosophy, or of any other science on earth; nor has the society he has kept been such as to supply the void of education. It has been of the lowest, the most illiterate and profligate persons of the kingdom, without choice of rank or mind, and with whom the subjects of conversation are only horses, drinking-matches, bawdy houses, and in terms the most vulgar."[101]

Matters of debt public and private seemed to hang over Jefferson's London visit, which lasted six weeks—twice as long as he had anticipated. Inevitably, he came into the orbit of Lucy and John Paradise, whose financial problems, growing out of Lucy's heavily encumbered Virginia estate, had been exacerbated by their spectacular improvidence. They had lived in London for some time and moved in the same fashionable circle as the Cosways. Lucy Ludwell Paradise, with her impressive Tidewater genealogy, charmed the susceptible envoy. He dined with the Paradises and even attended a ball in their company at the French embassy, no doubt all part of Lucy's strategy to enlist his help with their creditors. In the end, he spent far more time than he should have on this trivial matter, perhaps drawn into it, as Herbert Sloan has suggested, by its painful resemblance to his own complicated financial affairs.[102]

The Virginian's personal balance sheet did not improve during his London trip. Before leaving America he had invested in a copying machine in order to duplicate his enormous correspondence, but he had long wanted a portable model that he could carry on trips. In London he arranged to have one specially made to his own design, and his enthusiasm for the improved machine proved infectious: Madison, William Carmichael in Madrid, Lafayette, Chastellux, and even the papal nuncio in Paris eventually ordered Jeffersonian presses.[103]

When he brought the new copy press through customs on his way back to Paris, Jefferson encountered the usual problem of importing prohibited goods and had to ask Vergennes for special dispensation. In a letter thanking William Smith for expediting the shipment of the press, he asked Smith to look into the purchase of yet more contraband, "a pair of chariot harness...plated, not foppish but genteel, handsome without being tawdry." He had not been able to find either carriages or harness to his exacting taste in Paris. Lafayette found out about the order from the Foreign Ministry and apparently questioned the propriety of this undiplomatic transaction, drawing a candid if defensive reply from his somewhat embarrassed friend. "The reason for my importing harness from England," the Virginian wrote back, "is a very obvious one. They are plated and plated harness is not made in France as far as I have learnt. It is not for the love of the English but a love of myself that I sometimes find myself obliged to buy their manufactures." He did not miss the opportunity, however, to point out that America's free-trade policy gave the French minister in Philadelphia unlimited privileges to buy goods from any country in the world.[104]

Jefferson continued to be concerned about the welfare of the Barbary captives. Although publicly opposed to paying ransom, he surreptitiously attempted to secure the release of the Americans held in Algiers by arranging indirect payments. Not long after the treaty with Morocco was signed with the help of Spain, Jefferson learned of a religious order whose mission was to free captives from the "Infidels" by begging alms to pay for their release. A secret meeting was arranged with the general of the Mathurian order and congressional funds were set aside for the clandestine ransom.

After long and devious maneuvering—including the planting of false information that the United States was no longer interested in the hostages in Algeria, a ruse designed to drive down the price of tribute—the strategy came to naught.

Jefferson, however, never relinquished his idea of organizing a multinational naval force to bring the "pettyfogging nest of robbers" to heel. In his *Autobiography*, he outlined a plan for a "concerted operation among the powers at war with the Piratical States of Barbary."[105] The Confederation's inability to levy support from individual states for a military operation in the Mediterranean, of course, made American participation out of the question. As late as August 1788, Jefferson continued to hope that France and others would "join in a league for keeping up a perpetual cruize against these pyrates, which tho a slow operation, would be a sure one for destroying all their vessels and seamen and turning the rest of them to agriculture. But a desire of not bringing upon themselves another difficulty will probably induce the ministers to do as their predecessors have done."[106]

By that summer, the bankrupt French treasury and recalcitrant regional parliaments had forced Louis XVI to revive the Estates-General, defunct for over a century, in order to raise taxes. The city, Jefferson wrote, was a "furnace of politics" and the agitated government was in no position to enter into the joint military action that he continued privately to promote. The Barbary pirates remained an unsolved problem that he would have to wrestle with later, both as secretary of state and as president of the United States.

ON NOVEMBER 14, 1788 Jefferson forwarded to John Jay for congressional ratification the signed copy of the long-delayed consular convention between the United States and France. In this, his greatest diplomatic success, Jefferson demonstrated his skill in protecting the independence of the American Republic from the conflicting ambitions of its most reliable but unequally powerful friend.[107]

A history of misunderstandings between the countries underlines the significance of Jefferson's achievement. The Treaty of Amity and Commerce of 1778 had established reciprocal rights to appoint consuls, whose powers and functions would be the subject of a separate convention. While France regularly pressed for the new agreement, the United States just as regularly avoided dealing with it. The French consuls saw their duties as being both legal and commercial, but under United States law they were prohibited from engaging directly in trade, unlike their American counterparts in France. In a report to Congress in 1785, Jay, as secretary of foreign affairs, noted that friction in American ports over the authority of foreign consuls and their agents had repeatedly flared into ugly confrontations. In 1779 the French consul general, Conrad Alexandre Gérard, protested to Congress that these conflicts demonstrated a "want of proper regulations for maintaining the immunity of the flag, which is the foundation of free commerce." Violations of the principle of diplomatic immunity occurred regularly in both countries.[108]

Gérard's successor, La Luzerne, submitted a draft agreement to Congress to be considered "with all speed" in the summer of 1781, as the French and American troops were planning to meet at Yorktown and bring the war to a close. The following day Congress moved to set up a committee to consider the agreement. A year later a "Scheme for a Convention" was sent to Franklin, with instructions binding him to follow "the Matter thereof in all respects." Preoccupied by the peace treaty with England, the tired diplomat took no action until the spring of 1783, when various drafts of the convention began to circulate. The resulting Convention of 1784 left open the question of whether American consuls could also engage in commercial transactions—an issue that naturally affected the American commissioners' authority to negotiate commercial treaties.

French consuls, moreover, asserted privileges and immunities that challenged the supremacy of local American laws. In an incident involving a royal French frigate, a private U.S. citizen had a warrant served on a French cannoneer charged with stealing a watch just as the *Aigrette* was preparing to sail out of New York harbor. In March 1788 the French minister fired off a strong protest to Montmorin, then in the midst of his negotiations with Jefferson on a new convention. Another clash occurred in Norfolk, Virginia, when the French consul failed to rescue a French captain who had been arrested by the local sheriff for barratry, a serious charge under maritime law. French businessmen constantly complained of unfair treatment under what they viewed as a biased, chaotic system of conflicting laws in each state jurisdiction.

Eager to encourage trade in whale oil and tobacco, the American and French governments shared an interest in eliminating obstacles to free and open trade. Jefferson and his French counterpart, Rayneval, who was appointed to arrange the treaty, got along well and succeeded in working out, or around, the many questions that troubled the two parties. In his official report, Jefferson meticulously compared in parallel columns all the variations in the Conventions of 1784 and 1788, printing both English and French texts. His recommendations were reluctantly endorsed by a suspicious Jay, and the convention was finally ratified by the Senate on July 29, 1789. A key provision subjected "all persons, and property, to the laws of the land," sweeping away one of the major problems of the earlier conventions. Jefferson's reasonableness and candor had won the day; Jay was unable to find a single objectionable word or phrase to strike or quibble with.[109]

Jefferson's report also discussed the qualifications of foreign service personnel, comparing the merits of native-born and foreign consuls. "*Native* citizens, on several valuable accounts, are preferable to Aliens and to citizens alien-born. They possess our language, know our laws, customs and commerce, have generally acquaintance in the U.S. give better satisfaction, and are more to be relied on in point of fidelity." On the other hand, American representatives were limited in their language facility and their knowledge of the host country's government and judicial system. "But we should look forward to future times to have no more native citizens" in consulate jobs who "being bankrupt have taken asylum in France from their creditors, or young ephemeral adventurers in commerce without substance or conduct, or other descriptions which might disgrace the consular office, without promoting our commerce." Jefferson's appraisal was a sad indictment of the mediocre standards of the provincial American foreign service. It was one more issue that the future secretary of state and president would have to address.

JEFFERSON EXCELLED AS AN AMBASSADOR, advancing both the symbolic and the practical representation of the American experiment. It was the most satisfying public role of his life. It suited his personality

and character, his seeming candor and idealism, allowing him to participate fully in public affairs without the distractions of petty politics or
day-to-day management. His deep commitment was reflected in every
aspect of his activities as minister in Paris—advising, corresponding,
digesting information, holding meetings, maneuvering through the
tricky shoals of European court politics, drafting treatises on intricate
matters that were important to the American cause.

But the myriad details of diplomatic work did not divert the Virginian
from the larger lessons it had to teach—above all, that foreign policy gave
incalculable power to those who directed it. The necessity for secrecy, for
freedom from oversight, even for arbitrary authority—all characteristics
of the European chanceries where he had cut his diplomatic teeth—left
their marks and occasional scars on the susceptible student. Nor were they
at odds with his own operating style, when exercised in the name of liberty
and its empire. Jefferson had been hardened (and occasionally humiliated) in
the toughest of all diplomatic schools. By the time he became president of
the United States, his knowledge of Europe and the conduct of foreign policy would be greater than that of any other American.[110]

Chapter 7
The Women in His Life

WOMEN BECAME AN INCREASINGLY VITAL, leavening part of Jefferson's existence in the imaginative space of Paris. Their wit, manners, and sensibility softened his stereotyped reactions to European society, which often failed to meet his conventional Puritan standards. They regularly interrupted the long hours in his study in the rue de Berri with invitations, visits, dinners, and conversation. Few women outside his immediate family ever enjoyed such unrestricted access to his company. Since Henry Adams's day, biographers have speculated about the "wall of silence" Jefferson supposedly threw up to protect his privacy. But in Paris, when women played a more intimate part of his everyday life than ever before or after, he frequently let his guard down in teasing, confidential communications to women friends. They responded by expressing their own keen anticipation or recollection of his empathetic company.[1]

Temptation was an inescapable part of the glamorous, libidinous society of Paris. For the French in the late eighteenth century, adultery was a class issue, hardly a political or social problem. To Jefferson, however, such moral lapses reflected the corruptions of despotism and privilege; even marital infidelity could be traced to France's odious system of government rather than to any innate human flaw. As he often said in his letters, the French would surpass any people in the world if only they had "a better religion" and "form of government." Lacking what a later age would call firm family values, Parisians cultivated "pursuits which nourish and invigorate our bad passions, and which offer only moments of ecstasy amidst days and months of restlessness and torment."[2]

In Jefferson's various sermons on the perils of a foreign education for

American youth, European women as a type, promising seduction, intrigue, luxury, and infidelity, headed the list of hazards. His letter to John Bannister, Jr., becomes theological as he warns of dissipation, profligate spending, aristocratic pretensions, and "a passion for whores," all of which undermined "fidelity to the marriage bed."[3] In cautioning the presumed innocent Bannister, whose habits had not yet been fully formed, the provincial Jefferson revealed a deep anxiety about women that he had felt since early manhood. Only a pre-Enlightenment vision of eternal damnation was left out of his harangue.

By the time he traveled to the south of France, "the land of corn, wine, oil and sunshine," in 1787, Jefferson had developed a slightly more mature and mellow attitude toward French mores. Upon hearing that the husband of Lafayette's mistress had committed suicide, he told his secretary, William Short, that he didn't know "whether to condole with or congratulate the marquis." A man who would kill himself in the wonderful climate of Aix (where the distraught husband lived) must, he added, be a "bloody minded fellow indeed."[4]

Short's personal life presented the envoy with moral problems that couldn't be brushed aside as a social aberration. A few weeks after arriving in Paris, Short had moved to the suburb of Saint-Germain-en-Laye to work on his French. Boarding with a local family, he was immediately attracted to the daughter of the house. Jefferson, evidently suspicious, repeatedly urged him to "come home like a good boy," but Short returned only when he was officially appointed Jefferson's full-time secretary. It is not clear when, in Jefferson's old-fashioned euphemism, a "fixed attachment" developed between Short and Rosalie de La Rochefoucauld. Jefferson left no recorded comment, but the affair must have been a disappointing confirmation of what he considered one of the most serious threats to Americans in Europe.

The relaxed morals of Paris did not only pose a risk for young American men. In a well-known letter to the rich Philadelphian Anne Willing Bingham, whose manners and classic beauty had immediately caught Jefferson's eye when they met during her visit to France, the envoy compared the "empty bustle" of Paris with the virtuous domestic happiness of the chaste, republican women of America.

At eleven o'clock it is day, *chez madame*. The curtains are drawn. Propped on bolsters and pillows, and her head scratched into a little order, the bulletins of the sick are read, and the billets of the well. She writes to some of her acquaintances, and receives the visits of others. If the morning is not very thronged she is able to get out and hobble around the cage of the Palais Royal; but she must hobble quickly, for the Coiffeur's turn is come; and a tremendous turn it is! Happy if he does not make her arrive when dinner is half over! The torpitude of digestion a little passed, she flutters for half an hour thro' the streets by way of paying visits and then to the Spectacles. These finished, another half-hour is devoted to dodging in and out of doors of her very sincere friends and away to supper. After supper cards; and after cards, bed—to rise at noon the next day, and tread, like a mill-horse, the same trodden circle over again. Thus the days of life are consumed, one by one, without an object beyond the present moment; ever flying from the ennui of that, yet carrying it with us; eternally in pursuit of happiness, which keeps eternally before us. If death or bankruptcy happen to trip us out of the circle, it is matter for the buz of the evening, and is completely forgotten by the next morning.

In America, on the other hand, the society of your husband, the fond cares for the children, the arrangements of the house, the improvements of the grounds, fill every moment with a healthy and useful activity. Every exertion is encouraging, because to present amusement it joins the promise of some future good.... This is the picture in the light it is presented to my mind; now let me have it in yours.[5]

Jefferson's letter to Bingham presents an early version of "the great trans-Atlantic legend,"[6] a myth of the ideal family held together by women and their hard-working husbands, yeoman farmers who would in turn become the backbone of republican society. Given his parochial upbringing and his steady diet of classical readings, the Virginian's caricature was predictable, as was his belief—shared by all of the founding fathers—that women carried the entire burden of the family and, by extension, social harmony. John Adams was even more sweeping in his convictions about the critical role women had played in the success or failure of republics throughout history. "The Manners of Women, are the surest Criterion by which to determine whether a Republican Government is practical in a Nation or not. The Jews, the Greeks, the Romans, the Swiss, the Dutch, all lost their Republic Principles and habits, and their Republican Forms of Government, when they lost the Modesty and Domestic Virtues of their Women."[7]

No doubt Jefferson was aware of the upsurge of interest among French intellectuals on the eve of the Revolution as to what a woman's role and rights should be in a rational, modern republic. But his paean to the domestic world of American women paraphrased a passage from Horace describing the ideal pastoral wife, which Jefferson had copied into his *Commonplace Book* as a young man: "If a modest wife shall do her part in tending home and children dear, piling high the sacred hearth with seasoned firewood against the coming of her weary husband, penning the frisking flock in wattled fold, draining their swelling udders, and drawing forth this year's sweet vintage from the jar, preparing an unbought meal... what joy to the sheep hurrying homeward from pasture, to see the wearied oxen dragging along the upturned ploughshare... and the homebred slaves, troop of a wealthy house, ranged around the gleaming Lares!"[8]

Anne Bingham, like Abigail Adams, did not hesitate to challenge the Virginian's biases. She came to the defense not only of French women but of the rights of women generally, calling his "candor... rather overcharged" and in need of a strong rebuttal. Her lively riposte sheds light on the growing spirit of equality that the women in Jefferson's international circle were asserting:

> The state of Society in different countries requires corresponding Manners and Qualifications. Those of the french Women are by no means calculated for the Meridian of America, neither are they adapted to render the Sex so amiable or agreeable in the English acceptation of those words. But you must confess that they are more accomplished, and understand the Intercourse of society better than any other country. We are irresistibly pleased with them, because they possess the happy Art of making us pleased with ourselves; their education is of a higher Cast, and by great cultivation they procure a happy variety of genius, which forms their Conversation to please either the Fop or the Philosopher.

In what other Country can be found a Marquise de Coigny, who, young and handsome, takes a lead in all fashionable Dissipation of Life, and at more serious moments collects at her House an assembly of the Literati, whom she charms with her Knowledge and her bel Esprit. The Women of France interfere in the politics of the Country, and often give a decided Turn to the Fate of empires. Either by the gentle Arts of persuasion, or by the commanding force of superior Attractions and Address, they have obtained that Rank and Consideration in society, which the Sex is intitled to, and which they in vain contend for in other Countries. We are therefore bound in Gratitude to admire and revere them, for asserting our Privileges, as much as the Friends of Liberties of mankind reverence the successful Struggles of American Patriots.[9]

Even Diderot was not prepared to admit women to the highest circles of the philosophes, still the preserve of enlightened gentlemen. In his essay "On Women," he argued that women's apparent inferiority was due to their legal subordination and poor education rather than to any innate differences between the sexes.[10] But it was Condorcet who led the attack on the exclusion of women from the full rights of society in his essay "On the Admission of Women to the Rights of Citizenship." The aristocrat's discourse, heavy with appeals to reason and justice, was as uncompromising as his assault on slavery. "Now the rights of men result from the fact that they are sentient beings, capable of acquiring moral ideas and of reasoning concerning those ideas. Women, having these same qualities, must necessarily possess equal rights." To the argument, implicit in Jefferson's position, that public responsibilities imposed by equality would take women away from their duties at home, Condorcet had a ready answer: an enlightened, educated woman exercising her political rights would be better equipped to raise children as free citizens. Neither Condorcet nor Jefferson wanted to encourage women to take public roles.[11]

The perspective of the high-strung philosophe undoubtedly had been broadened by his recent marriage to the chic, intelligent Sophie de Grouchy. This remarkable woman had not only helped translate Filippo Mazzei's history of the United States from Italian into French; she would also translate into French Adam Smith's *Theory of Moral Sentiments*.[12] In

Lavoisier and His Wife
by Jacques-Louis David, 1788.
Jefferson's friend and fellow member of
the American Philosophical Society was
one of the founders of modern chemistry.
His beautiful wife, Anne-Piettette—
shown here with him in their
laboratory—actively collaborated in his
revolutionary experiments. One of
Jefferson's "martyrs" of liberty, Lavoisier
was among the last victims of the
guillotine during the Terror in 1794.
(Metropolitan Museum of Art. Purchase,
Mr. and Mrs. Charles Wrightsman Gift,
in honor of Everett Fahy)

the Condorcets' apartment in the Hôtel de la Monnaie, the issue of equal
rights was eagerly discussed and the hosts could test their arguments
with the best minds available. The Condorcets were by no means unique
in having complementary intellectual interests and international reputa-
tions. For example, the marquis de Lavoisier and his talented wife worked
side by side on scientific experiments in their splendidly appointed laboratory. Arthur Young, the English agronomist, found Madame Lavoisier
"a lively, sensible, scientific lady" and was deeply impressed by her discussions of the latest scientific treatise of the Irish chemist Richard Kirwin,
which she was translating into French.[13]

The Parisian salon was another unfamiliar public sphere in which Jefferson would have to learn to navigate while acknowledging an uncomfortable equality between the sexes. The atmosphere of wit, intrigue, and
intellectual cross-fertilization, stimulated by a constant supply of new faces
drawn from literature, science, the arts, and politics, was orchestrated by
women of extraordinary intelligence and guile. In the waning years of the
ancien régime, the "reign of women" in the drawing rooms was absolute. It
was in the salons of Madame d'Houdetot, Madame Helvétius, and the

duchess d'Enville that Jefferson first felt his way under the guidance of expert teachers.[14]

As "tumult and contest" mounted in Paris during the spring of 1789, he reported to Maria Cosway in London that love had "lost it's part in conversations." Unable to resist drawing moral conclusions, he claimed that the subject was no longer spoken of in salons and at dinner tables because great cities offered too many distractions that made true love and friendship impossible. In America, by contrast, love was "felt in it's sublimest degree." In other words, it was not so much the political revolution as the unhealthy urban environment that had taken its toll on human affection.[15]

Many aspects of life in the French capital stirred interests and feelings that Jefferson could explore most fully with women. Their sympathetic manners and hospitality to strangers, intellectual independence, and sensitivity to the creative pursuits so dear to Jefferson encouraged him to savor the best of European culture. Abigail Adams, Anne Willing Bingham, Angelica Schuyler Church, Madame de Tessé, Madame de Tott, Madame de Corny, Madame de Bréhan, Madame d'Houdetot, Maria Cosway: each in her own way fortified the lonely widower with emotional and intellectual support. And each found his company irresistible. They, more than any of the men that Jefferson knew well, with the exception of John Trumbull and probably Baron Grimm, shared Jefferson's passion for music, art, and architecture.

In the Jefferson Papers at the Library of Congress, there is a single, undated sheet of paper containing a draft of an outline labeled "On Sending American Youth to Europe." It is not a sketch for one of Jefferson's periodic attacks on European decadence. Rather, it enumerates contributions that Jefferson considered cynosures of high European culture— wine, painting, sculpture, music, poetry, architecture, public gardens. Beginning with "Government. Pure Despotism" and ending with "Soil, Climate and Agriculture," the outline appears to be a loose framework for a projected essay on contemporary France. But the categories also serve as an index to the experiences and qualities that Jefferson often identified with his close women friends. Under the heading "Society," he jotted down the following:

Love	Theatres
Friendship	Concerts
Charity	Balls
Religion	Meals
Children	Talkativeness
Dogs	Sexes have changed business[16]

Painting, sculpture, architecture, and gardens appear elsewhere in the outline. Most of the activities Jefferson lists are pursuits shared with another person. (Dogs were a conspicuous part of upper-class Parisian society, and apparently he did not know where else to slot them in.) Above all, they imply a relationship with the opposite sex. Outside of the salons, theater, opera, and concerts represented the most adventurous new public spaces open to women. They were part of the *beau monde* where women could go on their own or with men they were not married to. Maria Cosway, Abigail Adams, and Marie Antoinette were all devotees of the theater who attended performances without their husbands. The subtly erotic atmosphere of the theater, with its conversations, flirtations, assignations, and love notes, had become an accepted part of the theater-going experience. The *demi-monde* sat side by side with the *haut monde*. Plays and operas such as *The Marriage of Figaro* explored love, adultery, divorce, and other major social and political issues that concerned women.[17]

In putting love and friendship at the top of his list, and conversation—"talkativeness"—at the end, Jefferson highlighted the social activities at which French women excelled. A century earlier, love and friendship had been the central themes of Madame de La Fayette's novels. It was an undercurrent of intimate, often clandestine emotions which animated the flow of ideas in the salons that women had invented in the seventeenth century. In their candid conversation, women set the tone of French social life that Jefferson so admired. "Women accustom us to discuss with charm and clearness the dryist and thorniest subjects," Diderot noted. "We talk to them unceasingly: we listen to them: we are afraid of tiring or boring them. Hence we develop a particular method of explaining ourselves easily that passes from conversation into *style*."[18] Politics and political intrigue were never far below the surface of these exchanges.

As Gouverneur Morris remarked after a brisk exchange with the politically savvy Madame de Corny, France was "the Woman's country."[19]

Although Jefferson retreated sporadically into old patriarchal attitudes—it is surprising that he did not do it more consistently—his close and unprecedented engagement with female society was among the major legacies of his European experience. Significantly, the husbands of the strong, independent women in his growing circle of friends seem to have remained in the background. Jefferson usually acknowledged them politely, but they were not members of his "coterie." Anne Bingham's pushy husband actively stirred the envoy's dislike. "*He* will make *you believe he* was on the most intimate footing with the first *characters in Europe* and versed in the *secrets* of every *cabinet*," Jefferson wrote Madison. "Not a word of this *is true. He* had a rage for being *presented* to *great men* and had no *modesty* in the methods by which he could effect it. If *he obtained access* afterwards it was with such as who were susceptible of impression from the *beauty of his* wife."[20] The italics represent the coded portion of his unflattering portrait.

William Bingham had made a huge fortune in the war and in 1780 married the well-connected Anne Willing, whose father had also done well financially as a partner of Robert Morris. Bingham was twelve years older than Anne, who was sixteen when they were married. In 1783 the restless, ambitious husband was ready to make a splash in European capitals when he and his glamorous wife embarked for London and Paris. Their extravagant style attracted attention wherever they went. To the Adamses and Jefferson, their display of wealth was not only unbecoming, it contradicted all of the propaganda about American republican virtue that Adams and Jefferson had worked so hard to spread. There was quiet satisfaction when Nabby Adams reported to a Boston friend that the Binghams had galloped out to Versailles one day in their coach and four to be presented at court, only to find that they had picked a day when the court was not receiving.

ABIGAIL ADAMS WAS THE FIRST WOMAN to play a part in the Virginian's emotional life in Paris. He regularly called on the Adamses at the Hôtel de Rouhault in Auteuil, a large house with a garden of five acres. John Adams considered it adequate to his station, but Abigail complained of having to scrape by with seven domestics. They would have been

Abigail Adams by Ralph Earl (?), ca. 1785. Although the subject of the portrait was not identified until 1948, Earl, whose name is on the canvas, was in London when she passed through on her way to Paris in the fall of 1784. The severity of the portrait belies the warmth and humor that so captivated Jefferson when he first met Abigail. (New York State Historical Association, Cooperstown)

"hooted at as ridiculous" if they had made do with fewer, she told her sister, Mrs. Cranch. The Spanish ambassador to France had a staff of seventy servants, and the English ambassador had at least fifty.[21] No doubt Abigail taught Jefferson about the aggravating "etiquette" and rigid hierarchy of French servants; he had encountered similar difficulties in trying to set up his own household. Encouraged by her warm interest in his personal affairs, he introduced Abigail and her daughter Nabby to the latest fashions in the Paris shops. The silk hose made by the Hermits of Mont Calvaire were an immediate hit, and Jefferson continued to supply the Adams women with Parisian hosiery after they moved to London.

Abigail's staunch New England personality was animated by a droll sense of humor and a tart tongue. She held independent, forthright political views and became an ardent disciple of Edmund Burke. Although she had never gone to school in her life, her strong intellectual constitution and self-confidence allowed her to express opinions freely. Her assessments of

Interior of the Hôtel de Rouhault.
The Adams' residence in Auteuil in 1784–85 was a large mid-eighteenth-century house that Jefferson visited often before his friends moved to London. "There are few houses with the privilege which this enjoys, that of having the saloon, as it is called, the apartment where we receive guests on the first floor," Abigail Adams reported to her sister. (Photo by Adelaide de Menil)

public figures were often critical; Molière, she said, may have been an honest man, but if so, he had not "coppied from his own heart." Seventeen-year-old John Quincy Adams was living with his family in Auteuil and often visited Jefferson. The Adamses in turn took an interest in Patsy Jefferson's adjustment to the convent atmosphere of Panthémont; Abigail and Nabby accompanied Patsy and her father to witness the ceremony of the taking of the veil.

Adapting quickly to social and diplomatic customs, the Adamses were soon giving at least one dinner a week for visiting Americans. According to Abigail, the other American ministers were expected to do the same. When Jefferson entertained, he respected French customs that Abigail found peculiar. "Men rarely sit down before dinner and often block the fireplace in the winter," she complained. "At dinner, the ladies and gentlemen are mixed, and you converse with him who sits next you, rarely speaking to persons across the table.... Conversation is never general, as with us, for when the company quit the table, they fall into *tête-à-tête* of two and two, when the conversation is in a low voice."[22]

When the Adamses moved to England in the spring of 1785, Abigail regretted leaving the friend whom she considered "one of the choice ones of the earth."[23] In her first letter to Jefferson, she wrote that she wished he could have shared his "favorite passion" with her at a performance of Handel's *Messiah* in Westminster Abbey. His reply is full of the bantering, conversational charm reserved for his women correspondents. Quoting some uncomplimentary verses about a Saxon princess composed by the French ambassador to Saxony, he reported that the diplomat had promptly been arrested and the French newspaper in which the verses had appeared closed down. Ironically, Jefferson praised the "energy" of the French censor in acting so quickly. He had met "the old Countess d'Hocquetout" (Madame d'Houdetot) at her country place in Sannois, where she lived with her husband and her lover. He had heard a nightingale singing in the garden, but chauvinistically pronounced its music inferior to "our [American] mockingbird, and fox-coloured thrush." He closed by asking Abigail's advice on submitting his house rent to Congress as part of his ministerial expenses.[24]

Abigail didn't hesitate to send the envoy on shopping expeditions for shoes and three decorative *plateaux de dessert* for her dining table, firmly specifying which gods and goddesses she wanted in bisque to embellish them. "With respect to the figures," he replied,

> I could only find three of those you named, matched in size. These were Minerva, Diana, and Apollo. I was obliged to add a fourth, unguided by your choice. They offered me a fine Venus; but I thought it out of taste to have two at the table at the same time. Paris and Helen were presented. I conceived it would be cruel to remove them from their peculiar shrine. When they shall pass the Atlantic, it will be to sing a requiem over our freedom and happiness. At length a fine Mars was offered, calm, bold, his faulchion not drawn, but ready to be drawn. This will do, thinks I, for the table of the American Minister in London...offering adoration to that titular god also who rocked the cradle of our birth, who has accepted our infant offerings, and has shewn himself the patron of our rights and avenger of our wrongs.

Having delivered this flirtatious tribute, Jefferson inquired about the economies of buying tablecloths and napkins in London.[25]

Following their reunion in London in the summer of 1786, the two friends traveled together to several of England's renowned stately houses and gardens. Afterward, their correspondence recommenced with news, political gossip, and shopping lists. But Abigail's hawkish reaction to Shays' Rebellion in western Massachusetts early the following year brought a perceptible coolness to their letters. She strongly opposed Jefferson's "laudable" but misguided spirit, supporting instead "vigorous measures to quell and suppress" the "mobbish insurgents."[26] The uprising of debtors and farmers in 1786, finally put down the following year, was a diplomatic embarrassment to Jefferson: it undermined European confidence in the American experiment. While he opposed "irregular interpositions of the people," he was instinctively sympathetic to the grievances expressed by the insurgents and argued for a light punishment when the troublemakers were arrested. He was divided on a little rebellion, "a storm in the Atmosphere."[27]

ABIGAIL DID NOT WRITE AGAIN FOR FOUR MONTHS. On June 26, 1787, her warm, maternal spirit revived briefly in a letter announcing the safe arrival of Jefferson's daughter Polly, who was staying with the

Adamses on her way from Virginia to Paris. Abigail was immediately captivated by the bright eight-year-old. Polly, unhappy about leaving her familiar Virginia, had crossed the Atlantic with a servant who appeared to Abigail scarcely older than her mistress. "The old Nurse whom you expected to have attended her was sick and unable to come," Abigail wrote to Jefferson. "She has a girl 15 or 16 with her, the Sister of the Servant you have with you." James Hemings's sister, Sally, was actually fourteen years old. She had been substituted at the last minute to act as Polly's traveling companion. It is difficult to imagine why Jefferson's in-laws in Virginia chose a child to undertake such a difficult mission. Certainly, Sally was not the mature chaperone Jefferson had requested.

Sally Hemings had not only been Polly's maid and close friend for seven or eight years, she was probably her aunt as well. According to family tradition, John Wayles, Martha Jefferson's father, was also the father of Sally by his slave Betty Hemings. When Wayles died, the Hemings family, including James and Sally, had passed with some 130 other slaves to the Jeffersons.[28] This family connection may have influenced the Eppeses in entrusting Polly to Sally's care. The Hemings children's reputation for intelligence and dependability may also have figured in their decision.

On June 27 Abigail wrote to Jefferson that she was at a loss to know what to do with little Sally, who seemed to be in a state of shock in a strange country after the long sea voyage. Sally was "quite a child" and, frankly, needed more care than Polly. Though good-natured, she was "wholly incapable of looking after" Jefferson's daughter. According to the ship's captain, she had been no help whatever on the crossing. "Captain Ramsey is of the opinion will be of so little Service that he better carry her back with him," Abigail reported. Jefferson, who had just returned from the south of France, sent his servant Adrien Petit to escort the two girls from London to Paris. Abigail, shocked that he had not come himself, described the tearful departure, observing that Polly "did think you would have taken the pains to have come here for her, and not have sent a man whom she cannot understand."[29]

Polly and Sally finally arrived at the Hôtel de Langeac on July 16, two weeks before Polly's ninth birthday. Abigail had suggested that Jefferson arrange for a tutor to teach Polly at home instead of sending her to join her sister at Panthémont. "I regret that such fine spirits must be spent behind the walls of a convent," Abigail wrote to her sister. But "Mademoiselle Polie" was enrolled at Patsy's school, where, according to her father, she made an instant hit with students and faculty.[30] Somewhat defensively, Jefferson explained to his relatives in Virginia that the convent had "as many protestants as Catholics, and not a word is spoken to them on the subject of religion."[31]

Despite the attention she has received from historians, Sally Hemings remains a shadowy presence in the envoy's life. Until Fawn Brodie's biography of Jefferson appeared in 1974, she was referred to stereotypically as "Dusky Sally," "Monticello Sal," or just plain Sally. Her identity has been further obscured by historians determined to refute the claim that she became the Virginian's mistress in Paris. But the evidence is meager. Apart from nine notations in Jefferson's *Memorandum Book* recording purchases of clothing, her servant's pay, and a fee for smallpox vaccination, Sally Hemings is completely absent from the Paris record. We know nothing of her living arrangements or duties at the rue de Berri. Her wages were twelve livres a month, the same as her brother's until he finished his training as a chef. The record shows payments for only ten months of work, although she was in Paris for twenty-six. Jefferson's notation in April 1789—"Dupré 5 weeks board of Sally washing etc."—is of little help. Given her lack of training and education, it is difficult to imagine how Sally fitted into the arcane hierarchy of French servants, although she did manage to learn some French. She was known to at least one of Polly Jefferson's classmates at the convent, and there has been reasonable speculation that she acted as maid for the Jefferson girls while they were in school.[32]

In 1873 Sally Hemings's son Madison recalled to a newspaper interviewer in southern Ohio that his mother had told him that Jefferson was his father and that she had become the envoy's "concubine" in Paris.[33] This claim cannot be conclusively substantiated. But Madison's assertion that Sally and James Hemings had refused to accompany Jefferson back to Virginia until he promised to free her children at age twenty-one (according to Madison, Sally was pregnant when she left Paris) is supported by the fact that her four surviving children were indeed freed at that age. Rumors of an affair circulated as early as Jefferson's first term as president. That none of his French acquaintances ever alluded to a liaison in their diaries is not necessarily conclusive. As Annette Gordon-Reed has observed, "caution is certainly required when making judgments about an aspect of human life—sexuality—that is so personal and likely to be influenced by a myriad of hidden subtleties and nuances."[34]

On purely practical grounds, it is difficult to see how Jefferson could have kept an affair with Sally Hemings secret. The Hôtel de Langeac was a relatively small, semipublic establishment always open to visitors: the second floor had only two bedrooms in addition to the large oval room where the minister worked and slept. William Short was a full-time resident, house guests regularly put up, and Patsy and Polly also lived at the rue de Berri during their last six months in Paris. The daily traffic of visitors, tutors, guests, and servants has not left a single shred of evidence of the putative liaison. Jefferson scholars, however, have not lacked imagination in exonerating him. Garry Wills, for example, accepting the possibility of an affair, has likened Hemings to "a healthy and obliging prostitute" who presumably led her master on. Conjectures about the supposed relationship have also provided material for the fertile inventions of novelists and film makers.[35]

MARIA COSWAY'S BRIEF ENTRY into Jefferson's life during the fading days of summer and early fall of 1786 has also attracted the interest of biographers and novelists. John Trumbull first introduced them, but the crucial four pages of his diary beginning on August 19, documenting the date and circumstances, are unfortunately missing. Trumbull discreetly recalled years later "that this time was occupied with the same industry in examining whatever relates to the arts, and that Mr. Jefferson joined us almost daily; and here commenced the acquaintance with Mrs. Cosway; of which very respectful mention is made in his correspondence."[36]

Jefferson leaves no doubt that he was carried away by the "golden-haired Anglo-Saxon, graceful to affectation and highly accomplished in music," as one contemporary described her. From the moment they met at the Halle aux Bleds, his "Heart" (as it tells the "Head" in the famous dialogue that he would send her after their first parting) was "dilating" with its "new acquaintances, and contriving how to prevent a separation from them." No time was lost in canceling a full day of engagements on the spot. "Lying messengers were...dispatched into every corner of the city" with flimsy excuses, including one to the duchess d'Enville rudely regretting a dinner invitation at the last minute, telling her that some dispatches had arrived that needed immediate attention.[37]

Of all the women in Jefferson's circle of friends in Paris, Cosway stands out for her exotic background, her deeply religious yearnings, and her serious but unfulfilled creative talents in painting and music.[38] A note of self-doubt and emotional confusion is heard in several of her letters to Jefferson. She confessed in her memoirs that her early inclination was to be a nun. The middle-aged Virginian, sixteen years older than Maria, had never met anyone quite like her before, and the aura of the cosmopolitan demimonde which surrounded her and her friends no doubt added to her attraction. As a guileless American, Jefferson too exuded an exotic quality of a different brand, but his complex, intellectual inner world was one that Cosway could not fully comprehend or comfortably enter. One gets the impression that the qualities each saw in the other were something different than their actual personas.

Both Jefferson and Cosway enjoyed the opera and theater, where they could privately partake of each other's company. In a particularly moving passage in one letter, he longed for a message from her "brimful of affection" and promised to read it "with the dispositions with which Arlequin in les deux billets, spelt the words 'je t'aime'"—an allusion to an aria they had heard together at the Théâtre des Italiens.[39]

Maria Cosway had been born in Florence, where her father, Charles Hadfield, had moved from Britain in the 1740s and opened a popular inn, a favorite stopping place for English nobility and gentry on the Grand Tour. Tragedy struck when Maria was quite young: of six brothers and sisters, only she and two others escaped the hands of a mad nurse acting under a delusion that she was dispatching the Hadfield children to an early heavenly reward. This early trauma no doubt contributed to Maria's intense religious bent.

At the convent where she first studied music, languages, and drawing, Maria's precocious talent in painting was encouraged, winning her election to the Florentine Academia del Disegno in 1778, when she was

Maria Cosway. Mezzotint by Valentine Green after self-portrait, 1787. Deeply Catholic, Cosway defiantly displays the cross as she looks the viewer squarely in the eye in this bold, self-confident image, unusual for the crossed arms. (Collection of William S. Adams)

eighteen. She studied with Johann Zoffany and, during an extended trip to Rome in 1778–79, was able to work with Pompeo Batoni, his rival Raphael Mengs, and Henry Fuseli. Her musical gifts were also promising, and she served for a time as the organist in the Florentine Monastery of the Visitation.[40]

Three years after her father died in 1776, Maria and her mother moved to London, where the painter Angelica Kauffmann introduced her to prominent artists, writers, politicians, and collectors. Kauffmann also found her a sponsor, the antiquarian/collector Charles Townley, whom Maria had first met in Florence. Townley was the center of a small circle that included Francesco Bartolozzi, the Virginia expatriates Lucy and John Paradise, James Boswell, and Richard Cosway. Another regular guest at Townley's Park Street house was the antiquarian Pierre-François Hugues, whom Jefferson and Maria called "mr. Danquerville" (d'Hankerville). An enterprising, vaguely disreputable dabbler in cults, d'Hankerville had worked his way into Townley's confidence, no doubt entertaining him with the erotic illustrations he had copied from William Hamilton's Greek vases to illustrate his luridly titled *Monumens de la vie privée des douze Césars* and

Monumens du cult secret des dames romaines. He was to catalogue the impressive collection of ancient sculpture that Townley had acquired in Italy. The future Mrs. Cosway probably met her husband at Townley's house in 1780.

Maria downplayed her artistic and musical abilities, treating them as amateur social accomplishments useful in promoting her husband's career. She frankly admitted that "the novelty and my Age Contributed more than the real Merit" of her art. "Had Mr. C. permitted me rank professionally I should have made a better painter but left to myself by degrees instead of improving I lost what I had brought with me from Italy of my early studies." Maria Cosway's marriage in 1781 was negotiated by her mother with a generous settlement, according to a contemporary, James Northcote. The family was running out of money and the ridiculous but highly successful miniaturist, who was a year older than Jefferson, had offered the highest price, to the envy of some of his rivals. He was now ready to exploit his royal connections, becoming the prince of Wales's chief artistic advisor and decorator.[41]

The Cosways' marriage appeared congenial for the first few years and Maria exhibited at the Royal Academy. Her subjects were drawn largely from mythology, such as the *Works of Ossian*, the fictitious epic that Jefferson had shared with Chastellux during the marquis' visit to Monticello. Whatever domestic tensions smoldered beneath the surface, the pair adroitly papered over them with a glittering social life, often masquerading as historical figures such as Heloise and Abelard; Cosway claimed to own the poet's skull. Schomberg House, their establishment on Pall Mall, had already earned a reputation before the Cosways moved in as the headquarters of the sex therapist Dr. James Graham, who lectured on his "Grand Celestial Bed" that decorated his notorious "Temple of Health and Hymen." William Hazlitt, who frequented their bizarre soirées, wrote that the Cosways "kept house in style, in a sort of co-partnership, of so novel a character, as to surprise their new neighbors, astonish their old friends, and furnish wonderment for the table-talk of the town."[42]

A friend of Angelica Church told Gouverneur Morris that Schomberg House was "considered as one of those where, from the very mixed Companies which frequent it, dangerous connections may be formed."[43] Horace Walpole spent a memorable evening at "Mrs. Cosways' Diet," where he

met Prince Oghinski, "who has so great a share in the revolution of
Poland, and was king of it for four-and-twenty hours." Other "person-
ages" spotted by Walpole were the profligate politician John Wilkes and
the notorious transvestite, spy, and diplomat Mademoiselle la Chevalière
d'Eon, who gave fencing exhibitions for the guests. Walpole also mentioned Rev. Benjamin Latrobe, "chief of the Moravians" and the father of
the future architect of the Capitol in Washington. Maria Cosway was, by
any definition, an international hostess.

Yet Maria grew deeply dissatisfied with her London life, so far from
the world she had known in Italy. "I must return as soon as possible to my
occupations in order not to feel the rigor of the Melancholy which is
inspired by this unpleasant climate," she confessed (in Italian) to Jefferson
in her first letter to him from London, written on October 30.[44] Feeling
isolated and alien in England, she also missed the comforting milieu of
Catholic churches and religious institutions. "There are no Monasteries
which contain men of God who at all hours pray for us and for all of those
who do not pray, all who are lost." A small cross on a long black ribbon
rests on her folded arms in the self-portrait she painted the year she met
Jefferson in Paris. In its bold, almost twentieth-century directness, the
portrait brings to mind Tiberius Cavallo's description of Mrs. Cosway as
"the Magnetic muse"—a reference to mesmerism, which the Cosways had
enthusiastically taken up. Jefferson realized that Maria "joined enthusiasm
and religion," as he delicately put it, but he was surprised when Angelica
Church reported in 1793 that their friend had abruptly left her small
daughter and husband in London to study painting in Italy and to retire
for a time to a convent in Genoa. "I thought that very enthusiasm would
have prevented her from shutting up her adoration of the God of the universe within the walls of a cloister," he wrote back.[45]

Rumors swirled around the prince of Wales, and the Cosways' house
was an easy target. Mistresses and hangers-on were openly welcomed by
the eccentric painter and his wife, prompting George III to rebuke his son,
"Among *my* painters there are no fops."[46] Not only was Maria Cosway
linked romantically with the dissolute prince, the Italian castrato Luigi
Marchesi's name was added to her alleged list of conquests. The Corsican
hero Gen. Pasquale Paoli seems to have occupied a special place in her

Madame de Tessé, artist unknown. Jefferson was immediately attracted by Madame de Tessé, who shared his enlightened ideas and his passion for gardening. Known as a philosophe, she was, as one acquaintance put it, "a skeptic except about her own infallibility." (Collection of François Schlumberger)

heart. Richard Cosway's Titianesque portrait of Paoli hung in her bedroom in London, and she later took it to Italy, along with Trumbull's portrait of Jefferson that she was given in 1788. Eyebrows had also been raised over Townley's too paternal interest in the fatherless Maria Hadfield when she first arrived in London. Although she had many women friends as well, her striking looks and alluring manners aroused envy and may have contributed to her racy reputation.

IN CONTRAST TO THE NEUROTIC, mercurial, often light-headed Maria Cosway, Madame de Tessé, like Abigail Adams, provided the Virginian a solid friendship underpinned by her warm, firm, generous hospitality. Two years older than Jefferson, she was born Adrienne-Catherine de Noailles. She was the aunt of Adrienne de Lafayette, and it was through the Lafayettes that she met the American envoy. Their common interests in gardening and liberal ideals insured that their friendship would last until the countess's death in 1814. Madame de Tessé wore her political convictions on her sleeve; Gouverneur Morris pronounced her "a republican of the first feather." Her natural grace and dignity deflected attention

The Hôtel de Tessé.
Built in the 1720s, it was the home of Jefferson's friend the countess de Tessé and her
husband from 1769 until 1790, when they were forced to flee. Jefferson was a regular visitor.
(Photo by Adelaide de Menil)

from the nervous tic that gave her mouth a slight grimace when she talked. "She was one of those ladies of the Old Regime," wrote her niece, the marquise de Montagu, "captivated by the philosophical ideas of the century, and intoxicated by the seductive innovations which were to bring about, in their eyes, the regeneration and happiness of our country. In philosophy, Voltaire, with whom she was closely connected was her master; in politics M. de La Fayette, her nephew was her hero." Another family memoir describes Madame de Tessé's conversation as "sophistical, paradoxical and obscure." Her encounter with Voltaire reportedly had caused her to lose religious faith at an early age, although she "never failed to cross herself in privacy when ill and taking medicine."[47]

In her first surviving letter to Jefferson, dated July 20, 1786, Madame de Tessé thanked him for "un acte qui déploie les privilèges de l'homme" (an act expressing the rights of man), probably referring to the recent French translation of the Act for Establishing Religious Freedom.[48] He had sent her the text along with a catalog of Virginia plants—two quintessentially Jeffersonian gifts. Earlier, Filippo Mazzei had given Madame de Tessé a copy of the first draft of the Declaration of Independence, making her probably the only person in Europe who had access to Jefferson's preferred original text.

Madame de Tessé and her husband had traveled widely in Italy and Sicily; no doubt she advised Jefferson on his archeological tour in the south of France. A letter he wrote to her from Nîmes on March 20, 1787 contains the most lyrical account of his discovery of Roman antiquities. He instinctively knew that she would receive his observations with more sensitivity and understanding than Abigail Adams, whose reading in the Bible, Shakespeare, Swift, and Sterne was more conventional. Jefferson confessed that the Maison Carrée had ravished him like a mistress and that "the sublime triumphal arch" had filled him with such "rapture" as he had experienced on their first meeting.

In the same letter, Jefferson revealed what Bernard Bailyn has called his characteristically "direct, tactical involvement with public affairs." It was this quality that allowed him to cut through the tangled politics of the Assembly of Notables then under way at Versailles. Jefferson knew that Madame de Tessé would be keenly interested in his strategy for breaking the deadlocked assembly. He proposed to restructure the unworkable assembly into a kind of constitutional convention, reducing the number of committees from seven to two. The assembly should then persuade the king, instead of choosing the deputies of the commons himself, to summon those "chosen by the people." "Two Houses, so elected, would contain a mass of wisdom which would make the people happy and the King great," Jefferson declared.[49]

SOPHIE-ERNESTINE DE TOTT—addressed by the courtesy title of madame, though she was unmarried—became acquainted with Jefferson through the de Tessé household. Plain and unfashionable, she was closer to the bluestocking stereotype than most of Jefferson's more stylish female friends. In his first letter to her, dated November 28, 1786, the Virginian thanked Madame de Tott for allowing him to study with her "the rhythm of Homer." He sent her "a few rules of Greek prosody" and enclosed "the best edition extant of your divine countryman Homer"—a teasing reference to her mother's possible Greek ancestry.[50]

Madame de Tott was an amateur painter and didn't hesitate to offer Jefferson critical advice on contemporary painting. Responding to a letter that reached him in Marseilles, he provided a glimpse of the supremely satisfied traveler at the end of an exhilarating day in comparing Chaville to the auberge where he had been staying:

> True it is not the charming gardens of Chaville without, nor its
> decorations, nor its charming society within. I do not seek therefore for the
> good things which it has not but those which it has. 'A traveler, sais I,
> retired at night to his chamber in an Inn, all his effects contained in a single
> trunk, all his cares circumscribed by the walls of his apartment, unknown
> to all, unheeded, and undisturbed, writes, reads, thinks, sleeps, just in the
> moments when nature and the movements of his body and mind require.
> Charmed with the tranquillity of his little cell, he finds how few are our real
> wants, how cheap a thing is happiness, how expensive a one is pride. He
> views with pity the wretched rich, whom the laws of the world have
> submitted to the cumbrous trappings of rank; he sees him labouring
> through the journey of life like an ass oppressed under ingots of gold, little

Les Plaisirs de Chaville, attributed to baron de Tott, ca. 1785.
Madame de Tessé is seen conducting one of her readings in the salon of the Château de
Chaville. (Collection of François Schlumberger)

of which goes to feed, to clothe, or to cover himself; the rest gobbled up by
harpies of various descriptions with which he has surrounded himself.
These, and not himself, are it's real masters. He wonders that a thinking
mind can be so subdued by opinion, and that he does not run away from his
own crowded house, and take refuge in the chamber of an Inn.' Indeed I
wonder so too, unless he has a Chaville to retire to.[51]

Madame de Tessé's superb neoclassical château, designed by Etienne-
Louis Boullée, became a regular stopover for the American envoy as he
rushed back and forth between Paris and Versailles during the hectic days
of 1788 and 1789. At Chaville and in her townhouse in the rue de
Varenne, Madame de Tessé and her friends often indulged in interminable
readings, devoting a month to Samuel Richardson's *Clarissa Harlowe,* followed by Jefferson's favorite *Tristram Shandy* and Plutarch's *Lives.* The
painting entitled *Les Plaisirs de Chaville,* probably by baron de Tott, gives

an intimate view of Boullée's noble salon as the countess reads to her captive, half-asleep audience.

The very sound of the word *Chaville* evoked a perfect world to Jefferson musing in his "little cell" in Marseilles. Later, as president, he would recall the château as a symbol of a vanished civilization where, as Henry Adams wrote, he had "breathed with perfect satisfaction as nowhere else" in his life.[52] The longing to withdraw recurred sporadically at moments of discouragement in Jefferson's public life, and he often expressed it in his intensely private, philosophical letters to women. Only they, he seemed to feel, understood both his antisocial side as a "sublimated philosopher" and his idealism as a man who could "grasp visionary happiness." As he had written to Maria Cosway:

> The most effectual means of being secure against pain is to retire within ourselves, and to suffice for our own happiness. Those, which depend on ourselves, are the only pleasures a wise man will count on: for nothing is ours which another may deprive us of. Hence the inestimable value of intellectual pleasures. Ever in our power, always leading us to something new, never cloying, we ride, serene and sublime above the concerns of this mortal world, contemplating truth and nature, matter and motion, the laws which bind up their existence, and that eternal being who made and bound them up by these laws. Let this be our employ. Leave the bustle and tumult of society to those who have not talents to occupy themselves without them.[53]

THE NEED FOR SOLITUDE SEIZED JEFFERSON AGAIN in October 1787, following his return from the south of France. "The sky is clearing and I shall away to my hermitage," he wrote to Madame de Corny, alluding to his suburban retreat at Mont Valérien. Jefferson sent with his note a recently published memoir of Calonne, the deposed finance minister, now living in exile. Knowing of her interest in public affairs, he could be sure that the book would be welcome, although he warned that she would find it slow going.[54]

Marguerite-Victoire de Corny was married to Ethis de Corny, who had followed Rochambeau to America and became Lafayette's aide in the Revolution. Corny and his delicate, vivacious second wife—Morris called her a "lively and sensible Woman"—were serious supporters of the American experiment.[55] Her gentle, well-bred manners, coupled with her catholic tastes in men, attracted Jefferson and Morris. She seems to have adored them both. Playing the energetic hostess in her house in the chaussée d'Antin, Madame de Corny built a formidable social network that extended from her husband's circle of friends in high government posts to Angelica Church, Maria Cosway, and Adèle de Flahaut, whose circle in turn included Talleyrand and other court mandarins.

Because the Cornys lived not far from the Virginian's first house and their door was always open to Americans, letters between Jefferson and Madame de Corny are rare. She appears briefly in the letters of Cosway and Church and throughout Morris's diary, which records regular visits and dinners but gives few details of her personality. At Adèle de Flahaut's urging, she had arranged for Morris and the uninhibited countess to have their first dinner together at her house, inaugurating their lusty affair. Jefferson and Madame de Corny often walked together in the Bois de Boulogne. His first surviving letter to her, written while she was in London in the summer of 1787, flirtatiously reminded her how much she was missed. "The Bois de Boulogne invites you earnestly to come and survey it's beautiful verdure, to retire to its umbrage from the heats of the season. I was through it to-day, as I am every day. Every tree charged me with this invitation to you."[56]

MADAME DE CORNY, Maria Cosway, and the other European women Jefferson met in Paris did not fit in any way his mythical image of the "republican" wife and mother, devoted to home and family. Martha Wayles Jefferson had been his exemplar of reserve and modesty. Unlike Abigail Adams, Martha apparently had no interest in her husband's political fortunes or in public affairs. Jefferson did not have the nerve to remind Abigail, as he did Angelica Church, that "the tender breasts of ladies were not formed for political convulsion; and the French ladies miscalculate much their own happiness when they wander from the true field of their influence into that of politics."[57]

Jefferson's confusion over the role of women in public life is revealed in a letter to George Washington reporting on the early course of the French Revolution. After declaring his conviction that the first meeting of the Estates-General would go well, the envoy abruptly turned to the destructive influence of women on politics. "The manners of the nation allows them to visit, alone, all persons in office, to solicit the affairs of the husband, family, or friends, and their solicitations bid defiance to laws and regulation." Without "the evidence of one's own eyes," he added, one would not believe "the desperate state to which things are reduced in this country from the omnipotence of an influence which, fortunately for the happiness of the sex itself, does not endeavor to extend itself in our country beyond the domestic line."[58]

Jefferson's unresolved conflict is most apparent in letters to his daughters. Although Patsy was doing well at the Panthémont school, he insisted to her aunt that she return to Virginia soon in order to master "domestic economy." He left no doubt that it was in running a household and raising a family that a woman's republican virtues would shine and her true service to the new society would be properly rewarded. When Polly arrived in Paris and was also enrolled in the convent school, Jefferson reminded Patsy that she must set an example by teaching her younger sister "industry and useful pursuits. I will venture to assure you that, if you inculcate this in her mind, you will make her a happy being in herself, a most inestimable friend to you, and precious to all the world."[59]

Scolding Patsy for using a crib to translate Livy, Jefferson sternly admonished her to remember that, in the best American tradition, she would be equal to whatever she undertook "with resolution." Even conquering Livy would yield practical benefits when she returned to Virginia by teaching her how to surmount difficulties in managing her house and family. Music, drawing, and books were not simply genteel embellishments; they would also help her to deal with the inevitable boredom of plantation life. Sometimes, he reminded Patsy, reading "in dull company" was "ill-mannered," so she must also learn to sew when there was nothing else to do. "The needle is then a valuable resource. Besides, without knowing how to use it herself, how can the mistress of a family direct the work of her servants?"[60]

Jefferson's ideal Virginia housewife inhabited a far different world than his cosmopolitan Paris friends. For the first time, women of means in the late eighteenth century began to travel widely, freely, and often alone. In

breaking out of the old confines of family and home, women were increasingly asserting a power that men had always enjoyed. Jefferson himself
found that traveling "unheeded," "unknown," and "undisturbed" gave him a
feeling of paring his existence to the essentials, an ecstasy that not even the
rich could purchase. This well-being is evident in the notes he made on his
tour through southern France and Italy. It is not simply the recitation of
exotic, interesting sites but an inner calm, a newly discovered emotional
harmony that is conveyed in the subtext. The only drawback, as he told
Angelica Church, was his inability fully to share his pleasure, since the
spirit of friendship was part of "a body which ties it to time and place."[61]

Jefferson's assumption that at least some of the women in his Paris life
were available to travel long distances is evident by the ardor of his letters
urging them to join him. The language he uses is not merely the conventional, playful hyperbole or gush of the period. Madame de Tessé, Madame
de Corny, Angelica Church, and Maria Cosway all seemed to go wherever
and whenever they chose. Jefferson encouraged their new freedom by
sharing with them as equals his own love of travel and the emotional lift it
gave him. Each woman received a warm invitation (husbands are not
mentioned) to come and spend time at Monticello.

The list of "Objects of Attention" in Jefferson's "Hints on European
Travel" is clearly addressed to men, not women. Otherwise he hardly would
have dismissed painting and sculpture as "useless" and "worth seeing but
not studying," given his critical dialogues with women who considered art
an essential ingredient of their civilized world.[62] Maria Cosway, Madame de
Tott, and Madame de Corny were all painters; their interest in and knowledge of contemporary art was more than a passing fad. The conventional
explication of Jefferson's dismissive comment is that it reflects his belief
that connoisseurship and appreciation of the arts should not be high on the
list of priorities in a new country with limited financial resources. This, in
spite of the fact that he would turn Monticello into a veritable museum of
paintings, sculpture, drawings, and prints collected in Europe.

IN A LETTER TO MARIA COSWAY, Jefferson mentioned meeting Angelica Schuyler Church for the first time in Paris in the winter of 1787. She
was, he wrote, equal to "all the good the world has given her credit for." A

sister-in-law of Alexander Hamilton, Angelica had been born in New York to a distinguished Hudson River family. Her father, Philip Schuyler, had been a major general in the Revolution. At age eighteen she had eloped with the Englishman John Barker Church. Returning to London after the war, the couple lived in great elegance. Church became a member of Parliament. Nabby Adams thought Angelica's personality reflected her name but found her husband failing high Adams standards.

Angelica's quiet, unassuming, sympathetic manner made an immediate impression on Jefferson (a friend called her sympathies "democratical"). As many women had discovered, the reserved Virginian could be communicative, confidential, and instructive on many subjects. Angelica responded in kind. In August 1788, six months after they met, Jefferson wrote begging her to return to Paris. "Your slender health requires exercise, requires amusement, and to be comforted by seeing how much you are beloved everywhere.... If you will install me as your physician, I will prescribe to you a journey a month to Paris."[63] That fall, as Jefferson was beginning to plan his American vacation, he boldly proposed that they travel to the United States together:

> Think of it then, my friend, and let us begin a negotiation on the subject.
> You shall find in me all the spirit of accommodation with which Yoric
> began his with the fair Piedmontese. We have a thousand inducements to
> wish it on our part. On yours perhaps you may find one in depositions we
> shall carry with us to serve and amuse you on the dreary voiage. Madame
> de Corny talks of your brother coming to Europe for you. How much
> easier for him to meet you in Williamsburg! Besides, I am your brother.
> Should this proposition be absolutely inadmissible. I will flatter myself
> with the hope of seeing you at New York, or even at Albany if I am master
> enough of my time.[64]

In alluding to Yoric and "the fair Piedmontese," the staid, diffident Virginian had introduced a scene charged with sexual innuendo from Sterne's best-selling *Sentimental Journey*, which Angelica Church had no doubt read. In the novel, Yoric and his traveling companions take shelter in an overcrowded country inn on a "wet and tempestuous night." The parson is forced to share a room with a lady from the Piedmont who has

Angelica Schuyler Church with Son Philip and Servant by John Trumbull, ca. 1785.
Although Angelica Church appeared comfortable in the fashionable circles of London and Paris, her well-bred reserve appealed to Jefferson's own ascetic tastes when they first met in 1787. (The Belvidere Trust)

"a glow of health in her cheeks." After "two hours of negotiations" culminating in a "treaty of peace," Yoric separates himself from the lady by a sheet, but both are left tossing and turning. Finally, Yoric can stand it no longer and breaks the silence. Though he utters "no more than an ejaculation," the lady accuses him of "an entire infraction of the treaty."[65]

The allusion may have been no more than a coy literary fantasy, but Jefferson kept the prospect of the American trip alive for a year. In May 1789, "hourly" anticipating his leave of absence, he taunted Maria Cosway with the possibility that Angelica might still accompany him. His short note closes with a poignant reference to the waning of their own romance: "Be our affections unchangeable, and if our history is to last beyond the grave, be the longest chapter in it that shall record their purity, warmth and duration."[66] That fall, he scribbled a parting invitation to Maria to meet him in Paris when he returned from America. "I count certainly to be here in May. It is a charming month, and should tempt you to travel." By then "perfect freedom and tranquillity" should have been restored to the French capital. Even if that should not be the case, she at least would be "free and tranquil" with him.[67]

LATE IN THE SUMMER OF 1787, Maria had returned to Paris for four months without her husband. Her attraction without her bohemian "coterie" was not the same for the Virginian as it had been the year before. Unlike the fall of 1786, there would be no escapes to follies, royal gardens, or fireworks displays, nor does Jefferson's account book reveal any purchases of opera or theater tickets. Staying with her friend the princess Lubomirski, Maria seems to have served as resident art critic at the princess's salon, where she held court "like the fair Aspasia of old, and FIAT stamped honour on every work she condescended to approve."[68] She also renewed her friendship with Jacques-Louis David, praising the artist so passionately that one observer remarked that her "violent contentions" had blotted out "all remembrance of that law of reason which confers freedom of opinion on all rational creatures."[69]

Near the end of Maria's second visit to Paris, Jefferson asked her to help organize a dinner in her own honor at the Hôtel de Langeac. The brilliant guest list included Princess Lubomirski, Baron d'Hancarville, the Polish patriot Julien Niemscewiski, and the dashing Count Potocki. The latter's interests were, like his host's, encyclopedic, ranging from agronomy to zoology. A distinguished amateur architect, he would shortly begin work on a hair-raising gothic novel.[70] At age eighteen, while traveling in the Mediterranean, Potocki had given chase to the American envoy's nemesis, the Barbary pirates, and for his daring was made a Knight of Malta. But in Jefferson's eyes the count's most fascinating project was undoubtedly his commission to reconstruct in drawings Pliny's fabled Laurentine villa, which the Virginian knew well from the Roman gardener/statesman's letters.[71]

In a note to Jefferson reporting on the progress she was making with the dinner party, Maria blamed him for the infrequency of their meetings over the past several weeks.[72] Whatever romance had drawn the two together a year earlier had definitely cooled; time and distance had taken their toll. Maria impetuously returned to London a few days after the party without giving Jefferson the farewell breakfast she had promised— another sign of their deteriorating relationship. Admitting that she had been "Confu'd and distracted" on their last evening together, she hoped that their correspondence would be "More frequent and punctual" than

Count Potocki
by Jacques-Louis David, 1781.
The portrait of the Polish nobleman
created a sensation when it was first
exhibited in 1781. Potocki was
introduced to the envoy in Paris by
their mutual friend Maria Cosway.
The count's portrait expresses the
romantic, patrician spirit that so many
of Jefferson's circle shared. (Muzeum
Narodowe w Warszawie)

their meetings in Paris had been. She believed she understood Jefferson's
indifference. "I suspected the reason, and would not reproach you since I
know your Objection to Company. You are happy you can follow so Much
your inclinations. I wish I could do the same."[73]

Jefferson did not reply to Maria's letters for several weeks; then he
lamely explained that he had had trouble finding a reliable courier. He
excused his behavior in Paris by saying that she had attracted so many
admirers that she could no longer "move more extempore." How different
things had been on her first visit, when they had "so unpremeditately
mount[ed] into the Phaeton and hie[d] away to the bois de Boulogne, St.
Cloud, Marly, St Germains &c."[74] The line evokes a romantic but enigmatic
passage in Jefferson's first letter to Maria in 1786. After the "follies" of
their first day together, the two "lovers" had ridden out in the late autumn
afternoon "to St. Cloud, from Ruggieri's, from Ruggieri's to Krumpholtz;
and if the day had been as long as a Lapland summer day, you [Jefferson's
"heart"] would still have contrived means, among you to have filled it."[75]

The Terrace of the Château at Marly by Hubert Robert.
The artist captures the decaying, seductive state of Louis XIV's retreat in the 1780s, when Jefferson and Maria Cosway visited it. The château and pavilions were pulled down during the Revolution. Jean-Baptiste Pigalle's *Mercury*, seen at the right of the terrace, was never in the garden but was added by the artist. (Nelson-Atkins Museum of Art, Kansas City, Missouri. Purchase, Nelson Trust)

IN DECEMBER 1787, shortly after Maria's abrupt departure, John Trumbull arrived from London to paint the portraits of the French officers who had been present at the surrender in Yorktown. He had accepted Jefferson's invitation to view the Salon exhibition and his offer of a bed at the rue de Berri. Traveling with the painter was Angelica Church, who stayed with the Cornys. "Have you seen, yet the lovely Mrs. Church?" an unhappy Maria wrote to Jefferson on Christmas Day. "If I did not love her so Much, I should fear her rivalship."[76] Her concern may well have been justified.

During Angelica's two-month visit to Paris, Jefferson discovered a woman who was far less demanding and complicated than Maria Cosway. Like him, Angelica enjoyed both the classics and quiet country life. Knowing that Jefferson admired her good taste, Trumbull engaged Angelica to inspect the elegant new carriage that the envoy had ordered in London, before sending it on to Paris. She presented Jefferson with a silver tea urn—he called it "a perfect beauty"—in hopes that it would "sometime at Monticello remind you of your friend." Both Angelica and Maria asked John Trumbull for copies of the small portrait of Jefferson that he had painted for his *Declaration of Independence.* Angelica acknowledged that Maria's likeness was superior but consoled herself that she possessed a "better elsewhere."[77] Understanding Angelica to mean that she held a better likeness of him in her heart, Jefferson replied immediately: "The memorial of me which you have from Trumbull is the most worthless part of me. Could he paint my friendship to you, it would be something out of the common line....I never blame heaven so much as for clogging the ethereal spirit of friendship with a body which ties it to time and place. I am always with you in spirit; be you with me sometimes."[78]

In his first letter to Angelica, on February 17, 1788, Jefferson confessed: "The morning you left us, all was wrong. Even the sun shine was provoking, with which I never quarelled before. I took it into my head he shone only to throw light on our loss: to present a chearfulness not at all in unison with my mind." Deciding to take his daily ride earlier than usual on the morning of Angelica's departure for London, he had mounted his horse and taken "by instinct the road you had taken. Some spirit whispered this to me." He had ridden as far as St. Denis before turning back. But instead of going home, he had sought solace in Madame de Corny's company, before returning to his study to put his thoughts together in the letter. After these opening gallantries, Jefferson vented his nostalgia for Monticello, reminding Angelica that she had promised to visit him there. His reveries of the American landscape echo the descriptions that he had sent to Maria Cosway little more than a year earlier:

> Indeed, madame, I know nothing so charming as our own country. The
> learned say it is a new creation; and I believe them; not for their reasons,
> but because it is made on an improved plan. Europe is a first idea, a crude
> production, before the maker knew his trade, or had made up his mind as
> to what he wanted. Let us go back to it together then. You intend it a visit;
> so do I. While you are indulging with your friends on the Hudson, I will
> go to see if Monticello remains in the same place. Or I will attend you to

the falls of Niagara, if you will go on with me to the passage of the
Patowmac, the Natural bridge &c. This done, we will come back together,
you for a long, and I for a lesser time.[79]

MARIA, DEEPLY HURT THAT SHE HAD NOT HEARD from Jefferson
while Angelica was in Paris, wrote again in March 1788 reproaching him
for neglect. Although his "long silence" was "unpardonable," she still
wanted permission for Trumbull to copy his portrait. "It is a person that
hates you that requests this favor," she added teasingly. Years later, Maria
took the little portrait with her to Lodi, where it hung in her convent
apartment among other reminders of her former life in Paris and London.[80] One souvenir not found among her belongings was the most astonishing letter in all of Jefferson's correspondence. The original of the
famous dialogue between Jefferson's "Head" and "Heart" is missing, but he
carefully made a press copy before dispatching it to Maria in London. This
singular document, awkwardly written with the Virginian's left hand and
dated October 12, 1786, the day the Cosways returned to London, has been
mined by historians for its maddeningly opaque glimpse into its author's
personality. It has also been closely and profitably read for clues to Jefferson's political philosophy.[81]

The letter was baffling to Maria Cosway as well. After showing it to
several friends, she struggled to answer her admirer, but the words were
confused and incoherent. "Your letter could employ me for some time, an
hour to Consider every word, to every sentence I could write a volume,
but I could wish that my selfishness was not reproaching to Me, for with
difficulty do I find a line but after having admired it, I recolect some parts
concern Me."[82] Then she shifted somewhat more comfortably into Italian.

For one brief moment, Jefferson seemed to have emerged from the
inner sanctum of his private feelings. The ostensible subject of the artful,
spirited debate is whether he should see the Cosways again. The Head com-
plains that the Heart should not have made friends with these strangers,
as "we had no occasion for new acquaintances." But the letter is riddled with
other possible interpretations. Jefferson examines "the divided empire" of
his persona, revealing a man torn between passion for the rigors of science
and reason and an equally strong attraction to sensibility, friendship, and

love. That the dialogue represents an attempt to resolve, or at least dampen, this interior conflict seems as clear as any other explanation.[83]

To the Head's mathematical balance, weighing and trading off pain against pleasure, "miserable arithmetic" and "frigid speculations," the Heart's "generous spasms" reply: "Respect for you has induced me to enter into this discussion and to hear principles uttered which I detest and abjure. Respect for myself now obliges me to recall you into the proper limits of your office. When nature assigned us the same habitation, she gave us over it a divided empire. To you she allotted the field of science, to me that of morals....Morals were too essential to the happiness of man to be risked on the uncertain combinations of the head. She laid their foundation therefore in sentiment, not in science."

Notwithstanding Jefferson's charming invention that he composed the letter while sitting "solitary and sad" before his fire, the careful spacing of lines on the pages suggests that it was the product of meticulous labor. In fact, its composition may well have taken place over several days; there was undoubtedly an earlier draft in addition to the fair copy that Jefferson duplicated. This is important to keep in mind when reading the theatrical opening lines: "Seated by my fire side, solitary and sad, the following dialogue took place between my Head and my Heart....Overwhelmed with grief...I would willingly meet whatever catastrophy should leave me no more to feel or to fear." If the Heart wins the debate, as I believe it does, it is the rational, calculating Head, drafting, correcting, and copying over several days, that has composed the exercise, making sure a copy is preserved for posterity.[84]

Whether Jefferson believed that his dialogue—disguised in a fairly conventional literary device and inspired particularly by Sterne's *Tristam Shandy*—would be understood and appreciated by Cosway is unclear. Maria was accustomed to the sentiments of admirers and suitors, and she often expressed her own emotions, however awkwardly. But she seemed intimidated by the intense feelings expressed in the letter. When she finally attempted to answer it, she found her own heart "mute," saying she could express herself in "friendship."

There are further problems with labeling the dialogue a "love letter" in the conventional sense. At least at the beginning, it seems to be addressed

not to Maria personally but to "Mr. and Mrs. Cosway...the lady and gentleman to whom we had been presented." Jefferson refers to "these good
people," "their merit," and "their friendship," and expresses the fanciful
hope that they will visit Monticello: "Perhaps you flatter yourself they
may come to America?" The dialogue was in fact enclosed with another
short letter and addressed to Mrs. Cosway with instructions for her to
divide the "three mortal sheets" into "six doses of half a sheet each, and
every day, when the toilette begins, take a dose, that is to say, read half a
sheet."[85]

Although Richard Cosway apparently went along for the ride on
some of the Paris outings in the fall of 1786, there is no doubt whom the
Heart is referring to in a lyrical passage recalling

> the transactions of that day.... How beautiful was every object! the Pont
> de Neuilly, the hills along the Seine, the rainbows of the Machine of Marly,
> the terras of St. Germains, the chateaux, the gardens, the [statues] of
> Marly, the pavilion of Lucienne. Recollect too Madrid, Bagatelle, the
> King's garden, the Dessert. How grand the idea excited by the remains of
> such a column! The spiral staircase too was beautiful. Every moment was
> filled with something agreeable. The wheels of time moved on with a
> rapidity of which those of our carriage gave but a faint idea, and yet in the
> evening, when one took a retrospect of the day, what a mass of happiness
> had we travelled over![86]

These lines alone reveal the depth of the author's feelings. Jefferson
had carefully selected the secluded locales outside of Paris not only for
their seductive beauty, mysterious past, and vaguely erotic associations
but also for the pleasure they would give Maria. Both the new *jardins
anglais* in and around Paris and the now unfashionable older gardens and
parks, in their overgrown neglect, represented inviting retreats for an
increasingly liberated public. Like the theater, gardens had become entic-
ing places offering an aura of privacy to couples for brief escapes
together, as paintings and engravings of the period amply document.
The garden rendezvous became a set-piece in opera. The aging Madame
du Barry's little pavilion of Louveciennes, designed by Ledoux as a present from the king, "a monument to the concupiscence of Louis Quince,"

View of the Pavilion of Louveciennes by
Claude-Nicolas Ledoux.
Built near Saint Germain-en-Laye for
Madame du Barry, it was among the
"beautiful objects" the enraptured
Virginian showed to Maria Cosway as they
explored the Paris suburbs in the fall of
1786. (Musée de l'Ile de France. Photo
Giraudon)

attracted a certain notoriety, both prurient and aesthetic. John Adams
dubbed it the "elegant retreat for devotion, Penitence and mortification of
Madam Dubarry."[87] Louis XIV had built the château and gardens of nearby
Marly as a private escape from his own suffocating court etiquette. The
severe lines of the original seventeenth-century terrace and water courses
had fallen into fashionable dishabille through neglect and ever-tightening
royal budgets.

Bagatelle, another extravagant folly, had recently been thrown up in a
record sixty-one days by the king's brother, the count d'Artois, in a reckless
wager with his rumored lover, Marie Antoinette. Just inside the gate, visitors were startled by what appeared to be a preposterous garden embellish-
ment—a model of an American fort on the Indian frontier. The count had
built it for his children to supplement the serious anthropological collection
in Versailles, where he had helped to establish a study cabinet of American
Indian artifacts.[88]

The most romantic stop on this excursion of nascent romance was
the Désert de Retz, built and largely designed by the rich voluptuary
Monsieur de Monville for his own very private pleasures and those of his
friends. The centerpiece of the jardin anglais was an elegant, four-story
apartment set in a wooded glen and concealed by the trunk of a supposedly antique column. The entrance to the amorous little theme park was
its most erotic element: a gate placed in the mouth of a stone grotto
guarded by two naked lead satyrs holding flaming torches.

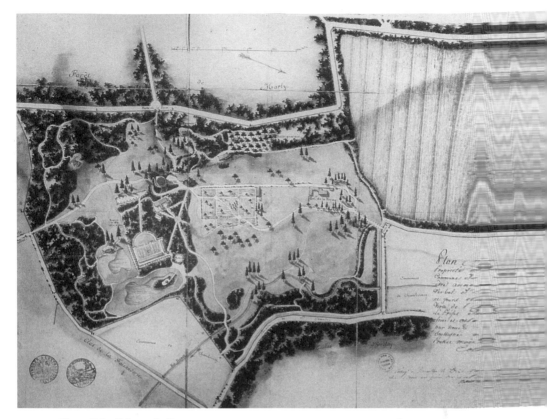

Plan of the Désert de Retz.
The recently built garden that Jefferson and Maria Cosway visited in 1786 is located
edge of the Forest of Marly. Jefferson mentions only the famous Column House, but
were more than twenty other exotic garden structures. (Collection of the author)

The polemical passage about America's superior landscape as s
ized by "our own dear Monticello," so central to Jefferson's ideal repu
society, can be read as a self-conscious attempt to preserve his identity
being assaulted by unsettling emotions of love. The Heart's praise
republican virtues of freedom, friendship, and felicity reveals which si
ferson was on. Even the Heart's references to "digging navigable
making roads, building public schools, establishing academies, ere
busts and statues to our great men, protecting religious freedom, aboli
punishment, reforming and improving our laws generally" become fo
able republican propaganda, although odd in a love letter. It was as

author expected its distraite recipient to show the letter around to all the anti-American "lying newspapers of London."

Having already won the argument in favor of sentiment, the Heart clinches the moral debate by taking credit for the righteous leadership of the American Revolution itself: "If our country, when pressed with the wrongs at the point of the bayonet, had been governed by its heads instead of its hearts, where should we have been now? hanging on a gallows as high as Haman's. You began to calculate and to compare wealth and numbers: we threw up a few pulsations of our warmest blood: we supplied enthusiasm against wealth and numbers: we put our existence to the hazard, when the hazard seemed against us, and we saved our country: justifying at the same time the ways of Providence, whose precept is to do always what is right, and leave the issue to him."

Pulling himself out of reverie to close his "tedious sermon," Jefferson mentions in closing that his friend Jean Henri Latude, the eccentric old raconteur, came often to take soup at the rue de Berri, entertaining his host with accounts of his years in prison. Latude had allegedly been thrown into the Bastille—the marquis de Sade was already there—for writing a few uncomplimentary verses about Madame de Pompadour. Jefferson quotes a few lines, adding a predictable moral to the tale: "How fertile is the mind of man, which can make the Bastille and Dungeon of Vencennes yield interesting anecdotes!"[89]

IN AN AGE RIFE WITH *LIAISONS DANGEREUSES*, Jefferson may not have realized how many complications would arise from his connections and friendships. The embarrassing Williamos affair, when he may unwittingly have harbored a spy under his own roof, occurred when he was still very much a novice on the diplomatic stage. But there was often a touch of naiveté in his first impressions of strangers to whom he was immediately drawn. This was particularly true of beautiful women such as the clever Madame de Bréhan, whose past bore more than a passing resemblance to Laclos' novel. Jefferson could never understand what to him was ingrained French cynicism when it came to romantic love.

If, as he regularly predicted, freedom and peace had indeed been restored to France when he planned to return in the spring of 1790, there seems little doubt that women would have continued to a play a significant role in his life. Angelica Church would most certainly have reappeared, not only to see him but to visit her daughter Kitty, who had been a classmate of the Jefferson girls at Panthémont; Jefferson once invoked Kitty's name to lure her mother back to Paris. Madame de Tessé, Madame de Corny, and Madame de Tott would have carried on their political, horticultural, and aesthetic exchanges with the Virginian. And Madame de Bréhan would have been back with tales of her unhappy experiences in the uncivilized society of New York and Philadelphia. In the relaxed Virginian she would have found a warm, if slightly bemused and wiser, listener who was secretly glad to have escaped the society she described.

With Maria Cosway, however, it is unlikely that Jefferson could have picked up where he had left off. Given her growing estrangement from her husband and the strong religious inclinations that drew her to Italy, neither Jefferson's shoulder nor his embrace was the haven she was looking for. Maria had never understood the Virginian's complex, enigmatic personality clearly enough to enter his life fully, although her half-articulated struggle to do so comes through in her letters. One senses that, in the end, Jefferson never would have allowed his feelings for someone he loved to divert him from the path he had marked out for himself. Theirs was one liaison that was past and would no longer threaten either his heart or his head.

The myth of Europe represented one pole of Jefferson's cultural world; the myth of America—of his "country," Virginia, and Monticello—represented the other. Between them, they generated an energy that illuminated five extraordinary years. He often reacted sharply to the Old World, as in his letter to Carlo Bellini comparing the chaste, domestic state of republican America to the decadence of Paris's female-dominated society. Women, as he told Washington, might undo the holy cause of liberty. Yet he could not deny the enchantment they had given him as he

Column House, Désert de Retz.
More than any other structure at the Désert, the Column House, with its elegant apartment on four floors, appealed to the Virginian's imagination. "How grand the idea excited by the remains of such a column!" he recalled in a letter to Maria Cosway. "The spiral staircase too was beautiful. Every moment was filled with something agreeable." (Photo by Adelaide de Menil)

attempted to come to terms with the new relationship between Europe and America.

In years to come, the encounter between New World innocence and Old World experience, played out by men and women from both worlds, would become one of the central themes of American literature. Jefferson had experienced what Henry James later would call the "banquet of initiation." Like a character in a James novel, Jefferson had confronted in the maze of European society his own deepest anxieties, fears, attractions, and prejudices. He had found, as American writers would later attest, that the "vaunted scene of Europe" was rich in moral content at many different levels. Above all, he had discovered a new type of woman abounding in meaningful, seductive, poetic, even dangerous possibilities.

Chapter 8

"Storm in the Atmosphere"

> Thinking people were content to talk of abolishing all the abuses.
> France, they said, was about to be re-born. The word "revolution"
> was never uttered.
>
> —Madame de La Tour du Pin, May 1789

IN AUGUST 1785, on the first anniversary of his arrival in Paris, Jefferson confided to his friend and former landlady in Philadelphia, Elizabeth House Trist, his candid assessment of French society. His affection for the French people was clear: "The roughnesses of the human mind are so thoroughly rubbed off with them that it seems as if one might glide thro' a whole life among them without a justle. Perhaps too their manners may be the best calculated for happiness to people in their situation." But the repressive French government was another matter. "Bad in form," its authoritarian structure was incapable of producing human happiness. Although some of its administrators were reasonably civilized, the inherent "vices" of the despotic system ground the majority to an ineffectual powder. "Of twenty millions of people supposed to be in France, I am of opinion there are nineteen millions more wretched, more accursed in every circumstance of human existence, than the most conspicuously wretched individual of the whole United states." James Madison, with whom Mrs. Trist shared Jefferson's letter, remarked with surprise that his friend had never "been so full to me on that subject" and warned that such private comments should be handled with care.[1]

Jefferson offered no cure for what he later called the "monstrous abuse of power under which these people were ground to powder." The causes of their suffering were many: the "weight of their taxes, and inequality of their distribution"; the "oppressions of the tythes; the shackles on Commerce by monopolies; on Industry by gilds & corporations; on the freedom of conscience, of thought, and of speech; on the Press by the Censure, and of persons by lettres de cachet"; and the "enormous expenses of the Queen, the princes & the Court; the prodogalities of pensions; & the riches, luxury, indolence & immorality of the clergy."[2]

No one, Jefferson included, believed that the nineteen million wretches at the bottom of the heap were capable of carrying out political reform on their own. In this respect, it would be a long time before the French and American peoples would be political equals. The overthrow of the system by force did not yet appear to be an option. Nor had Jefferson or anyone else figured out how a country of more than twenty million people that had never known a moment of real freedom could be transformed on such a scale into a functioning republic of responsible citizens.

As Jefferson watched the pressure for change bubble up among the liberal nobility and bourgeoisie, and even among the younger members of the powerful clergy, he came to believe that a consensus might be reached on a written constitution that would at least modify the despotic French government, if not sweep it completely away. Still, turning the liberal rhetoric and ideals into action was not in the cards. As late as 1789 Jefferson wrote Madison that the French were "versed in theory and new in the practice of government...acquainted with man only as they see him in their books and not in the world."[3] Even after the unexpected violence of that summer and fall, he reminded an anxious Lafayette that "we are not to expect to be translated from despotism to liberty in a featherbed." Only much later did he admit that "surely under such a mass of misrule and oppression, a people might justly press for a thoro' reformation, and might even dismount their rough-shod riders, & leave them to walk on their own legs."[4]

On August 22, 1785, Jefferson reported to St. John de Crèvecoeur that Cardinal de Rohan, an intimate of the queen, had been arrested and thrown into the Bastille for complicity in a scheme to sell her, for an exorbitant sum, a diamond necklace that she had not ordered. Marie Antoinette's appetite for luxury was reputedly insatiable and, as always when the queen was involved, Jefferson was prepared to believe the worst. "The

Hameau, Petit Trianon, Versailles.
Marie Antoinette's charming stage-set Norman farm village was inspired by Flemish and
Dutch genre paintings. In 1789, Gouverneur Morris saw its true folly: "Royalty has here
endeavored at great Expense to conceal itself from its own eye but the Attempt is vain. A
Dairy furnished with Porclaine of Sèvre is a semblance too splendid of rural life." Members
of the Estates-General walking in the garden ought to recognize "that the Expense and
others like it occasioned their Meeting." (Photo by Adelaide de Menil)

public is not yet possessed of the truth of the story, but from his character and all other circumstances I have little doubt that the final decision
must be against him."[5]

The "Affair of the Diamond Necklace" was the major set-piece of the
pre-Revolutionary drama. The ensuing new wave of scurrilous, satirical
libelles portraying Marie Antoinette as a greedy, spendthrift slut would
ultimately contribute to her downfall and that of the monarchy. The truth
is murky, but Jefferson's rush to judgment was consistent with his deep

antipathy toward the queen and her circle. Nonetheless, he admitted to Abigail Adams that in this case "the Queen had been compromitted without the smallest authority" and the Cardinal, a "debauchee, and a booby," had himself been duped.[6]

In the same letter to Abigail, Jefferson passed on a piece of gossip with political overtones. Fascinated by Parisian couture, he subscribed to the *Cabinet des modes* and occasionally sent fashion plates to women friends in America. He had proposed to send Anne Bingham a box of "caps, bonnets &" chosen by the queen's dressmaker, Rose Bertin. Marie Antoinette, he reported to Abigail, was now wearing only Bertin's gowns made of French cotton gauze, and he wondered "how many English looms" might be decommissioned as a result. But the change in the queen's dress may well have had more subtle implications in France than in the textile business of England.[7]

Before Jefferson arrived in Paris, the queen had struck out on an independent course unprecedented in royal households, taking up with a series of courtiers, *chevaliers servants* who could amuse and distract her from the dull ceremonies at Versailles and the boorishness of the king. Conspicuous in this group was the elegant count de Vaudreuil, who, with the queen's urging and his own West Indian fortune, had mounted for her the notorious production of *Le Mariage de Figaro*. Loving the stage, Marie Antoinette had created near the Petit Trianon a small theater where she sometimes acted. In Paris she frequented the theaters that Jefferson enjoyed so much—the Comédie Française, the Opéra, and the racier Théâtre des Italiens. Such unseemly exposure provided fodder for the pornographic hacks who were busily churning out scandalous doggerel and caricatures of the queen for sale in the stalls and alleyways of the Palais Royal. At another level, the queen's involvement with the theater confirmed Rousseau's earlier attack on the theater and women who frequented it: they became "public women," no better than prostitutes.[8]

Although the open, "natural" manner of dress now flaunted by the queen may have been very much in the new pastoral mode that Jefferson frequently extolled, it was not what the public wanted or expected in its queen. In the political context of her traditional role as exemplar of the obedient, submissive consort of the king, her public independence was unsettling. Marie Antoinette was not only redefining the royal identity, she was threatening the established relations between men and women, husbands and wives, by dramatizing her own femininity. Neither her subjects nor the American envoy liked what they saw, though for different reasons.[9]

For Jefferson, who had much stricter standards than most French people, the queen's demeanor contradicted his belief that a wife should dedicate herself to her husband's well-being and to a happy family life, the foundation on which the virtues of a republican society ultimately rested. Jefferson's passing reference to the queen's preference for simple, loose lawn dresses suggests a personal unease. This new, relaxed fashion, portrayed in the ravishing portraits of the queen by her close friend Vigée-Lebrun, represented a dramatic break with the stiff, conventional, symbolic image demanded by her royal office. As the queen's brother in Vienna bluntly warned her, she wanted all the privileges of the monarchy while pretending to be a private person, and she had better change her ways.

The Virginian's drumbeat criticism of the queen can be regularly sampled in his correspondence. Writing to Madison in June 1787, he remarked that "the king loves business, economy, order and justice," but that he allowed himself to be governed by the "capacious" queen, who, though "devoted to pleasure and expense," was "not remarkable for any other vices or virtues." In early August, sensing that the country was speedily sliding toward the brink, he told Madison that the queen was now "detested and an explosion of some sort is not impossible." It was the envoy's first reference to the likelihood of civil violence.[10]

There were other disturbing signals as well. On his first outing with Maria Cosway in the fall of 1786, Jefferson had driven out to the palace of Saint Cloud, with its secluded, overgrown avenues and lavish water pieces. There they had seen a recent example of the queen's reckless indifference to the country's financial problems. The year before, she had instructed Calonne to hand over millions of francs from the hard-pressed Treasury to purchase the former Orléans property. As one of her friends tactlessly explained, she only wanted the palace to bring "her closer to the amusements of Paris." This, and the sign reading "By Order of the Queen" that she had prominently posted at the gates of Saint Cloud, further fueled public criticism.

Jefferson always blamed Marie Antoinette's extravagance, and particularly her influence over the king, for the Treasury's inability to balance its budget. But he knew that the country's financial crisis stemmed from deeper causes. Most embarrassing for him was France's costly financial support of the American war, which, according to Calonne, had added millions to the national deficit. Interest on the loan ate up 50 percent of the annual budget. The "wall of circumvallation" that Calonne erected around Paris in 1785 to increase tax revenue daily reminded Jefferson of the unpaid American debt. It was not just foul urban air, carrying disease and plague, that many believed would now engulf Parisians trapped behind the ominous tax wall. To many, it signaled a deeper malaise, producing an avalanche of pamphlets, satirical verses, and derisive puns linking the wall to the government's financial plight.

Diamond-necklace scams in high places, new customs duties collected beneath neoclassical porches, and a queen's run on the state's treasury did not necessarily announce the collapse of the social order. As Jefferson closely observed the changing scene, particularly in 1788 and 1789, he saw little cause for alarm. On the surface, American relations with France appeared stable. The gift of Lafayette's bust by Virginia to the citizens of Paris in the fall of 1786 had been a well-timed public relations coup. Jefferson's sincere tribute and the equally stylish response delivered by Ethis de Corny had all the overtones of a ceremony in the Roman Senate. The impeccably staged civic ritual marked a high point in French-American friendship.

A month after the fête at the Hôtel de Ville, an official letter from Calonne, actually masterminded by Lafayette and Jefferson, arrived at the Hôtel de Langeac. In it, the French government gave formal approval to more relaxed trade with the United States. Although the new regulations did not break the farmers-general's monopoly of the tobacco trade, Robert Morris's export monopoly was seriously damaged by requiring the farmers to buy additional American tobacco from other sources. It was a partial victory and Jefferson remained confident that, as Lafayette reported to Washington, the monopoly "must fail by the slower method of mines."[11]

On January 24, 1787 a letter from John Jay brought Jefferson up to date on the recent troubles in western Massachusetts, where disaffected farmers and debtors had been staging their own populist revolt, later to be known as Shays' Rebellion. The trouble had started when the state attempted to raise taxes, sparking resistance by farmers and laborers already deeply in debt. John Adams had predicted with bluff confidence that the "commotion" would not get out of hand. "Don't be alarmed at the late Turbulence in New England," he assured Jefferson. "The Massachusetts Assembly had in its zeal to get the better of their debt, laid on a tax, rather heavier than the people could bear. But all will be well, and this commotion will terminate in additional strength to government."[12]

The rebellion did not end, however, until it was put down by Federal military forces early in 1787. This homegrown uprising against unjust government authority prompted some classic Jeffersonian aphorisms on rebellion, but it also reinforced his optimism about the fundamental nature of government. Jefferson being Jefferson, his sublime, abstract faith in the people made him confident that they alone could solve their problems, even if thousands died in the effort. If the Tree of Liberty needed a little blood of patriots from time to time to make it grow, he added ingenuously, it was a small price to pay.

As fragmentary reports of the Massachusetts rebellion drifted in, Jefferson assured Edward Carrington, a Federalist member of Congress, that Europe had responded positively to the clamp-down on the insurgents. The vigorous action of the state authorities had inspired "more confidence in the firmness of government." Then he launched into a virtual sermon on republican theology that has been reproduced in many collections of letters and anthologies. Among Jefferson's ringing lines is the often quoted charge: "Cherish therefore the spirit of our people, and keep alive their attention. Do not be too severe upon their errors, but reclaim them by enlightening them. If once they become inattentive to the public affairs, you & I, & Congress, and Assemblies, judges & governors shall all become wolves."[13]

Carrington, whom Jefferson had known from his days as governor of Virginia, was not a close friend, but Short had identified him as a "man of merit and patriotism" who was well positioned to act as a sympathetic and politically useful conduit for periodic "letters from Paris." After suggesting that the two men become correspondents, Short laid out some of the more troubling issues confronting Jefferson in Paris with respect to the

Confederation's power to regulate commerce and its ability to discharge its debts. Carrington, in turn, served as a bellwether on congressional thinking. Jefferson would also use him later as a messenger to express his reservations about the new constitution being debated in Philadelphia.

John Jay poured cold water on any "republican" (a word, like *revolution*, just coming into general use) compromise with the Massachusetts troublemakers, declaring that "a mere Government of Reason and persuasion is little adapted to the actual State of human nature in any Age or Country." Yet such attitudes dampened neither Jefferson's sympathy for the insurgents nor his later endorsement of the French Revolution.[14] For him, the future was full of hope and promise. As he told John Adams in 1816, he had always liked "the dream of the future better than the history of the past." But, lacking any real sense "of man's capacity for evil" and having "no tragic sense whatsoever," in the words of Gordon Wood, Jefferson inevitably saw his expansive optimism overtaken by harsh realities, both at home and in Paris.[15]

Abigail Adams replied bluntly to the Virginian's inquiry about the recent disorders in her native state: "Ignorant, restless desperadoes, without conscience or principals," she fumed, "have led a deluded multitude to follow their standard, under pretense of grievances which have no existence but in their imagination." Warming to her argument, she struck at the crux of the old debate: "Instead of that laudable spirit which you approve, which makes a people watchful over their Liberties and alert to the defense of them, these mobish insurgents are for sapping the foundation and destroying the whole fabrick at once."[16]

Jefferson tacitly agreed that, in the fine balance between liberty and order, government was sometimes justified in exerting its power to preserve liberty. But he allowed that he might not have all the facts to his "perfect satisfaction." Expressing his hope that Shays' "malcontents" would be pardoned after they had been subdued, he famously professed: "The spirit of resistance to government is so valuable on certain occasions, that I wish it always to be kept alive. It will often be exercised when wrong, but better so than not to be exercised at all. I like a little rebellion now and then. It is like a storm in the Atmosphere."[17] Adopting the mathematical terminology of the Enlightenment, he reassured David Hartley that a single insurrection in one out of thirteen states every eleven years added up to no more than "one in any particular state in 143 years, say a century and a half." Such distractions would not prevent democratic forces from rescuing mankind from feudal barbarism, religious superstition, and despotism.[18]

BY THE FALL OF 1786, Calonne realized that the fast redemption schedule on the loans taken out by the government during the American Revolution was partly responsible for the worsening financial situation. The annual deficit stood at over 100 million francs, and repayment of the debt had grown to an alarming 250 million a year. Calonne claimed, unconvincingly, that he had been working on his "plan for the improvement of the finances" for two years before presenting it to the king. To win a semblance of public support for the new tax that would have to be imposed, he persuaded Louis XVI to call the Assembly of Notables shortly after the New Year. Jefferson reported the development to Jay, unsure of its implications but noting that the assembly had not been convened in more than a century and a half. He could not provide any details, however, since "this government practices secrecy so systematically that it never publishes its purposes."[19]

Jefferson was pleased that Lafayette and du Pont de Nemours were included on the king's list as delegates, in spite of strong resistance from the marquis' enemies in court. Lafayette's "education in our school" had "drawn on him a very jealous eye from a court whose principles are the most absolute despotism," he wrote to Edward Carrington.[20] Two other members of the assembly, the vicomte de Noailles and Alexandre de Lameth, had actually witnessed the lowering of the British flag at Yorktown. Their presence in the republican camp seemed to confirm Washington's observation that the American Revolution had transformed the French aristocracy into reformers. Earlier in the year, La Rochefoucauld had told his old friend Franklin of his own deepening interest in American affairs: "I often speak of America with Mssrs. Jefferson and Mazzei, and especially with the Mis de La Fayette, with whom I have, since your departure, contracted a very intimate relationship which pleases me more every day, and I see with interest and pleasure that, although your states do not always do as well as possible, they nevertheless often win the right to serve as models for Europe and to restore the full lustre, sometimes on one point and sometimes on another, of the rights of mankind."[21]

The conversations between Lafayette, La Rochefoucauld, and their American friends had become crucial links in Jefferson's diplomatic intelligence network. Abigail Adams remarked that the marquis was the most reliable source of information about the United States when the American postal and courier system failed. Jefferson complained to Monroe that without his two well-connected French friends, he would know nothing at all about what was happening in America.[22]

The king convened the country's lackluster grandees in the Assembly of Notables on February 22, 1787, in a transparent attempt to avoid the far more dangerous step of calling the Estates-General. Everyone understood that the government's motivation was, as Lafayette put it, "at bottom a desire to make money some how or other, in order to put receipt on a level with the expenses." The "notables" included thirty-six great lords, fourteen prelates, thirty-three members of provincial parliaments, and some fifty other worthies representing municipalities outside of Paris. Jefferson unaccountably called them "the most distinguished characters of the nation."[23] Gathered in the Hôtel des Menus Plaisirs at Versailles, they listened to yet more grandiose rhetoric about the financial crisis, an exercise in futility that immediately became the butt of satires and jokes. In one print, a monkey is shown addressing a group of poultry: "My dear creatures, I have assembled you here to deliberate on the sauce in which you will be served."[24]

As much as Jefferson hoped the assembly might let the constitutional genie out of the bottle, leading to further reforms with at least a whiff of republican idealism, he was not encouraged by the Parisians' frivolous reaction to what he saw as an honest attempt to grapple with profound political problems. His attitude was shared by many Americans, who believed, as Henry Adams observed more than seventy years later, that "France was not serious."[25] Jefferson's report of the assembly to Abigail Adams reveals the gulf that existed between the unamused Virginian and a people he dearly loved:

The most remarkable effect of this convention as yet is the numbers of puns and bon mots it has generated. I think were they all collected it would make

Meeting of the Assembly of Notables Presided Over by Louis XVI and Held in the Hôtel des Menus Plaisirs at Versailles by J.-M. Moreau le jeune, 1787.
The call of the Assembly to deal with the Treasury's bankruptcy was the first of several critical steps leading to the collapse of the government. (Photo copyright Réunion des Musées Nationaux)

a more voluminous work than the Encyclopédie. This occasion, more than anything I have seen, convinces me that this nation is incapable of any serious effort but under the word of command. The people at large view every object only as it may furnish puns and bon mots; and I pronounce that a good punster would disarm the whole nation were they ever so seriously disposed to revolt. Indeed, madame they are gone. When a measure so capable of doing good as the calling of the Notables is treated with such ridicule, we may conclude the nation desperate, and in charity pray that heaven may send them good kings.[26]

A few days after the assembly's first session, Jefferson left on his trip to the south of France. Viewing the proceedings in Versailles from a distance, the ardent democrat recovered his optimism and even imagined that the assembly might somehow transform itself into two legislative bodies, vaguely resembling the English system, in exchange for a more equitably distributed tax increase. "Keeping the good model of your neighboring country before your eyes, you may get on step by step toward a good constitution," he wrote to Lafayette. "If every advance is to be purchased by filling the royal coffers with gold, it will be gold well employed."[27] At this stage Jefferson was willing to accept the old order, despite the inequities of a system that allowed the nobility and clergy to escape paying taxes and thus deprived the Treasury of more than half of its property tax revenues. The king might still be bought off and a "tolerably free constitution" put in place without resort to arms. The French, Jefferson declared, should take on only "as much liberty as they are capable of managing."

In a display of "popular absolutism," Calonne had divided the Assembly of Notables into seven tightly controlled committees, each headed by a prince of the blood. The "abuses of pecuniary privileges" were high on his legislative agenda. Jefferson, however, never raised the question of proportional representation in the assembly; nor did he broach the fundamental principle that "the people are not to be taxed but by representatives immediately chosen by themselves." Lafayette, Jefferson's chief source of information about the assembly, dismissed Calonne's claim that the government was bankrupt. In his view, the deficit had been caused by waste, corruption, and extravagance—"sums squandered on courtiers and superfluities"— not by tax loopholes or the underwriting of the American war. Calonne's proposed tax reforms, which would have introduced equality before the law, were defeated, and the provincial assemblies failed to pursue similar measures. Neither Jefferson nor Lafayette publicly addressed the core problem—the privilege embedded in the country's legal and social framework—and it would not surface in the Virginian's correspondence for at least another year.[28]

As the Assembly of Notables dragged on, participants and observers grasped at any indication of a possible shift in power in the direction of a parliamentary monarchy. An upbeat du Pont de Nemours, optimistically believing that the king had transferred some of his power to the assembly, declared that "on the 1st of May France was still a monarchy and the first in Europe. On the 9th of May...France became a Republic in which there remains a magistrate decorated with the title and honors of royalty but forever obliged to assemble his people to ask them to supply his wants, for which the public revenue without this new national consent would be forever inadequate. The King of France became a king of England."[29] Du Pont's fleeting illusion that constitutional monarchy was at hand was not unlike the vision Jefferson conjured in his letters to Lafayette and Madame de Tessé, describing how to transmute the Notables into a proto-Congress instilled with republican virtue.

Shortly after returning to the Hôtel de Langeac in mid-June 1787, Jefferson received a long letter from Madison outlining a plan to replace the old Articles of Confederacy, now in a terminal state, with the "foundation of the new system." First and foremost, the "federal head" was to be armed with the power to control state legislatures in key areas, not only to insure order but to protect popular liberty as well. "The effect of this provision would be not only to guard national rights and interests against invasion, but also to restrain the States from thwarting and molesting each other, and even from oppressing the minority within themselves by paper money and other unrighteous measures which favor the interest of the majority."[30]

To Jefferson, it appeared that his trusted friend and confidant was proposing a wholesale transfer of power to the federal government. Madison's plan, he believed, would concentrate far too much authority in the central administration by giving it veto power over the states, although 99 percent of state laws did not in fact concern the Confederacy.

Three separate copies of the proposed constitution—one from Washington, one from Franklin, and one from Madison—had been dispatched to Paris, and Jefferson studied the text eagerly. Assuring one Frenchman that it was a "wonderfully perfect instrument," he liked the idea of a federal government that could perpetuate itself "without needing continual recurrence to the state legislatures." He also approved of assigning authority for levying taxes to the "greater house," thus preserving the fiction that the people were not to be taxed without representation. But the absence of a bill of rights disturbed him deeply. "A bill of rights," he wrote to Madison in December 1787, "is what the people are entitled to against every government on earth, general or particular, and what no just government should refuse." Such a bill, he went on, should provide "clearly and without sophisms for freedom of religion, freedom of the press, protection against standing armies, restrictions against monopolies, the eternal and unremitting force of habeas corpus laws, and trials by jury in all matters of fact triable by the laws of the land and not by the laws of Nations."[31]

Jefferson could not understand why Madison, who had fought so valiantly for the Virginia Declaration of Rights, now appeared indifferent to including a bill of rights in the constitution. As he wrote to another American friend, "The enlightened part of Europe have given us the greatest credit for inventing this instrument of security for the rights of the people, and have been not a little surprised to see us so soon give it up."[32] To John Adams's son-in-law, William Smith, he expressed a more profound dismay: "But I own it astonishes me to find such a change wrought in the opinions of our countrymen since I left them, as that three-fourths of them should be contented to live under a system which leaves to their governors the power of taking from them the trial by jury in civil cases, freedom of religion, freedom of the press, freedom of commerce, the habeas corpus laws, and the yoking them with a standing army. This is a degeneracy in the principles of liberty to which I had given four centuries instead of four years."[33] In Paris, Jefferson had observed and documented the French government's flagrant violation of each of these sacred freedoms. This first-hand experience gave him a different perspective than Madison, who believed that mere "paper" or "parchment barriers" to dictatorial abuses were inessential, and that the real threat to republican government came from "overbearing majorities."

Jefferson strongly objected as well to the constitution's failure to provide for rotation in office, particularly the office of president. This and the bill of rights were the two basic tenets of his enlightened political theology. The people must remain inviolate in their fundamental rights as citizens and on constant guard against the bugaboo of "monarchy" and privilege. Elected officials could not be trusted and were quite capable of abandoning the virtuous citizens who elected them. Jefferson already detected signs of trouble. As he told Benjamin Hawkins, he was shocked that some of his countrymen were considering "a kingly government as a refuge." He advised them to read La Fontaine's fable of the frogs who, bored with democracy, asked Jupiter to send a new king. The god taught them a lesson by sending a crane who proceeded to dine on his subjects. If that didn't work, he added, "send them to Europe to see something of the trappings of monarchy.... If all the evils which can arise among us from the republican form of our government from this day to the day of judgment could be put into a scale against what this country suffers from monarchical form in a week or England in a month, the later would predominate."[34]

Lafayette, who had also received a copy of the Constitution in December 1787, was generally impressed, though he shared the conventional liberal concern about the power granted to the executive. Still, the American Constitution seemed a "bold, large frame" that might inspire a similar experiment in France if only a truly representative national assembly were called. He realized, however, that a French charter would "bear no comparison with the worst constitution that may be pointed out within the United States."[35] He was also realistic enough to recognize that a French constitution would undoubtedly also be "poisoned with abuses which it is impossible, and perhaps improper for the present to irradicate."

The arrival of draft copies of the American Constitution in Paris stirred up new speculation and exchanges between Jefferson and Lafayette, a kind of informal seminar on political theory in which the American document was analyzed as a model for constitutional reform in a far different setting. They were shortly joined by a distinguished gadfly from London, who had come to Paris to promote an iron bridge he had invented. Thomas Paine, the author of *Common Sense*, had met Lafayette in Philadelphia. The marquis, with Jefferson's approval, was trying to sell Paine's bridge scheme to French interests, but politics quickly took over their deliberations. "Mr. Jefferson, Common Sense, and myself are debating [the proposed constitution] in a convention of our own as earnestly as if we were to decide upon it," Lafayette wrote Gen. Henry Knox, his old military colleague, now secretary of war for the Confederation.[36]

The French crisis continued to deepen in the fall and winter of 1787–88. After attending a dinner in Paris, Arthur Young wrote in his diary: "One opinion pervaded the whole company, that they were on the eve of some great revolution...a strong leaven of liberty, increasing every hour since the American revolution."[37] The government of Louis XVI had desperately tried to strike a bargain with the powerful Parliament in

Paris: in return for its approval of new loans essential for the government to continue to function, the king promised to convene a more representative Estates-General sometime in the future. Parliament balked, however, and on May 2, 1788, the king precipitated a further crisis by commanding the Parliament to act forthwith on his request for loans. When rumors spread that Louis planned to break the deadlock by force, Parliament issued what Jefferson euphemistically, and mistakenly, called a bill of rights. Among the "rights" it asserted was the prerogative of the Estates-General, which had not been convened since 1614, to levy taxes. The only justification for Jefferson's optimism was Parliament's denunciation of *lettres de cachet* and the declaration that judges could not be removed from office.

Reporting to Madame de Bréhan in New York, Jefferson complained that the turmoil was ruining the civilized pleasures of Paris to which they were both addicted. "The confusion here at present is really distressing. Society is spoilt by it. Instead of that gaiety and insouciance which has distinguished it heretofore, all is filled with political debates into which both sexes enter with equal eagerness." Forced to at least appear to be a spectator rather than a participant in the political drama, the envoy was miserable.[38] He told Anne Bingham that the once "gay and thoughtless" city had become "a furnace of Politics," and "men, women and children talk nothing else." Although Philadelphia too had its "political fevers," he trusted that "our good ladies...have been too wise to wrinkle their foreheads with politics." Instead of a political tract, Jefferson enclosed recent issues of the *Cabinet des modes*, along with "some new theatrical peices."[39]

Stung by criticism voiced in the Assembly of Notables of the American government's inability to pay the interest on its French loans or the stipends it owed French veterans of the Revolution, Jefferson had made a fast trip to the Netherlands in March to attempt to consolidate and extend the American loans. His meetings with the Dutch bankers were successful, and by the time he left Paris in 1789, he had secured loans to discharge at least some of the obligations to the French officers. Returning from the Netherlands via Germany, he continued to report to Jay and Madison about developments in Paris, while receiving their views on the slow, zigzag progress being made across the Atlantic to ratify the new American Constitution.

The anxious diplomat again raised with Jay, and unofficially with Madison, the question of reimbursement for his personal expenses in Paris. Aware that the government in Philadelphia was about to be replaced, he was concerned that it might not act before it closed down. "My furniture, carriage, apparel are all plain," he protested to Madison. But "plain" does not describe the twenty pieces of table silver, including ten dinner plates and two tureens, that Jefferson had recently ordered from Mathew Boulton in England, or the extensive collection of new china he had bought for his dining room, or the handsome carriage he was planning to have made in London, for which he had already purchased a fine but not "foppish" set of English harness.[40]

In May 1788, Jefferson confirmed to Moustier the rumor that the desperate king was planning to call the Estates-General, on the heels of a series of disturbances in Paris and the provinces. "The public mind is manifestly advancing on the abusive prerogatives of their governors, and bearing them down," he reported to the king's American representative in Philadelphia. "No force in the government can withstand this in the long run. Courtiers had rather give up power than pleasures: they will barter therefore the usurped prerogatives of the king for the money of the people. This is the agent by which modern nations will recover their rights." Some members of the court party were worried that the Estates-General might get out of hand. "The Ton of Society," Morris noted, adding his usual corrective to the Virginian's optimism, "seems to be that it was not worth while to call the States General for such a Trifle as the Deficit in the Revenue amounts to."[41]

Going to his study on the upper floor of the Hôtel de Langeac, every morning Jefferson wrote countless letters, emerging "worn down" to "sally at 12 o'clock into the bois de Boulogne and unbend my labours."[42] Whenever he broke away from the routine of diplomatic business to reply to a letter from Abigail Adams, Angelica Church, or Maria Cosway, the relaxed pleasure and playfulness in his manner was palpable. One of his letters to Maria opens: "I am never so happy as when business smoothing her magisterial brow, says 'I give you an hour to converse with your friends.'" Complaining that things had turned "gloomy" in the summer of 1788, he longed to savor her company—"an asylum for tranquility"—away from serious conversations that were taking on an increasingly partisan character.

In his close, if uncritical, commentary on the convulsions of the French nation, Jefferson habitually put the best gloss on a deteriorating situation. "While our second revolution [the American Constitutional Convention] is just brought to a happy end with you," he wrote to the "American farmer," Crèvecoeur, in August 1788, "yours is but cleverly under way. For some days I was really melancholy with the apprehensions that arms would be appealed to, and the opposition crushed in it's first efforts. While the opposition keeps at its highest wholesome point, government, unwilling to draw the sword, is not forsed to do it." As the pace of change accelerated, however, a new dimension emerged in Jefferson's thinking. He told Crèvecoeur that France, like Holland, was witnessing "a contest between the monarchical and aristocratic part of the government against the people." He admitted to John Cutting that an all-powerful king would remain a despot, no matter how benevolent. On the other hand, "priests and nobles" were "barriers between the king and people," making a privileged aristocracy as great an obstacle to political reform as the crown.[43]

The friends with whom he was in almost daily contact—Lafayette, du Pont, and Condorcet—were likewise becoming more radical in their thinking. The normally cool, well-bred voices heard in the Assembly of Notables were increasingly sharp and agitated. Taxation and its relation to public policy were openly debated. Broader authority for the provincial assemblies was tabled for discussion at the second meeting of the Notables in November 1788. As the calling of the Estates-General approached, liberal aristocrats became more vocal in opposing its tripartite structure of nobility, clergy, and bourgeoisie, or Third Estate. In their eyes, transforming the Third Estate into an assembly of citizens equal in votes to the other two orders was a critical step on the path to revolution. Filippo Mazzei summarized the situation in his newsletter to the king of Poland: "Aristocratic tyranny is struggling against despotism and monarchy. The pretext is the good of the people, to which, however, the aristocracy here, as it is everywhere else, and always has been, is far more opposed than the monarchy is."[44]

Ignoring the critical issue of equal representation in the selection of members of the convocation, Jefferson still believed that the calling of the Estates-General might lead to the adoption of a bill of rights, "so that the nation may be acknowledged to have some fundamental rights not alterable by their ordinary legislature." A "well-tempered constitution" could follow, "without its having cost a drop of blood," he wrote Monroe in August 1788. The crown had yielded "one right after another to the nation. They have given them provincial assemblies which will be very perfect representations...and stand somewhat in the place of our state assemblies. They have reformed the criminal law, acknowledged the king cannot lay a new tax without the consent of the states general and they will call the states general the next year."[45]

The Virginian's euphoric letter represents the high-water mark of his resilient faith that all would end well under a constitutional monarchy. The very prospect of the Estates-General had spread "the most perfect tranquillity" through the kingdom, he told John Cutting in November.[46] The debates inside (and outside) the Assembly of Notables did indeed seem a long way from the free-for-all of American democracy. Yet there was a growing feeling that an elected body ought to be formed to represent the entire French populace. The question of representation, of the "relationship between the leaders and the led," would, of course, be a central issue in the French Revolution. In America, however, the controversy over class and privilege had ceased to be a concern once all political ties with England had been severed and the leadership was firmly in the hands of recognized leaders.

By the late fall of 1788, organized opposition to the government of Louis XVI had become more conspicuous. In November a group of nobles formed the Society of Thirty, a political club that would later become the influential Patriot party. Condorcet, Lafayette, and La Rochefoucauld were among its charter members. They called themselves a "conspiracy of well-intentioned men" organized to work for reform along republican, constitutional lines by pressuring the government and the Assembly of Notables. One of their favorite meeting places was Madame de Tessé's drawing room in the rue de Varenne. The king, now checked in his powers, nevertheless remained the symbolic centerpiece of the unfolding drama.

By the ancient ground rules favoring the status quo, voting in the reconvened Estates-General was to be by bloc, each of the three orders making its decisions separately. By virtue of their greater numbers, the nobility and clergy—Madame de Staël called them "obscure eminencies"—would of course be the masters of the show.[47] But the Patriots had committed themselves to doubling the membership of the lower Third Estate. This "doubling of the Third" would undercut the ability of the traditional establishment, concentrated in the upper orders, to control the proceedings. Thus a truly national assembly would emerge as a tribunal to debate and settle the country's grievances.

On December 27, in what Jefferson called "a Siberian degree of cold," the worst in memory, cosmic signs converged with national bankruptcy. Louis XVI did the unthinkable: ignoring a last-minute plea from the royal princes, he agreed to the doubling of the lowest estate "by order of the [king's] council." It appeared that public pressure had finally triumphed. Fatally, however, the method of voting was not specified. Jefferson saw that, as he told Paine, the opening of the Estates raised questions that could "never be surmounted amicably."[48] The Third Estate assumed that delegates would vote individually rather than by orders, a misunderstanding that led directly to the Oath of the Tennis Court less than a year later.

Several members of the Society of Thirty were also involved in the new Société des Amis des Noirs. Lafayette had been in the forefront of the organization of the society and its efforts to abolish slavery. Although Jefferson hid behind diplomatic protocol in declining to join, Lafayette's international prominence encouraged antislavery leaders in England and America to establish ties with their French counterparts. Condorcet, another outspoken member, had published a polemic on abolition under a pseudonym in 1781. Linking the peaceful constitutional revolution with the struggle for black freedom, he wrote to Lafayette: "It is in the Estates General that the cause of the Negroes should be pleaded, and it is to you, the hero of American liberty, the wise and zealous advocate of the noble resolution on behalf of Negroes, the generous man who has devoted part of his fortune and some of his brilliant youth to the search for ways to break the chain that his eyes ought never to see—it is to you that belongs the defense there of Liberty and the Rights of man, which are the same for all, no matter what their color or their country may be."[49]

In late December 1788 Jefferson told Francis Hopkinson that "all hands are employed in drawing plans of bills of right." Shortly after the New Year, he added to his library a copy of Condorcet's *Essais sur la constitution des assemblées provenciales*, which had been banned by the increasingly edgy government. On January 8 he sent Richard Price in London a lengthy account of the calling of the Estates-General, giving full credit for the apparent progress to the Patriots, who had been "able to keep up the public ferment at the exact point which borders on resistance without entering on it." The reformers would not win all the rights they sought in the first rounds; rather, "the nation must be left to ripen itself more for their unlimited adoption." John Adams took a more pessimistic view. "I know not what to make of a republic of thirty million atheists," he told Price. "Too many Frenchmen, after the example of too many Americans, pant for equality of person and property. The impracticality of this, God almighty has decreed, and the advocates for liberty who attempt it will surely suffer for it."[50]

Lafayette had long been eager to draft a bill of rights and already had the empty frame waiting for it in the entry hall of his house in the rue de Bourbon, next to his copy of the American Declaration. The marquis worked secretly on his text, not even telling his mistress and confidante Adélaide de Simiane, though Jefferson seems to have known about it. On January 12 the envoy dispatched a copy to Madison, noting its faithfulness to the American model. "You will see that it contains the essential principles of ours accommodated as much as could be to the actual state of things here."[51]

While the country was preoccupied with provincial elections of delegates to the Estates General, Jefferson enjoyed his Olympian detachment from the partisan debates in both France and Philadelphia. To Francis Hopkinson's report that he had been accused of being an antifederalist, the Virginian retorted: "I am not a Federalist, because I never submitted the whole system of my opinions to the creed of any party of men whatever in religion, in philosophy, in politics, or in anything else where I was capable of thinking for myself. Such an addiction is the last degradation of a free moral agent. If I could not go to heaven but with a party, I would not go there at all."[52] On the same day that he was declaring himself the patrician individualist, above and beyond party, he surveyed the French political scene in a letter to Moustier in New York: "The difficulties of procuring money and of preventing bankruptcy, continue always at such a point as to leave the administration no resource but that of appeal to the nation. The nation availing itself of their advantageous position presses on sufficiently to obtain reasonable concessions." Jefferson remained convinced that "the dispute between the privileged and unprivileged orders" as to "how they shall divide these concessions between them" ultimately would be settled in favor of the people without bloodshed.[53]

In a letter written the next day to Madame de Bréhan, the Virginian boasted that a "king with 200,000 men at his orders, is disarmed by public opinion and the want of money." While keeping his eye on political reforms, Jefferson savored the cultivation of the senses in the best Epicurean tradition. Paris, he told Moustier's homesick mistress, was "enlarging and beautifying" with the onset of spring, in spite of Ledoux's tax walls. Fine, broad boulevards had recently been laid out in a circuit of fifteen or twenty miles, exposing the city's unrivaled radiance. A new theater called the Opéra Buffons was serving up Italian operas. Jacques-Louis David was by all odds the reigning painter. Jefferson's inner equilibrium is palpable, taking on a neoclassical symmetry that seems to balance all of his exuberant interests and energy, from David's pencil to the bloodless transfer of political power.[54]

Confined to his house on account of a sudden spring chill, he relaxed by practicing his drawing, producing a design for an avant-garde silver coffee urn to be executed by Jean-Baptist-Claude Odiot. Recalling the elegant equipage he had seen in Paris, and knowing how much Jefferson's Virginia taste prized a smart turnout, his old friend Baron Geismar had asked the envoy to make detailed drawings of a cabriolet and a phaeton for a carriage maker in Germany. As soon as the weather improved, Jefferson drew up plans of "scrupulous exactness," including a sketch for raising the axle of the vehicle. He included them with a letter to the baron in which he reported that the American Constitution was about to go into operation. As for "the revolution in this country (for such we may call it)," it was moving along smoothly and would "end in rendering the nation more free and more powerful."[55]

The recent political turmoil, he told David Humphreys, had improved the normally giddy social life of Paris, lifting the level of dinner conversation. "The frivolities of conversation have given way entirely to politics" and partisan pamphleteering was rampant. "The press groans with daily productions, which in point of boldness make an Englishman stare, who hitherto has thought himself the boldest of men. A complete revolution in this government has, within the space of two years (for it began with the Notables of 1787) been effected merely by public opinion, aided indeed by want of money which the dissipations of the court had brought on." In stressing the importance of "public opinion," Jefferson had identified a central, transforming element of politics on the eve of the Revolution.[56]

IN APRIL 1789, A LATE THAW FINALLY ENDED the devastating winter that had killed off countless people living, homeless and starving, in the streets of the capital. The opening of the Estates-General was postponed several times because of the spring floods and other excuses. A new stage set replacing the one built for the Notables had to be prepared in the Hôtel des Menus Plaisirs, the court's warehouse for props. The election of delegates was complicated and tedious. In Paris, the process first entailed the selection of electors, who would then pick the delegates, giving them firm instructions on constitutional issues. Lafayette was chosen to represent the Auvergne but not his district in Paris. On April 22 he made his way "in Dishabille" to Jefferson's house, where Gouverneur Morris joined them to review the snag in their plans. Morris urged Lafayette to assert his leadership in the city, where he sensed trouble brewing, by increasing the number of French troops relative to mercenaries. Jefferson thought such reinforcements were unimportant. All agreed, as Morris noted, that Lafayette should hold his fire in the Estates-General, speaking only on "important Occassions" in order to make the greatest impact.[57]

Suddenly, without warning, around midday on April 27 the bookseller Hardy was startled by a sharp explosion that rattled his shop near the Faubourg Saint Antoine. Workers in the nearby Réveillon wallpaper factory and in the Hanriot saltpeter plant had marched off the job and into the streets, carrying a gibbet with an effigy of the factory owners. To alarmed bystanders, the unruly throng, armed with sticks and stones and shouting threats against the rich and privileged, appeared to be a full-scale insurrection of the proletariat. The first popular uprising of the Revolution had begun.

The origins of the uprising are obscure, but there is no dispute that the roughly 350 workers in the wallpaper factory were being paid, on average, a paltry twenty-five sous a day. Réveillon had suggested that if the tax imposed on goods leaving the district were reduced, he could cut their wages even more. The manufacturer's application of trickle-down economics became further garbled by the time it reached the factory floor, where the employees knew only that they were on the edge of starvation. On first hearing about the riot, Jefferson dismissed the dispute as "a pretense" on the part of the workers and in no way related to the grand political debates that were consuming the attention of his friends in high places.[58]

A crowd of about three thousand soon gathered in front of the Hôtel de Ville, and the mêlée quickly spread to neighboring districts. Egalitarian cries of "Vive le roi! Vive Monsieur Necker [Controller General Jacques Necker]! Vive le Tiers Etat!" added a comic touch to what appeared to be an alarming confrontation. Returning from the races at Vincennes, Madame de La Tour du Pin and her friends were cheered as the crowd waved their carriage through in the rue Saint Antoine: their coachman was wearing the livery of the popular troublemaker, the duke d'Orléans.

As the riot gained momentum, without much leadership or direction, Hanriot's house was stripped and the contents burned in the street. When the workers, now several thousand strong, were finally dispersed, they turned on Réveillon's factory and gutted it. A detachment of soldiers stationed at the gates of the manufacturer's house was unable or unwilling to save it from the rampage. His furniture, paintings, and library of fifty thousand volumes were dragged out and put to the torch. At last, a large company of mounted troops arrived with two field pieces and, in a swift, violent charge, cleared the narrow, congested streets of all except the wounded and dying. The marquis de Ferrières, a delegate to the Estates-General from

Poitou who saw the Gardes Françaises fire point-blank into the crowd, called it a massacre.

Twelve soldiers were killed and eight wounded in this prelude to civic carnage. Assuming roughly ten times as many civilian deaths and injuries, a total of 150 casualties seems a reasonable guess, making it one of the bloodiest single days of the entire Revolution. Jefferson, who estimated the number at between one and two hundred, calmly assured Madison that "this execution has been universally approved."[59] His reaction to the urban rioters contrasted starkly to his sympathy for the dissidents of Shays' Rebellion in Massachusetts. Nervous officials surveying the catastrophe were shocked to realize that order could no longer be maintained by the city's standing complement of six thousand troops, many of them hated mercenaries. From now on, an army would be needed to protect the people of Paris.

Much later, in his autobiography, Jefferson conceded that such "acts of popular violence" had been "part of the history of the day." In his contemporary report to Jay, however, he distinguished the workers' riot from "the great national reformation going on." The demonstrators were a "mob" of "the most abandoned banditti...unprovoked and unpitied." Clearly, the urban proletariat had none of the picturesque appeal that the Virginian found among the rural peasantry of southern France or Fontainebleau. Strolling in the Bois de Boulogne and along the grand Parisian boulevards, or driving through the city in his new "crane-neck" carriage, the light softly filtered through the slats of venetian blinds, Jefferson had remained unmoved by the terrible conditions of the city's poor. Nor had he urged American visitors in Paris, as he had those traveling through the countryside, to enter "the houses of the laborers, and especially at the moment of their repast; see what they eat, how they are clothed," and whether they were obliged to labor too hard.[60] The grubby tenements and sweat shops of the Faubourg Saint Antoine were not sunny Provence.

Moreover, as Jefferson had argued in his *Notes*, disturbances were exactly what could be expected when people were piled on top of one another in a large city. In the chapter on manufacturing, he had warned that city life was "pestilential...to the liberties of man" and would infect the body politic. That specter had now emerged in the terrible "careers of mischief" bred in the bloody streets of Paris. No amount of rational constitutional rhetoric, bills of rights, and declarations could save the faceless crowds that would inevitably appear in America if large cities were allowed to develop there.

Two days after the riot was quelled, two men caught looting were summarily convicted and hanged outside the Bastille. Others were rounded up and branded on the shoulder with the letter "G" before being sent to the galleys for life. At supper with friends on May 2, Gouverneur Morris heard a full report from a guest who "entertain[ed] the Ladies with a Description of the Magnificence of the hanging Match." Baron de Bezenvald, who gave the orders to crush the mob, was said to be "vastly pleased with his Work....It is therefore agreed on all Hands that the Baron is a great General, and as the Women say so it would be folly and Madness to controvert the Opinion."[61]

"WHILE IN PARIS PEOPLE WERE CUTTING EACH OTHER'S THROATS," the marquis de Ferrières wryly reported to his wife, "in Versailles they were deciding the details of the delegates' attire." On May 5 the Estates-General finally opened with all of the panache and dignity the exhausted old regime could muster. The anxious nobility tried to ignore the menacing words scrawled on walls, the scurrilous broadsides circulating in the Palais Royal, and the bodies hastily buried in the catacombs of Saint Antoine in the wake of the riots.

The day before, king, court, and delegates had attended a solemn mass in the Cathedral of Notre Dame at Versailles. The procession of the Holy Sacrament to the church had followed the strict hierarchy of the orders: the Third Estate, dressed in severe black with white muslin cravats, and denied even the small ceremonial swords to which they were entitled, stood out against the tawdry scarlet, purple, and gold costumes of the two upper orders. Harking back to 1614, a hat *à la Henri IV*, with the brim turned up in front, had been designed for the king and nobles, signaling their traditional alliance. Leading the parade for the last time were the royal mounted falconers, medieval in splendor and dress, each carrying a hooded bird on his wrist, followed by heralds blowing fanfares. The warm sun glinted on their silver trumpets hung with purple banners, and a dazzled Gouverneur Morris was sunburned but enthralled as he walked around bareheaded, carried away by the pageantry.

Jefferson and Morris set out early the next morning for the opening session. Morris was on the road to Versailles by six A.M. and in his seat in the Salle des Menus Plaisirs a little after eight. Some three thousand people were packed into the large room decorated with three hundred Gobelin tapestries. Offending pagan scenes depicted on the hangings had been politely censored by being moved to more obscure walls away from the clergy. "The senior clergy, glittering with gold, and all the great men of the kingdom, crowding around the dais…displayed the utmost magnificence, while the representatives of the Third Estate looked as if they were dressed in mourning," recalled Rabaut de Saint Etienne, a Protestant member of the Third Estate. "Yet their long line represented the nation, and the people were so conscious of this that they overwhelmed them with applause. They shouted 'long live the Third Estate!' just as they have since shouted 'long live the nation!'"[62]

Twelve frantic ushers tried to herd the milling crowd into their assigned bench seats. The orders were seated separately, nobility and clergy according to rank, the Third Estate merely according to their respective *bailliages*, or administrative districts. Louis XVI took his place on the throne, resplendent in the diamond-encrusted robes of the Order of the Holy Ghost. Short, graceless, and nearsighted—he refused to wear glasses and often screwed up his face—the king was transformed on state occasions. The queen sat on a platform below him, wearing a blue *panier* gown. During her husband's address, Morris noticed her weeping quietly and urged the delegates standing near him to give her a cheer, but without success.

The grand theater of the opening ceremony was marked by a moment of unintended comedy. After speaking, Louis doffed his hat in salute to the audience, and the nobles did the same. To their horror, some members of the Third Estate responded by first putting their hats on and then slowly removing them, whereupon the king took his off again. The perplexed nobles then removed theirs, as the queen convulsively waved her fan and whispered in the king's ear to put his great plumed chapeau back on. "If the Ceremonial requires these Manoeuvres the Troops are not yet properly drilled," Morris remarked sardonically.[63]

After gusts of windy rhetoric from Necker and others, much of it inaudible, the king finally left the hall, admonishing the assembly to avoid "dangerous innovations." "Here drops the curtain on the first great Act of this drama," Morris wrote. "His Courtiers seem to feel that he seems to be insensible of the Pang of Greatness going off." Jefferson declared the king's brief speech "exactly what it should have been and very well delivered....Viewing it as an opera it was imposing," he reported to William Carmichael, the American consul in Spain.[64] To both Jefferson's and Lafayette's disappointment, however, the "new constitution" was completely ignored during the opening session. By implication, it was a secondary matter to be taken up after the more pressing fiscal problems had been dealt with.

Even before the Estates-General opened, many nobles had gone over to the popular order, especially those from Paris and other large cities, "whose greater intercourse with enlightened society had liberalized their minds and prepared them to advance up to the measure of the times," as Jefferson wrote in his memoirs. Many of the younger clergy recruited from the rural peasantry, disgusted by the "princely revenues" their superiors spent on "palaces of luxury and indolence," had also defected. But the spirit of change had not caught up with the country peers, reactionary and limited in both thinking and experience, who represented perhaps a third of the Second Estate. "Residing constantly on their patrimonial feuds, and familiarized by their daily habit with Seigneural powers and practices, they had not yet learned to suspect their inconsistence with reason and right." Despite his anti-urban bias, Jefferson implicitly recognized that the city provided a more congenial atmosphere for enlightened political growth.

For several days, Jefferson made the two-and-a-half-hour trip to Versailles to follow the debates in what he called "the Commons," where the serious effort to organize a constitutional government was taking place. While the meetings of the nobles were "impassioned and tempestuous," the members of the Third Estate were models of rectitude and good judgment, always remaining "temperate, rational and inflexibly firm." The nobles had decided that they alone would verify their own credentials, rather than submitting them to a joint commission of the three estates. Lafayette had pushed for the commission, contrary to the strict instructions of his constituents in Auvergne. It was a major setback for the marquis, who saw himself as the French Washington, and Jefferson immediately grasped his friend's dilemma. If Lafayette sided with the nobles, he would undermine his political popularity. If he shifted his support between the nobles and the "Commons," he would be looked upon as a self-serving trimmer carefully watching the wind. By the time he inevitably joined the Third Estate, it would be too late to assert real leadership.

In intervening in this purely domestic situation, Jefferson was not merely ignoring diplomatic protocol; he was urging a member of the legislature of the country to which he was accredited openly to disregard the instructions of his own constituents. The only alternative, he advised Lafayette in a letter dated May 6, was to move quickly to work out a compromise by which the three estates would transform themselves into a bicameral legislature—a lower body made up of the Third Estate and an upper house comprising the nobility and clergy. Lafayette must "take at once that honest and manly stand" that his "own principles" dictated. "This will win their hearts for ever, be approved by the world which marks and honours you as a man of the people, and will be an eternal consolation to yourself."[65]

Lafayette, however, could not yet bring himself to turn on his constituents, and for the next two weeks the three orders remained stalemated over the "great preliminary question" of voting. The Third Estate refused any compromise short of unconditional recognition that they were the de facto "Commons." In the drawing rooms of Madame de Tessé and the duchess d'Enville, the search continued for a way to remodel the existing government without stirring up uncontrollable violence. Here Jefferson the master strategist took charge of Jefferson the ideologue. On May 19 and 20 he wrote outlining his plan to Thomas Paine, Richard Price, and Crèvecoeur. The reformers would once again push for joint verification of credentials. When this failed, as it was sure to do, a minority of nobles and clergy would go over to the Third Estate, which in turn would notify the king that it was ready to do business. Unless Louis consented to a limited monarchy—the first step toward a republic—tax collections would be suspended throughout the country and civil war would follow.[66]

At the end of May the nobility voted to "maintain the deliberation by order," and on June 2 Jefferson and William Short met with Lafayette and Rabaut de Saint Etienne in Versailles. The breathtaking scheme that emerged from their discussions violated diplomatic code even more blatantly than Jefferson's letter to Lafayette. The king was to be persuaded to summon a plenary session of the three orders—Jefferson called it a *séance royale*—at which he would spring on the stunned assembly a "Charter of Rights," declaring by royal fiat the Estates-General to be the national legislature of France. Jefferson himself would draft the charter. The following morning in the rue de Berri, he drew up a short, ten-point document "containing all the good in which all the parties agree." In reality, it was nothing less than an instrument of abdication. The king, in Jefferson's words, declared the Estates-General alone empowered to levy taxes and control the budget of the country.[66] Copies of the charter were immediately dispatched to Lafayette and Rabaut, to whom Jefferson wrote: "You will carry back to your constituents more good than ever effected before without violence, and you will stop exactly at the point where violence would otherwise begin. Time will be gained, the public mind will continue to ripen and to be informed, a basis of support may be prepared with the people themselves, and expedients occur for gaining still something further at your next meeting and for stopping again at the point of force."[67]

Exhausted and bewildered, Lafayette thanked Jefferson for his "Excellent idea" but confessed that it was "very hard to navigate in such a whirling." France was not yet ready for a Virginia-bred national charter. Only God knew what would happen next when men quibbled over whether they should be called "the Commons" while the more serious problems of the growing food shortage, the empty treasury, and the constitution went unaddressed. Not too convincingly, he assured Jefferson that he would "endeavor to Bring Matters to the Issue you point out." A few days later, Lafayette asked the envoy directly whether he should invite the liberal minority of the nobility to join the Third Estate after issuing one more ultimatum for the three bodies to unite. Once again, Jefferson's ideology conflicted with his pragmatic instincts. The daring revolutionary suddenly became reserved and vague, claiming that he was "unable to form an opinion" for himself.[68]

It may be that Jefferson had finally sensed that the potential for violent confrontation was greater than he had been willing to admit a few days earlier. In the confused atmosphere of crisis, as he told Rabaut de Saint Etienne when he sent him the draft of the proposed charter, he was painfully anxious "lest Despotism, after an unaccepted offer to bind it's hands, should seize you again with tenfold fury."[69] If Jefferson had wandered into the Palais Royal and had seen the flood of political tracts pouring out, he might have been even more alarmed. An amazed Arthur Young noted:

Every hour produces something new. The spirit of reading political tracts, they say, spreads into the provinces, so all the presses of France are equally employed. Nineteen-twentieths of these productions are in favour of liberty, and commonly violent against the clergy and nobility....But the coffee-houses in the Palais Royal present yet more singular and astonishing spectacles; they are not only crowded within, but other expectant crowds are at the doors and windows, listening *a gorge deployée* to certain orators...the eagerness with which they are heard, and the thunder of applause they receive for their sentiment of more than common hardness or violence against the present government, cannot easily be imagined.[70]

Twenty-five years later, Jefferson confessed to Lafayette that his interim proposal had indeed fallen short of the representative constitution that his old friend had favored, but he felt it was all that the French were then "able to bear, soberly and usefully to themselves." Some of their most enlightened friends, Jefferson recalled, had pressed Lafayette to go even further. Being "closet politicians merely, unpracticed in the knowledge of man," they "did not weigh the hazards of a transition from one form of government to another, the value of what they had already rescued from

those hazards, and might hold in security if they pleased, nor the impru-
dence of giving up the certainty of such a degree of liberty, under a limited
monarchy, for the uncertainty of a little more under a republic."[71]

On June 17, by a decisive five-to-one majority, the Third Estate
declared itself a self-appointed National Assembly representing the entire
nation, breaking all ties to the old orders. The nobility was no longer an
essential part of the government. That same day Jefferson wrote to Jay: "A
tremendous cloud hovers over this nation. If the King and his ministers
were to side openly with the Commons the revolution would be completed without a convulsion, by the establishment of a constitution, tolerably free, and in which the distinction of Noble and Commoner would be
suppressed. But this is scarcely possible. The king is honest and wishes to
the good of his people, but the expediency of an hereditary aristocracy is
too difficult a question for him." Jefferson's on-the-scene assessment is
shared by most historians today.[72]

Two days later a majority of the clergy accepted the assembly's invitation to join. On the morning of June 20, members of the Third Estate
found the door of their meeting hall guarded and a notice posted that
their meetings had been suspended. The night before, Talleyrand had
been given a secret audience with the king's brothers, who warned him
that unless Louis dissolved the assembly, it would destroy the monarchy.
Jean-Sylvain Bailey, the president of the assembly, took the government's
act as an insult, and the members agreed to adjourn to a nearby building,
an indoor tennis court. In the famous Oath of the Tennis Court, all but
one of the deputies, in Jefferson's words, bound "themselves to each other
by an oath never to separate of their accord till they had settled a constitution for the nation on a solid basis." Jefferson quickly saw that the clash
was not between Louis and the people but between the people and the
aristocracy supported by a weak, vacillating king. The struggle no longer
resembled the Glorious Revolution of 1688, the anniversary of which had
been celebrated the year before by some of Jefferson's friends in Paris.[73]

Jefferson assured Madison that the Commons had all the country's talent, "cool, temperate and sagacious," but he failed to mention that their
friend Lafayette was not yet among them. On June 23 Morris dined at
Madame de Tessé's, where the frustrated marquis criticized him to his face

for failing to support the Patriot party. "I seize this opportunity," Morris recalled in his diary, "to tell him that I am opposed to the Democracy from Regard to Liberty." The liberals were rushing "Headlong to Destruction." Their democratic ideas were hopelessly at odds "with the materials" they had to work with, and under the circumstances "the worst Thing which could happen would be to grant them their Wishes."[74] Morris expanded on his misgivings in a letter to Jay a few days later. The French, having no "Education and Habit for the Enjoyment of Freedom," were sure to "greatly overshoot their Mark."[75]

Not until July 1, two months after the opening of the now defunct Estates-General, was Washington's adopted son finally made an accredited member of the National Assembly. At the same time, rumors were spreading that twenty-five thousand soldiers loyal to the king were assembling at Versailles; grizzled veterans strolling on the palace terraces boasted that their sabers would make short work "of the ambitious lawyers, the profligate noblemen, and unfrocked priests who were ruining the country." Still, Jefferson felt confident enough to tell Jay that, with the Third Estate in the hands of the majority, the "great crisis" was over. "I shall not have matter interesting enough to trouble you with as often as I have done lately."[76]

To celebrate the thirteenth anniversary of the American Declaration of Independence, Jefferson invited Lafayette, Morris, and twenty other guests to dinner on July 4. Morris had no deep regard for the French aristocracy, saying that "when a Man of high Rank and importance laughs to Day at what he asserted yesterday, it is considered as in the natural Order of things." At the party he warned the marquis that destroying the constitutional authority of the nobility would leave no one to defend the liberty of the people. He foresaw a disaster if something was not done quickly. Three days before, Morris had written Jay that he did not believe the French troops in the city would "act against the people."[77] Although Jefferson would not have put it quite that way, at this stage the two Americans were both willing to accept some degree of the old political inequalities to avoid setting off a fatal reaction.

By the beginning of July the wheat shortage had driven bread prices to volatile levels and mass famine seemed imminent. While Jefferson prepared to leave on his vacation at a moment's notice, he discussed with the French minister of foreign affairs the possibility of obtaining food supplies from America—an offer that combined humanitarian goals with American commercial interests. American merchants, Jefferson hinted, could deliver such aid if it were needed. Rumors of the offer quickly embroiled the envoy in an embarrassing dispute when the popular count de Mirabeau attempted to use it to discredit Necker, the controller general, who he claimed had rejected it. Although the assembly had appointed a Committee on Subsistence, it seems not to have known of the American offer, and Mirabeau grabbed the chance to attack the government.

Necker had a large following in Paris. His fall would play into the hands of Mirabeau, who counted on the not-so-secret backing of the Orléans faction to bring the government down. At this point, everyone was playing with fire. Jefferson had nothing but contempt for the duke d'Orléans, describing him to Jay as unprincipled and "sunk in debaucheries of the lowest kind, and incapable of quiting them for business. Not a fool, yet not head enough to conduct any thing." Mirabeau, the "chief" of the Orléans clique, who were "persons of wicked and desperate fortune," was merely smarter than the rest and more dangerous, capable of stirring up "confusion and even a temporary civil war."[78]

With Lafayette's help, Jefferson composed a diplomatic letter exculpating Necker. Mirabeau was satisfied, although the letter did not tell the whole story of the envoy's efforts to bring in surplus American grain for the relief of the beleaguered country. Jefferson later dismissed the episode as being of little consequence, but he did not know that the king, without Mirabeau's assistance, soon would oust Necker from the royal council in a poorly timed preemptive strike. The charge that the minister had missed an opportunity to lower food prices with American aid may have forced the king's hand, allowing Mirabeau and the duke d'Orléans to seize control of the government with the envoy's unwitting help.[79]

On July 6 Lafayette sent Jefferson a note: "Will you send me the Bill of Rights with your notes? I hope to see you tomorrow. Where do you dine?" Jefferson replied that he was dining with the duchess d'Enville and would bring the papers with him. Three versions of Lafayette's Declaration of the Rights of Man and Citizen are known. Jefferson had sent the first draft to Madison in January. The second was the one he planned to bring

Burning of Tollhouse, Barrière de la Conférence, July 12, 1789. Engraved by Berthault after Prieur. Ledoux's "little palaces" were sacked and burned the same day Prince de Lambesc's cavalry, which Jefferson saw near the Place Louis XV, prepared for the first clash of the Revolution. (Bibliothèque Nationale de France, Paris)

to the duchess's house. On July 9 Lafayette sent Jefferson another note saying that he hoped to introduce his proposed declaration in the National Assembly the following day and asking again for any last-minute observations. He closed with the news that Versailles was outraged with him for opposing the recent troop movements; Jefferson might well have to claim him as an American citizen should the government suddenly arrest him.[80]

While awaiting permission to leave for the States, Jefferson wrote to Paine and Price on July 11 and 12, respectively, confidently telling them that Lafayette's Declaration of the Rights of Man (he left off "and Citizen") would be the assembly's first order of business. Although Jefferson had been consulted at various stages, it is not possible to identify his specific suggestions in the surviving drafts. The provision to have an amending convention was undoubtedly his. As he told Paine, the whole outline of the assembly's priorities, including the declaration, represented "the materials of a superb edifice." During the next several weeks, members of the assembly conscientiously reviewed the texts of many American charters, including the constitutions of Virginia, Pennsylvania, Massachusetts, and Maryland, as well as Jefferson's Declaration of Independence. On the eve of the French Revolution, they were looking not for a new theory of government, as Gilbert Chinard observed, but for empirical evidence of the success of the American experiment, which had now safely passed the laboratory stage.[81]

On the morning of July 11 Lafayette laid the draft of his declaration on the assembly desk. His timing could not have been worse. That evening Necker left his house in Versailles with his wife, ostensibly to dine with friends in Saint-Germain-en-Laye. Instead, they headed directly for the Belgian border, changing to a post chaise at Le Bourget to cover their tracks. Necker had been fired that afternoon and, like his predecessor Calonne, he did not intend to wait around to be arrested or to serve as a rallying point for the opposition. In the wake of this bombshell, Lafayette's Declaration of the Rights of Man—the culmination of his career, "fruit of my past, gage of my future"—would not be discussed for weeks.[82]

On July 13 Jefferson flashed the news to Paine in London that the controller general had been dismissed late on the afternoon of the 11th. Trouble had erupted in Paris when word arrived in the middle of the afternoon on Sunday, the 12th. The Palais Royal, headquarters of the duke d'Orléans' faction, had exploded instantly. Speakers mounted the tables of the cafés and the cry "To arms" echoed through the galleries, amid dark rumors of a St. Bartholomew plot. Upon entering the city, the king's foreign troops had been attacked by mobs. The first incident had taken place on the afternoon of July 13, just as Jefferson was passing near the Place Louis XV (soon to be rechristened the Place de la Révolution), "where a body of German cavalry being drawn up the people posted themselves upon and behind the piles of stones collected for the bridge." As the envoy approached the square, the angry crowd formed a lane and allowed him to pass through a moment before they "attacked and drove off the cavalry with stones."[83] In that file of sullen, defiant Frenchmen, Jefferson had made his closest contact with the raw forces of the French Revolution.

Back at the Hôtel de Langeac, Jefferson heard the fire of the mercenary troops in the distance after they had rallied and returned to the attack near the Tuileries garden. Unknown to him, a unit of Gardes Françaises (National Guards) in battle order had suddenly arrived, determined to help in the crowd's defense of the city against the king's troops. Morris, who had also been in the Place Louis XV when the confrontation took place, reached the rue de Berri a little later, bringing more details of the skirmish. "In Effect, the little City of Paris is as fine a Tummult as any one could wish. They are getting Arms wherever they can find any," he wrote in his diary that evening.[84] It wasn't much of a clash, but it meant that lines had now been drawn over the sovereignty of Paris. The center of power had shifted from Versailles to the Palais Royal.

Jefferson's on-the-spot reports of the civil eruptions are notable for their terse, detached tone, as well as their accuracy. Two days after the fall of the Bastille, which he did not actually witness, he wrote:

> The tumults in Paris which took place on the change of ministry, the slaughter of the people in the assault of the Bastille the beheading the Governor and Lieutenant Governor of it, and the Prevost de Marchands, excited in the king so much concern, that bursting from the shackles of his ministers and advisers, he went yesterday morning to the states general with only his two brothers, opened his heart to them, asked them what he could to restore peace and happiness to his people, and shewed himself ready to do every thing for that purpose, promising particularly to send away the troops. The heat of this city is as yet too great to give entire credit to this, and they continue to arm and organize the Bourgeoisie.[85]

Jefferson was at Hôtel de Corny on the evening of July 14 when Ethis de Corny arrived with a first-hand account of the clash at the Bastille. That morning, as head of a deputation from the city's volunteer guard, Corny had gone to the already besieged fortress, where more than thirty thousand guns were stored, requesting arms to defend the city. The crowd had threatened to break down the gates and help themselves to the

Cavalry of Prince de Lambesc, July 12, 1789, Charging the Crowd in the Tuileries. A few minutes after Jefferson had passed near the Place Louis XV on his way home, Prince de Lambesc faced the menacing crowd near the entrance to the Tuileries garden. When the Garde Française arrived, the first pitched battle for the control of the city occurred. (Department of Special Collections, Stanford University Libraries)

arms, but Corny asked the marquis de Launay, governor of the prison, for a truce. De Launay had welcomed the delegation and invited the group in for dinner. A few hours later, Corny had received permission to return to the Hôtel de Ville for consultation. As his carriage drove out of the Bastille, the crowd had surged into the inner courtyard, where four civilians near Corny's deputation were shot. On that signal, the crowd had overrun the prison, killing the governor, six soldiers, and ninety-eight others. Nearly a hundred had been wounded in the clash. The country was on the brink of open insurrection. The governor's head hoisted on a pike, Jefferson reported to Jay, had "worked powerfully thro' the night on the aristocratical party, insomuch that in the morning those of the greatest influence on the Count d'Artois represented to him the absolute necessity that the king should give up evry thing to the states."[86]

On July 15 Lafayette, the most popular figure in the city, was acclaimed commander of the National Guard, swearing before the altar in the Cathedral of Notre Dame to "defend with his life the precious liberty entrusted

The Bastille During the First Days of Demolition by Hubert Robert, 1789.
The day before the fall of the Bastille, Jefferson serenely wrote his neighbor sending her a book on gardening: "As Mme. Broutin cares for an English garden, Mr. Jefferson thought she might find pleasure in a book translated from the English in which this subject is superbly treated." But the same day, he wrote Thomas Paine that when the news of Necker's resignation hit Paris, the mobs forced the theaters to close and "foreign troops were advanced into the city" in anticipation of greater trouble on July 14. City planners had long wanted the old prison demolished to make way for new improvements but volunteer wreckers under Lafayette's orders accomplished the job for more political purposes. (Musée Carnavalet. Copyright Photothèque des Musées de la Ville de Paris)

to his care." Like so much else in the Revolution, the ceremony was a synthesis of the old France and the new. Lafayette presented to his citizen-soldiers their insignia, a cockade in the red and blue colors of the city of Paris, between which he had placed white, the color of the king. Two days later, it would be pinned on the king himself.[87]

Taking up his post in the Hôtel de Ville, Jefferson's friend moved firmly to restore order. He immediately directed the demolition of the Bastille, which was in fact already under way. On July 16, when the crisis again threatened to overwhelm the city authorities, the king was invited to Paris. Lafayette sent a note offering to meet the royal delegation at the Pont-du-Jour and escort it safely into the center of the city. Jefferson watched the procession of the king and fifty deputies, led by Lafayette on horseback, move slowly through streets lined with some sixty thousand citizens brandishing "pistols, swords, pikes, pruning hooks, scythes." Morris was struck by the members of the assembly, who walked "promiscuously together in the Procession." The display of more serious ordnance taken from the Bastille and the Invalides emphasized the city's determination to defend itself.

When Louis returned safely to Versailles after his ordeal, wearing the new cockade, the day had, in Jefferson's words, "concluded an amende honorable as no sovereign ever made, and no people ever received." The envoy did not witness the tragic dénouement of the drama, but as he reflected on the events of 1789 in his old age, Marie Antoinette's responsibility grew in his mind, until finally she became the proximate cause of the Revolution itself:

> This angel, as gaudily painted in the rhapsodies of the Rhetor Burke, with some smartness of fancy, but no sound sense was proud, distainful of restraint, indignant at all obstacles to her will, eager in the pursuit of pleasure and firm enough to hold to her desires, or perish in their wreck. Her inordinate gambling and disapations, with those of the Count d'Artois and others of her clique had been a sensible item in the exhaustion of the treasury, which called into action the reforming hand of the nation; and her opposition to it her inflexible perverseness, and dauntless spirit, led herself to the Guillotine, & drew the king on with her, and plunged the world into crimes & calamities which will forever stain the pages of history. I have ever believed that had there been no queen, there would have been no revolution.[88]

A few days later, the "astonishing train of events" momentarily ebbed and Jefferson returned to the role of legal scholar. He had a fire laid in his study and relaxed by taking up one of his favorite subjects, writing a short, learned essay on juries under the American system. In the form of a letter to the abbé Arnoux, it opened with a bibliography of English sources on the subject, followed by a succinct explanation of the role and function of the jury in a republican government. Asked "to decide whether the people had best be omitted in the Legislative or the Judiciary, I would say it is better to leave them out of the Legislative. The execution of the laws is more important than the making of them," Jefferson told the abbé.[89]

He assured friends that through all the recent "ferment" he had never lost a night of sleep. "I have been thro' it [the city] daily," he wrote on August 3, "have observed the mobs with my own eyes in order to be satisfied of their objects, and declare to you that I saw so plainly the legitimacy of them, that I have slept in my house as quietly thro' the whole as ever I did in the most peaceful moments."[90] Finding time to order from London replacements for the four pair of candlesticks stolen from his house, he assured John Trumbull that the city was now tranquil. The sculptor Houdon offered the envoy another diversion with a revised proposal to undertake an equestrian statue of Washington. As for the agitated public, the business of making a constitution would absorb everyone's attention and divert them "from the bloody objects which have lately occupied their minds."[91]

Two weeks after he had "joined the crowds to watch the razing of the Bastille stone by stone," it occurred to Jefferson that the French Assembly, like the American Congress, might have a "a clean canvas to work on" in overhauling the machinery of government without further disturbances. He was confident that the American model would be followed. Morris, of course, thought just the opposite, believing that the assembly was "too democratical and should wind up its work immediately."[92] It was far too full of "all those romantic Ideas of Government, which happily for America, we were cured before it was too late," he told Washington. As Morris had pointedly remarked to Lafayette earlier apropos his Declaration of Rights, "it is not by sounding words that revolutions are produced."[93]

Yet ugly tensions persisted in the streets not far from the rue de Berri. Taking their cue from the unrest in the Saint-Antoine district, journeymen tailors at the Louvre and wigmakers in the Champs-Elysées, complaining that business had suddenly fallen off after the assembly abolished all signs of ranks in early August, decided to demonstrate against their masters. Mass hysteria in the city was fed by rumors that foreign troops gathered on the outskirts were planning an invasion and looters were already pillaging the countryside. On August 13 Jefferson reported to Jay with detachment: "Abundance of chateaux are certainly burned and burning and not a few lives sacrificed."[94] Long lines outside the bakery shops were another sign that growing food shortages could spark trouble without warning.

On the afternoon on August 25, a messenger delivered another urgent note to the Hôtel de Langeac from Lafayette. He asked Jefferson "for liberty's sake" to host a secret dinner the next day for a group of deputies attempting to sort out their differences before the situation deteriorated further. As Jefferson well knew, schisms were developing among the patrician Patriots, breaking the party "into fragments of very discordant principles." The divisions fell along the old fault lines of liberty versus order and freedom versus the rule of law. Whether progressive or reactionary forces would prevail was by no means clear, either to the Virginian or to his unexpected dinner guests. It was becoming far more difficult to predict the outcome in Paris than it had been in Williamsburg or Philadelphia.

At that very moment, isolated districts outside of Paris were either threatened or under attack. In the crucial dispute over the king's powers, some wanted it as absolute as necessary to preserve order, while others would retain no royal veto at all. An increasingly alarmed Lafayette warned in his note that "total dissolution and a civil war" would follow if a compromise were not found. His plan was to meet with key assembly members "of honest but differing opinions" over dinner at the American's house and try to work out an agreement on basic constitutional principles.[95]

The dinner began at four and continued until ten in the evening on August 25. Jefferson later claimed that he listened in impressed silence to "logical reasoning and chaste eloquence" of classical proportions, a memory that would remain vivid into his last years at Monticello. How could such an Attic group not fail to find an Attic solution? After six hours of deliberation, ending in the American fashion with wine served on the bare table, "a compromise is finally reached giving the king a suspended veto while the legislature will be a single body elected by the people." Jefferson, still trying to bolster his hopes of a peaceful transition from despotism to republic, declared that not "even a war could prevent their establishing finally a good constitution."[96]

Another issue undoubtedly touched on in the long meeting at the Hôtel de Langeac was whether the fundamental law of the French constitution could be revised, and if so, how. Should it be changed at stated, periodic times or as the need arose? If it was made difficult or impossible to alter, then the past would lay heavily over future generations. The right to change the constitution had been spelled out in the final paragraph of the draft declaration that Lafayette had written with Jefferson's help. Of the forty-eight proposed declarations of rights considered by the assembly or informally discussed in the summer of 1789, nineteen contained a right of revision, but only two bestowed it on successor generations. Revision had been strongly urged by a number of assembly members and had been the subject of pamphlets. As early as 1787, Condorcet had argued for the need to provide for constitutional changes. Yet on August 26 the assembly approved a Déclaration des droits de l'homme et du citoyen that did not provide for making future changes.[97]

Then and later, Jefferson never wavered in his belief in the "droit des générations qui se succèdent," the principle that one generation cannot bind its successors by law or constitution. The vexing question of what Herbert Sloan has called the "crippling effects" of legacies fascinated the Virginian as a theorist, and the exchange at his dining table may well be another link in the evolution of his remarkable essay "The Earth Belongs in Usufruct to the Living," cast in the form of a letter that he wrote two weeks later to James Madison.[98] Jefferson's arguments are explicitly directed to conditions in France, but he was clearly exploring universal principles.[99] From the first day he had set foot in Europe, he had been made aware of the "corrupt" legacies of the past on the fabric of society. The United States, he wrote, had so far escaped Europe's "contagious and ruinous errors." The assembly's recent attempt to deal with the dead hand of the past by dismantling feudal rights and privileges had addressed some, but not all, of the issues.

The questions raised by Jefferson, and explored earlier by Condorcet and others, constitute a radical polemic on political relativism. His essay, citing as it did examples of entrenched French abuses, supports the theory that the American envoy was making a final undercover foray into the internal affairs of the sovereign state to which he was accredited before leaving for Virginia. On August 27 the assembly postponed further consideration of the Declaration of Rights until the constitution was finished. Jefferson placed "The Earth Belongs in Usufruct to the Living" in Lafayette's hands sometime after September 5. Thus, he may well have felt that there was still a chance for his arguments to be used in the floor debates in laying entirely new foundations for the nation.

Jefferson's essay was profoundly relevant to the constitutional issues facing French society. It pointed out the consequences of the principle that representatives elected by the people have no inherent power to restrain succeeding bodies. The principle was not only central to the problem of the crushing national debt, it "enter[ed] into the resolution of the questions Whether the nation may change the descent of lands, holden in tail? Whether they may change the appropriation of lands given antiently to the church, to hospitals, colleges, orders of chivalry and otherwise in perpetuity? Whether they may abolish the charges and privileges attached to lands, including the whole catalogue ecclesiastical and feudal?" The principle struck at the power of the crown itself, pertaining to "hereditary offices, authorities and jurisdictions; to hereditary orders, distinctions, and appellations; to perpetual monopolies in commerce, the arts and science; with a long train of et ceteras; and it renders the question of reimbursement [of the government's debts] a question of generosity and not of right."[100]

In the last days before Jefferson and his family left Paris, rumors of violence, conspiracies, and capricious bursts of anger continued to spread. To Jefferson they were passing distractions from the main goal that seemed so close at hand. If the reactionaries, in a desperate effort to preserve their privileges at Versailles, tried to interfere with constitutional reform, "the national militia (that is by their commander)" could simply step in and declare the constitution by fiat, giving the military countercoup "regular sanction" later, following the style of every coup throughout history.

Early on October 5, while the Jefferson party was waiting in Le Havre for the storms to calm, a ferocious political tempest swept across Paris from the Place de Grève. A crowd had gathered in front of the Hôtel de Ville, listening to a market woman blame Marie Antoinette for the shortage of food. Crying "Du pain, du pain!" five or six thousand Parisians, mostly women, armed with the impromptu tools of revolution prepared to march on Versailles and bring the king and queen back to Paris as hostages. Lafayette was forced to follow with his troops. Upon reaching the royal apartments, Lafayette led the queen and the young dauphin onto the balcony of the palace to appease the restive mob below.

By one o'clock on the afternoon of October 6, Louis XVI, Marie Antoinette, and other members of the royal family were on their way to Paris. Lafayette rode beside the royal carriage, surrounded by a mass of some sixty thousand people, whose tattoo was now "À Paris, à Paris." Short reported to Jefferson that the wet, bedraggled column of "women, children, men of all sorts, in the condition you may suppose…arrived at half after eight" that evening, as rain continued to fall. The captives and their captors had been received "in great order." Lafayette's courageous maneuvers had managed to steer the mob, the assembly, and the royal family toward what appeared to be a safe mooring. So far, at this unpredictable stage of the hurricane, Lafayette had held the rudder with a firm grip.

THE TIMING OF JEFFERSON'S DEPARTURE FROM PARIS, before the mobs and demagogues had seized control, allowed him to preserve his dogged optimism and the reforming zeal of a believer in the "true god" of reason and liberty. For him, the French Revolution would become a sacred idea that transcended its individual leaders, including his closest friends. This idea was part of the baggage he brought back to Virginia. As he had declared in a letter to Paine on July 11, the National Assembly was ready with "coolness, wisdom, and resolution to set fire to the four corners of the kingdom and to perish with it themselves rather than relinquish an iota of their plan of a total change of government."[101]

Jefferson understood the use of terror and the need to perish in the "fire," if necessary, to bring about revolutionary change. During Shays' Rebellion, he had spoken of watering the Tree of Liberty with the blood of patriots, and he had tacitly approved of the sobering display of waving heads carried on pikes in the streets of Paris. But he did not fully comprehend the political limits of the application of terror, or its dangers to those who employed it. Those fatal lessons would be learned by many of the men and women he had known in Paris. As the revolution roared out of control in 1792 and 1793, sweeping away some of his closest friends and colleagues, Jefferson refused to admit that their tragedies and those of countless others belied his simplistic faith that constitutional reform, in France and elsewhere, would produce enlightened human happiness.

Before the revolutionary storms subsided, Lafayette would be charged with treason, flee the Jacobin madness in 1792, and languish for more than five years in the dungeons of Olmütz, the Austrian prison. The two other friends who attended Jefferson's farewell dinner in the fall of 1789 would both suffer death as enemies of the people. On September 4, 1792, the duke de La Rochefoucauld, passing through the town of Gisor, was seized, stoned to death, and disemboweled by a mob in the presence of his wife, Rosalie, and his mother, the duchess d'Enville. That same week, the duke's nephew (and Rosalie's brother), the count de Chabot, died in the Prison de l'Abbaye during the September Massacres. The duchess's distraught letter to Jefferson reporting the brutal murders unaccountably went unacknowledged.

The La Rochefoucauld family never forgave Condorcet for refusing to intervene on Chabot's behalf. Later the philosophe himself was cornered by Robespierre's police. Before taking poison in his hiding place at Bourg-Egalité in 1794, Condorcet wrote out testamentary instructions for his daughter on the flyleaf of the copy of Homer he was carrying. She was to be taught English in case she had to flee to America for safety. If this should happen, she was to seek protection from Franklin's grandson, Benjamin Franklin Bache, or from Condorcet's friend Jefferson.

The spring of 1794 would claim other victims from Jefferson's circle as well. On April 22, the seventy-six-year-old Malesherbes, with whom the Virginian had exchanged quantities of seeds—Jefferson had praised him for his "zeal to promote the general good of mankind by an interchange of useful things"—was the last member of his family to be beheaded. He had been forced to watch while his daughter, her husband, and his granddaughter each preceded him onto the scaffold.

Jefferson seems to have been unable or unwilling to accept these personal tragedies. His friends were simply unfortunate martyrs to the cause of liberty and humanity. In view of the universal issues at stake, the price they had paid was not too great. When as secretary of state he received Short's graphic accounts of the September Massacres, "too horrid and disgusting to behold," Jefferson severely reprimanded his former secretary and loyal friend for exaggerating the savagery of the Paris mob. "The liberty of the whole earth was depending on the issue of the contest, and was ever such a prize won with so little innocent blood?" he wrote. "My own affections have been deeply wounded by some of the martyrs to this cause, but rather than it should have failed, I would have seen half the earth desolated." Then, in the grim words of a religious fanatic, he added: "Were there but an Adam and an Eve left in every country, and left free, it would be better than as it now is."[102]

In early 1793, when he learned that the monarchy he had once supported had been overthrown the previous August and the French Republic established by order of the Commune, Jefferson's enthusiasm for the Revolution reached new heights. At each stage of the rebellion, both during and after his Paris years, he responded uncritically to the unfolding saga, even as it veered dangerously out of control and away from his idealized scenario. But the possibility of rewriting the drama in the language of the Enlightenment or changing its outcome was long past. Not until he was confronted with the dictatorship of Napoléon did Jefferson finally recover from his purblind allegiance and admit, albeit grudgingly, that his indiscriminate faith in the cause of French liberty might have been misplaced.

THE REFINEMENTS AND INTELLECTUAL ACHIEVEMENTS of the European Enlightenment concentrated in cosmopolitan Paris had enlarged Jefferson's aspirations for an ideal world. With all of its faults and failures as a just and humane society, still France had, in the extraordinary men and women he knew and admired, the possibilities of "an aristocracy of virtue and talent." He was far from certain of the details, but if France could complete the reformation of its oppressive government after the American model, its enlightened manners and taste would ensure a triumphant new beginning. All of Europe would follow, joining the American republic in a great transatlantic civilization without boundaries or passports. It was this seductive mirage that had kept alive his liberal hopes in the face of repeated disappointments.

In Paris, Jefferson's expanding dream had overwhelmed all vestiges of the provincialism he had arrived with. It now reached beyond the ambition of nationality, to define a new era for the future of mankind. His ideal society, domesticated, educated, and refined along modern lines, would be led by a natural aristocracy not unlike his Parisian friends. They, like he, would govern as if a golden age were at hand. "A more benevolent people I have never known," he wrote in his old age, "nor greater warmth & devotedness in their select friendships. Their kindness and accommodation to strangers is unparalleled, and the hospitality of Paris beyond anything I had conceived possible in a large city. Their eminence too in science, the communicative dispositions of their scientific men, the politeness of the general manners, the ease and vivacity of their conversations, give a charm to their society to be found nowhere else."

Jefferson desperately yearned somehow to translate these virtues—civility, sensibility, and taste—to America and its government, oblivious in his efforts, as Henry Adams remarked, to "the disease of omniscience." He yearned to project his experience and aspirations into the new nation's collective dreaming, beyond the vibrant, decadent facade of a complex ancient order, secure in its identity. He was prepared for his calling when Washington asked him to stage-manage the planning of the new Federal City, the setting for a government ordered to the Enlightenment's hopes and philosophical design. In ten years, at the turn of the new century, the former diplomat would in fact become the last philosopher-statesman to preside over the uncompleted city and the still uncertain destiny of its government. The memories of Paris had added a new promise and beguiling aura to his undying illusion of that most perfect society on earth.

Notes

Chapter 1. Taking Leave

1. Gouverneur Morris, *The Diary of the French Revolution*, ed. Beatrix C. Davenport, 2 vols. (Boston, 1939), 1:222. On Sept. 17 and 18, Morris says it is so cold that fires are necessary.

2. Merrill D. Peterson, *Thomas Jefferson and the New Nation* (New York, 1970), 21. TJ was aware of his habit of counting and computing, wryly telling Abigail Adams, "I have compared notes with Mr. Adams on the score of progeny, and find I am ahead of, and think I am in a fair way to keep so. I have 10 1/2 grandchildren and 2 3/4 great-grand-children; and these fractions will ere long become units." *The Adams-Jefferson Letters*, ed. Lester J. Cappon, 2 vols. (Chapel Hill, 1959), 2:367.

3. TJ to Maria Cosway, Jan. 14, 1789, *Papers*, 14:446.

4. TJ to John Jay, Sept. 19, 1789, *Papers*, 15:459.

5. TJ to David Humphreys, Aug. 14, 1787, *Papers*, 12:32–33.

6. TJ to Maria Cosway, July 25, 1789, *Papers*, 15:303.

7. TJ to Thomas Paine, Sept. 13, 1789, *Papers*, 15:424.

8. TJ to Maria Cosway, July 25, 1789, *Papers*, 15:305.

9. Henry Adams, *History of the United States during the Administrations of Thomas Jefferson* (New York, 1984), 1:188.

10. Keith M. Baker, *Condorcet: From Natural Philosophy to Social Mathematics* (Chicago, 1975), 25.

11. Ibid., 27.

12. Condorcet's essay has been translated by Durand Echeverria and can be found with a perceptive introduction in the *William and Mary Quarterly*, 3d Series (1968), 25:85–108. See also *Condorcet: Selected Writings*, ed. Keith Baker (Indianapolis, 1976), 71–83.

13. Baker, *Condorcet*, 371.

14. Morris, *Diary*, 1:xviii–xix. Mme de Flahaut is conspicuous throughout the diary.

15. Stanley Elkins and Eric McKitrick, *The Age of Federalism* (New York, 1993), 317.

16. Morris, *Diary*, 1:259.

17. John Adams, as usual, was more outspoken than TJ regarding personalities, call-ing Morris "a Man of Wit" and a writer of "pretty verses—but a Character trés legere."

The Diary and Autobiography of John Adams, ed. Lyman Butterfield, 4 vols. (Cambridge, Mass., 1961), 2:390.

18. Text of tribute in *Papers*, 15:239–44.

19. Jared Sparks, *The Life of Gouverneur Morris* (Boston, 1832), 284.

20. Morris, *Diary*, 1:220.

21. Crèvecoeur to TJ, July 15, 1784, *Papers*, 7:376.

22. *Diary and Autobiography of John Adams*, ed. Butterfield, 4:66–67.

23. See Gilbert Chinard, "Notes on the French Translations of the 'Forms of Government or Constitutions of the Several States,'" *Year Book, American Philosophical Society* (1943): 88–106. Chinard's research traces the text of the French version of the Virginia Bill of Rights taken from the first draft, which differed from the final text. Franklin, with his canny eye for propaganda, arranged to present copies to members of the royal family. Printed in quarto and bound in red morocco, Marie Antoinette's copy with her coat of arms survives in the Bibliothèque Nationale. See *Creating French Culture*, ed. Marie-Hélène Tesnière and Prosser Gifford (New Haven, 1995), 353–54.

24. James Madison to TJ, Oct. 17, 1784, *Papers*, 7:446; TJ to James Madison, March 18, 1785, *Papers*, 8:39; TJ to James Madison, Jan. 30, 1787, *Papers*, 11:95. Short's biographer believes that as early as the winter of 1788 TJ knew of Short's infatuation and may have encouraged him to take a long tour of southern France and Italy in order to cool the romance. George Green Shackelford, *Jefferson's Adoptive Son* (Lexington, Ky., 1993), 114.

25. The count de Ségur, a close acquaintance of the marquis, noted his "cold and grave" manner, giving him "an air of timidity and embarrassment, which did not really belong to him," a quality of startled mien seen in the portraits, as if a flash bulb had exploded in his face. *Memoirs and Recollections of Count Louis Philippe de Segur*, 3 vols. (1825; rpt., New York, 1970), 1:106.

26. TJ to Lafayette, April 2, 1790. *The Letters of Lafayette and Jefferson*, ed. Gilbert Chinard (Baltimore, 1926), 167.

27. Ibid., 51.

28. *Lafayette in the Age of the American Revolution*, ed. Stanley J. Idzerda, 5 vols. (Ithaca, 1979), 1:7.

29. TJ to Diodati, Aug. 3, 1789, *Papers*, 15:326. TJ told Thomas Paine on July 17, 1789, that "A more dangerous scene of war I never saw in America, than what Paris has presented the 5. days past." TJ to Paine, July 17, 1789, *Papers*, 15:279.

30. On Sept. 19, 1789, TJ reported to Jay that "a person whose information would have weight [Lafayette?] wrote to the Count de Montmorin adjuring him to prevent it [the flight to Metz] by every possible means, and assuring him that the flight would be a signal of a St. Barthelemi against the aristocrats in Paris and perhaps throughout the whole kingdom." TJ to Jay, *Papers*, 15:459–60.

31. Morris, *Diary*, 1:221.

32. Ibid., 1:223. Morris admired Lafayette's abilities during the American war, but

later in Paris found his devotion to both the monarchy and the republican cause decidedly equivocal. See Idzerda, *Lafayette*, 2:116–17.

33. Morris, *Diary*, 1:221.

34. "Autobiography," *Thomas Jefferson: Writings*, ed. Merrill Peterson (New York, 1984), 98.

35. In his *History of the United States during the Administrations of Thomas Jefferson*, 1:127–28, Henry Adams paints a convincing picture of the president's social and political domination of the village-capital through his select and careful entertaining with the best food and wine in town.

36. TJ to F. W. Gilmer, 1816, *The Writings of Thomas Jefferson*, ed. Paul L. Ford, 10 vols. (New York, 1892–99), 10:33. Thomas Mann Randolph recalled TJ's manners as being "those of the polished school of the Colonial Government, so remarkable in its day—under no circumstances violating any of those minor conventional observances which constitute the well-bred gentleman and considerate to all persons." Henry S. Randall, *Life of Thomas Jefferson*, 3 vols. (New York, 1858), 3:674.

37. Morris, *Diary*, 1:159, n.

38. William Maclay, *Diary and Other Notes on Senate Debates*, ed. Kenneth R. Bowling and Helen E. Veit (Baltimore, 1988), 275. Dumas Malone attempts to soften the classic caricature in *Jefferson and His Time*, 6 vols. (Boston, 1948–81), 2:258–59, but Maclay's fresh vividness cannot be wholly dismissed.

39. Randall, *Jefferson*, 1:421.

40. Abigail Adams (Smith), *Journal and Correspondence of Miss Adams* (New York, 1841), 14.

41. Margaret Bayard Smith, *The First Forty Years of Washington Society* (New York, 1906), 387–88.

42. A. Adams, "Memoir of William S. Smith," *Miss Adams*, 132.

43. The text of the agreement dated September 1793 can be found in *Thomas Jefferson's Farm Book*, ed. Edwin Morris Betts (Chapel Hill, 1955), 15–16. See also Paul Finkelman, "Jefferson and Slavery," in *Jeffersonian Legacies*, ed. Peter S. Onuf (Charlottesville, 1993), 205, and James Bear, Jr., *The Hemings Family of Monticello* (Ivy, Va., 1980), 9–12.

44. See n. 24 above.

45. TJ to Carlo Bellini, Sept. 30, 1785, *Papers*, 8:569.

46. The complete list of baggage shipped by TJ from France is reproduced in *Papers*, 15:375–77.

47. In his last letter to John Jay, written from Le Havre on Sept. 30, TJ wrote that he proposed to "go directly to my own house, get through the business which calls me there, and then repair to New York where I shall be ready to reimbark for Europe." *Papers*, 15:501.

48. "Memorandum Books."

49. Extract from the diary of Nathaniel Cutting at Le Havre and Cowes, *Papers*, 15:490.

50. TJ to William Short, *Papers*, 15:509.

51. "List of Baggage Shipped by Jefferson from France" and notes, *Papers*, 15:375–77. George Green Shackelford, *Thomas Jefferson's Travels in Europe, 1784–1789* (Baltimore, 1995), 157, gives the number as 86 pieces, but this figure probably includes baggage shipped later by Short.

52. TJ to Thomas Paine, Oct. 14, 1789, *Papers*, 15:522.

53. TJ to Maria Cosway, Oct. 14, *Papers*, 15:521.

Chapter 2. A Provincial Prelude

1. TJ to Filippo Mazzei, May 31, 1780, *Papers*, 2:405.

2. "Autobiography," *Writings*, ed. Peterson, 58.

3. *Papers*, 2:528.

4. Philip Rahv, *Discovery of Europe* (New York, 1960), viii.

5. TJ to Lafayette, Aug. 4, 1781, *Papers*, 6:112. Even though he was quickly vindicated in his performance as governor, the humiliation would rankle him the rest of his life. Democracy in practice had taken its toll on its chief philosopher-priest. "Would anyone believe," he wrote in 1820, six years before his death, "that flight has become, in the minds of party men, the subject of I know not how many volumes of insults. It has been sung in verse, and told in humble prose how, forgetting the noble example of the hero of La Mancha and his windmills, I refused to do battle alone against a legion."

6. Thomas Jefferson, *Notes on the State of Virginia*, ed. William Peden (Chapel Hill, 1955), 153.

7. TJ to Giovanni Fabbroni, June 5, 1778, *Papers*, 2:196. Fabbroni was a friend of Filippo Mazzei. The letter was intercepted by the British, so he was not able to pursue the request. The two men continued to correspond over the years but never met.

8. Douglas L. Wilson, "Thomas Jefferson's Library and the Skipwith List," *Harvard Library Bulletin*, n.s. 3, no. 4 (Winter 1992–93): 56–72.

9. *Jefferson's Literary Commonplace Book*, The Papers of Thomas Jefferson, 2d ser., ed. Douglas L. Wilson (Princeton, 1989), 146–47.

10. TJ to Henry Lee, May 8, 1825, *Writings*, ed. Peterson, 1501.

11. TJ to Robert Skipwith, Aug. 3, 1771, *Papers*, 1:78.

12. Fiske Kimball, "List of Architectural Books Owned by Thomas Jefferson," *Thomas Jefferson Architect* (rpt., New York, 1968), 90–101.

13. Marquis de Chastellux, *Travels in North America in the Years 1780, 1781 and 1782*, ed. Howard C. Rice, Jr., 2 vols. (Chapel Hill, 1963), 2:389–96.

14. "Autobiography," *Writings*, ed. Peterson, 46.

15. James Madison to Edmund Randolph, June 28, 1782, *The Papers of James Madison*, ed. Robert A. Rutland et al., 5:150–51.

16. TJ to Samuel Henley, Nov. 27, 1785, *Papers*, 9:65.

17. TJ to Chastellux, Nov. 26, 1782, *Papers*, 6:203.

18. Malone, *Jefferson and His Time*, 1:398.

19. In October TJ wrote Elizabeth Eppes that his "miserable existence is really too burthesome to be borne, and were it not for the infidelity of deserting the sacred charges left me, I could not wish it's continuance a moment" (Oct. 3?, 1782). It is significant that this deeply personal confession was made to a woman who was not a member of the family. That he was struggling with aggravated depression was clear in his effort to bury himself in work.

20. TJ to James Madison, Feb. 20, 1784, *Papers*, 6:350.

Chapter 3. The City

1. Michel Gallet, *Stately Mansions*, trans. Adam Ferguson (New York, 1972), 4.

2. Hugh Honour, *Neoclassicism* (London, 1969), 17—18.

3. Marc-Antoine Laugier, *An Essay on Architecture*, trans. Wolfgang and Anni Herrmann (Los Angeles, 1977), 95. See also Michael Dennis, *Court and Garden* (Cambridge, Mass., 1986), 128.

4. Dennis, *Court and Garden*, 128.

5. Ibid., 136—76.

6. TJ to the Virginia Delegates in Congress, July 12, 1785, *Papers*, 8:290. See also Gordon Wood, "The Trials and Tribulations of Thomas Jefferson," in *Jeffersonian Legacies*, ed. Onuf, 404. Wood comments on TJ's connoisseurship in the role of an impresario to improve American taste. See also Garry Wills, "The Aesthete," *New York Review of Books*, Aug. 12, 1993: 6—10.

7. TJ to Mme de Bréhan, March 14, 1789, *Papers*, 14:655.

8. Arthur Young, *Travels in France* (London, 1890), 94—95.

9. *Papers*, 11:111—12 and 197—98.

10. Simon Schama, *Citizens: A Chronicle of the French Revolution* (New York, 1989), 73—76. See also George Mathews, *The Royal General Farms in Eighteenth-Century France* (New York, 1956).

11. "Ledoux par lui-même," *L'Oeuvre et les rêves de Claude-Nicolas Ledoux* (Paris, 1961), 154; *The Eye of Thomas Jefferson*, ed. William Howard Adams (Washington, 1976), 176.

12. Schama, *Citizens*, 73.

13. TJ to Patrick Henry, Jan. 24, 1786, *Papers*, 9:214.

14. John Jay to TJ, June 16, 1786, *Papers*, 9:651.

15. Allan Braham, *The Architecture of the French Enlightenment* (Berkeley, 1980), 11.

16. *Memorandum Books*, ed. Bear and Stanton, August 20, 1784.

17. *Papers*, 8:270—73, n.

18. TJ to James Monroe, Nov. 11, 1784, *Papers*, 7:512.

19. TJ to James Monroe, June 17, 1785, *Papers*, 8:230.

20. TJ's problems with debt and its impact on his political philosophy are brilliantly explored in Herbert Sloan's *Principle and Interest: Thomas Jefferson and the Problem of Debt* (New York, 1995).

21. TJ to John Jay, Paris, June 21, 1787, *Papers*, 11:490.

22. Malesherbes to TJ, May 5, 1786, *Papers*, 9:452–53, n.

23. Francis Steegmuller, *A Woman, a Man, and Two Kingdoms* (Princeton, 1993), 185. See also Gallet, *Mansions*, 95–103, for a discussion of follies and pavilions.

24. Sébastien-Roch Nicolas Chamfort, *Products of a Perfected Civilization: Selected Writings of Chamfort*, ed. and trans. W. S. Merwin (San Francisco, 1984), 40.

25. F. Kimball, *Architect*, 148, correctly identifies the drawing (fig. 118) as being related to the Hôtel de Langeac, but at the time contemporary plans had not been discovered. Kimball incorrectly identifies the acute angle in the drawing as representing the corner of the Champs-Elysées and the rue de Berri.

26. Howard Rice, Jr., *Thomas Jefferson's Paris* (Princeton, 1976), 43; Luc-Vincent Thiéry, *Guide des amateurs*, 140–41.

27. Rice, *Jefferson's Paris*, 14.

28. Schama, *Citizens*, 134–35.

29. Ibid., 136.

30. Ségur, *Memoirs*, 3:495.

31. Robert Darnton, *The Literary Underground of the Old Regime* (Cambridge, Mass., 1982), v. See also his more recent study *The Forbidden Best-Sellers of Pre-Revolutionary France* (New York, 1995). Darnton's landmark thesis on the impact of Grub Street's influence on the eve of the Revolution has been extended by a number of historians; see Sarah Maza, *Private Lives and Public Affairs* (Berkeley, 1993), 30–34.

32. Alexis de Tocqueville, *The Old Régime and the French Revolution*, trans. Stuart Gilbert (New York, 1955), 138.

33. TJ to David Humphreys, Aug. 14, 1787, *Papers*, 12:32.

34. TJ to James Currie, Jan. 24, 1785, *Papers*, 7:604–6, 635.

35. Elkins and McKitrick, *Age of Federalism*, 163–93. Chap. 4, "The Republic's Capital City," is an original and perceptive discussion of the problems of a capital city as they relate to the idealism of the period. Although the capital was often called "Washington's Folly," it was TJ who carried out the important task of overseeing the "New Town" that was, in Benjamin Latrobe's words, "neither a village, town or city."

36. *Notes*, ed. Peden, 165.

37. Ibid., 153.

38. Edward C. Carter II, "Benjamin Henry Latrobe and the Growth and Development of Washington, 1798–1818," *Records of the Columbia Historical Society* (Washington, D.C., 1971–72): 128–49.

39. Paul F. Norton, "Thomas Jefferson and the Planning of the National Capital," *Jefferson and the Arts: An Extended View*, ed. William Howard Adams (Washington, 1976), 215.

40. John Trumbull, *Autobiography of Colonel John Trumbull*, ed. Theodore Sizer (New Haven, 1951), 110.

41. TJ to Mme de Tessé, March 20, 1787, *Papers*, 11:226.

42. "Jefferson's Draft of Agenda for the Seat of Government," *Papers*, 17:461–62.

43. TJ to Pierre Charles L'Enfant, April 10, 1791, *Papers*, 20:26.

44. For an original study of the musical theater during TJ's period and later, see James H. Johnson, *Listening in Paris* (Los Angeles, 1995).

45. Thomas E. Crow, *Painters and Public Life in Eighteenth Century Paris* (New Haven, 1985), 226.

46. Marvin Carlson, *The Theatre of the French Revolution* (Ithaca and New York, 1966), 1–6.

47. TJ to George Wythe, Aug. 13, 1786, *Papers*, 10:244; *Writings*, ed. Peterson, 666.

48. Ségur, *Memoirs*, 1:39–40.

49. TJ to James Madison, March 18, 1785, *Papers*, 8:39.

50. Ségur, *Memoirs*, 1:101. Ségur included Silas Deane and Arthur Lee as well as Franklin in his picturesque description.

51. *The Works of John Adams*, ed. C. F. Adams (Boston, 1856), 10 vols, 1:660.

52. TJ to Abigail Adams, June 21, 1785, *Papers*, 8:241.

53. Claude-Anne Lopez, *Mon Cher Papa: Franklin and the Ladies of Paris* (New Haven, 1967), 146.

54. *Letters of Mrs. Adams, the Wife of John Adams*, ed. Charles F. Adams (Boston, 1840), 56.

55. *Diary and Autobiography of John Adams*, ed. Butterfield, 4:58–59. Adams complained of Franklin's work habits, saying that he often had to wait several days for his signature because every "evening was spent, in hearing the Ladies sing and play upon their Piano-fortes and other instruments of Music, and in games of cards, chess, Backgammon &c &c."

Chapter 4. The Patriot Aesthete

1. Karl Lehman, *Thomas Jefferson, American Humanist* (New York, 1947), 217.

2. Morris, *Diary*, 1:83.

3. In 1766, at age 23, TJ made his first trip out of Virginia to Philadelphia, where he was to be inoculated "against smallpox" by Dr. John Morgan. The physician was also a connoisseur and collector who had made the Grand Tour after his five years of medical studies in Edinburgh. In Rome he had followed a "Course of Antiquities" and met the artist Angelica Kauffmann, who painted his portrait in 1764. The record is silent on TJ's visit or later acquaintance with one of the most cultivated men in the colonies, but he could not have failed to note the worldly doctor's catholic library, as well as the drawings and engravings Morgan had brought back with him. *Eye*, ed. W. H. Adams, 96–97. See also *Jefferson and the Arts*, ed. W. H. Adams, 105–32.

4. The duke de Liancourt noted in his journal that although Virginians "of the first class were better read than any other part of the country," the "populace is perhaps more ignorant there than anywhere else." Quoted in *The Works of John Adams*, ed. C. F. Adams (Boston, 1856), 1:92.

5. Wills, *Inventing America*, 13.

6. Buford Pickens, "Mr. Jefferson as Revolutionary Architect," *Journal of the Society of Architectural Historians* 34 (December 1975), 268–71. The project has been dated ca. 1776–78.

7. TJ to William Carmichael, Dec. 26, 1786, *Papers*, 10:633.

8. Monroe was persuaded to settle in Albemarle County, and Madison was not far away in Orange County when he was not in public service. "Without society and a society to our taste," TJ wrote Monroe from Paris, "humans are never contented." Certainly Paris provided a society to his taste.

9. F. Kimball, *Architect*, fig. 79. A page from the notebook is reproduced in facsimile.

10. See Randall, *Jefferson*, 1:32–33. Jacob Rubsamen sent TJ a letter dated Dec. 1, 1780, quoting General Riedasel on the unexpected cultural life at Monticello when he was a guest there during his parole. Seeing TJ's father's map of Virginia on the wall, the general concluded that "this learned man was also a favorite of the Muses." *Papers*, 4:174. The Jefferson household was equipped with an "elegant Harpsichord Piano forte and some Violins," one visitor reported, and later TJ bought at least two violins in Paris. His account book has regular entries for concerts and operas, and his music library grew while he was abroad.

11. *Notes*, ed. Peden, 25.

12. Ibid., 80–81.

13. Chastellux, *Travels*, 2:391.

14. TJ to Rayneval, March 3, 1786, *Papers*, 9:313. These tools may have been the same ones Margaret Smith noted later in the president's office.

15. *Thomas Jefferson's Garden Book*, ed. Edwin Morris Betts (Philadelphia, 1944), 17.

16. Although unremarked by TJ, one would have to note a single exception, the marble statue of Lord Botetourt that stood in the entrance of the capitol building at Williamsburg until it was mutilated during the Revolution. It now stands in the basement of the library of the College of William and Mary in Williamsburg.

17. TJ estimated that the 148 titles comprising 379 volumes on the Skipwith List would cost approximately £100 sterling. He estimated the value of the library he lost in the fire at £200. This would translate into 600 volumes in his first library.

18. H. M. Kellen, "The Arts and Thomas Jefferson," *Ethics* 53, no. 4 (July, 1943): 281.

19. *Signa et Statua antiqua Perrier* (Rome, 1638–53). Perrier spent a number of years in Rome in the first half of the seventeenth century and documented ancient sculpture then extant in Rome, where the book was published. The list of casts in TJ's building notebook has been dated about 1771, and more than half of his nineteen selections are illustrated in Perrier.

20. See Garry Wills's "The Aesthete," reviewing an exhibition of the furnishings of Monticello.

21. These articles eventually filled the 86 crates that returned to the United States. Besides books, the goods included 7 plaster busts by Houdon, 63 oil paintings of various sizes, 48 chairs, tables, Sèvres bisque table decorations, 120 porcelain plates, 4 full-length gilt mirrors, 5 sofas, and silverware, besides table linen, damask hangings, and countless other bibelots. See *Eye*, ed. W. H. Adams, 215–19, for an account of French decorative arts collected by TJ and his American contemporaries. Even Washington could not resist a few French decorative pieces. See F. J. B. Watson, "Americans and French Eighteenth-Century Furniture in the Age of Jefferson," *Jefferson and the Arts*, ed. W. H. Adams, 273–93. The Monticello inventory of 1815 includes two gold-leafed settees, and it has been assumed that they were purchased in Paris. They would have been appropriate for the Hôtel de Langeac, his stylish second house.

22. *The Works of Jonathan Richardson* (London, 1773), 226.

23. Benjamin Harrison to TJ, July 20, 1784, *Papers*, 7:374–78.

24. TJ to Benjamin Harrison, Jan. 12, 1785, *Papers*, 7:599–601. Patrick Henry had succeeded Harrison by the time his reply was received.

25. TJ does not mention the date or circumstances of the modeling of his own bust, but it was finished in time for the Salon exhibition of 1789 that TJ attended, as his friend Baron Grimm noted in his newsletter.

26. Short reported to a friend afterward that "Mme. de la Fayette…did not receive more pleasure on the night of her wedding. Many tears were shed." Shackelford, *Adoptive Son*, 27.

27. TJ's letter of Sept. 27, 1786, and a detailed note on the presentation can be found in *Papers*, 10:407–10.

28. Joseph Ellis, *After the Revolution* (New York, 1979), 36. The two opening chapters deal critically with the paradox of the uncertain role of the arts in the early republic and provide useful colonial background.

29. "Jefferson's Hints to Americans Traveling in Europe," June 1787, *Papers*, 13:264–76.

30. TJ to Thomas Sully, Jan. 8, 1812, *The Writings of Thomas Jefferson*, ed. A. A. Lipscomb and A. E. Bergh, 20 vols. (Washington, 1903), 8:120. The marquis de Chastellux's essay attempting to predict the future of the arts and sciences in America, where the Enlightenment's political philosophy would be put to the test, exposed a troubling issue as far as the arts were concerned, and the limited evidence in the 1780s was not particularly encouraging. Chastellux, Epilogue, *Travels*, 2:529–48.

31. TJ to James Madison, Sept. 20, 1785, *Papers*, 8:534–35. Patrick Henry's letter to TJ dated Sept. 10, 1785, reports that the building already under way "will be the most magnificent in the 13 states by far, unless the Design is alter'd, or ill timed Frugality curtails its Execution. The length is 148 feet—Breadth 118 feet—with four elegant (not

to say magnificent) Fronts. To one who has seen Paris this is nothing; but I give you the Descriptions and I know your predilections will place it in a point equally pleasing with the Structures upon which Architecture hath lavished every thing beautiful and grand" *(Papers*, 8:509). TJ had learned an important lesson in France, far different than his cavalier idea in 1783, when he proposed that Virginia and Maryland build a seat of government and then present it to the Confederation.

32. Marie Kimball, *Jefferson: The Scene in Europe* (New York, 1950), 70–77; *Eye*, ed. W. H. Adams, 225–29.

33. Trumbull, *Autobiography*, 92–93. Before he left Paris in late 1789, TJ offered Trumbull a job as his secretary.

34. Helen A. Cooper, *John Trumbull* (New Haven, 1982), 76–81; TJ's sketch is reproduced as fig. 26. Probably the first copy of the text to reach Paris was a rough, amended manuscript TJ had sent to Filippo Mazzei, then in Paris, who passed it on to Mme de Lafayette's aunt and TJ's later friend the countess de Tessé. *Writings*, ed. Ford, 10:345.

35. TJ to the editor of the *Journal de Paris*, Aug. 29, 1787, *Papers*, 12:61–65. See also editorial note, *Papers*, 1:299–336, for a discussion of TJ's part in drafting the Declaration and the questions surrounding the signing on July 4, 1776. As for his role in the drafting, he merely says in his letter to the *Journal* that "a Committee to prepare a declaration of independence" was appointed by the Congress.

36. TJ's acerbic comments on Dickinson were made while correcting François Soulés' *Histoire des troubles de l'Amérique anglaise;* "Comments on Soulés' *Histoire*," *Papers*, 10:378. As a part of his ongoing propaganda strategy to consolidate political and philosophical support for the Revolution among French intellectuals, Franklin had masterminded the translation of Dickinson's book and adroitly made sure that it was widely circulated. The *Letters* had made a timely appearance just as America, representing "the hope of the human race," in Turgot's words, was beginning to fill the French imagination. When Benjamin Rush visited Paris the year Dickinson's book appeared, he was delighted and surprised to hear enthusiastic praise for it among the philosophes.

37. See Wills, *Inventing America*, 345–51, sorting out the rise of the myth of the Fourth of July, including Jefferson's involvement in the painting. TJ, in his *Notes*, states categorically that the Declaration was signed by all present on the Fourth, but this account has been challenged. See Boyd's note, *Papers*, 1:299–308.

38. Louis Gottschalk, *Lafayette Between the American and French Revolutions* (Chicago, 1950), 53–54. A copy of the Declaration could also be seen in George Washington's hand in a portrait of the chief divinity of the house that hung in Lafayette's shrine. Appropriately, the shrine's acolytes were two young American Indians, Otsiquette and Kayenlala, whom the Frenchman had first encountered in the wilds of upper New York State when he had gone there in 1783 to help negotiate a treaty with the Indians for the American Congress in order to force the British to evacuate some military posts. The "enterprising" marquis had arranged for the two young boys—one twelve, the other slightly older—to

be brought to Paris to serve as mascots and pages in his new house in the rue de Bourbon. Lafayette, as the representative of the French "father," the king, had always been popular with the Indians and had been given the name "Kayewla" after one of the great warriors when he was adopted into the Iroquois tribe in 1778. Kayenlala actually performed an Indian dance for guests in the neoclassical salon of Mme de Tessé's Chaville.

39. R. R. Palmer, "The Dubious Democrat," in *Thomas Jefferson: A Profile*, ed. Merrill Peterson (New York, 1967), 86–103. TJ is not consistent in this position.

40. TJ to Rev. Charles Clay, Jan. 27, 1790, *Papers*, 16:129.

41. Robert M. S. McDonald, "Thomas Jefferson's Anonymous Authorship of the Declaration of Independence," essay based on master's thesis, University of North Carolina, typescript (n.d.). The sermon was printed first in New Haven and later in Worcester, Mass. Joel Barlow may well have seen the reference at that time, inspiring the later tribute in Paris.

42. "A Fourth of July Tribute to Jefferson," *Papers*, 15:239–41.

43. TJ to John Paradise, July 5, 1789, *Papers*, 15:242.

44. *Papers*, 15:240–41, n. Morris refused to join the other Americans in signing the tribute to TJ, without recording a clear explanation. The editors point out that other Americans in Paris who did not sign the tribute were all connected to the commercial activities of Robert Morris, whose "deranged" business had given TJ some official concern. John Adams to Benjamin Rush, June 21, 1811, *The Spur of Fame: Dialogues of John Adams and Benjamin Rush* (San Marino, Cal., 1966), 182.

45. TJ to James Madison, quoted in Julian Boyd, *The Declaration of Independence* (Princeton, 1945), 11.

46. John Trumbull to TJ, Nov. 28, 1817, Trumbull, *Autobiography*, 311.

47. *Eye*, ed. W. H. Adams, 103.

48. Trumbull, *Autobiography*, 152.

49. Anita Brookner, *Jacques-Louis David* (New York, 1980), 68.

50. TJ to Mme de Bréhan, March 14, 1789, *Papers*, 14:656. An artist herself, Mme de Bréhan, sister-in-law and mistress of the French minister to the United States, was a member of Maria Cosway's small circle of Parisian friends. She seems to have been regularly in Trumbull's party in August and September 1786.

51. TJ to John Trumbull, Aug. 30, 1787, *Papers*, 12:69.

52. Brookner, *David*, 82.

53. TJ to Mme de Tott, Feb. 28, 1787, *Papers*, 11:187 and April 5, 1787, *Papers*, 11:270. See also Thomas Crow, *Emulation: Making Artists for Revolutionary France* (New Haven, 1995).

54. Trumbull, *Autobiography*, 105.

55. Stephen Lloyd, ed., *Richard and Maria Cosway: Regency Artists of Taste and Fashion* (Edinburgh, 1995), 23. In a letter written to Sir John Soane in 1830, Maria Cosway expressed concern that if the snuff box were found in her possessions when she died, it

"would no doubt go in the fire." Her portrait of TJ by Trumbull survived in her apartment until it was given to the people of the United States as a gift by the Italian government in 1976 in celebration of the American Bicentennial.

56. Trumbull, *Autobiography*, 105.

57. TJ was familiar with Vigée-Lebrun's work, particularly in the Salons of 1785 and 1787, where her portraits of the queen were featured. But he did not like her portraits. In 1790 he wrote Short to have Lafayette's portrait "drawn" for his collection "of American worthies." "I do not like Mme. le Brun's fan colourings," he cautioned Short, adding that "of all possible occasions it would be worst applied to a hero." TJ's prejudice prompted Short to commission Joseph Boze, a run-of-the-mill artist, to carry out an inferior job. TJ specified that it be the same size as the Washington portrait (by Wright but finished by Trumbull) that was still hanging in the dining room of the Hôtel de Langeac.

58. "Autobiography," *Writings*, ed. Peterson, 110–11. Trumbull does not specifically mention that Jefferson or the Cosways were with him at Vigée-Lebrun's dinner but says that after dinner David and the party "did make me the honor to visit my pictures."

59. Cosway's reputation as a rake with a highly developed sexual appetite is confirmed in a letter to the collector Townley, who was in Italy in 1772: "Italy for ever I say—if the Italian women fuck as well in Italy as they do here, you must be happy indeed—I am such a zealot for them, that I'll be damned if ever I fuck an English woman again (if I can help it)." Lloyd, *Richard and Maria Cosway*, 29.

60. Ségur, *Memoirs*, 2:28.

61. Honour, *Neoclassicism*, 21–22. The author's penetrating analysis of the relationship of the antique to late eighteenth-century art has been liberally tapped here and elsewhere in this study.

62. Francis Haskell, *Past and Present in Art and Taste* (New Haven, 1987), 31–45.

63. TJ's friend Joel Barlow, who had met d'Hancarville, became intrigued by the growing literature on phallic cults and advanced the theory that the Trees of Liberty sprouting in America and revolutionary France went back to the myth of the dismembered penis of Osiris cast into the Nile to insure fertility—a myth which the baron had resurrected. See Simon Schama, *Landscape and Memory* (New York, 1995), 251–55. As secretary of state, TJ appointed Barlow special emissary to rescue American hostages in Algiers. While on this mission, Barlow furthered his investigations on the rites and religions of Egypt.

64. TJ to Mme de Tessé, March 20, 1787, *Papers*, 11:226; TJ to James Monroe, Dec. 18, 1786, *Papers*, 11:612.

65. *Papers*, 13:264–76.

66. TJ to Mme de Tott, April 5, 1787, *Papers*, 11:271.

67. Fremyn de Fontenille to TJ, Oct. 23, 1787, *Papers*, 12:258–59; trans. in Rice, *Jefferson's Paris*, 107; see also pp. 105–7 and *Papers*, 12:199, "Note on Mont Calvaire." For a sense of Valérien's history, see the fine passage in Schama's *Landscape and Memory*, 431–44, irresistibly called "Calvaries of Convenience."

68. "Jefferson's Hints to Americans Traveling in Europe," *Papers*, 11:417.

69. TJ to Mme de Tessé, March 20, 1787, *Papers*, 11:226. The piece that caught his eye was actually called *Diana and Endymion*. He told Mme de Tessé that it was the second time he had fallen in love in France. The first time was with a piece of architecture, the Maison Carrée at Nîmes. He was only "violently smitten" with the Hôtel de Salm, he told his correspondent. She replied that she had read his letter to all her friends, as "they used to read those of the apostles at the gatherings of the early Christians." Rice, *Jefferson's Paris*, 98.

70. Biographical note, *Papers*, 10:157–60.

71. See *Eye*, ed. W. H. Adams, entries 151–53 and 527–31 for a detailed discussion of TJ's silver designs.

72. TJ to Thomas Johnson, March 8, 1792, *Papers*, 23:237.

73. These measurements are in *Papers*, 11:423–25. See also "Creative Architecture," chap. 10 in Lehman, *Humanist*. The "Epilogue" in Wills, *Inventing America*, contains a brief but pregnant interpretation of TJ the practical idealist.

74. TJ to Maria Cosway, July 1, 1787, *Papers*, 11:519–20.

75. TJ to William Short, April 7, 1787, *Papers*, 11:214.

76. TJ to Maria Cosway, July 1, 1787, *Papers*, 11:520.

77. For a definitive reconstruction of the Italian trip, see Shackelford, "Peep into Elysium," in *Jefferson and the Arts*, ed. W. H. Adams, 235–69. Shackelford suggests that TJ commented sparsely on sightseeing because he had all the information in his guidebooks. These guidebooks with city plans were in his library at Monticello and were loaned to Major L'Enfant when he began to lay out the Federal City.

78. TJ to William Short, May 21, 1787, *Papers*, 11:371–72.

79. TJ to Lafayette, April 11, 1787, *Papers*, 11:283.

80. TJ to John Page, May 4, 1786, *Papers*, 9:445.

81. See Edward Dumbauld, "Jefferson and Adams' English Garden Tour," in *Jefferson and the Arts*, ed. W. H. Adams, 135–57. All quotations are taken from this text.

82. *Papers*, 13:269.

83. Trumbull, *Autobiography*, 116.

84. TJ to Mme de Corny, June 30, 1787, *Papers*, 11:509.

85. Elkins and McKitrick, *Age of Federalism*, 199–204. I am indebted to the authors here and elsewhere for their illuminating discussion of the concept of the "middle state" and TJ's idealism. See also Leo Marx, *The Machine in the Garden* (New York, 1964), to which I express a great debt.

Chapter 5. The Liberal, Literary, Scientific Air of Paris

1. François Jean, marquis de Chastellux, *Voyages de M. le Marquis de Chastellux dans l'Amérique Septentrionale dans les années 1780, 1781 & 1782* (Paris, 1786, first authorized

edition). A limited edition of 24 copies had been privately printed, probably in 1782, before Chastellux left America. When a pirated edition was printed in Kassel, the authorized printing of 1786 followed. TJ received a copy of the limited edition in 1784. See *Catalogue of the Library of Thomas Jefferson*, ed. Millicent E. Sowerby, 5 vols. (Washington and Charlottesville, 1983), 4:201–3; for extended note, Chastellux, *Travels*, ed. Rice, 393–96.

2. TJ to Chastellux, Sept. 2, 1785, *Papers*, 8:467.

3. John Dos Passos, "A Portico Facing the Wilderness," in *Profile*, ed. Peterson, 65. TJ's sensitivity to the avant garde of his day makes Dos Passos's simile fitting.

4. Marquis de Chastellux, *Travels in North America*, trans. George Grieve (London, 1787), 2:43.

5. Introduction, *Notes*, ed. Peden, xi. TJ's friend Charles Thomson thought he ought to find a better title. For a brief but suggestive passage on the relationship between economics and politics in the *Notes*, see Richard Mathews, *The Radical Politics of Thomas Jefferson* (Lawrence, Kan., 1995), 35–45.

6. TJ to D'Anmour, Nov. 30, 1780, *Papers*, 4:167–68.

7. Amable and Alexander Lory to TJ, Dec. 16, 1780, *Papers*, 4:211; TJ to John Fitzgerald, Feb. 27, 1781, *Papers*, 5:15; John Fitzgerald to TJ, April 1, 1781, *Papers*, 5:311–12; TJ to James Hunter, May 28, 1781, *Papers*, 6:25; note, *Papers*, 6:258; Wilson, "Jefferson and the Republic of Letters," 55; Robert Darnton, *The Business of the Enlightenment: A Publishing History of the Encyclopédie, 1775–1800* (Cambridge, Mass., 1982), 318–19. Darnton gives TJ credit for promoting the *Encyclopédie* in America, although he did not actually buy his own copy until 1786, after he got to Paris. Darnton's account of the publication of the Lucca edition is in *Business*, 34.

8. TJ to Chastellux, Jan. 16, 1784, *Papers*, 6:467. TJ had first considered a Philadelphia printer, but decided it would be cheaper in Paris.

9. TJ to Charles Thomson, June 21, 1785, *Papers*, 8:245; Thomson to TJ, March 9, 1785, *Papers*, 8:16. Thomson's emendations would be added to later editions.

10. Adam Ferguson, *An Essay on the History of Civil Society* (Edinburgh, 1767), 375.

11. Lord Henry Home Kames, *Six Sketches on the History of Man* (Philadelphia, 1776), 1:525.

12. TJ to William Short, March 15, 1787, *Papers*, 11:215.

13. TJ to Chastellux, June 7, 1785, *Papers*, 8:184; TJ to Madison, May 11, 1785, *Papers*, 8:147.

14. John Adams to TJ, May 25, 1785, *Adams-Jefferson Letters*, ed. Cappon, 1:21.

15. The presentation inscription on the flyleaf of the copy sent to Richard Price is reproduced in *Papers*, 9:246.

16. For details concerning the distribution of the first edition of the *Notes*, see Coolie Verner, "Mr. Jefferson Distributes his *Notes*: A Preliminary Checklist of the First Edition," *Bulletin of the New York Public Library* 4 (April 1952): 159–86. At least forty copies of the private edition are unaccounted for, and many unrecorded copies undoubtedly

were sent to European colleagues and friends. TJ's letter to Madison was on Sept. 1, 1785, *Papers*, 8:462.

17. Gilbert Chinard, "Eighteenth-Century Theories on America as a Human Habitat," *Proceedings, American Philosophical Society* 91 (1947): 30.

18. Quote from Buffon's *Natural History of Man* as in Chinard, "Eighteenth-Century Theories."

19. Ibid., 31.

20. Condorcet, "The Influence of the American Revolution on Europe," in *Selected Writings*, 85–108. This is the first translation of Condorcet's entry in the essay competition. European governments that were losing subjects by emigration were also, as a matter of principle, interested in discouraging it through negative propaganda.

21. *Notes*, ed. Peden, 55.

22. Ibid., 63–64.

23. Ibid., 275.

24. Ibid., 64.

25. Abbé de Raynal, *Histoire Philosophique et Politique des Etablissemens, et du Commerce des Européens dans les deux Indes*, 4 vols. (Amsterdam, 1770). The work went through many editions, and TJ listed a copy in his library. See *Catalogue of the Library*, ed. Sowerby, 1:214–15, n.

26. Buffon to TJ, Dec. 31, 1785, *Papers*, 9:130–31. See Malone, *Jefferson and His Time*, 2:99–100, where the incident is discussed.

27. TJ to Buffon, Oct. 1, 1787, *Papers*, 12:195. For details of the transaction, see "From John Sullivan with Account of Expenses for Obtaining Moose Skeleton," *Papers*, 11:320–21.

28. Condorcet, *Selected Writings*, 81.

29. Claude Manceron, *Blood of the Bastille* (New York, 1989), 249. The pamphlet *Sentiments d'un républicain sur les Assemblées provençal et les Etats Généraux* was actually published anonymously.

30. On the Declaration, see Condorcet's essay "On the Influence of the American Revolution on Europe," *Selected Writings*, 76–83. His comment on the Virginia Bill of Rights was made in "Idées sur le despotisme…," in N. A. J. M. Caritat de Condorcet, *Oeuvres*, ed. Arthur O'Connor and Dominique Arago (Stuttgart, 1968), 9:168. TJ was also aware of the quality of his native tongue. In arguing against a foreign education, he warned: "I am of the opinion that never was an instance of man's writing or speaking his native tongue with elegance who passed from fifteen to twenty years of age out of the country where it was spoken." *Papers*, 8:636.

31. Jefferson had apparently sent the manuscript of his *Draught of a Fundamental Constitution for the Commonwealth of Virginia* to his Paris printer while the *Notes* were being printed, and copies of the constitution were appended to some but not all copies. See Verner, "Mr. Jefferson Distributes his *Notes*," 160.

32. Richard H. Popkin, "Condorcet Abolitionist," *Condorcet Studies*, ed. Lenora C. Rosenfield (Atlantic Highlands, N.J., 1984), 35.

33. John Chester Miller, *The Wolf by the Ears: Thomas Jefferson and Slavery* (Charlottesville, 1991), 17. I have relied particularly on chap. 6, "Slavery and the *Notes on Virginia*," in Lipscomb and Bergh, *Writings*, 1:72–73.

34. TJ to J. N. Démeunier, June 26, 1786, *Papers*, 10:63.

35. TJ to Paul Bentalou, Aug. 25, 1786, *Papers*, 10:296. It seems highly unlikely that the Hemingses were aware of the French law. James Hemings was freed by TJ when he returned from France on Feb. 5, 1796; *Farm Book*, 15.

36. Popkin, "Condorcet Abolitionist," 36.

37. Condorcet, *Selected Writings*, 76. *De l'influence de la Révolution* was first published in 1786. For TJ's attempted translation, see *Papers*, 14:494–98. Although the translation was never completed, four pages survive.

38. TJ to Dr. Edward Bancroft, Jan. 26, 1788, *Papers*, 14:492–93. TJ continued to explore and test a tenant system that could replace the slaves or at least transfer his responsibility for them by including them in the terms of the lease, hardly an act of emancipation. See *Farm Book*, 161–85.

39. TJ to Brissot, Feb. 11, 1788, *Papers*, 10:577–78.

40. Short to TJ, Dec. 25, 1789, *Papers*, 16:46.

41. Manceron, *Blood of the Bastille*, 225–35.

42. *Notes*, ed. Peden, 223. The Act for Establishing Religious Freedom, translated into French, was published by TJ as a pamphlet in 1786. TJ's original language of the Preamble is stronger than that adopted and quoted here; see *Papers*, 2:309.

43. Malone, *Jefferson and His Time*, 1:274–75.

44. See *Notes*, ed. Peden, 291–92, n. 7.

45. Ibid., 159.

46. TJ to James Madison, Dec. 16, 1786, *Papers*, 10:604.

47. TJ to George Wythe, Aug. 20, 1786, *Papers*, 10:244.

48. TJ to Mirabeau, Aug. 21, 1786, *Papers*, 10:283. The letter is undated; *Writings*, ed. Ford, 4:283, quoted in Malone, *Jefferson and His Time*, 2:104, assigns the date of Aug. 20.

49. Mazzei's "Memoranda Regarding Persons and Affairs in Paris," n.d., *Papers*, 7:385.

50. Kimball, *Scene*, 97.

51. *Notes*, ed. Peden, xviii.

52. The review appeared in the *Mercure de France*, June 2 and 9, 1787; quoted in Malone, *Jefferson and His Time*, 2:106. There was still no mention of TJ's authorship of the Declaration.

53. Manceron, *Blood of the Bastille*, 177–81.

54. Darnton, *Forbidden Best-Sellers*, xix.

55. TJ to John Rutledge, Jr., Feb. 2, 1788, *Papers*, 12:557.

56. See Philip Mazzei, *Researches on the United States*, trans. Constance D. Sherman

(Charlottesville, 1976), xi–xvii. See also William Short to TJ, March 14, 1788, *Papers*, 12:667–68.

57. Malone, *Jefferson and His Time*, 2:110. Malone concludes that the paper's *privilège* was revoked.

58. Elkins and McKitrick, *Age of Federalism*, 304.

59. This discussion is largely based on the editorial note on TJ and the *Encyclopédie*, *Papers*, 10:3–11, and the documents that follow.

60. TJ to Adams, Aug. 27, 1786, *Papers*, 10:303.

61. Count Mirabeau, *Considérations sur l'ordre de Cincinnatus* (Paris, n.d.).

62. "Autobiography," *Writings*, ed. Peterson, 44. Even though the noun *aristocrat*, according to R. R. Palmer, was not used widely in English before 1789, TJ employed it before that date in his commentary for the *Encyclopédie*.

63. TJ to Rev. James Madison, Oct. 28, 1785, *Papers*, 8:681–82. See also Sloan, *Principle and Interest*, 50–85.

64. Chastellux, *Travels*, 2:438.

65. TJ to James Madison, Sept. 6, 1789, *Papers*, 15:396; see also editorial note, 15:384–91. See Sloan's discussion of the letter in "The Earth Belongs in Usufruct to the Living," *Jeffersonian Legacies*, 281–315.

66. *Papers*, 10:50.

67. TJ to John Adams, Aug. 27, 1789, *Papers*, 10:302–3.

68. See editorial note, *Papers*, 10:364–83. Also see *Catalogue of the Library*, ed. Sowerby, 1:223. It is not clear how TJ and Soulés first met.

69. TJ had similar disturbing reports on American manners and had apologized to Mme de Bréhan that she might encounter Americans trying to ape European etiquette. When he heard that Boston ladies were indulging in too much fashion, he suggested to Abigail Adams that they adopt sensible republican uniforms.

70. TJ to Du Pont de Nemours, March 2, 1809, *The Correspondence of Jefferson and Du Pont de Nemours*, ed. Gilbert Chinard (New York, 1979), 144–45.

71. The definition of "peuple" in the *Encyclopédie* did not, as Chartier points out, recognize "the workers and plowmen" as political agents. See Roger Chartier, *The Cultural Origins of the French Revolution*, trans. Lydia G. Cochrane (Durham, N.C., 1991), 29.

72. TJ to Samuel Kercheval, July 20, 1816, *Writings*, ed. Ford, 12:4–7.

73. Joseph F. Kett, "Education," *Thomas Jefferson: A Reference Biography*, ed. Merrill Peterson (New York, 1986), 244.

74. This brief summary of the Du Pont–Jefferson friendship is drawn largely from the Introduction of *Correspondence of Jefferson and Du Pont de Nemours*, ed. Chinard, ix–cxxiii.

75. Manceron, *Blood of the Bastille*, 377. Napoleon made Volney "count of the Empire" in 1808.

76. *Catalogue of the Library*, ed. Sowerby, 4:155.

77. See ibid., 2:2–3.

78. David N. Mayer, *The Constitutional Thought of Thomas Jefferson* (Charlottesville, 1994), 135–41. Mayer's discussion is able and succinct.

79. H. Adams, *History*, 1:99.

80. Smith, *First Forty Years*, 80–81.

81. See Morton and Lucia White, *The Intellectual Versus the City* (Cambridge, Mass., 1962), 16–17. The authors quite rightly point out that at the time of this remark in 1800, TJ was also working on scientific means to control the disease.

82. TJ to Baron Geismar, Sept. 6, 1785, *Papers*, 8:500. See also Drew McCoy, *The Elusive Republic Political Economy in Jeffersonian America* (Chapel Hill, 1980), chap. 2, "The Republican Revolution."

83. Richard Hofstadter, *The American Political Tradition* (New York, 1948), 24.

Chapter 6. The Diplomat

1. Randall, *Jefferson*, 1:114.

2. Morris, *Diary*, 1:100.

3. "Autobiography," *Writings*, ed. Peterson, 62.

4. G. K. van Hogendorp to TJ, April 6, 1784, *Papers*, 7:81–82.

5. *Journal of the Continental Congress*, 34 vols. (Washington, D.C., 1976), 26:269–70.

6. Sloan, *Principle and Interest*, esp. chap. 1, "The Thralldom of Debt," which should be read as background to TJ's diplomatic mission.

7. Adam Smith famously intended for his *Wealth of Nations* to demolish Denham's mercantilist doctrine.

8. TJ to Chastellux with enclosure, Sept. 2, 1785, *Papers*, 8:467–70.

9. Van Hogendorp's Memorandum, *Papers*, 7:296–98. TJ's "Notes on Commerce of the Northern States" and related documents can be found in *Papers*, 7:323–55.

10. Albert Sorel, *Europe under the Old Regime*, trans. Francis H. Herrick (Los Angeles, 1947), 16. See also Robert W. Tucker and David Hendrickson, *Empire of Liberty: The Statecraft of Thomas Jefferson* (New York, 1990), 13.

11. TJ to Chastellux, Jan. 16, 1784, *Papers*, 6:467.

12. TJ to Samuel Smith, May 18, 1806, *Writings*, ed. Ford, 10:264.

13. TJ to Madison, Dec. 29, 1787, *Papers*, 12:442. See also Walter Lafeber, "Jefferson and an American Foreign Policy," in *Jeffersonian Legacies*, ed. Onuf, 377–378, n. The point is elaborated in *Notes*, ed. Peden.

14. TJ to John Jay, Aug. 14, 1785, *Papers*, 8:373. This suggestion is made in Lafeber, "Jefferson and an American Foreign Policy," 375. See also TJ to John Paul Jones, Aug. 3, 1785, *Papers*, 8:339.

15. *Notes*, ed. Peden, 164–65.

16. TJ to John Jay, Aug. 23, 1785, *Papers*, 8:426–27.

17. Abstract of Gouverneur Morris's Letters on Commerce copied in TJ's hand, *Papers*, 7:350–55.

18. *Profile*, ed. Peterson, 106. My interpretation is influenced by Merrill Peterson's essay "Thomas Jefferson and Commercial Policy, 1783–1793," *Profile*, 104–34.

19. McCoy, *Reference Biography*, 105.

20. Sloan, *Principle and Interest*, 38–39. Jefferson, of course, excluded himself from the effects of the virus, although his spending is documented in his *Memorandum Books*, ed. Bear and Stanton.

21. Marx, *Machine*, 73–144. See also Mathews, *Radical Politics*, 31–52.

22. McCoy, *Reference Biography*, 104.

23. Marx, *Machine*, 132.

24. TJ to John Bannister, Jr., Oct. 15, 1785, *Papers*, 8:15.

25. Editorial note, "Jefferson's Contemplated Mission to Europe," and documents that follow, *Papers*, 6:210–16.

26. Kimball, *Scene*, 17–18.

27. See "Report on Letters from Europe," *Papers*, 6:394, 401, n. 3, and "Jefferson's 'General Form' of a Treaty," *Papers*, 7:463–70.

28. TJ to William Short (extract), [April 30, 1784], *Papers*, 7:149.

29. Shackelford, *Adoptive Son*, 16.

30. *Diary and Autobiography of John Adams*, ed. Butterfield, 4:118–19.

31. *Adams-Jefferson Letters*, ed. Cappon, 1:13.

32. Adams to Arthur Lee, Jan. 31, 1785, in P. Smith, *John Adams*, 2:616.

33. Abigail Adams to Mrs. Shaw, Dec. 14, 1784, *Letters of Mrs. Adams*, ed. C. F. Adams, 67–70.

34. *The Book of John and Abigail*, ed. Butterfield et al., 389–90. Abigail Adams reported to her sister Mrs. Cranch on Dec. 9, 1784 that TJ had "been sick, and confined to his house for six weeks." (*Letters of Mrs. Adams*, ed. C. F. Adams, 62). TJ wrote von Hogendorp on Nov. 20 that he "had few hours wherein I could do any thing, and these were devoted to duty of public business" (*Papers*, 7:545). Earlier he had confessed to the Dutchman that the chronic uncertainty of his health had caused him to retire "from fashionable society" and to concern himself "with affairs of public interests, his sole diversion being that offered by belles lettres." Quoted in *Papers*, 7:82, n.

35. Adams to Elbridge Gerry, Dec. 12, 1784, *Papers*, 7:382n.

36. TJ to Madison, Jan. 30, 1787, *Papers*, 11:94–95.

37. Wills, *Inventing America*, 32–33.

38. See "Report on Letters from the American Ministers in Europe," *Papers*, 6:394 and 7:267. As formulated by Tocqueville, a "democracy can only with great difficulty regulate the details of an important undertaking," such as foreign policy, "preserve in a fixed design, and work out its execution in spite of serious obstacles. It cannot combine its measures with secrecy or await their consequences with patience." Quoted in Lafeber, *Jeffersonian Legacies*, 377, where "the Tocqueville problem" is discussed.

39. TJ to Monroe, June 17, 1785, quoted in "Jefferson's 'General Form' of a Treaty," *Papers*, 7:470, n.

40. "Autobiography," *Writings*, ed. Peterson, 57.

41. The text noting the "reasons in support of the new proposed Articles" is found in *Papers*, 7:491–93. Marie Kimball attributes the text to TJ; see *Scene*, 25–27.

42. Kimball, *Scene*, 27.

43. *Papers*, 7:465–66, n.

44. The reciprocal citizen proposal was first published by Julian Boyd with extended notes in *Papers*, 8:315–20, and my account follows it.

45. TJ to James Monroe, June 17, 1785, *Papers*, 8:227–33.

46. TJ to John Adams, July 28, 1785, *Papers*, 8:317.

47. TJ to Henry Skipwith, July 28, 1787, *Papers*, 11:636. The letter ends with a plea for a policy of "pay as you go," something TJ privately never managed to do throughout his life, notably when faced with the temptations of Europe.

48. "Autobiography," *Writings*, ed. Peterson, 57.

49. James Currie to TJ, Nov. 20, 1784, *Papers*, 7:538–39.

50. P. Smith, *John Adams*, 45.

51. TJ to Francis Eppes, Feb. 5, 1785, *Papers*, 7:635.

52. TJ to Monroe, March 18, 1785, *Papers*, 8:43.

53. TJ to John Jay, June 17, 1785, *Papers*, 8:226.

54. Kimball, *Scene*, 36–37. Ibid., 38–39, quoted from *Mémoires du Comte de Cheverny*, 1:82–84.

55. Ibid., 38. Although there has been speculation about TJ's conversational French, there can be no doubt that he could carry on everyday exchanges at both diplomatic and social levels, as he regularly reports in his correspondence. He also believed that a command of the local language was essential for American foreign officers.

56. No doubt TJ recalled that American protocol might upset the count when the Frenchman arrived in New York as minister in 1787. "It would have been better, therefore in a new country, to have excluded etiquette altogether." TJ to Count de Moustier, May 17, 1788, *Papers*, 13:173.

57. *Writings*, ed. Peterson, 705. See also Henry Adams's amusing account of the social chaos and bad feelings precipitated by the rules when the new English minister arrived in town. There is some indication that he perceived the insult was deliberate. *History*, 546–51.

58. H. Adams, *History*, 552–53.

59. Randall, *Jefferson*, 1:421. The "un-English particulars" Randall refers to were his fastidious reserve where manners were concerned and his inability to listen to an off-color story without blushing, according to William Short.

60. TJ to Abigail Adams, June 21, 1785, *Papers*, 8:239.

61. Malone, *Jefferson and His Time*, 1:35.

62. TJ to Madison, Jan. 30, 1787, *Papers*, 11:96.

63. *Papers*, 12:302, n.

64. TJ to John Jay with enclosure, Jan. 2, 1786, *Papers*, 9:136–46.

65. TJ to Vergennes, Aug. 15, 1785, *Papers*, 8:386.

66. Gottschalk, *Between the American and French Revolutions*, 202. Chap. 15, "Driving Jefferson's Nails," 202–21, is a useful discussion of the background on French-American trade politics. See also Lafayette's letter to Lambert giving the history of the committee in *Letters of Lafayette and Jefferson*, ed. Chinard, 114–22. See also Lafayette to TJ with enclosure, "From Lafayette with 'Avis au Comité du Commerce,'" *Papers*, 9:337–446. Condorcet may have helped draft the document. TJ recommended to Madison that Lafayette be given a gift of land in Virginia for all of his assistance, adding that he might need it as an asylum. TJ to James Madison, Feb. 8, 1786, *Papers*, 8:266.

67. *Papers*, 14:242–56.

68. Document with endorsement "on sending youth to Europe," which the editors believe was intended as an outline for an essay. *Papers*, 8:638.

69. American Commissioners to De Thulemeier, March 14, 1785, *Papers*, 8:27.

70. Rice, *Hotel de Langeac*, 9. TJ's house was in the city, but taxes were collected at the gate attached to the corner of the house at the Champs-Elysées and the rue de Berri.

71. TJ to John Adams, July 1, 1787, *Papers*, 11:516.

72. *Writings*, ed. Peterson, 792.

73. TJ to Nicholas Lewis, Sept. 17, 1787, *Papers*, 12:134–36; TJ to Lewis, July 11, 1788, *Papers*, 13:343. The homesick envoy had been in Paris only a few weeks when he placed the first of many orders for Virginia hams.

74. TJ to Geismar, July 13, 1788, *Papers*, 13:357.

75. TJ to Alexander Donald, *Papers*, 12:594.

76. TJ to John Adams, Aug. 30, 1787, *Papers*, 12:67–68.

77. TJ to John Jay, Oct. 8, 1787, *Papers*, 12:217.

78. Chinard, *Trois amitiés*, 13–14.

79. TJ to Abigail Adams, Aug. 30, 1787, *Papers*, 12:66.

80. TJ to Count Elie de Moustier, Oct. 9, 1787, *Papers*, 12:224; TJ to Madison, Oct. 8, 1787, *Papers*, 12:219.

81. Madison to TJ, Dec. 8, 1788, *Papers*, 14:340–41.

82. TJ to Maria Cosway, Jan. 14, 1789, *Papers*, 14:446.

83. TJ to John Adams, July 1, 1787, *Papers*, 11:517.

84. As Julian Boyd has pointed out in a long editorial note, "Proposals for Funding the Foreign Debt" (*Papers*, 14:190–97), historians have shied away from the complex subject. In 1996 Herbert Sloan confronted some of the knotty problem in *Principle and Interest*.

85. See Sloan, *Principle and Interest*, 50–85 and Sloan's essay "The Earth Belongs in Usufruct to the Living," *Legacies*, 281–315.

86. BFAR, 338–41. See also Schama, *Patriots and Liberators*, 58–128.

87. *Papers*, 12:77 n.

88. TJ to David Humphreys, Aug. 14, 1787, *Papers*, 12:33.

89. John Adams to Abigail Adams, March 14, 1788, *Papers*, 11:517.

90. TJ to Washington, May 2, 1788, *Papers*, 12:33.

91. Joyce Appleby, "What Is Still American in the Political Philosophy of Thomas Jefferson?" *William and Mary Quarterly*, 3d ser., 39 (April 1982): 287–309.

92. "Autobiography," *Writings*, ed. Peterson, 72.

93. American Commissioners to the President of Congress, *Papers*, 7:496.

94. TJ to James Monroe, Nov. 11, 1784, *Papers*, 7:512; Feb. 6, 1785, *Papers*, 7:639.

95. TJ to William Carmichael, May 5, 1786, *Papers*, 9:449.

96. John Adams to Carmarthen, March 13, 1786, *Papers*, 8:327.

97. TJ to William Carmichael, May 5, 1786, *Papers*, 9:449.

98. American Commissioners to John Jay, April 25, 1786, *Papers*, 9:407. Again, Sloan, *Principle and Interest* provides a useful background to the London negotiations.

99. "Autobiography," *Writings*, ed. Peterson, 57–58.

100. Ibid., 57. TJ's recollections of the presentation 35 years later have become a durable part of American mythology, but his version has been challenged by Charles Ritcheson. Ritcheson's argument hinges largely on the fact that John Adams was silent on the event at the time and that there is no contemporary evidence to support TJ's recollection. He also argues that the reputed insult was contrary to British court etiquette.

101. TJ to John Jay, Jan. 11, 1789, *Papers*, 14:430.

102. Sloan, *Principle and Interest*, 41–42. TJ also met with his private creditors while he was in London.

103. Bedini, *Jefferson and His Copying Machines*, 1–30.

104. TJ to William Stephen Smith, July 9, 1786, *Papers*, 10:116; TJ to Lafayette, July 18, 1786, *Papers*, 10:505. Lafayette's chiding letter to TJ is missing.

105. "Autobiography," *Writings*, ed. Peterson, 59–60.

106. TJ to John Jay, Aug. 12, 1788, *Papers*, 15:500–501.

107. Malone, *Jefferson*, 2:199–200.

108. The summary of the Consular Convention of 1788 is based chiefly on notes and documents in *Papers*, 14:56–180. TJ cleverly got Montmorin to agree that both the French and English texts would be treated as "original and authentic in all courts of justice." *Papers*, 14:90.

109. TJ to John Jay, Nov. 14, 1788, *Papers*, 14:58. TJ's emphasis on the representative's fluency in the local language implies that he met his own standards in conversational French.

110. I have greatly benefited from Bernard Bailyn's short but penetrating essay "Jefferson" in *Faces of Revolution*, 22–41, summing up TJ's diplomatic career in Paris.

Chapter 7. The Women in His Life

1. *Commonplace Book*, ed. Wilson, 14.

2. TJ to Carlo Bellini, Sept. 30, 1785, *Papers*, 8:569. The issue of adultery among *le gratin* during this period is ably discussed in Sarah Maza's *Private Lives and Public Affairs* (Berkeley, 1993), 282–86.

3. TJ to John Banister, Jr., Oct. 15, 1785, *Papers*, 8:636.

4. TJ to William Short, March 27, 1787, *Papers*, 11:247.

5. TJ to Anne Willing Bingham, Feb. 7, 1787, *Papers*, 11:122–23.

6. Rahv, *Discovery*, 296. I have liberally consulted Rahv's introduction and selections of literature, which include six of TJ's letters from Paris.

7. *Diary and Autobiography of John Adams*, ed. Butterfield, 4:123.

8. *Commonplace Book*, ed. Wilson, 139–40. Horace, Epode 2. See also Carl Richard, *The Founders and the Classics* (Cambridge, Mass., 1994), 161–62; Peter Gay, *The Enlightenment: An Interpretation*, 2 vols. (New York, 1966–69), 2:39.

9. Anne Willing Bingham to TJ, June 1, 1787, *Papers*, 11:392–93.

10. Joan B. Landes, *Women and the Public Sphere in the Age of the French Revolution* (Ithaca, 1988), 45.

11. Condorcet's essay on the rights of women is reprinted in *Selected Writings*, 97–104. Although it did not appear until 1790, Condorcet had already outlined his argument in his reception address for the academy. His positions on public education as well as on the rights of women were widely discussed during TJ's stay in Paris.

12. Mazzei also reprinted Condorcet's *Influences of the American Revolution in Europe* and *Letters from a Citizen of New Haven* in his history.

13. Young, *Travels*, 94. TJ had ordered a copy of Kirwin's work in 1787, the year Young visited the Lavoisiers. See *Catalogue of the Library*, ed. Sowerby, 1:307–8.

14. Dena Goodman, "Enlightenment Salons: The Convergence of Female and Philosophic Ambitions," *Eighteenth-Century Studies* 22, no. 3 (1989): 329–50.

15. TJ to Maria Cosway, May 21, 1789, *Papers*, 15:143.

16. Note with undated document, *Papers*, 8:637–38. It is placed by the editors between Oct. 15 and 17, 1785. Wine is listed elsewhere under "Production." The fine arts get their own separate schedule. Perhaps only the subjunctive prurient is applicable to the last item, "Sexes have changed business...." Even Fawn Brodie, in *Thomas Jefferson: An Intimate History* (New York, 1974), passed over it in silence. My reading is that TJ perceived women to have moved into spheres of activity formerly reserved exclusively for men, while men identified with the court had become more effeminate. TJ was by no means alone in his concern about the perceived masculinization of women and feminization of men, a sign of society's decline beginning with the ineffectual king. See Maza, *Private Lives and Public Affairs*, 180–81.

17. Maza, *Private Lives and Public Affairs*, 290–95.

18. Landes, *Women and the Public Sphere*, 45.

19. Morris, *Diary*, 1:250. The sole woman on record to have personally expressed an active dislike of the American envoy while he was in Paris was the audacious countess de Flahaut, mistress of Gouverneur Morris and the bishop of Autun. Morris quotes his mistress's cutting remark in his diary: "Cet homme est faux et emporté." Mme de Flahaut spoke perfect English, so it is interesting that she emphasized her peculiar characterization in French. Morris, *Diary*, 1:256.

20. TJ to James Madison, Jan. 30, 1787, *Papers*, 11:95.

21. *Letters of Mrs. Adams*, ed. C. F. Adams, 48. Built earlier in the century, the Hôtel de Rouhalt had served as a *folie* and the setting for the amours of two sisters, actresses who had earned themselves a place in the *chronique scandaleuse* of eighteenth-century Paris.

22. *Letters of Mrs Adams*, ed. C. F. Adams, 87.

23. Ibid., 92.

24. Abigail Adams to TJ, June 6, 1785, *Papers*, 8:178–81; TJ to Abigail Adams, June 21, 1785, *Papers*, 8:240–41. Later he told Abigail that he had waited to send the letter by private conveyance because it was "full of treason." July 7, 1785, *Papers*, 8:264.

25. TJ to Abigail Adams, Sept. 24, 1785, *Papers*, 8:548.

26. Abigail Adams to TJ, Jan. 86, 1787, *Papers*, 11:502.

27. TJ to Abigail Adams, Feb. 22, 1787, *Papers*, 11:174.

28. Bear, *Hemings Family*, 4–5. Not all scholars agree that John Wayles was Sally Hemings's father. According to Bear, although it is uncertain just when TJ learned of Betty Hemings's relationship with Wayles, it was before the family moved to Monticello in 1775. Bear gives no source for this claim. The literature, both popular and scholarly, on the alleged affair of TJ and Hemings is enormous and grows each year because it is, like so many contemporary conspiracy theories, built on speculation. Fawn Brodie developed her own theories in *Thomas Jefferson: An Intimate History*, a psychobiography. It should be added, however, that not all of her close readings of long-ignored material should be dismissed, as some historians have done, although they must be read with caution. As Brodie admits, the evidence is "subtle" and includes TJ's allusions to "mulatto"-colored soil during his travels, the reference to "Ora-ootan," which, according to Brodie, meant "wild man of the Woods," who at the time was believed to prefer "the black woman over those of his own species." These examples of "evidence" as well as other unprovable theories undermine her argument. Virginius Dabney has made the case for the defense in *The Jefferson Scandals: A Rebuttal* (Lanham, N.Y., and London, 1991), punctuating his argument with misplaced indignation. For a note and bibliography on the subject, see Lucia Stanton, "The Hemings-Jefferson Controversy: A Brief Account," Thomas Jefferson Memorial Research Department, March 1995.

29. Abigail Adams to TJ, June 27, 1787, *Papers*, 11:503; TJ to Mme de Corny, June 30, 1787, *Papers*, 11:509. Brodie and others have suggested that the captain was not disinterested and may have had other plans for the "dashing" mulatto on the return trip. Brodie, *Jefferson*, 216–17.

30. TJ to Elizabeth Eppes, July 28, 1787, *Papers*, 11:638.

31. TJ to Mary Jefferson Bolling, July 23, 1787, *Papers*, 11:612.

32. *Memorandum Books*, ed. Bear and Stanton, 685, 686, 690, 718, 721, 722, 725, 731. There is no evidence that TJ provided Hemings with a French tutor, as he did for her brother, who was expected to take over kitchen duties following his training as a cook. A classmate of the Jefferson girls sent greetings to Sally in a letter to Maria Jefferson after she had returned to Virginia. It is possible that Sally lived at the convent for a time and served as maid to the two girls, but the record is silent.

33. *Pike County Republican*, March 13, 1873.

34. Annette Gordon-Reed, *Thomas Jefferson and Sally Hemings* (Charlottesville, forthcoming).

35. Garry Wills, "Uncle Thomas' Cabin," *New York Review of Books* (April 18, 1974): 26–28.

36. Trumbull, *Autobiography*, 120.

37. *Papers*, 10:445; the entire letter can be found 10:443–54.

38. *Richard and Maria Cosway*, ed. Lloyd, 42. For the most thoroughgoing biographical background of Maria Cosway, which has been a valuable source for my own interpretation, see Stephen Lloyd, "The Accomplished Maria Cosway: Anglo-Italian Artist, Musician, Salon Hostess and Educationalist (1759–1838)," *Journal of Anglo-Italian Studies* 2 (1992): 109–39. One of the surviving children, George Hadfield, became an architect and was recruited by TJ to work on the Federal City.

39. *Papers*, 10:452.

40. *Richard and Maria Cosway*, ed. Lloyd, 41–42.

41. Ibid., 32, 41–45. While Cosway is known primarily for his miniature portraits, there is one well-known group portrait, *Charles Townley with a Group of Connoisseurs*. The commission from Townley grew out of his friendship with the artist, and the original composition was explicitly lecherous, with the six men sexually arousing themselves, while a seventh fondled a statue of Venus. For some unexplained reason, Maria Cosway took the racy original drawing for the painting with her to the convent in Lodi. The subject was cleaned up in the finished work. A note in *Richard and Maria Cosway*, ed. Lloyd, 108, says that the drawing was still at Lodi in the 1970s.

42. Ibid., 45–46.

43. Morris, *Diary*, 1:184.

44. Maria Cosway to TJ, [Oct. 30, 1786], *Papers*, 10:494.

45. TJ to Angelica Church, Nov. 27, 1793, *Writings*, ed. Ford, 7:78. In her old age, Cosway said that she had always wanted to be a nun. Lloyd, "Accomplished Maria Cosway," 124–25.

46. Helen D. Bullock, *My Head and My Heart: A Little History of Thomas Jefferson and Maria Cosway* (New York, 1945), 145.

47. *Papers*, 8:158, n. I have also relied on this note for other details regarding the de Tessé circle.

48. Mme de Tessé to TJ, July 20, 1786, *Papers*, 10:157–58.

49. TJ to Mme de Tessé, March 20, 1787, *Papers*, 11:228, n. 8.

50. TJ to Mme de Tott, Nov. 28, 1786, *Papers*, 10:553—54.

51. TJ to Mme de Tott, April 5, 1787, *Papers*, 11:270—73.

52. Adams, *History*, 101.

53. TJ to Maria Cosway, Jan. 30, 1787, *Papers*, 11:509.

54. TJ to Mme de Corny, Oct. 18, 1787, *Papers*, 12:246—47.

55. Morris, *Diary*, 1:2.

56. TJ to Mme de Corny, June 30, 1787, *Papers*, 11:509.

57. TJ to Angelica Schuyler Church, Sept. 21, 1788, *Papers*, 13:623.

58. TJ to George Washington, Dec. 4, 1788, *Papers*, 11:278.

59. TJ to Martha Jefferson, April 7, 1787, *Papers*, 11:278.

60. TJ to Martha Jefferson, March 28, 1787, *Papers*, 11:251.

61. TJ to Angelica Schuyler Church, Aug. 17, 1788, *Papers*, 13:521.

62. *Papers*, 13:269.

63. TJ to Angelica Church, Aug. 17, 1788, *Papers*, 13:521.

64. Ibid.

65. Andrew Burstein, *The Inner Jefferson* (Charlottesville, 1995), 101. Burstein takes a cautious position on TJ's relationship to Angelica Church. Here and elsewhere I have greatly profited from Burstein's thoughtful reading of TJ's personality. Burstein feels the relation was "without pronounced passion."

66. TJ to Maria Cosway, May 21, 1789, *Papers*, 15:142—43.

67. TJ to Maria Cosway, Sept. 11, 1789, *Papers*, 15:414. A year later, Maria Cosway would be free of her London life, if not tranquil. A few months after her daughter was born on May 4, 1790, Cosway suddenly bolted without husband or child to Italy, where she remained for four years. "Surely it is odd to drop a child and her husband all in a breath," Walpole noted. *The Yale Edition of Horace Walpole's Correspondence*, ed. W. S. Lewis, 48 vols. (New Haven, 1937—83), 11:285.

68. Bullock, *Head and Heart*, 78.

69. Ibid.

70. Count Potocki, *The Manuscript Found in Saragosa*, trans. Ian Maclean (New York, 1995). This is the first edition in English. In 1815, after fashioning a silver bullet and having it blessed by a priest, Potocki blew his brains out.

71. Pierre de la Ruffini, *The Villas of Pliny: From Antiquity to Posterity* (New York, 1983), 48—152; *Gallant and Libertine*, ed. Daniel Gerould (New York, 1983), 28—32.

72. Maria Cosway to TJ, [Dec. 1, 1787], *Papers*, 12:387.

73. Maria Cosway to TJ, Dec. 10, [1787], *Papers*, 12:415.

74. TJ to Maria Cosway, January [31, 1788], *Papers*, 12:540.

75. *Papers*, 10:445.

76. Maria Cosway to TJ, Dec. 25, [1787], *Papers*, 12:459.

77. Angelica Schuyler Church to TJ, July 21, 1788, *Papers*, 13:391.

78. TJ to Angelica Schuyler Church, July 27, 1788, *Papers*, 13:422–23.

79. TJ to Angelica Church, Feb. 17, 1788, *Papers*, 12:600–601.

80. Maria Cosway to TJ, March 6, 1788, *Papers*, 12:645.

81. Richard Mathews, *If Men Were Angels: James Madison and the Heartless Empire of Reason* (Lawrence, Kan., 1995), 245–56. In an original reading of the letter, Mathews casts Madison in the role of the Head's "fridgid speculations," while TJ reveals his philosophy in the "generous spasms of the heart."

82. Maria Cosway to TJ, [Oct. 30, 1786,] *Papers*, 10:494.

83. Appearing first in the *Virginia Advocate* on Aug. 23, 1828, the letter was reprinted in Thomas Jefferson Randolph, *Memoirs, Correspondence, and Miscellanies* (Charlottesville, 1829). The surviving press copy is mutilated, so the salutation "My dear Madam" was appropriated by the *Papers* editors from the Randolph version.

84. Most Jefferson scholars, beginning with Julian Boyd and the editors of the *Papers*, have declared the Head the winner. Richard Mathews and Garry Wills persuasively, but for different reasons, come down on the side of the Heart. The editors of the *Papers* speculate that the composition took place between Oct. 5 and 12, based on its carefully measured lines spaced over the twelve pages, but without any other evidence.

85. TJ to Maria Cosway, Oct. 13, 1786, *Papers*, 10:458. Julian Boyd in his note calls it "one of the notable love letters in the English language" (*Papers*, 10:444), but Douglas Wilson, in his perceptive essay "Jefferson and the Republic of Letters" (*Jeffersonian Legacies*, 69–70), raises questions about this characterization, suggesting that it may be due to our late twentieth-century preoccupations with sexual dimensions and subtexts. I agree.

86. Ibid., *Papers*, 10:445.

87. *Diary and Autobiography of John Adams*, ed. Butterfield, 4:121.

88. I am indebted to Edmund Carpenter, who called this remarkable early anthropological collection to my attention. Begun in 1786 by the marquis de Sérent, governor of the count d'Artois's children, it was first housed in the Bureau des Colonies d'Amérique at Versailles and then moved to the Hôtel de Sérent. It hardly seems possible that TJ did not know the collection, but the record, so far, remains silent. See *Cabinet de curiosités et d'objets d'art de la Bibliothèque publique de la ville de Versailles* (Versailles, 1869).

89. *Papers*, 10:453.

Chapter 8. "Storm in the Atmosphere"

Epigraph: Madame de La Tour du Pin, *Memoirs* (New York, 1971), 95. Mme de La Tour du Pin's recollection of the absence of the word *revolution* in conversation before 1789 reminds us that it and its encrusted meanings and images were not a part of the original script as events began to unfold before TJ's eyes that summer and fall. One of the most perceptive analyses of the subject is Keith Baker's essay "Inventing the French Revolution" in the collection of the same name.

1. TJ to Elizabeth House Trist, August [?], 1785, *Papers*, 8:404–6, n. "France, said Fénelon, is one enormous hospital," Lord Acton wrote. "French historians believe that in a single generation six millions of people died of want." J. E. E. Dalberg Acton, *The History of Freedom* (London, 1907), 49. I am indebted to Jim Holland for the Acton quote.

2. "Autobiography," *Writings*, ed. Peterson, 78.

3. TJ to James Madison, Aug. 28, 1789, *Papers*, 15:365.

4. "Autobiography," *Writings*, ed. Peterson, 78.

5. TJ to St. John de Crèvecoeur, Aug. 22, 1785, *Papers*, 8:421. The necklace, vulgar in its dripping opulence, was known as a *rivière* and popular as a souvenir for mistresses and courtesans. When someone in a Paris theater remarked that a particular rivière was flowing rather low over the décolletage of its owner, his companion replied that it was only returning to its source. Schama, *Citizens*, 203.

6. TJ to Abigail Adams, Sept. 4, 1785, *Papers*, 8:473. Sara Maza, in *Private Lives and Public Affairs*, has explored the complex issues surrounding the affair, arguing that the attack on the queen, who in fact knew nothing of the scam, demonstrates the public's conclusion that women in public positions were incompatible with a virtuous public sphere—a view close to Jefferson's own.

7. TJ to Anne Willing Bingham, Feb. 7, 1787, *Papers*, 11:124; TJ to Caspar Wistar, Jr., June 21, 1807, quoted in Rice, *Jefferson's Paris*, 23.

8. I am indebted to Maza's essay on this detail, and particularly on the growing fear of the power of women extending to the salon, where men were emasculated: "Every woman at Paris gathers in her apartment a harem of men more womanish than she."

9. Schama, *Citizens*, 215–16.

10. TJ to Madison, June 20, 1787, *Papers*, 11:482; Aug. 2, 1787, ibid., 664; Schama, *Citizens*, chap. 6, "Body Politics." See also Jan Lewis, "The Blessings of Domestic Society," *Jeffersonian Legacies*, 109–46, and Lynn Hunt, "The Many Bodies of Marie Antoinette," in *Eroticism and the Body Politic*, ed. Lynn Hunt (Baltimore, 1991), 108–30.

11. Gottschalk, *Between the American and French Revolutions*, 236. Gottschalk's chapter "Conflict with the Tobacco Cartel," 222–37, is useful on the tobacco trade problem.

12. John Jay to TJ, Dec. 14, 1786, *Papers*, 10:597; John Adams to TJ, Nov. 30, 1786, *Papers*, 10:557.

13. TJ to Edward Carrington, Jan. 16, 1787 *Papers*, 11:49.

14. John Jay to TJ, April 24, 1787, *Papers*, 11:313.

15. TJ to John Adams, Aug. 1, 1816, *Adams-Jefferson Letters*, ed. Cappon, 2:485; Gordon S. Wood, "Trials and Tribulations," in *Jeffersonian Legacies*, 413.

16. Abigail Adams to TJ, Jan. 29, 1787, *Papers* 11:86.

17. TJ to Abigail Adams, Feb. 22, 1787, *Papers* 11:174.

18. TJ to David Hartly, July 2, 1787, *Papers* 11:526.

19. TJ to John Jay, Jan. 9, 1787, *Papers*, 11:32.

20. TJ to Edward Carrington, Jan. 16, 1787, *Papers*, 11:48–49.

21. Gottschalk, *Between the American and French Revolutions*, 281.

22. Ibid., 164–65.

23. "Autobiography," *Writings*, ed. Peterson, 63.

24. Schama, *Citizens*, 238.

25. These are the words Henry Adams would use eighty years later to characterize the French after spending a few months in Paris in 1860. *The Education of Henry Adams* (Boston, 1918), 96.

26. TJ to Abigail Adams, Feb. 22, 1787, *Papers*, 11:174.

27. TJ to Lafayette, Feb. 28, 1787, *Papers*, 11:186.

28. For an excellent sorting out of the calling of the Notables, see Gottschalk's chapter "The Council of 'Not-Ables,'" *Between the American and French Revolutions*, 279–300.

29. Quoted in Schama, *Citizens*, 253. Schama and other historians see France's retreat from the role of a great power as evidence "that the monarchy was already a hostage to the deficit" and "would never regain its freedom of action through any palliatives....It was apparent from this painful moment, traditional absolutism was dead."

30. James Madison to TJ, March 19, 1787, *Papers*, 11:220. Adrienne Koch, *Jefferson and Madison: The Great Collaboration* (New York, 1950), 33–61.

31. TJ to Madison, Dec. 20, 1787, *Papers*, 12:440.

32. TJ to Francis Hopkins, March 13, 1789, *Papers*, 14:650–51. TJ's feelings about the sacred nature of a bill of rights may well have been strengthened by the mood of his liberal European friends, who had substituted such a declaration in the catechism of their new secular religion that now had replaced the church.

33. TJ to William Stephen Smith, Feb. 2, 1788, *Papers*, 12:558.

34. TJ to Benjamin Hawkins, Aug. 4, 1787, *Papers*, 11:684.

35. Gottschalk, *Between the American and French Revolutions*, 386.

36. Ibid., 374.

37. Young, *Travels*, 96.

38. TJ to Mme de Bréhan, May 9, 1788, *Papers*, 13:150.

39. TJ to Anne Bingham, May 11, 1788, *Papers*, 13:151.

40. *Papers*, 13:164, n.

41. Morris, *Diary*, 1:22.

42. TJ to Angelica Schuyler Church, July 27, 1788, *Papers*, 13:422. The Hôtel de Langeac had only two floors during TJ's residence.

43. TJ to St. John de Crèvecoeur, Aug. 9, 1788, *Papers*, 13:485; TJ to John Brown Cutting, July 24, 1788, *Papers*, 13:404.

44. Palmer, *Profile*, 95.

45. TJ to James Monroe, Aug. 9, 1788, *Papers*, 13:489.

46. TJ to John Cutting, Nov. 3, 1788, *Papers*, 13:47–48.

47. Jean Starobinski, *1789: The Emblems of Reason* (Charlottesville, 1982), 17.

48. TJ to Thomas Paine, May 19, 1789, *Papers*, 15:136.

49. Gottschalk, *Between the American and French Revolutions*, 424.

50. TJ to Richard Price, Jan. 8, 1789, *Papers*, 14:420–24; P. Smith, *Adams*, 2:286. See also Gottschalk, *Between the American and French Revolutions*, 397, n. 47.

51. TJ to James Madison, Jan. 12, 1789, *Papers*, 14:437.

52. TJ to Francis Hopkinson, March 13, 1789, *Papers*, 14:650.

53. TJ to Moustier, March 13, 1789, *Papers*, 14:652.

54. TJ to Mme de Bréhan, March 14, 1789, *Papers*, 14:655.

55. TJ to Geismar, Feb. 20, 1789, *Papers*, 14:582–83. See Baker, *Inventing the French Revolution*, 218–21.

56. TJ to David Humphreys, March 18, 1789, *Papers*, 14:676.

57. Morris, *Diary*, 1:49.

58. TJ to John Jay, May 9, 1789, *Papers*, 15:10.

59. TJ to Madison, May 11, 1789, *Papers*, 15:121.

60. "Hints to Americans Traveling in Europe," *Papers*, 13:269.

61. Morris, *Diary*, 1:64.

62. Starobinski, *1789*, 17.

63. Morris, *Diary*, 1:69.

64. TJ to Thomas Paine, May 19, 1789, *Papers*, 15:138.

65. TJ to Lafayette, May 6, 1789, *Papers*, 15:97–98; TJ to Washington, May 10, 1789, ibid., 118–19.

66. TJ to Richard Price, May 19, 1789, *Papers*, 15:137–39; TJ to Crèvecoeur, May 20, 1789, ibid., 139–40.

67. TJ to Lafayette, June 3, 1789, *Papers*, 15:165–66; TJ to Rabaut de St. Etienne, enclosing draft of charter of rights, June 3, 1789, ibid., 166–68.

68. Lafayette to TJ, [June 3–4,] 1789, *Papers*, 15:166; TJ to Lafayette, May 12, 1789, ibid., 179–89.

69. TJ to Rabaut de St. Etienne, June 3, 1789, *Papers*, 15:167.

70. Young, *Travels*, 153–54.

71. TJ to Lafayette, Feb. 14, 1815, *Letters of Lafayette and Jefferson*, ed. Chinard, 368.

72. TJ to John Jay, June 17, 1789, *Papers*, 15:188; Bailyn, *Faces of Revolution*, 38.

73. TJ to John Jay, June 24, 1789, *Papers*, 15:206.

74. Morris, *Diary*, 1:120.

75. Ibid., 130.

76. J. E. E. Dalberg Acton, *Lectures on the French Revolution* (London, 1910), 80–81. TJ to John Jay, June 24, 1789, *Papers*, 15:206.

77. Morris, *Diary*, 1:129.

78. TJ to Jay, Aug. 27, 1789, *Papers*, 15:359.

79. TJ to Madison, Aug. 28, 1787, *Papers*, 15:366. Although the characterization of Orléans and Mirabeau was made several weeks after the "Mirabeau Incident," TJ already had their number.

80. Louis Gottschalk and Margaret Maddox, *Lafayette in the French Revolution through*

the October Days (Chicago, 1969), 74–80. See also editorial note, "The Mirabeau Incident," *Papers*, 15:243–49, and letters that follow. Lafayette's second draft with editorial can be found in *Papers*, 15:230–31.

81. Gilbert Chinard, "Jefferson's Influence Abroad," *Mississippi Valley Historical Society* 30 (June 1943–March 1944): 15. Also see Chinard, "Notes on the American Origins of the 'Déclaration des Droits de l'Homme et du Citoyen,'" *Proceedings, American Philosophical Society* 98 (1954): 383–96.

82. Mme de La Tour du Pin was among the party at the maréchal de Beauvau's, where the Neckers said they were going. The next day, a footman from Versailles arrived at Le Val, the Beauvau house, and asked if the controller general and his wife had been seen since they disappeared the previous evening. Although she was beginning to hear "sharp remarks" in the salons, Mme de La Tour du Pin considered Necker's dismissal the first serious event leading to the Revolution. *Memoirs*, 107–11.

83. TJ to Thomas Paine, July 13, 1789, *Papers*, 15:273; "Autobiography," *Writings*, ed. Peterson, 89. See also Bailyn, *Faces of Revolution*, 38–39.

84. Morris, *Diary*, 1:146.

85. TJ to John Bonfield, July 16, 1789, *Papers*, 15:276–77. At the time that it was captured, the prison held many books confiscated by the old regime, including a number of titles that had already entered TJ's library. Helvétius, Diderot, Condorcet, and Raynal were all well represented.

86. TJ to John Jay, July 19, 1789, *Papers*, 15:288.

87. Georges Lefebvre, *The Coming of the French Revolution*, trans. R. R. Palmer (Princeton, 1976), 116. Like everyone writing about the French Revolution, I am indebted to this classic study and to Palmer's introduction.

88. "Autobiography," *Writings*, ed. Peterson, 92.

89. TJ to the abbé Arnoux, July 19, 1789, *Papers*, 15:282–83.

90. TJ to Diodati, Aug. 3, 1789, *Papers*, 15:326.

91. TJ to Lord Wycombe, July 25, 1789, *Papers*, 15:307.

92. TJ to Diodati, Aug. 3, 1789, *Papers*, 15:326.

93. Morris, *Diary*, July 28, 1:164–65, 170–71; Morris to Washington, July 31, 1789, ibid., 170–71; Sparks, *Morris*, 1:294–95.

94. TJ to Jay, Aug. 13, 1789, *Papers*, 15:340.

95. Lafayette to TJ, Aug. 25, 1789, *Papers*, 15:354–55, n.

96. TJ to Benjamin Vaughan, Sept. 13, 1789, *Papers*, 15:426.

97. As Sloan points out, Condorcet protested the assembly's omission in a letter to Mathieu de Montmorency on Aug. 30, 1789. See Condorcet, *Oeuvres*, 9:367–68, 371–72, and 389–90. If TJ was disappointed, he discreetly kept it to himself. Sloan believes his silence was to avoid being accused of meddling. Sloan, "The Earth Belongs in Usufruct to the Living," *Jeffersonian Legacies*, 307, n.34. Sloan's discussion of the letter is an indispensable addition to the literature.

98. Sloan, *Principle and Interest*, esp. chaps. 1 and 2.

99. Sloan, "The Earth Belongs in Usufruct to the Living," *Jeffersonian Legacies;* editorial note and documents, *Papers,* 15:384–99. The editors trace the proximate source of TJ's inspiration to an undated note from Dr. Gem with its brief outline, which they assign to around Sept. 1–6, 1789, when Gem was treating TJ for migraine. But the meeting at TJ's house with members of the assembly, where the question of changing the proposed constitution at fixed intervals was undoubtedly discussed (see *Papers,* 15:390–91, n.), while TJ's first draft was fresh in his mind, appears equally relevant.

100. TJ to Thomas Paine, July 11, 1789, *Papers,* 15:268.

101. TJ to William Short, Jan. 3, 1793, *Papers,* 25:14–17.

102. Adams, *History,* 100; "Autobiography," *Writings,* ed. Peterson, 98.

Bibliography

Primary Sources

ACCOUNT BOOKS

Jefferson's Memorandum Books: Accounts with Legal and Miscellany, 1767–1726. Ed. James
    A. Bear, Jr., and Lucia C. Stanton. *The Papers of Thomas Jefferson*, 2d ser.
    (forthcoming).

"Memorandum Books (1767–1826)." Typescript prepared by James Bear, Jr. Author's
    collection.

MANUSCRIPTS

Thomas Jefferson Papers. Library of Congress, Washington, D.C.

Thomas Jefferson Papers. Missouri Historical Society, St. Louis.

William Short Papers. Library of Congress, Washington, D.C.

Short Family Books and Papers. Price Collection. College of William and Mary,
    Williamsburg, Va.

Short-Jefferson Correspondence. College of William and Mary, Williamsburg, Va.

Short-Skipwith Papers. College of William and Mary, Williamsburg, Va.

DIARIES, AUTOBIOGRAPHIES, AND JOURNALS

Adams, John. *The Diary and Autobiography.* Ed. Lyman H. Butterfield. 4 vols.
    Cambridge, Mass., 1961.

Journals of the Continental Congress. 34 vols. Washington, D.C., 1976.

Morris, Gouverneur. *A Diary of the French Revolution.* Ed. Beatrix C. Davenport. 2 vols.
    Boston, 1939.

Trumbull, John. *Autobiography of Colonel John Trumbull.* Ed. Theodore Sizer. New
    Haven, 1951.

LETTERS

Adams, Abigail (Smith). *Journal and Correspondence of Miss Adams, Daughter of John
    Adams.* New York and London, 1841.

Adams, Abigail. *Letters of Mrs. Adams, the Wife of John Adams.* Ed. C. F. Adams. Boston,
    1840.

Adams, John. *The Works of John Adams.* Ed. C. F. Adams. Boston, 1856.

The Adams-Jefferson Letters: The Complete Correspondence between Thomas Jefferson and Abigail and John Adams. Ed. Lester J. Cappon. 2 vols. Chapel Hill, 1959.

Barbé-Marbois, François. *Our Revolutionary Forefathers: The Letters.* Ed. Eugene Chase. New York, 1929.

The Correspondence of Jefferson and Du Pont de Nemours. Ed. Gilbert Chinard. New York, 1979.

The Family Letters of Thomas Jefferson. Ed. Edwin Morris Betts and James A. Bear, Jr. Columbia, Mo., 1966.

The Letters of Lafayette and Jefferson. Ed. Gilbert Chinard. Baltimore, 1929.

Thomas Jefferson: Memoirs, Correspondence and Miscellanies. Charlottesville, 1829.

The Yale Edition of Horace Walpole's Correspondence. Ed. W. S. Lewis. 48 vols. New Haven, 1937–83.

PAPERS

Lafayette in the Age of the American Revolution: Selected Papers, 1776–1790. Ed. Stanley J. Idzerda. 5 vols. Ithaca, 1979.

The Papers of Thomas Jefferson. Ed. Julian Boyd et al. 26 vols. to date. Princeton, 1950–.

The Papers of James Madison. Ed. Robert A. Rutland, William M. E. Rachal, et al. 17 vols. Chicago and Charlottesville, 1962–91.

WRITINGS

Condorcet, N. A. J. M. Caritat de. *Oeuvres.* Ed. Arthur O'Connor and Dominique Arago. Stuttgart, 1968.

Du Pont de Nemours. *The Autobiography.* Trans. Elizabeth Fox-Genovese. Washington, Del., 1984.

Grimm, Baron. *Historical and Literary Memoirs and Anecdotes, Selected from the Correspondence of Baron Grimm.* Trans. Robert Bland. London, 1814.

Jefferson, Thomas. *Catalogue of the Library of Thomas Jefferson.* Ed. Millicent E. Sowerby. 5 vols. Washington and Charlottesville, 1983.

———. *Jefferson's Literary Commonplace Book.* Ed. Douglas L. Wilson. *The Papers of Thomas Jefferson,* 2d ser. Princeton, 1989.

———. *Notes on the State of Virginia.* Ed. William Peden. Chapel Hill, 1955.

———. *Thomas Jefferson: Writings.* Ed. Merrill D. Peterson. New York, 1984.

———. *Thomas Jefferson's Farm Book.* Ed. Edwin Morris Betts. Charlottesville, 1987.

———. *Thomas Jefferson's Garden Book.* Ed. Edwin Morris Betts. Philadelphia, 1944.

———. *The Writings of Thomas Jefferson.* Ed. Paul L. Ford. 10 vols. New York, 1892–99.

———. *The Writings of Thomas Jefferson.* Ed. A. A. Lipscomb and A. E. Bergh. 20 vols. Washington, 1903.

La Tour du Pin, Madame de. *Memoirs.* Trans. Felice Harcourt. New York, 1971.

Ledoux, Claude-Nicolas. *L'Architecture.* Ed. Kevin C. Lippert. Princeton, 1983.

Ligne, Prince de. *Letters and Memoirs.* Trans. Leigh Ashton. New York, 1927.

Maclay, William. *Diary and Other Notes on Senate Debates.* Ed. Kenneth R. Bowling and Helen E. Veit. Baltimore, 1988.

Ségur, Louis Philippe de. *Memoirs and Recollections.* New York, 1970.

Vigée-Lebrun, Elisabeth. *Memoirs.* Trans. Lionel Strachey. New York, 1989.

Secondary Sources

BOOKS

Acton, J. E. E. Dalberg. *The History of Freedom.* London, 1907.

———. *Lectures on the French Revolution.* London, 1910.

Adair, Douglass. *Fame and the Founding Fathers.* New York, 1974.

Adams, Henry. *History of the United States during the Administrations of Thomas Jefferson.* New York, 1984.

Adams, William Howard. *Jefferson's Monticello.* New York, 1984.

Adams, William Howard, ed. *The Eye of Thomas Jefferson.* Washington and Charlottesville, 1976.

———. *Thomas Jefferson and the Arts: An Extended View.* Washington and Charlottesville, 1976.

Arnason, H. H. *The Sculptures of Houdon.* London, 1975.

Badinter, Elisabeth, and Robert Badinter. *Condorcet, 1743–1794: Un Intellectuel en politique.* Paris, 1988.

Bailyn, Bernard. *Faces of Revolution: Personalities and Themes in the Struggle for American Independence.* New York, 1990.

Baker, Keith Michael. *Condorcet: From Natural Philosophy to Social Mathematics.* Chicago, 1975.

———. *Inventing the French Revolution.* Cambridge, Mass., 1990.

Baker, Keith, ed. *Condorcet: Selected Writings.* Indianapolis, 1976.

———. *The French Revolution and the Creation of Modern Political Culture.* 2 vols. Oxford and New York, 1987.

Bear, James, Jr. *The Hemings Family of Monticello.* Ivy, Va., 1980.

Bedini, Silvio. *Thomas Jefferson and His Copying Machines.* Charlottesville, 1984.

Bizardel, Yvon. *The First Expatriate Americans in Paris in the French Revolution.* Trans. June P. Wilson and Cornelia Higginson. New York, 1975.

Boyd, Julian. *The Declaration of Independence.* Princeton, 1945.

Braham, Allan. *The Architecture of the French Enlightenment.* Berkeley, 1980.

Branchi, E. C., ed. *Memoirs of the Life and Voyages of Doctor Philip Mazzei, William and Mary Quarterly,* 2d ser., 10, no. 1 (January 1930).

Brodie, Fawn. *Thomas Jefferson: An Intimate History.* New York, 1974.

Brookner, Anita. *Jacques-Louis David.* New York, 1980.

Buffon, Georges-Louis Leclerc. *Histoire naturelle, générale et particulière.* Paris, 1774–78.

Bullock, Helen D. *My Head and My Heart: A Little History of Thomas Jefferson and Maria Cosway.* New York, 1945.

Burstein, Andrew. *The Inner Jefferson.* Charlottesville, 1995.

Bush, Alfred. *The Life Portraits of Thomas Jefferson.* Charlottesville, 1987.

Butterfield, L. H., Marc Friedlander, and Mary-Jo Kline, eds. *The Book of John and Abigail.* Cambridge, 1975.

Carlson, Marvin. *The Theatre of the French Revolution.* Ithaca and New York, 1966.

Censer, Jack, and Jeremy D. Popkin, eds. *Press and Politics in Pre-Revolutionary France.* Berkeley, 1987.

Chamfort, Sébastien-Roche Nicolas. *Products of the Perfected Civilization: Selected Writings.* Ed. and trans. W. S. Merwin. San Francisco, 1984.

Chartier, Roger. *The Cultural Origins of the French Revolution.* Trans. Lydia G. Cochrane. Durham, 1991.

Chastellux, J. F., marquis de. *Travels In North American in the Years 1780, 1781 and 1782.* Ed. and trans.. Howard C. Rice, Jr. 2 vols. Chapel Hill, 1963.

Chinard, Gilbert. *Jefferson et les idéologues.* Baltimore, 1925.

———. *Thomas Jefferson: The Apostle of Americanism.* Boston, 1939.

———. *Trois Amitiés françaises de Jefferson.* Paris, 1927.

Clarke, Michael, and Nicholas Penny, eds. *The Arrogant Connoisseur: Richard Payne Knight, 1751–1824.* Manchester, 1982.

Cobban, Arthur. *The Social Interpretation of the French Revolution.* Cambridge, 1964.

Commager, Henry Steele. *Jefferson, Nationalism, and the Enlightenment.* New York, 1975.

Cooper, Helen A. *John Trumbull: The Hand and Spirit of a Painter.* New Haven, 1982.

Cripe, Helen. *Thomas Jefferson and Music.* Charlottesville, 1974.

Crow, Thomas E. *Emulations: Making Artists for Revolutionary France.* New Haven, 1995.

———. *Painters and Public Life in Eighteenth-Century Paris.* New Haven, 1985.

Dabney, Virginius. *The Jefferson Scandals: A Rebuttal.* Lanham, N.Y., and London, 1991.

Darnton, Robert. *The Business of Enlightenment: A Publishing History of the Encyclopédie, 1775–1800.* Cambridge, Mass., 1968.

———. *The Forbidden Best-Sellers of Pre-Revolutionary France.* New York, 1995.

———. *The Literary Underground of the Old Regime.* Cambridge, Mass., 1982.

Darnton, Robert, and Daniel Roche, eds. *Revolution in Print.* Los Angeles, 1989.

Dennis, Michael. *Court and Garden: From the French Hôtel to the City of Modern Architecture.* Cambridge, Mass., 1986.

Doyle, William. *The Origins of the French Revolution.* Oxford, 1980.

———. *The Oxford History of the French Revolution.* Oxford, 1989.

Duval, Marguerite. *The King's Gardens.* Trans. A. Tomarken and C. Cowen. Charlottesville, 1982.

Echevarria, Durand. *The Mirage of the West.* Princeton, 1937.

Elkins, Stanley, and Eric McKitrick. *The Age of Federalism.* New York, 1993.

Ellis, Joseph. *After the Revolution*. New York, 1979.

Fellows, Otis, and Stephen Miliken. *Buffon*. New York, 1972.

Ferguson, Adam. *An Essay on the History of Civil Society*. Edinburgh, 1767.

Gallet, Michel. *Demeures parisiennes: L'Epoque de Louis XV.* Paris, 1964.

———. *Ledoux et Paris*. Paris, 1979.

———. *Stately Mansions*. Trans. James C. Palmes. New York, 1972.

Gay, Peter. *The Enlightenment: An Interpretation*. 2 vols. New York, 1966–69.

Gerould, Daniel, ed. *Gallant and Libertine*. New York, 1983.

Gilchrist, J., and W. J. Murray. *The Press in the French Revolution*. New York, 1971.

Godechot, Jacques. *France and the Atlantic Revolution*. New York, 1965.

Gordon-Reed, Annette. *Thomas Jefferson and Sally Hemings*. Charlottesville, 1997.

Gottschalk, Louis. *Lafayette between the American and French Revolutions*. Chicago, 1950.

Gottschalk, Louis, and Donald Lach. *Toward the French Revolution*. New York, 1973.

Gottschalk, Louis, and Margaret Maddox. *Lafayette in the French Revolution through the October Days*. Chicago, 1969.

Haskell, Francis. *History and Its Images*. New Haven, 1993.

———. *Past and Present in Art and Taste*. New Haven, 1987.

Havens, George R. *The Age of Ideas*. New York, 1955.

Hofstadter, Richard. *The American Political Tradition and the Men Who Made It*. New York, 1948.

Honour, Hugh. *Neo-Classicism*. London, 1968.

Humphreys, Francis L. *Life and Times of David Humphreys*. 2 vols. New York, 1917.

Hunt, Lynn. *Politics and Culture and Class in the French Revolution*. Berkeley, 1984.

Hunt, Lynn, ed. *Eroticism and the Body Politic*. Baltimore, 1991.

Johnson, Douglas, ed. *French Society and the Revolution*. Cambridge, 1976.

Johnson, James H. *Listening in Paris*. Los Angeles, 1995.

Kames, Henry Home. *Six Sketches on the History of Man*. Philadelphia, 1776.

Kaplan, Justin. *Jefferson and France*. New Haven, 1967.

Kimball, Fiske. *Thomas Jefferson Architect*. New York, 1968.

Kimball, Marie. *The Furnishings of Monticello*. Charlottesville, 1940.

———. *Jefferson: The Scene in Europe*. New York, 1950.

Koch, Adrienne. *Jefferson and Madison: The Great Collaboration*. New York, 1950.

Landes, Joan B. *Women and the Public Sphere in the Age of the French Revolution*. Ithaca, 1988.

Laugier, Marc-Antoine. *An Essay on Architecture*. Trans. Wolfgang Herrimann and Anni Herrimann. Los Angeles, 1977.

Lefevre, Georges. *The Coming of the French Revolution*. Trans. R. R. Palmer. Princeton, 1974.

Lehmann, Karl. *Thomas Jefferson, American Humanist*. New York, 1947.

Lloyd, Stephen. *Richard and Maria Cosway*. Edinburgh, 1995.

Lopez, Claude-Anne. *Mon Cher Papa: Franklin and the Ladies of Paris*. New Haven, 1967.

Malone, Dumas. *Jefferson and His Time*. 6 vols. Boston, 1948–81.

Manceron, Claude. *Blood of the Bastille*. New York, 1989.

———. *Twilight of the Old Order*. New York, 1972.

Marx, Leo. *The Machine and the Garden*. New York, 1964.

Mathews, George. *The Royal General Farms in Eighteenth-Century France*. New York, 1956.

Mathews, Richard. *If Men Were Angels: James Madison and the Heartless Empire of Reason*. Lawrence, Kan., 1995.

———. *The Radical Politics of Thomas Jefferson*. Lawrence, Kan., 1984.

May, Henry F. *The Enlightenment in America*. New York and Oxford, 1976.

Mayer, David N. *The Constitutional Thought of Thomas Jefferson*. Charlottesville, 1994.

Maza, Sarah. *Private Lives and Public Affairs*. Berkeley, 1993.

Mazzei, Philip. *Memoirs of the Life and Peregrinations of the Florentine Philip Mazzei*. New York, 1942.

———. *My Life and Wanderings*. Ed. S. Eugene Scalia. Trans. Margherita Marchione. Morristown, N.J., 1980.

———. *Researches on the United States*. Trans. Constance D. Sherman. Charlottesville, 1976.

McCoy, Drew. *The Elusive Republic: Political Economy in Jeffersonian America*. Chapel Hill, 1980.

McKie, Douglas. *Antoine Lavoisier*. New York, 1952.

Ménétra, Jacques-Louis. *Journal of My Life*. Trans. Arthur Goldhammer. New York, 1984.

Mercier, Louis-Sébastien. *Tableau de Paris*. 12 vols. Amsterdam, 1783–88.

Middleton, Arthur Pierce, ed. *A Virginia Gentleman's Library*. Williamsburg, Va., 1952.

Miller, John Chester. *The Wolf by the Ears: Thomas Jefferson and Slavery*. Charlottesville, 1991.

Mintz, Max. *Gouverneur Morris*. Norman, Okla., 1970.

Montclos, Jean-Marie Pérouse de. *Etienne-Louis Boullée*. Paris, 1969.

Morellet, André. *Mémoires de l'abbé Morellet*. 2 vols. Paris, 1821.

Mornet, Daniel. *Les Origines intellectuelles de la Révolution française, 1715–1787*. Paris, 1967.

Nichols, Frederick D. *Thomas Jefferson's Architectural Drawings*. Boston, 1960.

Onuf, Peter S., ed. *Jeffersonian Legacies*. Charlottesville, 1993.

Parker, H. T. *The Cult of Antiquity and the French Revolutionaries*. Chicago, 1937.

Peterson, Merrill D. *Thomas Jefferson and the New Nation*. New York, 1970.

Peterson, Merrill D., ed. *Thomas Jefferson: A Profile*. New York, 1967.

———. *Thomas Jefferson: A Reference Biography*. New York, 1986.

Prey, Pierre de la Ruffini du. *The Villas of Pliny: From Antiquity to Posterity*. New York, 1983.

Rahv, Philip. *Discovery of Europe.* New York, 1960.

Randall, Henry S. *The Life of Thomas Jefferson.* 3 vols. New York, 1858.

Randolph, Sarah N. *The Domestic Life of Thomas Jefferson.* Charlottesville, 1985.

Revel, Jacques. *Fictions of the French Revolutions.* Evanston, Ill., 1991.

Rials, Stephane. *La Déclaration des droits de l'homme et du citoyen.* Paris, 1989.

Rice, Howard C., Jr. *L'Hotel de Langeac.* Charlottesville, 1947.

————. *Thomas Jefferson's Paris.* Princeton, 1976.

Richard, Carl. *The Founders and the Classics.* Cambridge, 1994.

Richardson, Jonathan. *The Works of Jonathan Richardson.* London, 1747.

Roche, Daniel. *The People of Paris: An Essay in Popular Culture in the Eighteenth Century.* Berkeley, 1987.

Rosenblum, Robert. *Transformations in Late Eighteenth-Century Art.* Princeton, 1967.

Rudé, George. *The Crowd in the French Revolution.* Oxford, 1959.

Schama, Simon. *Citizens: A Chronicle of the French Revolution.* New York, 1989.

————. *Landscape and Memory.* New York, 1995.

————. *Patriots and Liberators.* New York, 1977.

Schapiro, J. Salwyn. *Condorcet and the Rise of Liberalism.* New York, 1934.

Shackelford, George Green. *Jefferson's Adoptive Son: The Life of William Short, 1759–1848.* Lexington, Ky., 1993.

————. *Thomas Jefferson's Travels in Europe, 1784–1789.* Baltimore, 1995.

Shepperson, Archibald Bolling. *John Paradise and Lucy Ludwell of London and Williamsburg.* Richmond, Va., 1942.

Sloan, Herbert. *Principle and Interest: Thomas Jefferson and the Problem of Debt.* New York and Oxford, 1995.

Smith, Margaret Bayard. *The First Forty Years of Washington Society.* Ed. Guillard Hunt. New York, 1906.

Smith, Page. *John Adams.* 2 vols. New York, 1962.

Sparks, Jared. *The Life of Gouverneur Morris.* Boston, 1832.

Spurlin, Paul Merrill. *The French Enlightenment in America.* Athens, Ga., 1984.

Starobinski, Jean. *1789: The Emblems of Reason.* Charlottesville, 1982.

Steegmuller, Francis. *A Woman, a Man, and Two Kingdoms.* Princeton, 1993.

Tesnière, Marie-Hélène, and Prosser Gifford, eds. *Creating French Culture: Treasures from the Bibliothèque nationale de France.* New Haven, 1995.

Tocqueville, Alexis de. *The Old Régime and the French Revolution.* Trans. Stuart Gilbert. New York, 1955.

Tucker, Robert W., and David Hendrickson. *Empire of Liberty: The Statecraft of Thomas Jefferson.* New York, 1990.

White, Morton, and Lucia White. *The Intellectual versus the City.* Cambridge, 1962.

Williamson, George C. *Richard Cosway, R.A.* London, 1897.

Wills, Garry. *Inventing America: Jefferson's Declaration of Independence.* New York, 1979.

Wilson, Douglas L., and James Gilreath, eds. *Thomas Jefferson's Library.* Washington,
    1989.
Young, Arthur. *Travels in France.* London, 1890.

ARTICLES

Appleby, Joyce. "What Is Still American in the Political Philosophy of Thomas
    Jefferson." *William and Mary Quarterly,* 3d. ser., 39 (April 1982): 287–309.
Birn, Raymond. "Malesherbes and the Call for a Free Press." In Darnton and Roche,
    Revolution in Print, 50–66.
Carter, Edward C. "Benjamin Henry Latrobe and the Growth and Development of
    Washington, 1798–1818." *Records of the Columbia Historical Society,* 1971–1972:
    128–149.
Chinard, Gilbert. "Eighteenth-Century Theories on America as a Human Habitat"
    Proceedings, American Philosophical Society 91 (1947): 27–57.
———. "Jefferson among the Philosophes." *Ethics* 53, no. 4 (July 1943): 255–68.
———. "Jefferson's Influence Abroad." *Mississippi Valley Historical Society* 30 (June
    1943–March 1944): 171–87.
———. "Notes on the American Origins of the 'Déclaration des droits de l'homme et
    du citoyen.'" *Proceedings, American Philosophical Society* 98 (1954): 383–96.
———. "Notes on the French Translations of the 'Forms of Government or
    Constitutions of the Several States,' 1778–1783." *Year Book, American Philosophical
    Society,* 1943: 88–106.
Condorcet, N. A. J. M. Caritat de. "The Influence of the American Revolution on Europe."
    Trans. Durand Echevarria. *William and Mary Quarterly,* 3d ser., 25 (1968): 85–108.
Darnton, Robert. "The Facts of Literary Life in Eighteenth-Century France." In *The
    French Revolution and the Creation of Modern Political Culture.* Ed. Keith Michael
    Baker. Oxford and New York, 1987. Vol. 1, *The Political Culture of the Old Regime.*
Goodman, Dena. "Enlightened Salons: The Convergence of Female and Philosophic
    Ambitions." *Eighteenth-Century Studies* 22, no. 3 (1989): 329–50.
Howard, Seymour. "Thomas Jefferson's Art Gallery for Monticello." *Art Bulletin* 59
    (December 1977): 583–600.
Jackson, Donald. "The West." In Peterson, *Thomas Jefferson: A Reference Biography,*
    369–84.
Kallem, H. M. "The Arts and Thomas Jefferson." *Ethics* 53, no. 4 (July 1943): 260–83.
Kaplan, Lawrence. "Foreign Affairs." In Peterson, *Thomas Jefferson: A Reference
    Biography,* 311–30.
Kimball, Fiske. "Thomas Jefferson and the Public Buildings of Virginia." *Huntington
    Library Bulletin* 12 (1949): 303–10.
Lafeber, Walter. "Jefferson and an American Foreign Policy." In Onuf, *Jeffersonian
    Legacies,* 370–91.

Lewis, Jan. "The Blessings of Domestic Society." In Onuf, *Jeffersonian Legacies*, 109–46.

Lloyd, Stephen. "The Accomplished Maria Cosway: Anglo-Italian Artist, Musician, Salon Hostess and Educationalist (1759–1838)." *Journal of Anglo-Italian Studies* 2 (1992): 109–39.

Marraro, Howard R. "Philip Mazzei and His Polish Friends." *Quarterly Bulletin of the Polish Institute* (April 1944).

McCoy, Dennis. "Political Economy." In Peterson, *Thomas Jefferson: A Reference Biography*, 101–18.

McDonald, Robert M. S. "Thomas Jefferson's Anonymous Authorship of the Declaration of Independence." Master' thesis, University of North Carolina, 1994.

Norton, Paul F. "Thomas Jefferson and the Planning of the Nation's Capital." In Adams, *Thomas Jefferson and the Arts*, 191–232.

Palmer, R. R. "The Dubious Democrat." In Peterson, *Thomas Jefferson: A Profile*, 86–103.

Perkins, Buford. "Mr. Jefferson as Revolutionary Architect." *Journal of the Society of Architectural Historians* 34, no. 4 (December 1975).

Peterson, Merrill. "Thomas Jefferson and Commercial Policy, 1783–1793." In Peterson, *Thomas Jefferson: A Profile*, 104–34.

Pickens, Buford. "Mr. Jefferson as Revolutionary Architect. *Journal of the Society of Architectural Historians* 34, no. 4 (December 1975): 257–79.

Popkin, Richard H. "Condorcet, Abolitionist." In *Condorcet Studies.* Ed. Lenora Cohan Rosenfield. Atlantic Highlands, N.J., 1984, 35–47.

Rice, Howard C., Jr. "Poor in Love Mr. Short." *William and Mary Quarterly*, 3d ser., 21 (1964): 516–33.

Sloan, Herbert. "The Earth Belongs in Usufruct to the Living." In Onuf, *Jeffersonian Legacies*, 281–315.

Stanton, Lucia C. "The Hemings-Jefferson Controversy: A Brief Account." Thomas Jefferson Memorial Foundation, Research Department, March 1995.

Verner, Coolie. "Mr. Jefferson Distributes His Notes: A Preliminary Checklist of the First Edition." *Bulletin of the New York Public Library* 4 (April 1952): 159–86.

Wills, Garry. "The Aesthete." *New York Review of Books*, Aug. 12, 1993: 6–10.

Wilson, Douglas L. "Jefferson and the Republic of Letters." In Onuf, *Jeffersonian Legacies*, 50–76.

Wood, Gordon S. "The Trials and Tribulations of Thomas Jefferson." In Onuf, *Jeffersonian Legacies*, 395–417.

Index

Page numbers in *italics* refer to illustrations.